MARITIME MARYLAND

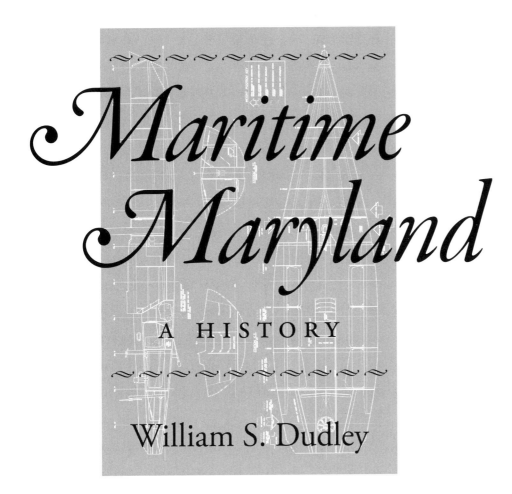

Maritime Maryland

A HISTORY

William S. Dudley

THE JOHNS HOPKINS UNIVERSITY PRESS
Baltimore

*In Association with the Maryland Historical Society
and the Chesapeake Bay Maritime Museum*

© 2010 The Johns Hopkins University Press
All rights reserved. Published 2010
Printed in the United States of America on acid-free paper
9 8 7 6 5 4 3 2 1

The Johns Hopkins University Press
2715 North Charles Street
Baltimore, Maryland 21218-4363
www.press.jhu.edu

Library of Congress Cataloging-in-Publication Data

Dudley, William S.
   Maritime Maryland : a history / William S. Dudley.
      p. cm.
   Includes bibliographical references and index.
   ISBN-13: 978-0-8018-9475-6 (hardcover : acid-free paper)
   ISBN-10: 0-8018-9475-1 (hardcover : acid-free paper)
   1. Navigation—Maryland—History.   2. Ships—Maryland—
History.   3. Maryland—History, Naval.   4. Shipping—Mary-
land—History.   I. Maryland Historical Society.   II. Chesapeake
Bay Maritime Museum.   III. Title.
   VK24.M3D835 2010
   387.09752—dc22   2009043634

A catalog record for this book is available from the British Library.

*Special discounts are available for bulk purchases of this book. For more
information, please contact Special Sales at 410-516-6936 or special
sales@press.jhu.edu.*

The Johns Hopkins University Press uses environmentally friendly
book materials, including recycled text paper that is composed of at
least 30 percent post-consumer waste, whenever possible. All of our
book papers are acid-free, and our jackets and covers are printed on
paper with recycled content.

To the memory of my parents,
Dorothy Lawson Dudley and William Henry Dudley

CONTENTS

Color plates follow page 138.

PREFACE

During the more than twenty-five years I have been sailing on Chesapeake Bay, I have had the pleasure of exploring many of the middle and upper bay rivers and creeks between Havre de Grace on the Western Shore and Crisfield on the Eastern Shore. From the bay itself, the beauty and charm of the Chesapeake is evident to anyone with an eye for the mingling of land and water. The ospreys and otters, the gulls, the crabs, and even the dreaded sea nettle are the natural inhabitants of these cruising grounds, where humans are the inevitable interlopers. I have observed the comings and goings of thousands of sailing yachts and power boats, many recreational, some of the working variety. One cannot help but notice over this period the increase in the number of vessels and types of vessel, the growth of waterside communities, the building and expansion of marinas, and the struggle of villages and towns to remain small and rural against pressures to enlarge and develop, exerted by those who proclaim that land always has a "higher and better use." At the same time, I followed accounts in the local and regional press about stress in the fisheries. Every year there is speculation about the portents of a good or bad crabbing season and about whether the oysters will make a comeback. Marine biologists and environmental enthusiasts earnestly warn us about the implications of seawater that has been polluted by the runoff from nutrient-saturated chicken and hog farms. In 1997, an outbreak of pfisteria in some rivers on the Eastern Shore led to devastating fish kills, and news of these events awakened concerns among average citizens that all was not well. Even if they did not normally follow the back-and-forth dialog of farmers and watermen and their representatives in the Maryland Assembly, people became aware of the closing of some seafood restaurants in the Annapolis, Baltimore, and Washington areas, and many wondered at the causes.

As a professional naval historian who treasures nature's offerings, I would like to think that the search for causes of things comes to me logically and naturally. In the mid-1980s, it occurred to me that one could use Maryland's current maritime problems to teach lessons in history. As a society we now enjoy or deplore what our predecessors have bequeathed to us. To the degree that we have choices to make, it is important that we inform ourselves about the nature of our legacy and why it came down to us as it did, for both good and ill. Let us then look at the picture of Maryland's maritime past through the widest possible lens so that we may detect the interactions of society, land, and water. In this way, we can identify the causes and effects of today's blessings and problems. Doing so, we may be able to impress upon those who govern that humans, fishes, plants, and animals operate as part of an organic tapestry. Humans are caught between balance and imbalance with the forces of nature. Challenge and response are in play, even though they may not be part of our conscious lives. Our basic needs are to be protected from the elements, to earn a living, and to find ever more satisfying recreational pursuits. We are responsible not only for our present physical and social environment but also for changes in climate, the disappearance of species of wildlife, the spread of new illnesses, the pauperization of watermen's families, and the inflated prices of waterfront properties.

This book evolved from a mix of historical curiosity, social observation, and a love of nature. Dr. William N. Still Jr., formerly of East Carolina University, attempted to interest a group of maritime historians in writing a history of maritime activities in the southern states. As he pointed out, there are an ample number of histories of American maritime activities among coastal states north of Chesapeake Bay but few for states below the Mason-Dixon Line. The South has been viewed by many observers as primarily agricultural and with little skill in seafaring. Yet, along the sounds, bays, and rivers of the Maryland, Carolina, Georgia, Florida, and Gulf tidewater regions, native Americans, blacks, and whites for generations worked the vessels that exported tobacco, rice, and indigo. They built canoes, skiffs, sloops, and schooners and employed them in fishing and in the riverine and coastal trades; they worked the water for shellfish and crabs and served as pilots for visiting vessels. They harvested the water and provided sustenance for societies in need of the protein that seafood uniquely offers. In addition, from Florida, Alabama, Mississippi, Louisiana, and Texas ports, these sailors were the maritime labor force that enabled the export of sugar and cotton to northern ports and Europe. When war broke out, these same people manned the vessels converted to warships that engaged in privateering and fought in the Revolutionary and Civil wars.

This work on Maryland will perhaps inspire a larger work on southern maritime history. Its scope is broad, from the maritime skills and work of native Americans before European settlement, to wars on the waters, to commercial and industrial uses of Chesapeake Bay and its tributaries, to today's boom in recreational boating. Overall, its focus is on seafaring people, their environment, and the impact of historical trends on the present and future of Maryland's waterways.

∾∾∾

I WISH TO ACKNOWLEDGE valuable assistance lent by some special individuals and institutions. Chris Becker, formerly the photographer and photo curator at the Maryland Historical Society, assisted in finding illustration art for this project, and Robert W. Rogers, a former director of the society, generously supported my use of its collections. To Pete Lesher, curator of the Chesapeake Bay Maritime Museum, I am indebted for his expertise and patience in answering my many questions and for providing assistance as I selected photographs from the CBMM collection. L. B. "Buck" Buchanan, chairman, and Jefferson Holland, executive director, of the Annapolis Maritime Museum, helped with their sustained interest in the heritage of Chesapeake Bay and their assistance in sharing the photographic materials in the museum's collection.

Professors Doreen Mack and Deborah Cebula, of Goucher College, encouraged me to develop a course on Chesapeake maritime heritage, which I taught at the Annapolis Maritime Museum during January 2005 and 2006. This encouraged me to gather my thoughts in a coherent pattern and discuss them with students in seminar fashion. I am indebted to Kathy Alexander, of the Johns Hopkins University Press, for her assistance in finding photos of *Chessie Racing,* and to Bruce Farr and the staff of Farr Yacht Design, for providing design data and line drawings of *Chessie Racing.* Lee Tawney, director of the National Sailing Hall of Fame in Annapolis, assisted by referring me to Jack Hardway, a freelance photographer who was most cooperative in providing a variety of beautiful yachting photographs, from which I selected a few for this book. I gained much historical insight into the commercial world of Baltimore's waterfront from conversations with Elizabeth Anne Hughes, the vice president, and her son, C. Duff Hughes, the president of Vane Brothers Company, in Fairfield, Maryland. Curator Beth Hanson of the Historical Society of Talbot County, in Easton, Maryland, was very responsive to my requests for the use of photographs in their collection, as was Louisa Watrous, intellectual property manager of the Mystic Seaport Museum in Mystic, Connecticut.

I am indebted to fellow naval historian William N. Still Jr., who encouraged this project from the beginning. Dr. Robert Neyland, the underwater archaeologist at the Naval History and Heritage Command, a colleague and friend for fifteen years, taught me much about the field of underwater archaeology and its usefulness for interpreting the maritime past. I appreciate the assistance of Susan Langley, the underwater archaeologist of the State of Maryland, and of Bruce Thompson, formerly Maryland's assistant underwater archaeologist, for acquainting me with the library of the Maryland Historical Trust and the many underwater archeological surveys the Trust undertook in Maryland waters. I wish to thank my longtime friend Fred Hecklinger for his deep knowledge of Chesapeake Bay watercraft and traditions and for his painstaking review of my manuscript at an early stage. L. Cory Reynolds, another old friend and fount of nautical knowledge, who accompanied me on many adventurous cruises on the bay over the years, was very supportive of this project. Donald G. Shomette, a prolific author of books on Chesapeake Bay history, has provided continuing advice and support. To Robert J. Brugger, senior acquisitions editor of the Johns Hopkins University Press, who believed in this project from the beginning and kept prodding when I sailed into the doldrums, and to Barbara Lamb, for her sharp editorial eye and keen queries, I am much indebted. For her sustained interest in and encouragement of my pursuit of "maritime Maryland," I am deeply grateful to my wife, Donna Tully Dudley, who patiently read and critiqued many chapters of this book.

MARITIME MARYLAND

Chapter One

Colonial Maritime Heritage

∽∽∽∽∽∽∽∽∽∽∽∽∽∽∽∽∽∽∽∽∽∽∽∽

THE INHABITANTS OF MARYLAND have depended, since earliest times, on the sea and its tributaries for their transportation, trade, and warfare. The geography of Maryland ordained it one of the most navigable of the thirteen original colonies. That distinction can still be claimed today, as Chesapeake Bay and its estuaries provide an estimated 8,100 miles of shoreline.[1] Almost 200 miles in length and relatively slender in breadth, ranging from 5 to 35 miles, the bay has an extraordinary wealth of tidal estuaries. Maryland shares with Virginia the blessings of Chesapeake Bay, characterized by historian Arthur P. Middleton as "the Mediterranean of America."[2]

Maryland's culture has had southern qualities during much of its history. It was a colonial plantation during the approximately 140 years of British rule (1634–1775), and Maryland's entrepreneurs developed industrial, mercantile, and financial concerns during the nineteenth century, gradually reorienting the state's economy toward the industrialized northern states.[3] But there are some compelling reasons for including Maryland among the states having a southern maritime orientation. Until the Civil War, Maryland's culture was predominantly southern, with the social attitudes and economic conditions common to other states that produced crops dependent on plantation slavery in the colonial period and the nineteenth century.

Middleton quotes colonists and Englishmen to the effect that Europeans saw tidewater Maryland and Virginia as one region and that the carving of Maryland from Virginia wrought more economic harm than good. He lays the blame at the feet of King Charles I, who "made the blunder of separating the Chesapeake region into two unnatural divisions."[4] Britain's closed mercantile system, which prohibited trade with other countries or their colonies, was intended to serve the mother country's purpose of creating a favorable balance of trade. Maryland planters had to deal with England's monopolistic trading companies.

The renewal of attention, in 2006–7, to Capt. John Smith's account of his voyage of discovery on Chesapeake Bay has awakened a new generation of Americans to the remarkable vision of the New World that Smith recorded. Within a year of the English landing at Jamestown, Smith had organized an expedition of some fourteen men to set out in a 30-foot shallop to explore the bay with a view to discovering more about this wondrous environment, its Native American people, the establishment of trading posts, and possibly a river leading to the long-sought northwest passage to the Far East. During the summer of 1608, he navigated the bay with skills born of his long years as a soldier of fortune and leader of men. Smith and his men covered some 2,500 miles of bay and shore line, probed the major rivers—Potomac, Patapsco, and Susquehanna—as well as the rivers Patuxent, Nanticoke, and the Rappahannnock during 1608–9, met with local native tribal leaders, traded goods for food, and demonstrated firearms. The maps he created after returning were a revelation to the Jamestown colonists and ultimately to England itself concerning the potential of these new lands. In our time, Smith's narrative shows readers the unmatched bounty of the Chesapeake Bay region, in contrast to current concerns over the health of the bay and its diminishing resources. It also demonstrates the degree to which Indians lived in harmony with their surroundings before the arrival of European settlers. Smith's explorations laid the groundwork for the founding of settlements in Maryland.[5]

The origins and subsequent development of Annapolis provide an example of Maryland's colonial history. When, in 1632, King Charles I of England granted to Cecil Calvert, the second Lord Baltimore, the lands of the Chesapeake north of the Potomac River, he did so knowing that the Calverts were newly converted Catholics. This was not viewed with enthusiasm in the Virginia Colony, from which the Calvert lands had been carved. Its inhabitants were mostly Anglicans who remembered the religious strife of sixteenth-century England and who were concerned about the arrival of Roman Catholics under the protection of the Crown. Baltimore gathered about him a group of Catholic gentlemen and others, including Protestants, who were experienced farmers to help found the colony. Fearing that in his absence something would go wrong, Lord Cecil Calvert sent his brother Leonard with the expedition to serve as governor. He also invited two Jesuit priests to become members of the party; they surreptitiously joined the *Ark* and *Dove* at the Isle of Wight after the ships' formal departure from London in 1633.

After a stormy Atlantic crossing, the expedition arrived safely at the mouth of the Potomac River and found an ample safe harbor in the St. Mary's River. After proper ceremonies, the settlers set about trying to create Calvert's vision of an "English town" culture in the New World. The Algonquin Indians who inhabited the region were remarkably peaceful, and even the Virginians cooperated in selling the Marylanders cattle, hogs, and slips for fruit trees. Calvert's settlers benefited from the unhappy example of Jamestown, founded more than twenty years earlier by settlers unprepared for work, and they also profited from the friendly relations they were able to create with those who already inhabited the land. Yet Calvert, too, had his challenge—from William Claiborne, an aggressive fur trader and official of the Virginia colony. Claiborne had voyaged far to the north in Chesapeake Bay before Calvert's arrival. In 1631, Claiborne had built fortifications, a church, and buildings on Kent Island as a base for dealings with the Susquehannocks and other Indians of the northern Chesapeake. He viewed Lord Baltimore as an interloper and rejected Gov. Leonard Calvert's overtures to join their colony. This led to conflict in 1635, when two vessels belonging to Maryland attacked one of Claiborne's on the

Eastern Shore of the lower bay. The Maryland vessels got the better of the fight, but in a later battle the odds were reversed. Finally, Governor Calvert sent a military expedition to Kent Island and captured the leaders. A truce of sorts was agreed upon, though Claiborne would be heard from again.

The powers that King Charles had granted Lord Baltimore were quite extraordinary in extent for the time. Lord proprietor, he owned all the property within the grant accorded to him; he could appoint all officials, receive rents, taxes, and fees, and grant lands to others, and he was head of the church. In short, he was empowered to behave like a medieval baron. In some ways, Lord Baltimore was to be disappointed. His ideal settlement was the English town, surrounded by fields that subjects would work during the day, returning to town at night. He expected the larger grantees, with two thousand or, later, one thousand acres, to establish manor houses. In St. Mary's County this pattern held, but to the north, with a few exceptions, the settlers opted for widely dispersed plantations, extending along rivers and creeks where ships could sail to pick up tobacco packed in barrels. As for religious matters, Lord Baltimore had promised toleration for Protestants among his Catholic settlers. This held, but he was concerned lest the Jesuit fathers he had brought to the colony become too ambitious and grasping. They held some very large grants, and he tried to keep them in check. This became an issue in the 1640s, when the quarrels of the English civil wars arrived in Maryland in the person of Richard Ingle, a Protestant shipmaster and supporter of Oliver Cromwell and Parliament as opposed to the king.

The English civil wars of the 1640s emerged from a contest between the pro-Catholic king and his loyalist supporters and the leaders in the House of Commons, most of whom were Protestants and firm believers that the king rules with the consent of Parliament. King Charles I was a weak though stubborn monarch married to Henrietta Marie, a French Roman Catholic. During the 1620s economic times had been hard, people had suffered from poor harvests, and plague had killed thousands of people. England's wars with Spain and France had gone poorly. As a result of these calamities, relations between King Charles and Parliament worsened. The Duke of Buckingham, the king's favorite and the only leader in whom he had confidence, was assassinated in 1628. Buckingham, a noble untutored in the art of war, had failed in military leadership, and his arrogance contributed to the enmity of many in Parliament and among the London populace. The king unwisely decided he would rule without consulting Parliament, and he did so until 1640. In that year, he reluctantly called Parliament into session so that he could obtain the funds to fight a war with Scotland. With the refusal of Parliament to provide funds, tensions came to the breaking point, and Charles withdrew from London in 1642 to prepare for war. The conflict lasted four years, with parliamentary forces gaining the upper hand in 1646. The king escaped from parliamentary control and briefly conspired with a Scottish group, but all came to naught. Charles was recaptured, imprisoned, tried, and executed in 1649. Parliament's Gen. Oliver Cromwell and his New Model Army were in the ascendancy by 1651, having defeated the late king's son, the future Charles II, at the Battle of Worcester. The political and sectarian bitterness that flowered in England during the civil wars could not help but find resonance in colonial Maryland, creating turbulence for Lord Baltimore and his family and followers.

Captain Ingle arrived at St. Mary's aboard the merchant ship *Reformation* in 1641. In that visit he offended the powerful Brent family, which was related by marriage to the Calverts. On Captain Ingle's return in 1644, Giles Brent, who was acting governor in Leonard Calvert's absence, ordered Ingle's arrest for speaking ill of the king. Ingle returned with armed men in 1645 and demanded that Marylanders take an oath of loyalty to the Parliament. He raided and plundered the estates of those who refused and laid waste the Jesuit plantations. About this time, Governor Calvert departed for Virginia, not to return until 1646, with an army he had raised for the purpose of reclaiming control of the province from those associated with Ingle. Meanwhile, William Claiborne took advantage of this confusion. Perhaps in league with Ingle, he returned to Kent Island and attempted to regain control of his former trading post. Governor Calvert returned in 1646 and forcibly expelled Claiborne, who returned to Virginia. In the midst of these difficulties Governor Calvert died, having in his last moments appointed Thomas Greene, a Roman Catholic, to succeed as governor and Margaret Brent to take care of his personal affairs and property. In 1648, Lord Baltimore (Cecil Calvert) soon removed Greene and appointed William Stone, a Virginia Protestant, as governor.[6]

Baltimore had realized that, in the aftermath of the civil wars, he would have to make changes to conform to the rule of Parliament and walk a narrow path in matters of religion. With the radical elements now in charge, Parliament took a dim view of Catholicism in Maryland. In order to survive, Baltimore had to appoint more Protestants to official positions, invite non-Catholics to populate Maryland, and severely limit the activities of the Society of Jesus. In 1648, he issued a new commission for the council and named five men to council seats, only two of them Catholics. With one exception, all had been active in supporting Leonard Calvert's return to Maryland and putting down Ingle's and Claiborne's rebellion. The one council member who had not previously settled in Maryland was Thomas Hatton, whom Baltimore chose to be provincial secretary, in effect the second most important post in the province. None of the new council members owned manors. Ingle's plundering and destruction in southern Maryland had undermined the manorial system. Baltimore's appointment of William Stone was a brilliant political maneuver. Stone was a wealthy tobacco planter and a long-time Protestant resident of Virginia, well connected in Parliament. He had promised Baltimore that he could bring more Protestant settlers to Maryland. By this move, Baltimore made his continued control of Maryland more acceptable to Cromwell's faction in Parliament.[7]

One of Governor Stone's first steps was to advance the Act Concerning Religion, passed by the Maryland Assembly in 1649, which guaranteed religious toleration. In doing so, he codified Lord Baltimore's wishes that his policies be extended in the colony. The act prohibited discrimination against any Christian sect and let it be known that religion was a private and personal matter. In view of the movement of nonconforming Protestants to Maryland in that same year, Stone may have drafted this act as much to attract Protestants to Maryland as to protect Catholics in the continuation of their religious practices. It was not until after the passage and promulgation of the act that a group of several hundred nonconforming Protestants emigrated from Virginia to found the settlement of Providence, at the mouth of the Severn River. Sir William Berkeley, a royalist Anglican and the new governor of Virginia, had made it clear that Puritans who chose not to accept the practices of the Church of England and the use of the Book of Common Prayer would not be tolerated. Thus, once Lord Baltimore, Governor Stone, and the Maryland Assembly declared their toleration policy, the way was clear for those who disagreed with Berkeley to embark and sail north to the Severn River.[8]

Some five hundred Puritans arrived at the mouth of the Severn River in 1649, many having received grants of land from Lord Baltimore near Whitehall Bay, on the Broadneck peninsula between the Severn and Magothy rivers. People settled in dispersed patterns along the water but used terms such as *town lands* and *town creek,* and they engaged in tobacco farming and fishing. A few had received grants of land across the river on the site that would soon be Arundeltown, the predecessor of Annapolis. Streams and creeks penetrated many areas of the peninsula and made water transport essential to life for those who settled there. An examination of inventories of the estates of deceased Providence settlers between the 1650s and 1690s shows the many maritime artifacts that were considered to have value, such as shallops, boats, ropes, sails, fishing hooks and lines, lead sinkers, canoes, oars, and anchors.[9] The settlers also traded furs with the Piscataway and Susquehannock Indians for items needed or wanted to make life more comfortable. Archaeologists working on lands once part of Providence have discovered ceramics and clothing items that could only have come from such trade, including those of Dutch manufacture available in New Netherlands. It is possible that Dutch ships penetrated the bay as far north as Providence in the mid-seventeenth century, even though this trade was prohibited under the English Navigation Acts.[10]

Sectarian strife interrupted the development of Providence in 1655. The leaders in Providence had for four years refused to swear an oath of loyalty and fealty to Lord Baltimore, a condition of their owning grants from the lord proprietor. Parliament was in a mood to punish anyone who pledged loyalty to Prince Charles as the rightful ruler of England. Maryland's council, in the absence of Governor Stone, had done so. Parliament authorized two commissioners, Richard Bennett and William Claiborne, to obtain the submission of Maryland to its will. Claiborne, an old enemy of Lord Baltimore, now found his moment. He and Bennett named a ten-man Puritan council as the proper governing body in Maryland. Former Governor Stone, finding his authority directly challenged, gathered about 130 men and sailed for the Patuxent River, where he seized the council's records. He determined that he would confront the Puritan leaders who had gathered at Providence.

Stone sent a body of men overland toward the Severn while he gathered several, perhaps eleven or twelve, boats and sailed for that destination. Meanwhile, the Puritans had been reinforced by the arrival of the *Golden Lion,* an armed merchant ship commanded by one Capt. Roger Heamans. What began on March 25, 1655, with Captain Stone's request for parley ended with gunfire from the ship, and a melee ensued. Heamans blockaded the enemy boats with *Golden Lion* and an unnamed second vessel while Captain William Fuller, of Providence, appeared with

120 men at arms. Stone's Catholic troops raised the cry "Hey for St. Maries," and the Puritans replied with "In the name of God fall on—God is our Strength." The battle was "fierce and sharp" but did not last long and ended with a Puritan victory. Captain Stone, wounded, surrendered along with most of his troops, but he had lost twenty in battle. The Puritans claimed to have lost two men killed outright and two more who died of wounds. Conflicting sources make it difficult to pinpoint the exact location of the battle; some fighting could have taken place on the right bank of the Severn River across from Providence. In the days that followed, the Puritans tried and condemned ten men to death, including Stone—though he was spared— and executed four. It is said that they would have killed the rest but for the pleas of the women and some of the soldiers. Ultimately, the Puritans under Bennett and Claiborne came to a settlement with Lord Baltimore, who had worked hard to placate Lord Protector Cromwell. Baltimore proclaimed an amnesty, and the Puritans agreed to take the oath and recognize Baltimore's authority as Proprietor. Had Stone's force been successful, it is possible Providence might have been destroyed, but more likely Stone would have confiscated the Puritan leaders' properties and placed the Catholics in charge of the settlement.[11]

In any event, Providence may well have been the source of the future population of Arundelton (or Arundeltown), but for the next thirty years it seems to have flourished as an agricultural and trading community. The rare 1671–72 journal of the ship *Constant Friendship,* commanded by William Wheatley, informs us of the perils of the long voyage, its intended destinations in Chesapeake Bay, the process of loading the ship, and its return voyage to London. The master's mate, Edward Rhodes, kept this journal through the seventy-five-day westward crossing that found *Constant Friendship* to be one of eighty-some ships that loaded tobacco in Maryland in 1672. Upon arrival in Chesapeake Bay, the ship put in first at St. Mary's, on the Potomac, to clear its papers with the colonial authorities, and then sailed north, stopping briefly in the Patuxent River and finally arriving at Providence, on the Severn, in what probably was Town Creek (today's Carr Creek), near Greenbury Point. The crew of *Constant Friendship* spent the next seventy-five days unloading the cargo brought from England and stowing the barrels of tobacco received from the Providence settlers. By March 25, when the ship departed Providence, she carried 440 hogsheads of tobacco in the hold and 110 hogsheads in the bread room and lazaretto near the vessel's stern. Stopping once again at Patuxent River, Captain Wheatley picked up additional tobacco and headed for St. Mary's to take on the final load of tobacco, totaling 724 hogsheads in all. After a relatively rapid passage of forty-seven days, *Constant Friendship* arrived at Plymouth on June 13, 1672. There the crew learned that England was again at war with the Netherlands and that they would have to sail in convoy, escorted by three warships, to ensure a safe arrival at London.[12]

Rhodes's journal, on which this account is based, is an important maritime document in its description of life at sea on board a seventeenth-century vessel trading with Maryland. The editor of this journal estimates that the *Constant Friendship* would have been about 64 feet in length, with a 26-foot beam and a depth of 13 feet. By standards then used, *Constant Friendship*'s capacity for cargo was 215 tons burden, and the captain would have required about twenty sailors to manage the vessel safely. This document puts the reader in touch with Providence, one of the "lost towns" of Maryland, which disappeared for reasons not clearly understood but probably relating to changes in economic and social conditions in a time of relatively poor communications.

Over time, the clearing of land and extensive planting of tobacco at Providence produced silting, and the use of the nearby creeks for deep-draft ships became difficult. The nearby harbors on the right bank of the Severn were more attractive. The first three known emigrants from Virginia to settle at Arundelton were Thomas Todd, Thomas Hall, and Richard Acton. Todd had been a shipwright living in Lynnhaven Parish, lower Norfolk County, Virginia. A survey of 1651 indicates that Todd established a 100-acre plantation on land running from Deep Cove (College Creek) eastward, including that of the present-day U.S. Naval Academy. Writing of Todd, Nancy Baker states that "Annapolis had its beginnings not in a tobacco market, but in a boat yard where a shipwright made and repaired the river craft essential to his planter neighbors."[13] Hall came from that portion of Norfolk along the Elizabeth River. His Arundelton property ran from Todd's to Spa Creek and north along the creek to Richard Acton's land. Acton, a former carpenter from lower Norfolk County, possessed 100 acres around the head of the creek and some acreage on the southern side. Those headwaters were called Acton's Cove, known for its deep water, which made it ideal for wharfs and shipping. This is where the town developed in its earliest years. In 1668, Cecil Calvert ordered the lieutenant governor and the Council to establish official ports of entry for the unloading and selling of imported goods. Richard Acton sold nineteen acres of his best land on Acton's Cove to Lord Baltimore's agents. This location was designated as one of the official Maryland ports of entry in 1669.

The further development of Annapolis followed as property was subdivided and passed from family to family. The Maryland Assembly contracted with surveyor Richard Beard to survey the town and lay out a new design for what in 1684 became Anne Arundell Town. Ten years later, under the guidance of the new governor, Sir Francis Nicholson, at St. Mary's City, the Assembly passed an act authorizing the removal of the capital and provincial courts to Anne Arundell Town. Once again, Richard Beard received a commission to resurvey and then redesign the town's plan. The Assembly approved the completed work and renamed the town Annapolis, in honor of Princess Anne, the heir to the English throne.[14]

Providence endured until the end of the seventeenth century but gradually lost population, while Arundelton attracted more and wealthier people to what was to become the colony's seat of government. Meanwhile, the ultimate source of the colony's wealth grew along with the annual tobacco trade, which was the basic economic link between the colonies and the mother country. Although records of this trade are fragmentary for the period before 1689, where they exist they are essential to understanding the trade and the dependencies involved. The trade had a seasonal dynamic driven primarily by weather, which directly influenced the growing seasons and produced the storms that ruled the latter months of the summer and early autumn. Research in the Public Records Office in London (Kew) indicates that a fairly complete run of customs records exists for the period 1689 to 1701. Of 1,033 voyages from Maryland, two-thirds were crossings to England and the remaining were voyages to other American colonies, including the island of Barbados. The naval officer who maintained these records was more like a merchant marine officer who kept records for the six ports of entry in Chesapeake Bay: Patuxent, Pocomoke, Annapolis, Potomac, Williamstadt (now Oxford), and Cecil County.[15]

The tobacco "fleets" did not cruise in company in the naval sense, except during the Anglo-Dutch Wars of the 1650s to 1670s. Usually the merchants would urge their shipmasters to sail when ready, from London, Bristol, or Liverpool, so as to obtain their cargoes on a timely basis. Ships would load their manufactured goods and sail for the colony during the winter months, arriving between January and March. They then found their way up the rivers and creeks to plantation wharfs to load the hogsheads of tobacco that had been packed in the late fall. At times, the masters of the tobacco ships had to ride overland to plantations in search of product. These were the so-called "riding captains." Once loaded, the masters would be anxious to put to sea before the hot, humid summer months, which brought diseases, malaria, and storms that could prevent or slow their passage back to England. For the period 1690–1700, customs records recorded 626 ships bound from Maryland to England, an average of 57 per year.[16] Once clear of the Virginia Capes, the tobacco vessel masters would find the Gulf Stream, flowing generally northeast, and usually be favored with southwesterly winds to push them homeward. On the other hand, the threat of piracy was ever present, and there was the real possibility of being captured by an enemy warship or privateer during one of the many conflicts involving England: the Anglo-Dutch Wars (1652–74), King William's and Queen Anne's Wars (1698–1701), the War of the Spanish Succession (1701–14), King George's War (1739–48), and the Seven Years' War (1756–63).[17]

Immigration also played a part in the tobacco trade. Many officials, planters, merchants, and indentured servants embarked on tobacco fleet vessels headed for Maryland ports. By far the majority of these passengers were indentured servants who obligated themselves to tobacco planters for three to four years to pay for their passages. Some became successful planters in their own right; others moved on to learn trades that were essential to growing towns like Annapolis. There were several different classes of indenture. The first were more or less independent souls of the lower middle classes who could purchase their fare on their own or borrow from better-off relatives in the colony for whom they would agree to work after arrival to pay off the debt. Others of the poorest and desperate but non-convict class were called Redemptioners, who could pay part passage, or the truly indentured, who would be transported and sold on arrival. The felons and other convicts on the bottom rung were military and political prisoners who were "transported" to be got rid of, as punishment for their participation in rebellions or mutinies, and convicts whose death sentences were commuted for certain periods depending on the gravity of their crimes. In the seventeenth century, all who were convicted of felonies could be subject to the death sentence, and there were about three hundred crimes in that category. Thus, many convicts stood in fear of execution and would view transportation as a magnanimous reprieve.[18]

It was not until the 1690s that the importation of African slaves became a significant element in the social and economic life of the colony. During the period 1660 to 1680 the planters discovered that they had overproduced tobacco. A glut on the European markets caused prices to drop, ruining some planters. In both Maryland and Virginia, tobacco farmers resorted to various measures to reduce production—restricting planting, culling before shipment, and sheer destruction of the crop. There was little call for increased labor at this time. But after 1690, the international demand for tobacco had increased, and when the slave trade was declared open to colonial traders and others beyond the Royal Africa Company, the numbers of slaves in colonial North America began to increase markedly. In Maryland, their numbers rose from 4,475 in 1704, to almost 8,000 in 1710, to 25,000 in 1720. In contrast, the number of whites in 1715 was 40,740. The slave and free black population grew rapidly in both relative and absolute terms. By 1790, the first census of the United States recorded the number of Maryland blacks at 111,079, more than half the white population, listed at 208,649.[19]

During the seventeenth century, the colony was dependent on trade with the mother country, but shipbuilding was slow to develop for lack of official encouragement. Planters largely depended on the availability of English-built vessels. As types, the largest was the ship, three masted and square rigged and of an average 130 tons burden. Smaller vessels with three masts were called barks, hag boats, flyboats, or pinks, depending on rig and size. Some of the smaller of these were Dutch-built double-enders, captured during the wars with Holland. Two-masted vessels in the tobacco trade included ketches, brigantines, and brigs, using combinations of square and fore-and-aft sails, and averaging about 39 to 33 tons burden. The sloop had one large sail on a single mast and one small sail forward of the mast, rigged to a bowsprit. The larger vessels usually carried guns for self-defense since they were unlikely to have a naval escort.[20] After the Glorious Revolution of 1688, when Maryland became a royal colony, the Assembly began to urge the construction of small ships and vessels of all types. According to a survey ordered in 1697, the sheriffs making inquiry found that most vessels, identified as shallops and sloops, were being built in Talbot and Somerset counties, with Anne Arundel County following next in line.[21] Shipwrights with training in English shipyards took advantage of the wealth of timber to establish building yards, principally on the Eastern Shore, where deep water on the shores of its many creeks and rivers provided convenient launching areas.

ON THE PATAPSCO RIVER, near where the town of Baltimore slowly took shape, William Fell established the first shipyard on Long Island Point in 1731. In time, this was to become a flourishing shipbuilding settlement. As for Baltimore, the earliest recorded shipyard was that of John Fraser, established on the margins of the stream known as Jones Falls in 1746. This was not an ideal location because of the accumulation of silt, which prevented launching except when rains increased the depth. From there, vessels would be hauled to the "basin" near what is today called the Inner Harbor, a place then plagued by shallows and inconvenient for wharfs and shipyards.

William Fell built his shipyard in a superior location on the Patapsco east of Jones Falls where there was adequate depth of water and an easy ebb and flow of the river. His son, Edward Fell, laid out the town of Fells Point (formerly Long Island Point), which was incorporated into Baltimore in 1773. Other shipwrights followed, such as Benjamin Nelson and George Wells in the 1760s and 1770s, David Stodder in the 1780s, and William Price and Thomas Kemp in the 1790s. These were among the most important shipwrights, who earned fame for the swift pilot schooners and other warships they built during the Revolutionary War and the War of 1812. In 1793, a large number of refugees arrived from the island of Saint Domingue (Haiti), where black Jacobins had arisen in revolution against the French. A number of these former French colonists and freedmen settled in Fells Point. One of these was Jean Despeaux, who quickly established himself as a shipyard owner and employed several of the black ship artisans who had accompanied him from the Caribbean. Others were Louis DeRochbrune, whose yard was located on Thames Street; Stephen Berrillant, at the foot of Bond Street; and Andrew Discandes, who worked with Despeaux in Fells Point and set up a shipyard of his own on Federal Hill in 1810.

Federal Hill, on the south bank of the Patapsco opposite early Baltimore, was another location rich in promise for shipbuilding. As of 1773, Thomas Morgan was the earliest shipyard owner to select the slope of Federal Hill for a construction site. It had good depth of water, no troublesome streams silting the water, and plenty of land forested in white oak and locust for ships' timbers. Nearby, on Light (then Forrest) Street, Darby Lux had built a ropewalk in the 1750s. The manufacture of ropes and cables, or cordage, of all sizes was an industry absolutely essential for shipbuilders. In earlier colonial times, the Crown had forbidden the establishment of such businesses, as they were competitive with British home industry and not desirable under the mercantilist doctrine that underlay the European colonial empires. Yet there was such a need for this product in the colony that its production was allowed to flourish. Morgan's son James attempted to continue his father's shipyard business but moved it to Fells Point. A further development for Federal Hill involved the entrepreneur Charles Hughes. He owned the land where Morgan had his shipyard. Hughes extended his holdings eastward along the Patapsco's south shore, built homes in the area, and began dredging and filling the basin where ultimately the Light Street wharves would be built.[22]

Shipwrights migrated to the Chesapeake port areas, including Annapolis, Londontown, Chestertown, Dorchester and St. Mary's counties, and Fells Point, at Baltimore. Ship chandlers, who supplied all manner of ships' equipment, also settled in these towns, as did craftsmen talented in the ways of the sea, sailmakers, rope makers, founders, and blacksmiths. An iron forge had been established near Principio, Maryland, three miles east of Havre de Grace in 1715. Ironworkers set up others on various branches of the Patapsco River. Likewise, another grew up on Virginia's Northern Neck, the Accokeek Furnace, which produced more than four hundred tons a year by 1750. Thus, the capability of building vessels for trade or war was well established in Maryland by the outbreak of the American Revolution.[23]

Annapolis, the colonial capital, was the focus of Maryland's prosperous tobacco trade in the eighteenth century. This town had advantages that Williamsburg, the Virginia capital, lacked: navigable water, shipyards, ship carpenters, ropewalks, block makers, sailmakers, and ship chandlers. Annapolis was the commercial and political capital city of the colony, although Baltimore, in the eighteenth century, was on the rise. Members of a growing merchant class established themselves in Annapolis to expedite the trade and handle the accounts of the planter-aristocracy in their trade with England. Sensing the imminent competition of Baltimore, Annapolis-based legislators were able to keep their city as the only official port of entry for the colony until the American Revolution.[24] Although Annapolis at the end of the seventeenth century was a relatively small town of two hundred fifty free whites,[25] it became a respected port of resupply, repairs, and fitting out for ships both entering and leaving Chesapeake Bay from a wider area on the Western Shore. This included anchorages on the South, Rhode, and West rivers, as well as on Herring Bay. The collector of customs and the district naval officer also had their offices in Annapolis.

Records in the Maryland State Hall of Records in Annapolis contain complete lists of ship entries and clearances given by the deputy collectors of customs from 1748 to 1775. The records include ships' papers showing vessels and cargo, owners and masters, port of origin and destination of cargo, as well as where and when the vessel was built. From this data, one can develop a good idea of the increased maritime activity in the Port of Annapolis during the quarter century before the American Revolution.[26] For example, in 1750, Philadelphia reported 320 ship arrivals, New York registered 302, and Boston showed 562 vessels, but only 64 entered at Annapolis. About twenty years later, in 1773, when Philadelphia was averaging 400 vessels per year, 200 ships put in at Annapolis, an increase of 212 percent, as compared with Philadelphia's increase of just under 25 percent. It is surprising to see the variety of destinations for ships clearing Annapolis in 1752: the 82 vessels, totaling some six thousand tons, included 23 bound for the Caribbean, 31 for the British Isles, 4 for Africa, Europe, and Madeira, and 24 for British North America. The clearances of 1758 were a low point, perhaps because of the ongoing war with France, but the customs records show gradual increases to 1774–75. In 1774, 250 vessels were cleared, while in the first six months of 1775, there were 155, indicating that 1775 could have been a banner year but for the outbreak of the Revolutionary War. In all, 2,981 vessels cleared customs outward bound from Annapolis during the years 1748–75.[27]

The sizes and types of vessel that called at Annapolis in the eighteenth century were highly diverse. The largest in size for the mid-eighteenth century were the letter of marque traders *Winchelsea,* of 500 tons burden, loaded with tobacco, iron, and lumber and carrying eighteen guns, and the *Winchester,* carrying the same cargoes but armed with twenty-four guns. These ships were bound for London, but the majority of vessels that put in at Annapolis were schooners, followed by ships, sloops, brigantines, and snows. Many were in the coastal trade, but the ships in coastal as opposed to transatlantic trade were about equal in number. As to shipowners, the dominant figures of mid-century Annapolis were Samuel Galloway, of Tulip Hill, near Galesville, and Patrick Creagh, of Annapolis. Galloway at one time or another owned upward of twenty-seven vessels and engaged in exporting iron and tobacco to England and grain or flour to the north. He imported manufactured goods, wine, rum, molasses, salt, slaves, convict labor, and indentured servants. Toward the end of the pre-Revolutionary period, the enduring tobacco export was still dominant, with 11,035 hogsheads being shipped, but grain and flour exports had risen sharply. With some fluctuations in the intervening years, grain exports from Annapolis increased from 82,684 bushels in 1749 to 472,783 bushels in 1774; likewise, flour exports grew from 1,598 barrels in 1749 to 70,164 barrels in 1774. The English had suffered from bad grain harvests and the migration of farm workers into the industrializing cities. Hence, Maryland planters on both Eastern and Western shores began to shift from tobacco to grain production, owing to the steadier market demand from the West Indies as well as the mother country.[28]

Along with the increase of shipping in and out of Annapolis, there were developments that positively affected Annapolis's business infrastructure. The town received its charter in 1708, and in the same decade, artisans began to arrive from other areas to work in the leather, cloth, and metal trades, creating a need for modest housing and workshops. As the colonial and county government grew, so did the number of officeholders, servants, and the gentry who found it advantageous to have residences in the capital. By 1715, the town population had nearly doubled, to four hundred, and by 1730 it had nearly redoubled, to seven hundred. This figure does not include the slave population. Most Annapolis craftsmen in this era were immigrants from England, Europe, or other colonies.

Craftsmen participating in the burgeoning marine trades helped to create the prosperity that came to characterize Annapolis and vicinity, including Londontown, on the South and West rivers, in the mid-eighteenth century. The first marine craftsmen in eighteenth-century Annapolis were shipwrights. Robert Johnson applied to the Assembly for permission to use the officially designated ship carpenter's lot in 1719. This was granted on condition that he engage only in shipbuilding and practice the trade continuously for the succeeding twelve months. The next was merchant Robert Gordon, who, in order to fulfill the terms, would have had to hire a shipwright, possibly Samuel Hastings. Not anxious to work, Hastings is recorded as having chopped off his own hand rather than continue sawing. Another, better-known shipwright is Ashbury Sutton, who was active in Annapolis before 1735 and bought rights to use the upper ship carpenter's lot from Gordon. Of the three, Johnson may have been the most successful, having accumulated enough wealth to have a small plantation on Thomas Point; in addition, at the time of his death he was building two houses in Annapolis. Among the property listed in the inventory of his estate were "a boat partly built and half a sloop."[29]

Several other marine trades flourished in Annapolis and nearby towns, such as Londontown, by the mid-eighteenth century. These included block (pulley) making, rope making, barrel manufacture (cooperage), sailmaking, ship carpentry, anchor manufacture, ship carving, and dealing in navigational instruments. Most of these trades involved skills that could be converted into landsmen's trades when maritime jobs were insufficient, and it was not uncommon for marine artisans to be found keeping taverns, working in tanneries, doing ordinary carpentry or metalwork, or helping with stables when the need arose. Indeed, diversification often provided additional income and was one path to upward mobility in Annapolis society. While Annapolis was not widely known as a shipbuilding port, it was renowned for being an efficient ship repair and outfitting community.

In the block-making trade, Thomas Fleming stood out as a master craftsman. He advertised himself in Annapolis's *Maryland Gazette* in 1745 as one who could make "blocks for shipping at reasonable rates—all gentlemen, planters, and others, may also be supplied with suitable blocks for tobacco prizes. Likewise, at the same prices are made and sold pumps for shipping and wells." He located his shop near both the marketplace and the city quay and was quite successful at his trade. The reference to making pumps has applicability to both shipping and domestic needs. Fleming hired assistant John Gordon in the 1750s and an indentured servant, Edward Clark, in 1755. Sometimes, to make some extra money, Fleming would purchase a barrel of limes or lemons and sell them on his premises. In 1752, he advertised imported goods for sale, such as New England hops, sugar, chocolate, tea, Carolina tar, and turpentine. About the same time, he advertised a 500-ton shallop for sale. In 1754 Fleming suffered a calamity that ruined his business; a fire broke out that consumed most of his shop and cost him dearly. An inventory of his remaining stock indicated the kinds of tools and wood he worked with: crosscut saws, augurs, chisels, an adz, compasses and calipers, mallets, a grindstone and wrench, sheave pins, two tons of lignum vitae, deadeyes, maple blocks, unfinished hand pumps, and parcels of iron. He sold his household goods in 1755 and left town to find a new beginning. His tools were given to William Roberts to satisfy a debt. Cabinetmaker Gamaliel Butler purchased Fleming's rebuilt shop and advertised that he had hired a good block maker from Philadelphia who would be able to carry on Fleming's work.[30]

Rope making, another essential maritime trade, was at first prohibited in colonial Maryland. Rope and cable were products traditionally provided by English firms and exported to Maryland, but in Annapolis the need was so great that colonials began to supply it on their own. Thomas Williamson and Barton Rodget, for example, bought hemp, hired workmen, assembled equipment, and purchased land for a ropeyard in Annapolis in 1747. In order to make rope, the proprietors had to purchase a supply of hemp, have it carried to Annapolis, hackle it, spin it into yarn, and then lay up the rope with the yarn. The hemp was found growing near Baltimore north of the Patapsco River. The ropewalk itself required a covered rope house of great length—more than 100 yards—in which to twist the yarn into strands and the strands into rope of varying diameters.[31] Three strands of hackled hemp would be attached to a wheel set up vertically, and this would be turned, twisting the strands into one length of rope. The building also required a furnace and chimney in which tar would be heated; the laid rope would then be dipped in the tar to preserve it from the corrosive effect of seawater. Williamson manufactured rope and twine for domestic purposes as well, in differing dimensions.

He was a very busy man; records indicate that he employed sailmakers, kept a tavern, and had a carting business. He was in this instance not just a rope maker but also an investor in various enterprises. His customers included men from other

Maryland counties as well as residents of Virginia and North Carolina. The latter included John Francis, a ship captain who regularly refitted his ship in Annapolis. Other ropewalks in the mid-bay area during these years included one owned by Stephen West in Londontown and another in Chestertown, owned by B. Hands & Company. By 1755, Christopher Lowndes was operating a ropewalk in Bladensburg and advertising his product in the *Maryland Gazette*. Competition in this trade was intense, as there were also merchants such as Nicholas Maccubin, Lancelot Jacques, James Dick, and Stephen West (the same) selling English-made cordage in Annapolis. Another competing firm, Golder and Thompson, was a partnership between Andrew Thompson, who had worked for James Dick's Londontown ropewalk and then moved to Annapolis, and John Golder, a local cabinetmaker and tavern keeper. This firm lasted from 1757 to 1764, when the partnership was dissolved.[32]

Where ropewalks and block makers are found, sailmakers will not be far away. One of the earliest sailmakers to work in Annapolis was John Connor, who had come to the town as early as 1736. Englishman William Bicknell, who had learned his sailmaker's trade while working in the Chatham shipyard, appeared in Annapolis in the summer of 1749. At that time he was working at Williamson's ropewalk. He advertised that he would "make sails for ships and other vessels in the best manner and at reasonable rates." His 1753 advertisement in the *Maryland Gazette* showed that he had done well and had taken on an indentured servant who could make or mend seines or nets.[33] In the very next year, Bicknell moved his business to Londontown, perhaps because of a new competitor in Annapolis, where Samuel Osband, a Rhode Islander, had set up as a sailmaker at the Creagh shipyard and at Williamson's ropewalk. In the 1760s, Osband also worked for Samuel Galloway, who was part owner, with Stephen Steward, of a shipyard on the West River, some fifteen miles south of Annapolis. William Johnson, possibly a brother of Robert Johnson, worked as a sailmaker "at the warehouse on Mr. Middleton's wharf . . . and he likewise makes cots, hammocks, and sacking bottoms for bedsteads."[34] Of the 585 ships that made voyages to Anne Arundel County during the first half of the eighteenth century, 38 percent went into the South River to trade at Londontown. In comparison, the Severn River received 20 percent and the West River only 13 percent of the county's overall shipping. Londontown's prosperity was due primarily to the tobacco trade, but merchants also exported wheat, corn, wood, and flaxseed from Londontown to British colonies in the Caribbean and elsewhere. Trade in the South River declined rapidly after the commencement of the Seven Years' War, in 1756, and never really recovered its earlier volume.[35]

The role of shipwrights in Annapolis and vicinity during the mid-eighteenth century deserves attention. In the port of Annapolis there were two important construction sites, the ship carpenter's lot where Patrick Creagh's yard was located, near the Market House, and on Dorsey's (College) Creek, at William Roberts's shipyard. It may seem peculiar for a town so linked to the sea, but few ships were actually being constructed in Annapolis. According to contemporary sources, there was already a shortage of local timber suitable for shipbuilding, Galloway and Steward's West River shipyard provided strong competition, and the Severn River was becoming increasingly shallow.

According to the traveler Rev. Andrew Burnaby, "there is very little trade carried on from this place, and the chief of the inhabitants are storekeepers and public officers. They built two or three ships annually but seldom more."[36] Creagh himself was not a shipwright but a merchant who hired skilled indentured servants or contracted with shipwrights to build on the ship carpenter's lot. Though he commissioned and launched the ship *Hanbury* in 1753, he owned many more ships than he built, amounting to thirteen vessels between 1734 and 1749. Ashbury Sutton, a shipwright who became a shipowner, had a share in the snow *Samuel,* 8 tons, in 1734. A few years later he purchased part of the upper ship carpenter's lot, and in 1746 he leased a ropewalk before leaving the town for Norfolk in 1748. Sewell Long, born in Somerset County, teamed with Edward Rumney in 1747 to build the ship *Rumney and Long,* 600 tons, for William Roberts. He also contracted with Patrick Creagh to construct the ship *Hanbury,* 150 tons, launched in 1753. Shipwright Benjamin Sallier was not quite as successful as those named, but he was quite the local character. A sheriff's notice of May 1752 read as follows: "Broke out of the Anne Arundel County gaol on the 14th instant, Benjamin Sallyer, ship carpenter by trade, a sour looking fellow about 30 years of age, brown complexion, impudent, talks bold, and wears handkerchiefs tied in a careless manner around his neck. Reward." Sallier had been imprisoned for debt relating to a job he had undertaken for William Cromwell in 1748 to complete work on a 48-foot vessel. He had had to hire his own workmen, pay for their accommodations, and use his own tools. Cromwell stopped work on the project because Sallier allegedly was not following instructions. The temperamental Sallier was then out of pocket and out of work when he was thrown in jail. He escaped, but the sheriff published a notice that if Sallier would surrender, he would not jail him again but would allow him to work out his debt working on another vessel.[37]

Annapolis shipwrights were itinerant and dependent on the yard owners for employment. They could go where there was a demand for their services. In the early 1770s, Annapolis shipbuilding and marine trades were in decline, perhaps in reaction to competition from nearby communities offering more opportunities for maritime tradesmen. Working from south to north, Herring Bay records show only a few vessels built in the 1730s, two schooners and two sloops, and they name Joseph Rawle, James Thompson, Samuel Read, and James Russel as the builders. West River showed significantly more activity, with members of the Norris, Steward, Foard (or Ford), Franklin, and Crandall families building boats and ships, intermarrying, and passing the skills down from father to son. Particularly notable is the marriage of Thomas Norris and Sarah Parrish in 1708. The Parrish family was one of the wealthiest families in the colony. When Thomas Norris died, Sarah married John Steward, and they inherited a parcel of the Parrish family property that eventually became the site of the shipyard owned by Samuel Galloway III and John's son Stephen Steward in the mid-eighteenth century. The Steward shipyard in West River was one of the most productive yards on the Western Shore of Chesapeake Bay. It produced as many as twenty-four vessels between 1753 and 1772, a few of them as large as 400–500 tons burden. Steward built two galleys for the Maryland State Navy and maintained those and others.[38] Yard construction came to a sudden halt in March 1781, when a British raiding party from HMS *Monk* and HMS *Hope* came ashore and burned vessels on the stocks and some of the yard buildings.[39]

On the South River, the marine trades and shipbuilding also showed growth during the mid-eighteenth century. Londontown was one of several ports that enjoyed favorable legislation of the Assembly during 1706–8. These laws exempted tradesmen from levies in their first four years of residence and included other incentives for settlement of towns. Shipwrights John Hill, William Chiffin, and John Moriarity lived and worked at Londontown during the years 1700 to 1720, as did ship carpenters William Wooten and Rodger Peele, who died a few years later. Ferry owner, tavern owner, and shipwright Edward Rumney also worked in Londontown. He was probably the father of Edward Rumney, the shipwright of Annapolis, and a relative of Nathaniel Rumney, a shipwright at Hammond's Ferry, on the Patapsco River. Only two vessels, the sloop *Biddy* and the ship *Frederick,* can definitely be counted as having been built (1733) on the South River in this period, although there may have been others.[40]

During the two decades (1755–75) prior to the American Revolution, Maryland shipbuilding grew to the point of providing a fair quantity of home-built vessels used for bay and oceanic transport. For that period, 386 Maryland-built vessels, listed in the port records of Annapolis, averaged 85 tons, including 98 ships, 37 snows, 66 brigs, 111 schooners, and 74 sloops. Next to the New England colonies, Maryland and Virginia were those most active in shipbuilding, producing together about 12 percent of the total tonnage of the North American colonies in the year 1769.[41]

This process did not cease with the advent of the Revolutionary War; rather, it increased. But prospective owners needed different types of vessels. The smaller schooners and sloops, built for speed, were much in demand. The "Virginia-built schooner," perhaps derived from the lines of Bermuda sloops, with low freeboard, masts raked aft, and smooth hulls, which could sail faster to windward than the heavier ships likely to be found in a blockading squadron, found a market in Chesapeake Bay. They were the forerunners of the "Baltimore Clippers," which reached their heyday during the War of 1812.

Baltimore, in the mid-eighteenth century, was only a village of two dozen houses and some two hundred people. By 1776, it was the ninth-largest town in British North America. The American Revolution disrupted ordinary economic life and brought new opportunities. The British occupation of New York and Philadelphia and their destruction of Norfolk precipitated merchant migrations to Baltimore.[42] By 1790, Baltimore was the fourth-largest city in the Republic. Its rapid increase in size can be attributed to trade with the British West Indies. The islands needed food supplies to support production of their cash crops: sugar, cocoa, tobacco, rice, and coffee. The North American colonies, from New York south, had traditionally provided corn, wheat, pork, beef, lumber, and iron. Baltimore's growth depended on exporting the wheat crops of Maryland and Pennsylvania farmers. A small iron industry and ship construction also emerged at about that time. Until the development of the steam dredge, Baltimore's progress as a deepwater port was delayed. Shoals in the Patapsco River prevented the largest ships, those over 300 tons, from nearing the city. Annapolis was no better off in this regard, but it was closer to the tobacco-producing lands of southern Maryland.

In the early 1770s, many Marylanders were still of a conservative bent and relatively fond of their royal governor, Robert Eden. Yet, as the reverberations of the Stamp Act crisis spread and the Townshend Act followed in its wake, hardships and popular protests broke out in the cities of the Northeast, particularly Boston. A harbinger of the trouble to come in Maryland can be seen in the burning of the *Peggy Stewart,* a merchantman that arrived at Annapolis from England with a cargo of tea, spices, and a number of indentured servants. The merchants of Baltimore, Annapolis, Londontown, and other Atlantic coastal cities had been in correspondence after the British closed the port of Boston in the wake of the "Tea Party" of 1773. Legend has it that, in May 1774, patriots in Chestertown took action that foreshadowed that in Annapolis. They boarded the brigantine *Geddes* and threw its tea overboard in a similar act of defiance. The historian Adam Goodheart has investigated the sources and found little existing evidence of the event, even though it is celebrated annually. However, if it did take place, it is likely that those who took part, having no desire that their names be known, found some way to eliminate the documentary evidence of their participation, so now all that is left is speculation and controversy.[43]

At a convention held in Annapolis in June, delegates voted to express sympathy with Boston's merchants, and as a protest, they agreed not to pay customs duties on certain imported goods. They also voted to send representatives to the First Continental Congress, to be held in Philadelphia in September. Merchants Anthony Stewart and James Dick, who owned the *Peggy Stewart,* had ordered two thousand pounds of tea to be consigned to T. C. Williams & Company, of Annapolis. When the ship arrived in October 1774, Stewart paid the tax to enable the passengers, mostly indentured servants, to come ashore. When it became known that Stewart had paid the customs duty, local patriots were outraged. As people gathered from out of town, some of the local lawyers and merchants counseled Stewart and Dick to destroy the ship as well as the shipment to prevent worse happening. At this, Stewart ordered the ship's captain to run *Peggy Stewart* aground off Windmill Point, where the owners themselves set fire to the ship, and she burned in front of hundreds of onlookers who had heard the news. This act soon became a symbol of colonial unrest in Maryland, and it found its parallels in other colonies, where protests broke out against British rule.[44]

Chapter Two

From the Revolutionary War to the War of 1812

∼∽∼∽∼∽∼∽∼∽∼∽∼∽∼∽∼∽∼∽∼∽∼∽∼∽∼∽∼∽∼∽

W ITH THE REVOLUTIONARY WAR came a surge in European demand for wheat and a relative decline in the demand for tobacco. Realizing this, some of Maryland's planters began to shift to wheat production. Baltimore was in a position to exploit this development. The quarter century after the Peace of Paris, in 1783, is marked by the gradual decline of Annapolis and the rise of Baltimore in the commercial and maritime life of the state. Maryland's maritime commerce grew before and after the American Revolution, but the war interrupted these developments. To continue importing badly needed goods and to export produce, Maryland had to create a navy. Her merchants and seafarers proved they would fight to defend their trade. As relations between the colonies and Great Britain strained to the breaking point in 1775, it became clear to merchants and others dependent on sea trade that American ports and shipping would suffer if they did not take steps to protect their livelihood. Almost all of the new states created navies. Some, like that of Massachusetts, were oceangoing. Others were simply naval militia, or "sea fencibles," as they were called, who rallied to defend the waterfront or the coastline at the sound of an alarm.

As the events of the American Revolution proceeded, royal government in the colonies broke down, and patriot leaders began to form improvised governments to cope with the crisis. In Maryland, Gov. Robert Eden, who was generally respected and well liked, tried to stay above the fray, while the Assembly, in June 1774, decided to participate in the First Continental Congress held in Philadelphia. The Assembly voted to form a convention to select the delegates. Those who were opposed to the governor and proprietary officials called themselves the "Popular Party," led by Charles Carroll, William Paca, Matthew Tilghman, Samuel Chase, and Robert Goldsborough. Each county could elect representatives to represent the convention in the Congress. These gentlemen, among others, went to Philadelphia, where they were generally among the moderates, that is, those who still opposed independence but wanted to send a protest to the Crown and to prepare for armed conflict should it come. During the winter of 1774–75, events took a turn toward outright conflict in New England, as towns stockpiled arms and ammunition and British troops marched out of Boston in search of these caches. From this came the clash of minutemen and British troops at Lexington and Concord in April 1775, precipitating the leftward surge of events toward war and revolution. Meanwhile, the Maryland convention voted itself to be what one historian has called a "semi-permanent legislature."[1]

Governor Eden, though still present in the colony, made no effort to regain control, but this left the government without an executive decision-making entity. To fill this vacuum, in May 1775, the convention created a Council of Public Safety, whose job it would be to maintain public security, to prepare defenses against outside threats, and to maintain law and order within the fabric of society. Many were worried about their property and the state of their finances. Borrowers were refusing to pay their creditors, and people were breaking friends and relatives out of debtors' prisons. On the Eastern Shore, landless tenant farmers, with loyalties in conflict, did not necessarily agree with the feelings of the landed gentry regarding a need for revolution. The spread of Methodism during the eighteenth century had created a bond of loyalty to John Wesley, the English founder of the sect. Others worried about the potential of a slave uprising, a real possibility where the slave and free-black population nearly equaled the whites. As events were to show, the Eastern Shore would remain an uncertain entity as the patriot revolution moved forward in Maryland.

In July 1775, the Continental Congress recommended that the committees of public safety in the colonies create navies to defend their ports and commerce. Soon thereafter, Congress began to establish its own navy, when, in an act of October 13, a committee voted send two armed vessels to intercept British troop transports and arms sailing for Quebec. Maryland's Council of Public Safety, headed by Daniel of St. Thomas Jennifer, authorized recruitment of seamen and marines, established salaries and bounties, outfitted and armed ships for war, and chartered vessels for service to the colony. A Baltimore Committee of Observation made up of leading merchants, chaired by Samuel Purviance Jr., assisted the Council of Public Safety in carrying out these naval tasks, with the cooperation of Continental Navy agent Jesse Hollingsworth. One of the council's earliest acts was to authorize the Committee of Observation to purchase the ship *Sidney,* owned by merchant John Smith, for £1,450 and to convert her to a warship. Thus was born the Maryland Navy's ship *Defence.*[2]

The mission of the Maryland Navy was to defend the state's harbors, protect commerce on the bay, and maintain communications with the Eastern Shore and Virginia. It would also perform a perhaps unexpected task—the transport of supplies and troops for the Continental Congress.[3] The council had in effect also created a state merchant marine, by chartering vessels to trade for the government and to return with munitions of war. Numerous voyages were made by Thomas Conway's sloop *Molly,* the schooners *Ninety-Two, Resolution, General Smallwood,* and *Friendship,* the brigs *Sam* and *Friendship,* the schooner-gunboats *Dolphin* and *Plater,* and the ship *Lydia.* Even the ship *Defence* made a trading voyage in 1778 before she was sold. Trading agents such as Richard Harrison, located at Martinique, and Abraham and Isaac Van Bibber, in St. Eustatius, or "Statia," worked for both Virginia and Maryland in obtaining needed war materials.[4]

British naval forces in the Chesapeake in the early months of 1776 were under the control of Captain Andrew Snape Hamond of HM frigate *Roebuck,* 44 guns, commander of the blockade of the Delaware and Virginia capes. Hamond was also responsible for protecting Lord Dunmore and his "floating city" of royalists in the lower Chesapeake Bay. The warships at his disposal were HM frigate *Liverpool,* 28 guns, HM sloop *Kingfisher,* 16 guns, and HM sloop *Otter,* 16 guns. Hamond learned that Maryland trading vessels were preparing to run the blockade under the protection of two armed vessels. On February 28, Hamond ordered *Otter,* under the command of Captain Matthew Squires, to sail up the bay and reconnoiter the Patapsco River.[5]

This set the scene for the first confrontation between patriot and British naval forces in Maryland waters. The Maryland Navy was at first limited to *Defence,* a small converted merchant ship, and her small schooner-tender *Resolution.* Commanded by Capt. James Nicholson, *Defence* sortied from Baltimore on March 9, 1776, to protect the port from attack by a small British squadron. Her approach threatened HM sloop of war *Otter,* whose captain had been ordered to cut out any ships capable of being armed, without risking loss of his ship. There was no battle. While *Otter*'s tenders attempted to take control of a grounded merchantman, *Otter* had grounded on Bodkin Shoal. As *Defence* drew closer, Squires worked *Otter* free, only to ground again, briefly. He recalled his tenders from the grounded merchantman and dropped down the bay.[6] Captain Nicholson returned to Baltimore and was hailed as the savior of the city. He had at least done his duty, and the ship *Defence* fully justified the expense of her commissioning as Maryland's first state warship. Three months later, the Maryland convention notified Governor Eden that "the public quiet and safety" required his departure from the colony.[7] Shortly thereafter, on June 23, HMS *Fowey* appeared off the mouth of the Severn River, picked up Eden, and carried him to Gwynn's Island, in the lower Chesapeake, where Virginia's Governor Dunmore and his few remaining followers had found refuge under the protection of the Royal Navy.

William Paca, a Maryland delegate to the Continental Congress, suggested to the Naval Committee of the Continental Congress that it commission two Baltimore merchant vessels, the sloop *Falcon,* commanded by Capt. William Hallock, and the schooner *Scorpion,* Capt. William Stone, for the Continental Navy. These vessels, renamed, became *Hornet* and *Wasp,* respectively, diminutive predecessors of a long series of distinguished U.S. Navy ships. After conversion for war, these vessels joined Commodore Esek Hopkins's squadron as it sailed forth on its first operation, the raid on the arsenal on New Providence in the Bahamas. The Council of Public Safety soon realized that the small, newly established Continental Navy would be unable to assist in the defense of the bay owing to its other missions. The council established the pay of the Maryland Navy as similar to that of the Continental Navy and commenced the construction of several row galleys, inspired by the type built for the defense of the Delaware River. Propelled by sails and oars, these shallow-draft vessels were ideal for many parts of the bay. They ranged from 50 to 70 feet in length, were sloop-, lateen-, or schooner-rigged, and were sailed by experienced seamen, supplemented by militia who handled muskets and swivel guns. Operating in divisions or squadrons, they could attack larger vessels in calms and could escape by hovering over the flats where larger vessels of the British navy could not reach them.

The Maryland Navy row galleries were built during 1777 at several yards, ranging from George Wells and Archibald's Baltimore shipyards, to Stephen Steward's at West River, and Thomas Smyth's at Chestertown, on the Eastern Shore. The galleys they completed were *Baltimore,* commanded by Thomas Walker, *Independence,* by Bennet Matthews, *Chester,* by Thomas Conway, *Conqueror,* by John David, *Plater,* by Benjamin King, and *Johnson,* by James Belt. The galley *Annapolis* was never completed. The galley commanders all had problems finding hands and provisions. Frequently, only two or three could be put in service at any one time because of such shortages. On June 8, 1778, Gov. Thomas Johnson appointed Thomas Grason commodore of the Maryland Navy.[8] He had a difficult task ahead.

Commodore Grason's most annoying enemies were loyalists who constructed and manned barges and galleys that operated from bases on the lower Eastern Shore. They sold food and provided water and intelligence to British warships patrolling the bay. The Tory bargemen preyed on trading vessels from Annapolis, Baltimore, Alexandria, and riverfront plantations that attempted to slip past the blockade.[9] On occasion, they raided plantations on the Patuxent, Nanticoke, and Wicomico rivers. The most notorious of these seagoing loyalists was Joseph Wheland Jr., who had first been arrested for carrying supplies to Lord Dunmore's fleet in early 1776. Freed on his bond, Wheland did his best to make life miserable for seagoing patriots. He and his men found comfort among other loyalists on the islands of the lower Eastern Shore. Some two hundred fifty of their number gathered in Somerset and Worcester counties and began to collect arms. When the state sent two thousand regulars and militia to disperse them and seize the arms, the loyalists melted away.

Each time the British came in strength into the bay, the loyalists revived. During Adm. Richard Lord Howe's campaign and the occupation of Philadelphia in 1777–78, the British promised them protection if they took an oath of allegiance to the king and attempted to recruit a Maryland Loyalist regiment. Seagoing Tories, including Wheland, manned barges and harassed shipping on Tangier and Pocomoke sounds. They were especially active when Benedict Arnold, whom the British had made a brigadier general, and his troops raided Virginia in 1780 and after the battle of Yorktown in 1781. Loyalist privateers, based on New York, also operated in the Chesapeake with the assistance of the Tories.

The earliest indication that the strategic balance of the war was changing was the appearance of a French naval squadron off the coast of Delaware in the summer of 1778. France had finally entered the war in alliance with the United States. This had been the main objective of Benjamin Franklin's diplomacy in Paris since 1777. Soon after signature of the Treaty, French Minister of Marine Sartine dispatched a squadron of twelve ships of the line and four frigates from Toulon under the command of the Admiral Comte d'Estaing. The overextended British navy observed but could not prevent the departure of the squadron from the Mediterranean. D'Estaing shaped his course for the mouth of the Delaware River, hoping to trap the British in their evacuation of Philadelphia. By his arrival in June, however, the British had marched north to New York after a bloody battle at Monmouth, New Jersey. Adm. Lord Richard Howe had deployed his smaller ships along the New Jersey and Delaware coast to provide early warning of the arrival of the French squadron. One of these ships was HMS *Mermaid,* a 24 gun (9-pounders) frigate that had been on the North American coast supporting naval operations and taking prizes since 1776. *Mermaid*'s commander, Capt. James Hawker, had anchored inside Cape Henlopen and was taking on water casks from HMS *Roebuck* when word of the French squadron arrived on July 9, 1778. *Roebuck* departed immediately for Sandy Hook, leaving Hawker to his own devices. What happened next has been revealed in other ships' logs and journals, both British and French. Hawker tried to slip out of the Delaware innocuously and escape the French by sailing southward along the Delaware-Maryland coast. Unfortunately for Hawker and the *Mermaid*'s crew, the wind was blowing from the southwest on that typical summer day. D'Estaing sent several frigates in chase, as *Mermaid* tacked along the coast, perhaps heading for the Virginia Capes and the safety of Chesapeake Bay.

After grounding briefly off Fenwick Island, Hawker sensed that the game was up and made for the Assateague Island shore. There, he knew, was an inlet used by the American sea captains as a way of avoiding the British blockade at the Virginia Capes. If they could bring supplies into Chincoteague Bay, the rebels would send their goods overland to Snow Hill, where they could be reshipped via the Pocomoke River to Cambridge, Oxford, Annapolis, or Baltimore.[10] Hawker's dilemma by now was to whom he should surrender, the French Navy ships in hot pursuit or the rebels just inside Sinepuxent Inlet. He chose the latter, probably in accordance with standing orders. On the early morning of July 8, having lightened ship as much as possible by heaving overboard cannon and excess baggage, Hawker drove *Mermaid* aground with all sails set. He then hoisted his ensign, lowered it, and ordered all his masts cut away, while the French frantically tried to reach his vessel. Before that could happen, an armed rebel schooner closed and boarded to hoist an American flag.

Col. Samuel Handy of Snow Hill accepted Captain Hawker's surrender and took custody of the prisoners, sending them on to Cambridge, where they would await further transportation. Gov. Thomas Johnson granted parole to Hawker and his officers. After being exchanged, Hawker eventually found his way to British-held New York, where he had to stand trial by court martial. The court, held on board HMS *Monmouth,* acquitted him for acting "consistent with his duty" by running his ship ashore rather than allowing her to fall prize to a French fleet. As for the *Mermaid* and her cargo, the Maryland Admiralty Court declared the ship condemned and sold at auction for the benefit of Colonel Handy and the Snow Hill battalion of the Worcester County Militia. The sale raised £14,233 to be distributed to the libellants; John Davidson & Company of Philadelphia bought the sole remaining cannon and ship's bell, and Jacob Morris & Company purchased the hull. The entire episode is important because it shows in dramatic fashion the importance of Maryland's Sinepuxent Inlet on Assateague Island and the Worcester County town of Snow Hill during the American Revolution. It is also the only example of the British surrendering a ship to the Americans while under pursuit by the French.[11]

After France entered the war, Maryland reduced the size of her small navy, selling off the ship *Defence* and several galleys. With complaints from Eastern Shore patriots and shipowners mounting, in 1779 the Council of Public Safety accepted the offer of Baltimore merchants to man two privateers to assist the Maryland

Navy's galleys. Nothing came of this, as the merchants heard that the port of St. Eustatius was completely blockaded. The General Assembly passed the Act for the Defence of the Bay, ordering severe measures. The militia was ordered to evacuate all residents of the islands below Hooper Strait by May 1, 1781. Likewise, St. Mary's County authorities were to strip nearby islands and the Potomac River shore of all that might be of value to Tory bargemen. At nearly the same time, a small British force of two sloops of war, HMS *Monk* and HMS *Hope,* were blockading Annapolis. In March 1781, these ships sent three barges into West River, some fifteen miles south, to find and destroy Stephen Steward's boatyard. Steward was a partner of the wealthy merchant Samuel Galloway, who lived near present-day Galesville in his classic colonial mansion, Tulip Hill. He had built several of the state's navy galleys and at the time of the raid had a 20-gun vessel on the stocks. The Royal Navy barges, armed with 100 marines, made their way up the West River at night. A small militia unit posted on Chalk Point at the entrance to Lerch Creek fired on them and fled as the marines landed to destroy the battery and then proceeded up the creek to Steward's yard. When the marines finished their work, there was not much left of the shipyard, the ship, the ways, the storehouses, and a dwelling. All burned, including Steward's books and papers.[12]

The state reestablished its navy, with barges instead of galleys. The barges were as lengthy as the row galleys of earlier years but were of shallower draft and were primarily oar-driven. They carried small cannons in bow and stern. The General Assembly authorized the governor and the Council of Public Safety to "purchase or build fitted with sails and oars and manned as soon as possible four large barges or row boats capable of carrying swivels and 25 men at least." The Tory barges, with their effectiveness in river raids, had made their point. Citizens on the Eastern Shore took the initiative of building several, since they were the ones who had suffered most. One barge, from Somerset County, 54 feet on the keel, 14 feet of beam, with a 3-foot depth of hold, was propelled by thirty-two oars and was capable of mounting up to ten swivel guns. Such a barge might also be equipped with platforms, forward and aft, for sliding carriages to hold 4- or 6-pounders. A list of these barges includes *Defence,* a Dorchester County barge commanded by a Maryland Navy officer; *Experiment,* provided by subscription of Eastern Shore residents; *Intrepid; Revenge,* commanded by Commodore Grason; *Protector,* commanded by Zedekiah Walley, who became commodore after Grason's death; *Somerset; Terrible;* and *Wye River,* which was personally owned by Thomas Groves, a commissioned officer in the Maryland navy.

The French Navy made its appearance in the bay, having fought the British fleet to a standstill at the Battle off the Capes on September 5, 1781. For a while, the French cooperated with the Maryland Navy in suppressing the enemy's barge warfare. Following the British surrender at Yorktown, however, the French presence shrank and the barges reappeared. In September 1782, Commodore Grason was killed in *Revenge* during a barge battle in the Potomac. The resulting furor brought four more barges into service under Commodore Zedekiah Walley, who was ordered to cruise with his "fleet" in Tangier Sound near James Island. The Maryland Navy got the worst of it in the famous "Battle of the Barges" on November 30, 1782, when six Tory barges met his four, *Revenge, Defence, Protector,* and the new *Fear-nought.* Due to a tactical failure, Walley's barge was isolated ahead of the others and the commodore was killed, as were twenty-five of his men, with twenty-nine others wounded.[13] This was the bloodiest battle the Maryland Navy fought during the war, but it was not the last, for barge warfare continued, essentially out of control, into March 1783.

Privateering, one of the strongest of Maryland's maritime traditions, was definitively established during the American Revolution, though it reached its peak during the War of 1812. The practice of privateering was often a resort of weaker maritime nations, whose public navies were small or poorly organized. By licensing mariners to arm their merchant vessels and hunt for the enemy, promising proceeds of the sale of the captured vessel or prize to privateer owners, officers, and crew, the government had a way of appealing to the profit motive and putting it to work in a patriotic way. Congress found that the prime disadvantages of sponsoring privateers during the American Revolution were that it drew experienced sailors away from the Continental Navy and that privateers were not answerable to naval command. They could not be depended upon to cooperate with the orders of a naval commodore. A privateer captain was responsible only to his ship's owners for his duty. Their primary targets were the enemy's merchant ships, not his public ships. Although examples are not lacking of privateers fighting ships of the Royal Navy, they usually avoided a contest in which they were matched against professional sea warriors and ships equipped exactly for that purpose.

Although Maryland had one of the smaller state navies, she provided far more privateers than her size would lead one to expect. She ranked just behind the ocean-going state of Massachusetts, accounting for approximately 20 percent of all privateers sent out. Many of Baltimore's merchants invested in privateering during the Revolution as a profitable way of using the capital they had accumulated in the war trade. Baltimore became the depot for Continental Army supplies of iron, flour, and salt. A good example was the firm of John Smith, a merchant from central Pennsylvania, who became a leader in the export-import trade before the Revolution. Smith incorporated his two sons, Samuel and John Jr., into the business and became one of the first to exploit the exchange of flour for military stores. Profits from war trade in excess of 100 percent were not uncommon, and demand remained constant. Other Baltimoreans became entrepreneurs in this fashion, including William Patterson, Jesse Hollingsworth, Jonathan Hudson, William Taylor, William Spear, and Daniel Bowley.[14]

Risky as it was, privateering also offered opportunities for enrichment if the owners invested in a stout, well-armed vessel, a skilled captain, and an experienced crew. The Continental Congress and the states issued more than 2,000 commissions, known as "letters of marque and reprisal," to privateersmen. The state of Massachusetts issued some 600. Maryland is credited with 224 commissions. These figures include some vessels reapplying under different names, different rigs, and new owners, so they are not certain but are fairly accurate.[15] While undoubtedly rooted in the colonial period, Maryland's modern seafaring traditions developed rapidly during the American Revolution. Its seaports attracted a concentration of maritime artisans, its shores provided abundant forests, and the state spawned an ample number of experienced mariners. The profitability of maritime pursuits in peace and war laid the groundwork for shipbuilding, the carrying trade, privateering, and related industries that flourished early in the nineteenth century.

The end of the Revolutionary War brought major shifts in political, economic, and social patterns in Maryland, affecting the state's maritime occupations. Despite optimistic predictions, Annapolis gradually lost her favored financial and social position but, as the state capital, retained a modicum of political importance. Conversely, Baltimore attracted the tobacco export trade. The city flourished in new affluence, tempered by competition with Alexandria, Philadelphia, New York, and Boston. In general, however, the late 1780s witnessed an economic depression that affected many areas of the Eastern seaboard. Merchants overcalculated the demand for luxury goods in the United States, and the outbreak of the European wars of the 1790s disrupted the continental market for all but the best Maryland tobacco. Georgetown, Piscattaway, and Port Tobacco, towns that had once flourished in this trade, went into decline, and Annapolis experienced a halt in population growth, becoming by stages a quiet market town.[16]

Not that the old firms died easily. The export firm of Wallace, Johnson & Muir had an interesting ploy. It employed some of its ship captains as "riding captains," whose job it was, between voyages, to ride about the area on horseback seeking cargo. They were also called "tobacco beggars" by unsympathetic souls, as "the usual practice was for a riding captain to bring a ship out from London early in the spring and spend the summer loading it and subsequent ships in the fall, when he returned to London with one of the last cargoes for the year."[17] To get business, the firm found it necessary to provide its agents with cash to pay planters an advance on what their tobacco would bring in London. The ships might remain at river landings for several months while small craft brought tobacco to the larger vessel from the Eastern and Western shores. In addition to working the Patuxent and Potomac rivers, their ships also made landings as far south as the York River, although their riding captains, not knowing the planters, did not do as well there. The major effort remained in Maryland. Planters with marginal tobacco crops began to grow wheat instead. Interestingly, Baltimore traders did not reap all the rewards. Wheat farmers in Frederick County discovered they could ship their crop more cheaply to the Georgetown landings on the Potomac than to those on the Patapsco near Baltimore. This encouraged competing consignment merchants, such as the partnership of Uriah Forrest and Benjamin Stoddert, which profited much from the Georgetown trade.[18]

In the long run, however, the tobacco trade suffered depression and planters shifted to wheat farming, plowing their fields deeper and silting the rivers. This made the tobacco trade more difficult. As the poorer farmers of southern Maryland failed, they migrated to richer farm areas in the west and north, reducing the population significantly in Charles and St. Mary's counties, thereby shrinking potential markets for finished goods. The affect on Annapolis, the former export capital of southern Maryland, was inevitable. The brilliant years were past, and the town had to wait nearly half a century, until the founding of the Naval Academy in 1845, to be stirred by a national event. In the decade after the Revolution, Maryland joined other states in debating the political future of the United States. Most of Maryland's leaders were Federalists at that time. When the Philadelphia convention met during 1787 to decide on the Constitution, the Maryland delegation, with the exception of two, voted to adopt the charter.

For many months during the winter of 1787–88, the nation debated ratification. Financial unrest in the northern states complicated the problem, but most Federalist shipping owners supported the movement. On April 22, 1788, the Maryland convention ratified the Constitution by a vote of 63–11, a resoundingly firm statement. Pro-Federalist citizens of Maryland celebrated in the streets of Baltimore, with seamen and the shipping trades well represented in a parade that featured a cart containing the *Maryland Federalist,* a miniature full-rigged ship, 15 feet in length, with seven sails, indicating that Maryland was the seventh state to ratify the Constitution.

This amusing idea was the brainchild of Capt. Joshua Barney, a Baltimore-born Revolutionary War hero. Barney had a successful career as a lieutenant and later as the captain of several ships in the Continental Navy, with privateers, and in the Pennsylvania Navy. Following the ratification celebrations, Barney was nominated by his fellow citizens to sail the tiny vessel down the bay and up to Mount Vernon on the Potomac, where he would present her to General Washington as a token of Maryland's esteem. This he did, impressing Washington with the ingenuity of American shipbuilders.[19] Barney eventually traveled to France, where he offered his services to the French Navy. After he returned in 1800 he would again make a major contribution to Maryland's maritime heritage.

Maritime trade, despite the collapse of the tobacco market, was accelerating in the early 1790s. The West Indies trade attracted Baltimore shippers, as it had during the Revolution. Likewise, trade was opening with the Far East. One year after the *Empress of China*'s historic voyage from Philadelphia in 1784, Colonel John O'Donnell's *Pallas* returned to Baltimore from Canton with a cargo of silks, teas, and spices.[20] In that year, Baltimore ranked fifth among the ports of the United States in terms of vessel clearances. From 1790 to 1800, Baltimore's exports increased sevenfold. Meanwhile, the maritime life of the nation had become exceedingly troubled.

The events in Europe and the Mediterranean gradually attracted American involvement in ways American merchants, shipowners, and sailors understood best. The Barbary states, formerly intimidated by Britain and her ally Portugal, made unrestrained attacks on American shipping in the Mediterranean. Between 1785 and 1793, fifteen American vessels were taken and their crews imprisoned and enslaved. At first, the new American republic had been too poor to render the tribute that was asked to guarantee safe passage. Then, having no navy to otherwise protect their ships, U.S. policy makers decided to yield to these demands, constructing the warship *Crescent* for the Dey of Algiers and making payments of money.[21]

Finally, in 1793, the Washington administration took the step that ultimately led to the final solution to the problem of piracy: building a national navy. Even that, however, was not readily accomplished. In 1794, Congress passed the Act to Provide a Naval Armament, which provided for the construction of six frigates under the authority of the War Department. The plan called for construction of these ships in various ports. One of them, the 38-gun frigate *Constellation,* came to life in David Stodder's Fells Point shipyard under the supervision of Capt. Thomas Truxtun. She was launched September 7, 1797. While the frigates were being built, relations between the United States and France were deteriorating. The United States had enjoyed a revival of trade with England and the British West Indies in the mid-1790s. After the outbreak of war between the French First Republic and Great Britain in 1793, the French undertook an attack against Britain's American trade. They sent frigates and commissioned privateers to attack Britain's West Indies trade. This reckless disregard of American neutral rights brought the United States and France to the point of war.

French navy ships and privateers attacked Baltimore's shipping, just as they did those of other American ports. One example will suffice. The schooner *Friendship,* commanded by Captain Harris, was twenty-six days out of St. Bartholomew's when it arrived in Norfolk with the news that a 12-gun American schooner from Baltimore had fallen in with the 10-gun French privateer *La Mère Patrie* off Antigua on March 25, 1797. The privateer ordered the Baltimore schooner to send over a boat with her papers. When the Americans refused, the French fired two broadsides. Unscathed, the Americans fired two broadsides in return, killing the French captain, a lieutenant, a doctor, and fifteen other men. The privateer then dropped her sails and struck her colors. The Americans, however, refused to accept the surrender and instead took possession of the Frenchman's prize, an American brig standing off to windward, and brought her into Antigua with a cargo of corn and flour. The French privateer put into St. Bartholomew's, where she was repaired, given a new captain, and sent out again. Since that time she had captured a New Haven brig loaded with molasses and sent her into Guadaloupe.[22] In this instance, the Marylanders were able to beat off an attack and get the better of the French privateer, but that was often not the case with unarmed or poorly armed American merchantmen. This was the kind of threat that compelled President John Adams to create the Navy Department in 1798, complete the construction of the six frigates, and embark on an undeclared naval war with France. The new frigates, which had been intended for use against the Barbary States in the Mediterranean, were soon escorting American merchantmen en route to and from the West Indies.

The U.S. Navy's new frigates were not numerous enough to stem the tide, however, so the new secretary of the navy, Benjamin Stoddert, purchased or chartered other ships to swell the navy's list. By the war's end, in 1801, the improvised navy included fifty-four vessels of all types. One of these, *Chesapeake,* was a 20-gun sloop of war later renamed *Patapsco* to avoid confusing her with the U.S. Navy's frigate *Chesapeake.* Under the command of Capt. Henry Geddes, she saw two years of active duty on several cruises serving in the squadron of Capt. Silas Talbot. *Maryland,* another sloop of war, was constructed in Price's Baltimore yard and launched in June 1799. Capt. John Rodgers, USN, a native of Havre de Grace, Maryland, was her commanding officer. He sailed under orders for Dutch Guiana (Surinam) to protect American merchantmen en route between French Guiana and Curacao. During two years of service, *Maryland* escorted convoys, made three captures, and carried diplomats to Europe for the Pinckney Treaty negotiations. She returned in August 1801 to Baltimore, where her crew was discharged. Rodgers sold her for the navy in October.

During the Quasi-War with France, American trade had suffered not only because of the danger of enemy warships; there was, simultaneously, financial panic during 1798–99 caused by a depression in Europe. Commodity prices had declined during British naval mutinies at the Nore and at Spithead, in England. British merchant houses collapsed, and merchants in continental ports began to fail because of the restriction of British credit. The worst was over by March 1800, and Baltimore's intercourse with the West Indies resumed, enlivened partly because of civil war and French intervention in St. Domingue, the French colony on the western end of the island of Hispaniola.

Maryland's shippers resumed trade with their European partners, though less with Great Britain than with the West Indies and the Continent. From 1802 to 1803, an uneasy truce lingered in Europe, but war broke out again, and Britain tightened her surveillance of the neutral American trade with France. From then on, British naval vessels were likely to board more American merchantmen and to confiscate them to prevent all trade with Napoleon's Empire.[23] The naval war between France and Britain soon made itself felt on the East Coast of the United States. In August 1806, a British squadron, in pursuit of French warships that had taken refuge in Chesapeake Bay, anchored off Lynnhaven Roads, just west of the Virginia Capes. The French frigate *La Cybelle,* 40 guns, took refuge at Norfolk, while the ship of the line *La Patriote,* 74 guns, put into Annapolis in desperate need of repair, having lost her topmasts in a hurricane. The British were to remain in the lower bay for many months while waiting for the French ships to attempt an escape.[24] The presence of these British warships led directly to one of the major international incidents that ultimately set the scene for the War of 1812.

The U.S. Navy at that time was operating in the Mediterranean trying to put an end to the Tripolitan War. The time had come for a new commodore to assume command of the Mediterranean Squadron. Navy Secretary Robert Smith named Capt. James Barron of Virginia to this post and provided the frigate USS *Chesapeake* to be his flagship. Under Barron's overall supervision, Master Commandant Charles Gordon was flag captain, in technical command of the ship. In ordinary circumstance, the commodore—such was Barron's temporary rank—would not interfere with Gordon's execution of his onboard responsibilities. The ship departed the Washington Navy Yard with many civilian passengers and encumbered with much dunnage, unstowed ship's stores, and passengers' baggage. Several days' passage was required for her to drop down the Potomac River to await the arrival of Commodore Barron. During this time, little progress was made in getting the ship ready for sea.

After the ship's arrival at Hampton Roads, Commodore Barron came on board twice to inspect the ship and get acquainted with the officers. On June 22, *Chesapeake* hoisted anchor, got under way with a southwest breeze, and proceeded out to sea, passing two British ships at anchor. Gordon then ordered the crew to clear the ship for sea, a task they were still at when the HMS *Leopard,* 50 guns, approached, and *Chesapeake* hove to, expecting a friendly exchange of information. This was not at all what the British captain, Salusbury Humphreys, had in mind. He was under orders to halt and search *Chesapeake* to discover if there were any British deserters among the crew. This was something that an American merchant ship could not have avoided, but a U.S. Navy warship was under no such compunction. To have allowed this would be a breach of sovereignty and national honor that neither Commodore Barron nor Captain Gordon could permit. Barron parlayed with a British lieutenant for close to an hour while *Leopard* stood by, with gun ports open and her captain seething with frustration at Barron's resistance to his demand. Unsuccessful at persuasion, the lieutenant returned to *Leopard,* which came alongside and, without further warning, delivered three broadsides into the unprepared *Chesapeake.* Neither Barron nor Gordon had taken the precaution of sending the crew to quarters (battle stations) although some of the other officers, suspecting that there might be foul play, had quietly urged this measure. The result was confusion and havoc on board the American ship. Barron hauled down his colors, and when a British boarding party appeared, he demanded to be allowed to surrender his ship. The senior British officer ignored this gesture and told him to muster the crew. This Gordon did, and the officer selected four men he identified as deserters and removed them from the ship. Captain Humphreys offered his regrets for any loss of life and then departed, returning not to Hampton Roads but to Halifax, to report his compliance with orders. At this point, the upset and embarrassed Commodore Barron had no choice but to return to Hampton Roads. The dishonored *Chesapeake* had received many shots between wind and water, had three feet of water in the hold, and had suffered sixteen men wounded and three dead.

From Norfolk to Washington and beyond, Americans reacted to the news with shock and anger. Once again, Great Britain had insulted the honor of the young republic. Naval officers wanted revenge, but they also wanted to cast part of the blame on the hapless Commodore Barron, who, despite his reputation as an expert sea officer, had failed to take normal precautions. *Leopard* had approached *Chesapeake* with open gun ports and guns run out. During the forty-five-minute parley with the British boarding officer, there was ample time for *Chesapeake* to have beat to quarters and prepared her gun crews for action. Later, in a court of inquiry and court-martial proceedings, Barron admitted knowing that recruiting officers in his ship had intentionally signed on deserters from the British squadron in Lynnhaven Roads. There had been numerous recent incidents of British warships halting American merchant ships and pressing sailors even though they had seaman's protections stating their American citizenship. In short, a warship in any circumstances should be always be ready to fight, and *Chesapeake*'s flag captain and commodore had failed to take these steps. Whatever might have happened in battle, had one occurred, it would have been more honorable than what had been allowed. As a result of the court-martial that followed, Commodore John Rodgers, as president of the court-martial, with several of the navy's senior officers as members, pronounced Barron guilty of failing to prepare his ship for battle on the probability of an engagement. His sentence was suspension from the navy for five years. This put him beyond the pale for participation in the War of 1812 and would have severe repercussions, culminating in the tragic duel between Capts. Stephen Decatur Jr. and James Barron in 1820.

The court ruled that Master Commandant Gordon was culpable of "negligently performing the duty assigned him" but gave him a surprisingly light sentence: to be privately reprimanded by the secretary of the navy. Gordon's Eastern Shore political connections may have protected him from a heavier sentence. His mother was a member of the influential Nicholson family and his aunt was the wife of Albert Gallatin, secretary of the Treasury. He was also related to Charles W. Goldsborough, chief clerk of the Navy Department. Marine Captain John Hall also came in for light punishment on the charge that he had "negligently performed the duty assigned," that is, provided musket cartridges that were too small for the bore of their weapons, but for this received only a reprimand. Gunner William Hook had failed to have the ships' guns properly mounted, the powder horns were unfilled, and the slow matches were not in the proper places. The court found Hook guilty of willful neglect and sentenced him to dismissal from the navy. In the final analysis, Barron seems to have been punished for the nonperformance of officers below him in the chain of command as well as a failure to lead. A fairer verdict would at least have held Master Commandant Gordon responsible for the disorganized condition of a ship that was hardly ready for sea, much less prepared for battle.[25] The aftermath of the *Chesapeake-Leopard* affair left the U.S. Navy thirsting for revenge. President Jefferson felt he had it within his grasp to wring concessions from Great Britain on the basis of this outrage. However, he overplayed his hand by demanding that Britain renounce impressment on the high seas, something the Crown would certainly not do in the midst of an ongoing European War, for which the Royal Navy needed every sailor it could find.

From 1807 to the outbreak of the War of 1812, Baltimore's merchants suffered along with those of the rest of the republic's port cities.[26] In response to the European powers whose navies were capturing and confiscating American ships, President Jefferson declared an embargo to coerce France and England into a diplomatic settlement on this issue. Under this law all American shipping to Europe or its colonies was prohibited. The embargo caused a sudden drop in Maryland's exports, from $14 million in 1807 to $2 million in 1808. In the following year, exports rose to $6 million, where they stayed until war brought further restriction in 1812.[27] For its part, the U.S. Navy, as small as it was, stressed preparedness, a lesson sadly learned from the *Chesapeake-Leopard* affair. The election of 1808 brought James Madison to the presidency. He appointed as secretary of the navy Paul Hamilton, a South Carolina planter with no special knowledge of naval affairs. But Hamilton was unafraid to ask for advice from senior naval officers, and he possessed a sense that the navy needed strengthening in the changed circumstances since 1807. Under his administration, the navy brought ships to active duty that had been left "in ordinary" during the Jeffersonian gunboat years—a time when his predecessor had expanded harbor defenses and built hundreds of lightly armed gunboats instead of heavy frigates and ships of the line.

During the years 1807–12, relations between the United States and Britain were tense, as the United States tried to steer the narrow course of neutrality during the war that had enveloped the European continent. The French emperor, Napoleon Bonaparte, had sent a large army into the Iberian Peninsula, with the result that the British sent an army under the command of Maj. Gen. Sir Arthur Wellesley to aid the beleaguered Spanish. The fighting in Portugal and Spain would continue into 1813. At the same time, Napoleon's other armies had extended his empire farther to the east, defeating the Austrian and Prussian armies. Meanwhile, the British navy continued its blockade of the difficult and often stormy French coastline of Normandy, Brittany, and the Bay of Biscay. American merchantmen, despite the embargo, attempted to trade with both France and Britain but were at risk of being captured by either nation if they were thought to be trading with the other. The British welcomed American ships supplying grain to their army in Portugal, a fact resented in France and portrayed as the United States' lack of impartiality. Within this stormy mix, the American government was drifting toward a war that many thought was unnecessary and avoidable. With this as background, it is time to shift attention to a leading naval personality from Maryland and the part he played in the conflict with Britain.

Commodore John Rodgers was born on a Maryland farm in Harford County, grew up in Havre de Grace, and went to sea in merchantmen out of Baltimore at an early age. His father, an acquaintance of Benjamin Folger, obtained an apprentice position for his son on the ship *Maryland,* which Folger co-owned with the merchant John Smith and his son Samuel, who later became a U.S. senator and civic leader of Baltimore in the War of 1812. As a result of this connection, John Rodgers Jr. became a close friend of Samuel's brother Robert, whom President Jefferson later selected as his secretary of the navy. Rodgers did well in merchant sail and in 1793 received his first command, the 300-ton ship *Jane,* owned by the Smith family. For the next four years, Rodgers frequented Caribbean ports and made profitable transatlantic voyages as well. With this background, it should be not be surprising that when he applied for a commission in the navy in 1798, during the Quasi-War with France, he was welcomed with the rank of lieutenant and assigned as second lieutenant under Capt. Thomas Truxtun on board USS *Constellation.*[28]

There is insufficient space to elaborate on Rodgers's naval career. Over the ensuing years, his rise was rapid and involved his first naval command in the sloop of war USS *Maryland* in the Quasi-War. He commanded USS *John Adams* in the first Mediterranean Squadron and then had temporary command of the squadron when Commodore Morris was recalled in 1803. Commodore Edward Preble superseded Rodgers when he arrived in his flagship USS *Constitution* in 1803. The prickly Rodgers held this against Preble because Rodgers was flying his own pendant when Preble arrived. Rodgers meanwhile had found success in combat, off the Tripolitan coast, capturing the Tripolitan vessel *Meshuda,* 20 guns, and destroying a corvette of 22 guns in 1803. In 1804, Rodgers gained command of the frigate USS *Congress* in the Mediterranean, this time under the new commodore Capt. Samuel Barron, recently arrived to succeed Preble, who was returning to the United States. Barron himself was not in good health and yielded command of *Constitution* to Rodgers in November 1805. When, six months later, the commodore's condition worsened, he relinquished command of the squadron to Rodgers. By this time, the Tripolitan situation had improved, with an American-led land-based expedition threatening the Bashaw of Tripoli if he did not agree to a peace settlement. In May 1806, by dint of war and astute diplomacy, the Tripolitan leader agreed to release the American prisoners he had held for nearly two years and establish diplomatic contacts, persuaded by a subvention of $60,000 from the American government. At virtually the same time, Rodgers brought his squadron to anchor off the coast of Tunis to overawe the bey of Tunis, who had been threatening war over Rodgers's seizure of two warships. After several exchanges, this tactic resulted in an agreement and induced the bey to send an emissary to the United States to regularize diplomatic relations. With this, and having received orders to sail for home, Commodore Rodgers could claim to have successfully achieved American aims in the Mediterranean, but not wholly on his own account. Several years of naval blockade, shore bombardment, gunboat warfare, the Eaton overland expedition, and Tobias Lear's (President Washington's secretary) diplomacy with Tripoli had preceded the settlements, but Rodgers was in charge at the end and received a letter of praise from President Jefferson.

It was Rodgers's fate to be the senior officer available on active duty for court-martial duty a few months after his return to the United States. It was in late 1807 that President Jefferson ordered Capt. James Barron to be tried by court-martial on several charges stemming from the poor showing of USS *Chesapeake* against HMS *Leopard*. Secretary of the Navy Robert Smith conferred with Rodgers, then selected him to be president of the court and other more junior officers to sit in judgment on Barron, Master Commandant Gordon, Marine Captain Hall, and Gunner William Hook. The trial took two long months of testimony and cross-examination, during which the "brotherhood" of the navy's officers was sorely tried. At the end of this ordeal, in late February 1808, Rodgers confessed to his wife that this was "the most unpleasant piece of duty I ever performed in the course of my life; and God forbid I should ever be employed in the same way again."[29]

Rodgers spent the next three years based at New York, commanding the frigate USS *Constitution* and performing such tasks as were appropriate to a senior officer, overseeing the condition and deployment of the Navy Department's miniscule gunboats, testing Robert Fulton's torpedo device, and dealing with problems in enforcing the government's non-importation act. In 1810, President Madison and Navy Secretary Paul Hamilton determined to make a more active use of the navy's ships. This involved refitting vessels that had lain in ordinary for several years and reorganizing the operational ships in two squadrons. As of June 1810, Hamilton assigned Rodgers, in the frigate USS *President,* to command a northern division, cruising from northern Maine to Cape Henry, Virginia, and ordered Commodore Stephen Decatur Jr., in the frigate *United States,* to command the southern division, cruising from Cape Henry to Florida. The secretary also gave clear indications of how he expected his commanders to behave. They were to defend and protect American merchant vessels within a marine league of the coast, seize and detain any suspicious private armed vessels in U.S. coastal waters, and "be prepared and determined at every hazard to vindicate the injured honor of our Navy." In the last phrase, Hamilton made an unmistakable reference to the *Chesapeake-Leopard* incident.[30] This set the scene for one of the precipitating events of the War of 1812.

Chapter Three

The War of 1812 in Chesapeake Bay

≈≈≈≈≈≈≈≈≈≈≈≈≈≈≈≈≈≈≈≈≈≈≈≈≈≈≈

BRITISH FRIGATES WERE IN THE HABIT of hovering off the American coast to pick off any visiting French merchant ships, privateers, or American merchant ships that might be carrying British deserters who could be pressed into service. On May 1, 1811, the frigate HMS *Guerrière* halted the American merchantman *Spitfire* and impressed one of her sailors. When word of this reached Washington, Secretary Hamilton immediately wrote to Commodore Rodgers who, as luck would have it, had brought *President* into the Chesapeake, anchored off Annapolis, and gone on leave to visit his wife at Havre de Grace. Hamilton ordered Rodgers to set sail as soon as possible toward New York, to confront *Guerrière,* and possibly to do battle. Rodgers left the Chesapeake and discovered a ship with the configuration of a frigate some fifty miles north of Cape Henry.

It was late afternoon on May 16 when the *President*'s lookouts sighted the frigate in the distance. Rodgers turned his ship toward her with all sails set and overhauled the ship in the darkness of early evening. He hoisted his colors and pendant and came closer. The strange ship hoisted its colors, but Rodgers could not distinguish them. Finally, at a distance of less than a hundred yards, Rodgers hailed "What ship is that?" and the answer came, "What ship is that?" Then, before he had time to answer, the stranger fired one shot, another, and then three in succession, plus musketry. Rodgers ordered *President*'s gun crews to open fire and did not cease for several minutes. The stranger opened fire again, as did *President,* and this went on for another five minutes. The result in human terms was nine killed and twenty-three wounded on board the attacking ship. For *President*'s crew, there were none killed and only one injured, with some damage to fore and main masts. Finally, Rodgers's opponent identified herself as HMS *Little Belt,* a light frigate (or corvette) of 21 guns.

This discovery changed the picture entirely. Instead of meeting a frigate of nearly his force, Rodgers had battered a lighter and more weakly armed opponent. He reported his deep regret to Secretary Hamilton, saying that such a deed was deeply repugnant and that he never would have done so had he known the ship's size and strength. From a distance it was difficult to tell a small frigate from a larger one because they had similar configuration. As it was, he felt he had no choice since he had been fired on. Hamilton responded that he approved of Rodgers's performance under the circumstances but that Rodgers should be on his guard from now on because the British would mark him for retaliation. In fact, the British newspapers called him a cowardly bully, and he realized that he would also be set up for ridicule by his counterparts in the Royal Navy. Rodgers requested a court of inquiry when British accounts of the incident became available and contradicted his version, particularly in the matter of who fired first. Captain Bingham insisted that *President* had fired first, that he had shown his colors from early afternoon, and that the firing had lasted forty-five minutes. Rodgers insisted that the firing had lasted no more than fifteen minutes. The court of inquiry, convened on board *President* in New York harbor, lasted for nearly two weeks and delved into specifics. The court's opinion was entirely favorable to Rodgers, and the case was considered closed, but its reverberations continued and contributed to the mounting bad feelings against Britain as war became a distinct possibility.[1]

In addition to the *Little Belt* incident, other factors were pushing the United States toward a confrontation with Great Britain. Settlers in the northwestern territories had been alarmed by the activities of the Shawnee chief Tecumseh, who had called on other tribes for collective resistance to American encroachment on Indian lands. The Indians had established a village encampment on Tippecanoe Creek near its confluence with the Wabash River in the Indiana Territory. Fearing a revival of frontier warfare, the citizens of Vincennes voted to ask the territorial governor, Gen. William Henry Harrison, to attack and disperse the Indians who, the settlers felt, were receiving aid from the British in Canada. Harrison gathered some thousand troops and marched on the Indian settlement. On November 7 the Indians attacked, and after an all-day battle, with severe losses on both sides, they withdrew, and Harrison's army razed the encampment. This, the Battle of Tippecanoe, was hailed as a great victory for Harrison and the frontiersmen, whetting the appetite of many in the west for further conquests, expulsion of the Indians, and possibly acquisition of land in Canada.

Since the inception of the wars of the French Revolution in 1792, British impressment of sailors from American ships had become a major grievance. It was most painfully felt in the Northeast and Middle Atlantic states, which provided most of the trading vessels and their sailors. A conservative estimate of the number of American seamen impressed from 1796 to January 1812 is 10,000. During the most severe period, from 1803 to 1812, some 6,000 sailors were impressed. Probably 750 to 1,000 were impressed annually between 1808 and 1812.[2]

Along with the humanitarian concerns for these sailors were the economic concerns raised with regard to the French Navy's seizure of American ships accused of trading with England. In order to squeeze the British economy as part of his blockade of Britain, Napoleon enacted the Berlin Decree of 1806 and the Milan Decree of 1807. These acts were intended to pinch off trade with Britain and specifically targeted American ships that were specially licensed to trade with Britain. French authorities were enabled to seize and confiscate any U.S. ships caught in this trade. In a further outrage, the emperor's Bayonne Decree of April 17, 1808, ordered the seizure all U.S. ships in European ports, on the pretext that they were in violation of the U.S. Embargo Act (December 22, 1807), and resulted in the confiscation of more than $10 million in American goods and ships.[3] It is a paradox that, as hurtful as the impressments were, the New England Federalists, representing the majority of shipowners, were decidedly pro-British in the showdown with Republicans over whether to go to war with either power. Perhaps this shows that it was the ship seizures, not the impressments, that really hurt the New England merchants. In their view, to side with Great Britain as opposed to France was to choose the lesser of two evils. For them, the British cause was still the ancient source of American liberties, and they looked with disgust on the idea of supporting a malign and deceitful dictator who was well on his way to dominating the world.[4]

President Madison called the Twelfth Congress into session in November 1811 to discuss what measures to take in preparation for a war with Great Britain or France. He urged Congress to strengthen the nation's defenses, to bring the army up to strength, to enlarge stockpiles of materials, and to improve the navy. Generally, the electorate had been critical of the Eleventh Congress for having done little to advance the nation's interests. A new breed of Republicans (called War Hawks) entered Congress, while fewer Federalists returned to office. Yet, there were still divisions in the ruling party on matters of defense. In the event, Congress did little to satisfy the need for effective armed forces and failed to pass all the financial measures that treasury secretary Albert Gallatin had proposed in order to fund the war. Navalists were unable to gain passage of a bill to commence building 74-gun ships of the line and new frigates. They had to be satisfied with funds only to repair and fit out the frigates *Constellation, Chesapeake,* and *Adams.* On the military side of the ledger, Congress passed legislation theoretically increasing the size of the army from 10,000 to 25,000 men. Actually, previous to this, the army's size had been only 6,700, one-third less than its authorized 10,000.

In early 1812, with war sentiment rising, the president asked Congress to authorize a sixty-day embargo on shipping in order to give notice to American merchant ships that they would be put at risk if they lingered in foreign ports. Congress responded, extending the embargo to ninety days. As late as May, there was still hope that in Great Britain the Privy Council would rescind the Orders in Council that so injured the neutral trade. Such a move had been rumored, was favored by British manufacturers, and was a matter of debate, but when the change of policy came, it was too late. In the final analysis, a majority of the congressional representatives from the Middle Atlantic and Southeastern states, from Pennsylvania to Georgia, felt there was no honorable alternative to war. The Federalists and anti-Madisonian Republicans from New Jersey, New York, Connecticut, Rhode Island, and Massachusetts provided the bulk of the antiwar votes. In response to President Madison's urging, Congress declared war on June 18, 1812. The vote was 79–49 in the House of Representatives and 17–13 in the Senate.[5]

The U.S. Navy's senior officer was ready to sail immediately. Commodore Rodgers had ordered the ships of the northern and southern divisions to assemble at Sandy Hook, where he combined them into one squadron under his command. By concentrating, he believed that he could get the jump on enemy warships then on station and interrupt the British merchant trade routes, which generally followed the Gulf Stream from the Caribbean to the English Channel. When Rodgers sortied on June 21, he was still missing one of his ships. The USS *Constitution,* under the command of Capt. Isaac Hull, had returned from Europe in early February. With his ship worn and sluggish from months at sea, Hull had made passage to the Washington Navy Yard for repairs, refitting, and careening. The yard finished its work in May, but Hull needed to complete his crew, so Secretary Hamilton authorized the ship to visit Annapolis for recruiting before leaving the bay. When Rodgers sailed from Sandy Hook, *Constitution* was still making her way down the Potomac. On his way to Annapolis, Hull wisely put his crew through their paces at exercising the great guns. After months of work in the navy yard, the men were bound to be out of practice. Once moored off Annapolis, he sent his recruiting officer ashore to induce the needed sailors to sign on, and by July 5 he was heading down the bay for the capes, anxious to get to sea before the British could set up a blockade off the entrance to Chesapeake Bay. Hull received his final orders from Hamilton, instructing him to take on the enemy unless he encountered a force superior to his own and to report to Commodore Rodgers, but "if he should not be in that port, you will remain there until further orders."[6]

Captain Hull never arrived to pick up those orders. As he proceeded from Chesapeake Bay toward New York, his course intersected that of a British naval squadron under the command of Commodore Philip B. V. Broke. At first sighting off Egg Harbor, New Jersey, Hull thought the ships might be those of Commodore Rodgers; however, he was quickly disabused of that mistake when another British ship, HMS *Guerrière,* approached from the north to join Broke. At that point the British launched their historic pursuit of *Constitution* as she fled to evade Broke's six ships, through calms, shifting breezes, and squalls. Hull escaped through clever seamanship and the determination of his crew until, two days later, the British gave up the chase. Hull then put into Boston to pick up further orders, but none awaited him. On his own initiative, he proceeded northeast toward Newfoundland and the Grand Banks to hunt for prizes. To his good fortune, one of the ships he found turned out to be *Guerrière,* detached from Broke's squadron and on her way to Halifax. The ships engaged in a three-hour battle, which ended in the destruction of the British ship in the United States' first successful frigate action of the war.

Only a few months later, Chesapeake Bay was the scene of a story depicting another of the nation's first frigates early in the war. With the declaration of war with Great Britain, Capt. Charles Stewart reported ready for duty at Washington, and Secretary Paul Hamilton did not hesitate. He ordered him to the brig *Argus* on June 22 with orders to "proceed to sea and scour the West Indies and Gulf Stream—consider yourself as possessing every belligerent right of attack, capture and defense of and against any of the public or private ships of the Kingdom of Great Britain, Ireland and other dependencies."[7] On Stewart's return, Hamilton ordered him to command USS *Constellation,* then undergoing an extensive rebuild at the Washington Navy Yard. This ship had been scheduled for a thorough overhaul in 1806, when she returned from the Mediterranean, but this must have been postponed because it was not until March 1812 that Commodore Thomas Tingey, commandant of the Washington Navy Yard, commenced the overdue repairs. Even then, the lack of timber, equipment, and ordnance delayed completion of the yard's work until at least October 11, when a gunboat captain noticed her ensign hoisted, indicating that *Constellation* had been recommissioned. During the weeks that followed, gunboats brought anchors, guns, and provisions for *Constellation,* apparently still in need of filling its complement as evidenced by the opening of recruiting rendezvous in Alexandria. While these preparations were going forward, Secretary Hamilton asked Stewart for help persuading Congress to authorize a new round of shipbuilding, to which he complied with a letter of November 12, arguing for the construction of heavy frigates and ships of the line.[8] This communication evidently had a positive effect. Congress authorized the building of four 74-gun ships of the line and six 44-gun frigates on December 23, 1812.

Stewart, concerned that ice forming on the Potomac might soon prevent his departure, dropped down the river in late December with his frigate still not completely ready for sea. He put in at Annapolis to continue preparations in accord with instructions from William Jones, the newly appointed secretary of the navy. Still not satisfied with his tests of gunpowder and lacking spare sails and other equipment, but anxious to escape the Chesapeake before British blockaders took position off the Virginia Capes, Stewart got under way for Hampton Roads. Unbeknownst to him, the British Admiralty, on December 26, 1812, gave orders for its ships to commence a blockade of Chesapeake and Delaware bays.[9]

To his great chagrin, Stewart discovered on February 2, the day he brought his ship into Hampton Roads, that seven Royal Navy war vessels (two ships of the line, three frigates, a brig, and a schooner) had arrived off Cape Henry, making their way into Chesapeake Bay. He had little choice other than to lighten the ship and haul her up the Elizabeth River, above (south of) Craney Island, where she could be protected by the guns of Fort Norfolk and the navy gunboat flotilla. In the three months that followed, Stewart exerted efforts to strengthen the gunboats' crews and armaments, a step that would pay dividends. The enemy ships remained in control of the waters of Hampton Roads for the next two years, although at certain times Baltimore privateers and the corvette USS *Adams* found it possible to slip out. *Constellation* remained where she was for the rest of the war. Her finest hour occurred on June 22, 1813, when Admiral Warren's forces made a deliberate attempt to thrust past the gunboats and the Craney Island defenses. Having anticipated the attack, Stewart's successor, Capt. Joseph Tarbell, had ordered *Constellation*'s guns, sailors, and marines landed to join the artillery batteries of Virginia militia on the island. With a coordinated defense, they repulsed the British attack in what was one of the few defeats inflicted on the British during their Chesapeake campaigns of 1813 and 1814.[10]

≈≈≈

THE WAR OF 1812 BROUGHT BOTH PROSPERITY and tragedy to Maryland. The wealthier merchants of Baltimore took advantage of the trading halt to pour their resources into entrepreneurial warfare. They invested millions of dollars in privateering, fitting out swift-sailing schooners with raked masts and low freeboard to attack the British carrying trade.[11] By capturing heavily laden merchantmen and sending them into friendly ports, Baltimore's businessmen turned many a patriotic dollar. On the other hand, when large British squadrons invaded Chesapeake Bay in 1813–14, amphibious troops laid waste to numerous plantations on the Eastern and Western shores and their rivers.[12] They attacked and burned the White House and other public buildings of the nation's capital and ransomed the city of Alexandria. Only Baltimore was well defended, thanks to the energies of her own citizens. There were but a handful of federal troops and sailors available for defense of the region. The U.S. Army was fighting mainly on the northern frontiers, where the war had begun in an ill-fated attempt to capture Canada.

Seafaring Baltimoreans armed and licensed 122 private vessels during the war, outnumbering all other states in this form of warfare. New Englanders, who had gone privateering in great numbers during the American Revolution, produced only a handful of such warships during the War of 1812. Of a total of 1,750 estimated captured British vessels, Baltimore privateers captured 556. Of these, perhaps as many as 170 actually arrived at port for adjudication. Most of the privateers were schooners built at Baltimore shipyards. For example, Thomas Kemp's yard produced 9 such privateer schooners, including *Rossie* (Joshua Barney), *Rolla* (James Dooley), *Comet* and *Chasseur* (Thomas Boyle), and the largest of Baltimore's schooners, *Mammoth* (Samuel Franklin). Eastern Shore builders like William Harrison, Impey Dawson, and Perry Spencer of Talbot County, Noah Richardson of Dorchester County, and Spry Denny of Queen Anne's County also contributed to this effort. Some Eastern Shore schooners were built on speculation, whereas others were commissioned by Baltimore builders and were fitted out in that city. Perhaps Baltimore's most unusual privateer vessel was the xebec-rigged *Ultor,* with three masts and lateen sails. While difficult to quantify, privateering may have cost the British an estimated $40 million in lost ships and increased insurance rates.[13]

One of the best examples of Baltimore's privateering prowess is the story of Capt. Joshua Barney's exploits in the privateer *Rossie.* Barney grew up on a Maryland farm but went to sea early in life, before the Revolutionary War. He had shown early proficiency as a teenager in taking command of a merchant schooner when the captain, his brother-in-law, fell ill in the Mediterranean. Barney not only brought the ship back but with a cargo in her hold and a profit for her owners. During the Revolution he served in privateers and in the Continental Navy. He sailed with Capt. Isaiah Robinson in the Continental Navy brig *Andrew Doria* when he made a voyage to St. Eustatius and received the famous "first salute" from the Dutch governor of that Caribbean Island. Barney was the first lieutenant under Capt. James Nicholson in the Continental frigate *Virginia* when she grounded on the "middle ground" shoal in trying to elude British blockaders one dark and stormy night in 1777. He was imprisoned by the British in England and managed to escape, not once but twice. After the Revolution he tried farming and but could not stay away from the sea. In the 1790s, the first secretary of war selected him as commanding officer of one of the first frigates, but Barney refused to serve. He would have been junior to Capt. Silas Talbot, an officer he did not respect. Instead, Barney sailed to France, a new republic then in full revolutionary fervor, where his naval feats were legendary. He was offered the rank of a senior captain and given command of a naval squadron in the French Navy. He participated in the war against the British in the Caribbean and was part owner in two French privateers. Barney's enemies in the United States later claimed that he tainted his American patriotism by serving under the French, against whom the U.S. Navy fought during the Quasi-War, though Barney denied that his ships had ever fought against those of his countrymen.

At the outbreak of the War of 1812, Barney was anxious for reinstatement in the U.S. Navy, but there was no place for him. Several Baltimore merchants felt that such great talent and experience should not go to waste. Their names are notable, for they included some of the city's leading merchants: John McKim Jr., Thomas Tenant, Robert Patterson, Levi Hollingsworth, Jeremiah Sullivan, and Christopher Deshon. They purchased the Thomas Kemp–built schooner *Rossie,* relatively small at 206 tons, converted her to a privateer, and offered Barney command. Barney's influence was such that he secured privateering commission number one and departed from Baltimore on July 11, 1812. During the next six weeks, *Rossie* captured eighteen vessels off Nova Scotia and Newfoundland. Barney put in at Newport on August 30, resupplied the ship, and departed again, this time cruising toward the Caribbean. Though less successful in his second cruise, he did capture the 8-gun mail packet *Princess Amelia,* which had a valuable cargo. He returned to Baltimore on October 22, having captured 3,698 tons of British shipping worth about $1.5 million, along with 217 prisoners. Barney's early success was at least partially due to the fact that many of his unfortunate prisoners did not know that war had been declared. Nonetheless, he returned to great acclaim and brought profits for the schooner's owners.

No treatment of Baltimore privateering in the War of 1812 would be complete without mentioning the redoubtable privateer commander Thomas Boyle, whose successes during the war exceeded Barney's, having encompassed cruises in two vessels over a longer period of time. Boyle hailed originally from the seafaring town of Marblehead, Massachusetts. He had sailed from Baltimore for a number of years in command of trading schooners and was well respected in the Fells Point community. The merchants Andrew Clopper, Levi Hollingsworth, Peter Arnold Karthaus, and Jeremiah Sullivan combined in a syndicate to purchase the 187-ton schooner *Comet,* built by Thomas Kemp, the constructor of *Rossie.* Boyle departed Baltimore on July 12, bound for a three-month cruise. Fourteen days later, he overtook the 400-ton ship *Henry* out of Hull, England, en route from St. Croix, in the Virgin Islands, to London, with a valuable cargo of sugar, fustic, and wine. Boyle placed a prize crew on board *Henry* and sent her into Baltimore.

He found another large ship in mid-August—the *Hopewell*—an armed merchantman that put up a stiff fight and exchanged broadsides until *Comet's* guns cut her up to the point of being unmanageable. *Hopewell* had come from Surinam loaded with sugar, molasses, cotton, coffee, and cocoa intended for her owners in London. She, too, then headed for Baltimore with a prize crew on board. *Comet's* next victim, the 364-ton ship *John* of Liverpool, armed with 14 guns, also refused to surrender without a struggle. Yet she finally succumbed to *Comet's* superior firepower and Boyle's deft handling. Boyle sent her and her cargo of sugar, rum, cotton, coffee, copper, and hardwood into Baltimore. At the completion of this cruise, he returned without a man killed and having encountered not a single British cruiser.

All told, he had captured four handsome prizes and had done so well for his owners that they offered him an owner's share.

Boyle refitted *Comet* and headed farther south. This time, off the coast of Brazil, he found a Portuguese warship escorting three armed British merchantmen. He was not one to shrink from a larger enemy force. *Comet* overawed the Portuguese ship, forcing her to sheer off while he concentrated fire on the merchant ships. Boyle captured his prizes, though the much larger Portuguese man of war got away. Boyle continued to send prizes toward the United States, but by January 1813, the British blockade was taking effect and their cruisers were on the alert. British records show that some prizes were recaptured before they could gain the safety of Chesapeake Bay, and a few of *Comet*'s prize crews ended up in prison at Barbados and in England. This created a problem for Boyle, and it was one that privateers always had to guard against. Once they took a prize and sent it toward a friendly port, the prizes had minimum crew, and the *Comet,* or any capturing ship, would have diminished her own crew by so many. Thus, it became more difficult to defend one's own ship. Boyle began to burn his prizes after first taking out any valuable cargo. In February 1813, *Comet* was lucky to escape from the pursuing British frigate *Surprise* and put into St. Bartholomew's in the Leeward Islands for repair to a damaged foremast. Boyle also had to outrun British warships in the Virgin Islands. He finally took *Comet* into Wilmington, North Carolina, because the Chesapeake, by March, was too heavily blockaded. His second cruise was not as successful as the first, and he had suffered three dead and sixteen wounded when he took on the more heavily armed *Hibernia* (800 tons and 22 guns). From this lesson, the Baltimore merchants learned they would need larger ships, more men, and more provisions for distant cruising over longer periods of time.[14]

Boyle's next privateer command, the one that brought him fame, was the 356-ton schooner *Chasseur.* She was the swiftest of the swift, built by Thomas Kemp for Williams Hollins. She at first had trouble breaking through the blockade, but finally did so under the command of William Wade, Boyle's first officer in *Comet.* From December 1813 until June 1814, she cruised the North Atlantic from Europe to the Caribbean and returned to New York with moderate success. The owners replaced Wade with Boyle, and he sailed *Chasseur* out of New York on July 29, 1814, for a cruise to the British Isles and European waters. On his way he captured the 14-gun brig *Eclipse,* the schooner *Fox,* and the brig *Antelope* and sent them to Baltimore for adjudication. He burned several Scottish fishing vessels for which he had no use. He sent two ships sailing in company from South America, loaded with hides, tallow, bark, and fur, into American ports.

It was about this time, in August 1814, that Boyle's sense of humor and patriotism joined in a gem of impudence. He drafted a proclamation announcing to the British that he and his ship had placed the British Isles under "state of strict and rigorous blockade." He further stated that he had ordered this proclamation be published so that it could be made known to the English public. He sent the notice in by cartel with instructions to post it at a coffeehouse near the famous insurance company Lloyd's of London. This was his answer to the ineffective blockade the British had imposed on the American coast. From then on Boyle toyed with the warships, usually small brigs of war, that the Admiralty sent to destroy him. *Chasseur*'s great speed and maneuverability were sufficient to remove him from danger if he felt the need, which he did on several occasions. He was fortunate that none of his pursuers was able to dismast *Chasseur* or cut up her rigging to bring him within reach. While cruising, his favorite tactic was to follow a convoy coming in from the West Indies, wait for an opportune moment—when a vessel lagged or the escorting warships were otherwise occupied—and then dash in to cut out a prize. He would then take out the most valuable of her goods and send her into an American port with perishables and the bulk cargo.

He was not always successful and sometimes lost well-armed ships with active gun crews. Like most privateers, he was not anxious to do battle with the Royal Navy's ships unless absolutely necessary. On one occasion, Boyle allowed his ship to be lured alongside an opposing schooner that showed only three guns, yet when *Chasseur* committed herself the enemy revealed a hidden tier of gun ports and many extra men who had hidden behind a bulwark. It was broadside to broadside for a few minutes while round shot and bullets flew across the decks. Finally, Boyle laid *Chasseur* alongside and ordered boarders away. Boyle's capture, the Royal Navy schooner *St. Lawrence,* 15 guns, had six killed and seventeen wounded, while *Chasseur*'s crew had five killed and seven wounded. Boyle reported that his enemy had originally been the stout American privateer *Atlas* out of Philadelphia. Out of feelings of respect and humanity, tempered by practicality, Boyle converted the *St. Lawrence* into a flag of truce and sent her into Havana, the closest port. This battle, one of the last naval actions of the war, took place on February 15, 1815, two months after the signing of the Treaty of Ghent, yet before word of ratification had reached all points on the globe. Five days later, *Chasseur* entered Baltimore harbor as the shores echoed to salutes offered by Fort McHenry. Even then, the public press referred to *Chasseur* as the "Pride of Baltimore," the ship that has become the icon of Baltimore's privateering during the War of 1812.

Within Chesapeake Bay, after establishment of the blockade, the inhabitants of the shores of both Virginia and Maryland suffered exceedingly from the dominance of the Royal Navy's presence and the lack of adequate support from the U.S. Navy. The strategy developed by the Madison administration for directing the War of 1812 involved three small American armies attacking Canada simultaneously during the summer of 1812. The navy's role in this was to protect American shipping and to attack British commerce on the Atlantic. Virtually no forethought had been given to naval warfare on the Great Lakes in support of the armies or on Chesapeake Bay, should the British choose to operate in American coastal waters. Without ships of the line to contend with the Royal Navy's 74-gun ships, and having only a handful of powerful well-manned frigates, the navy could not afford to have its major units blockaded in the bays and sounds along the Atlantic coast. However, that is exactly what happened to the *Constellation,* hauled out of reach up the Elizabeth River near Norfolk when Stewart found he could not escape from the bay. The same would also happen later that year when, after attempting to escape from Long Island Sound on June 1, Commodore Decatur's frigate *United States* and the prize frigate USS *Macedonian* were blockaded in the Thames River at New

London and unable to escape through the British squadron stationed in the sound and off Montauk Point. The only vessels of use to the navy in Chesapeake Bay were the Jeffersonian-era gunboats, most of which were deployed at Norfolk under the command of Capt. John Cassin, whose principal mission was the protection of the *Constellation.*

The British presence soon made itself felt along the shores of the middle and upper parts of Chesapeake Bay. The British raiding strategy in the Chesapeake had three major goals. The first was to divert American military resources from operations along the Canada–United States border. Anything that could be done in the Chesapeake to weaken American efforts to gain ground in Canada would, from a British point of view, be worth doing. Second, British presence in the Chesapeake Bay region would be a threat to the nation's capital in Washington. This would create confusion and fear among the poorly defended lawmakers, who might well be persuaded to sue for peace. Finally, the strategy targeted Baltimore, a growing, wealthy city whose private ships of war were making a mockery of the British blockade and creating a firestorm of criticism from merchants in London and Liverpool whose ships were being attacked and captured in unprecedented numbers. British naval officers referred to Baltimore as a "nest of pirates," which they greatly wished to be destroyed. Another target was the Virginia port of Alexandria, a wealthy entrepot of tobacco warehouses and granaries that would help pay for the war in America.

The Royal Navy officers who led the raids in the Chesapeake in 1813 were Vadm. Sir John Borlase Warren and his deputy, Radm. Sir George Cockburn. Warren had a large and difficult job as the commander of the Royal Navy's forces on the North American Station, extending from Halifax to the Caribbean. For the most part, he would leave the unpleasant work in the Chesapeake to his second-in-command. Of the two, Cockburn was the more aggressive and dangerous for Americans. He relished amphibious warfare and had been made an honorary Royal Marine for his efforts. Further, he had no fondness for the former British colonies and thought that American leaders were particularly hypocritical in their love both of freedom and of slavery—freedom for the planters and slavery for the masses of African black field workers who had been imported for the better part of 140 years.

Rear Admiral Cockburn arrived in Chesapeake Bay on March 3, 1813, in his flagship HMS *Marlborough,* 74 guns, in company with HMS *Dragon,* 74 guns, three frigates, and two sloops of war. Vice Admiral Warren joined him three weeks later in his flagship HMS *San Domingo* (74 guns), with three more frigates and additional supply ships. After an initial failed attempt to capture the frigate *Constellation,* Warren and Cockburn made the first of two sweeps of the northern Chesapeake, commencing in April. On their way, they sent a division of cutters and launches from their squadron into the Rappahannock River, where they attacked and captured four Baltimore privateer schooners (*Arab, Lynx, Racer,* and *Dolphin*), apparently waiting their chance to leave the bay. The prisoners taken in this attack provided Cockburn with the first intelligence of the Baltimore defenses. Bypassing the Potomac and Patuxent rivers, the appearance of their squadron as it passed up the bay must have had an unsettling effect on civilians ashore. The ships made no attempt to land near Annapolis but did look into the Patapsco River, sending tenders and smaller boats to sound the river and test the Baltimore defenses. As Cockburn wrote, "I am endeavoring to have the position of different Shoals and Knowls [*sic*] around us ascertained and buoyed off, and if I find it possible to get anything into the entrance of Patapsco I shall do so, and should it appear practicable to annoy the Fort or Vessels above it with Rockets, etc. I shall not hesitate in attempting it." In the following days, Warren's ships stretched into the northern bay, intending to visit Havre de Grace, but were unable to get anywhere near the port because of uncharted shoals. The ships of the line and frigates had to anchor off Turkey Point. From there Cockburn had to send out his squadron's launches in order to reconnoiter the Susquehanna River and resupply the ships' water.[15] On April 29 the armed boats approached Frenchtown on the Elk River, where the militia fired on them with small cannon and muskets. The sailors and marines retaliated by landing, charging the position, and then burning the town. Farther up the Susquehanna River, at Port Deposit, there was a well-defended battery, and, at Elkton, the militia sharply rebuffed a boat attack, thereby saving the town and a number of small craft from harm.

As British boats carrying the Royal Marines approached Havre de Grace on May 3, the local militia showed spirit, hoisting an American flag and firing off their small battery, thus showing their contempt for the enemy. This, of course, was precisely what Cockburn wanted so that he could display his intention of suppressing all opposition wherever it surfaced. The landing force dispersed the militia, captured its captain, then burned their abandoned houses. Cockburn explained that he wished to make them (the proprietors and militiamen) "understand and feel what they were liable to bring upon themselves by building Batteries and acting toward us with so much useless Rancor."[16] This was, in effect, a warning to Marylanders not to offer resistance at the risk of seeing their properties destroyed. For those townspeople and farmers who cooperated or at least did not resist, Cockburn's policy was to take what the fleet needed, paying with scrip (bills on the Royal Navy victualing office) and claiming he paid fair value for what was taken. What Cockburn described as fair value was usually just a fraction of the market value, and naturally, there was no practical way for the recipient to retrieve the compensation for his goods or livestock. One critical observer, a Royal Navy midshipman, noticed that farmers frequently refused payment for their stock. More often than not, the British "took what they wanted and left the unwanted scrip."[17] On that same day, Cockburn's troops scored an unexpected coup when they discovered the Principio Foundry as they probed up the Northeast River. Landing unopposed, they spent several hours destroying machinery—five 24-pounders intended to defend the foundry, twenty-eight 32-pounders, eight other cannons, and four carronades of varying calibers. In his report, Cockburn crowed that it was "one of the most valuable works of the kind in America."[18]

Three days later, Cockburn sent the frigate *Mohawk* to the mouth of the Sassafras River to stage a raid on Georgetown and Fredericktown, which lay seven miles upriver. As the boats approached within a mile of these towns, located on opposite shores, they found that the local militia had prepared a warm welcome:

galling musketry and cannon shot from both banks of the river. Cockburn, who enjoyed putting himself at the head of these expeditions, landed his marines with fixed bayonets. They rapidly dispersed the defenders. From that point on, Cockburn felt free to wreak destruction on the towns' collected fishing and trading vessels. He also destroyed stores of sugar, leather, and lumber. He did not mention in his report that, in addition to burning the lower part of the towns, his men had proceeded up the hill on the Georgetown side to a private residence and set it on fire. He was approached by the bold Catherine Knight, who pointed out that this was the home of an elderly woman, who was trapped within, and asked if he would have his men extinguish the fire. He did, but his men immediately set fire to a neighboring house. Knight said that the fire would spread to the house she had just saved, but Cockburn and his men turned and left, so she put the fire out herself. From that time, this rambling brick house (now a restaurant/bed-and-breakfast establishment) on the heights has been known as the "Kitty Knight" House.[19]

The British withdrew from the northern bay to carry out other attacks at Ocracoke, on the North Carolina coast, and at Norfolk, where an attempt to capture USS *Constellation* failed utterly in the face of stiff resistance from the disembarked *Constellation* gun crews and the artillery batteries of the Virginia Militia in the Battle of Craney Island. To efface this stain, Cockburn sent his troops against Hampton, Virginia, where two companies of former French prisoners of war ran amok among the defenseless citizenry, causing embarrassment to the British Army's local commander, Col. Sir Sidney Beckwith. Admiral Warren soon returned to Maryland's shores, after first probing the lower Potomac River. His ships of the line proceeded as far up as St. Clement's Island, where he ordered his marines to take possession to obtain water, cattle, and foodstuffs. He then sent three frigates and a schooner farther, to Cedar and Maryland points, "in order to make an impression if practicable upon the enemy's frigate and small vessels below Alexandria, as well as to create an Alarm at Washington and to embarrass the Enemy in the measures for the further invasion of Canada during the setting of Congress in that City. I am sorry to say that the Frigates could not get higher up, without being lightened."[20]

~~~

TWO OF THE MORE UNUSUAL MOMENTS of Maryland's War of 1812 occurred in Chesapeake Bay. In 1813, as the impact of the British blockade began to take effect, Master Commandant Charles Gordon, USN, who was stationed in Baltimore, suggested to Secretary of the Navy William Jones that he take advantage of the presence of several privateers to organize a defense for Baltimore shipping, using the privateers. With Jones's blessing, the privateer owners offered their vessels *Comet, Patapsco, Revenge,* and *Wasp* and their crews for Gordon's temporary command. They operated from March to September 1813, gathering intelligence and harassing the smaller enemy vessels, such as the armed tenders and launches that the British used for reconnaissance and scavenging along the rivers. Gordon's initiative may have staved off an attack against Baltimore in 1813 and set an example for the defense of the bay in 1814.[21]

Even as Gordon's improvised squadron set to work, Capt. Joshua Barney wrote to Secretary of the Navy William Jones on July 4, 1813. He described the military strength of the British squadron, estimating that with the marines, army artillery, and naval infantry units available, amounting to 8,200 men, they could carry out devastating raids on Washington, Norfolk, and Baltimore. He proposed that the Navy Department establish a flotilla of barges and gunboats on the bay, armed by the navy and manned by sailors from Baltimore. "Let as many of such barges be built as can be mann'd, form them into a flying squadron, have them continually watching and annoying the enemy in our waters, where we have the advantage of shoals and flats throughout the Chesapeake Bay . . . each boat ought to carry 50 officers and men and 25 soldiers; a squadron of twenty barges would require 1000 officers and men." Barney also suggested adding several light, fast-sailing vessels for use as fireships to harass the enemy's ships when at anchor. He further advised sinking vessels as obstructions in the Potomac and Patapsco rivers and appended a sketch of one of the proposed barges.[22] Secretary Jones took his advice and appointed Barney a master commandant (and later captain) in the U.S. Navy, responsible directly to him for the construction and operations of the flotilla. In August Jones wrote that he had ordered James Beatty, navy agent in Baltimore, to contract for "the building of eight barges or galleys, for the defense of the Chesapeake and its waters, four of which are to be 75 feet long and four of 50 feet long to be armed and equipped as this Department shall direct." He appointed Barney to supervise the project and promised to provide a number of 24-pounder guns as well as 42- or 32-pounder carronades, adding that he would also provide the U.S. Navy cutter *Scorpion* and the schooner *Asp* and two or three gunboats.[23]

In the spring of 1813, the unrestrained rampaging of the British on the bay had thoroughly alarmed the leadership of Maryland and the city of Baltimore, in particular. With little progress in the main theater of war on the Niagara–Lake Ontario border with Canada, the threat that the war might well last at least another year provoked action. Gov. Levin Winder and Sen. Samuel Smith anticipated that British plans included an attack on Baltimore. Senator Smith, one of the most powerful individuals in Maryland by virtue of his personal wealth and family connections, was also a major general in the Third Division of the state's volunteer militia. He had written to Governor Winder as early as March 1813, suggesting that the ease with which the British could suddenly appear "against the city makes it necessary to be in a state of preparation to repel any attempt that may be made." He and Winder made an inspection of Fort McHenry, finding it to be lacking in men and firepower, and the governor urged him make all arrangements necessary for the defense of the port. Smith then wrote to Secretary of War John Armstrong listing the fort's weaknesses, alleging that it was in no condition to repel a serious attack from the formidable British fleet. Colonel Swift, of the U.S. Corps of Engineers, made an inspection and recommended the construction of lower gun batteries, the placement of hot shot furnaces, the digging of a five-foot counterscarp around the fort, and the filling in of embrasures within the fort to allow cannon to be fired *en barbette*. From the French consul, the fort's commander, Maj. Lloyd Beall, obtained twenty-eight 36-pounder long guns and twenty-eight 18-pounders—a considerable addition to the fort's firepower. These guns had been salvaged from *L'Eole,* a French ship of the line that had grounded on the Virginia Capes in 1806.

After the appearance of the British squadron off the Patapsco in April, the City Council created a Committee of Public Supply to obtain loans from banks, enabling citizens to purchase arms and equipment, in the hope that they would later be reimbursed by the federal government. In May the governor placed Smith in charge of all Baltimore's militia troops, but the fort was under federal control and Smith did not respect Major Beall's abilities. A delegation from the Committee of Public Supply visited Secretary of War Armstrong and gained his commitment to reappoint the known and trusted Maj. George Armistead to this vital command. He had been in charge of the fort during the period 1809–12. Transferred to Fort Niagara, Armistead had distinguished himself in the capture of Fort George in May 1813, and Armstrong soon reappointed him to command at Fort McHenry.[24]

As if to confirm Marylanders in their worst fears, British warships reappeared off the Eastern Shore in August. Admiral Warren had learned that St. Michaels had erected a battery commanding the harbor; on August 10, he sent HM sloop of war *Conflict* to investigate. Her commander directed a division of eleven boats, under the command of Lt. James Polkinghorne, up the Miles River, where, according to his report, a militia patrol spotted them and gave the alarm. In fact, militia general Perry Benson had assembled a force of five hundred men of the Talbot County militia. They had reportedly constructed and thrown a chain-and-timber boom across the entrance of the harbor, protected by a gun battery. The militia fired on the British with canister and grape as they approached. The enemy sailors and marines landed at Parrott's Point, destroyed the battery (six 12- and 6-pounders), and pursued the gun crew as they retreated to the town. There, the Easton Artillery, under the command of Lt. Clement Vickers, manned another battery of two field guns and fired on the British, who suffered two wounded, thereby encouraging their departure. The British boats should have been supported by Colonel Beckwith's marines, but they had landed four miles away and were unable to coordinate. Without Beckwith's support, Lieutenant Polkinghorne had to withdraw and claimed to have sighted no vessels.[25] A local legend has it that the townspeople "fooled the British" by hanging lanterns in the trees so that, if fired, the cannon would overreach their targets. Yet, as Norman Plummer points out, the raid was made in daylight, and in the event, even if lanterns had been hung, they would not have made a difference. He regards this legend as a myth that may have been created about the time of the centennial of the attack on the town, in 1913.[26]

At about the same time as this attack, the British established an encampment on Kent Island. The Royal Marines and 102nd Army regiment landed, primarily to forage, collect cattle, and provide a temporary place for the many soldiers who had been brought low by sickness to recover their health. Early on the morning of August 12, the First Battalion of Colonel Beckwith's marines embarked in boats to make a reconnaissance at Queenstown, on the Chester River, where Maj. William H. Nicholson had deployed three hundred militiamen. In the predawn Nicholson sent forward Capt. Benjamin Massey and a platoon of eighteen men to probe for the British. The militia fired on the enemy troops, who panicked in the darkness and began firing on each other. Marylanders have called the place of this action "Slippery Hill." In the confusion, rather than plunging ahead in their usual manner, the British retreated to their boats and rejoined the others on Kent Island. Admiral Warren's report on his occupation of Kent Island does not enlarge upon the failed Queenstown raid, but it does state that Warren had decided against attempting further attacks on the Western Shore because of the large numbers of troops being mustered, namely, eleven thousand at Baltimore and five thousand at Annapolis. Both of these estimates seem exaggerated, perhaps from Americans spreading disinformation or because Warren, at this late stage, was anxious to be done with operations.[27]

But it was true that Gen. Samuel Smith had ordered special efforts to strengthen Baltimore's defenses, among them the creation of a unit of veteran seamen, known as the First Marine Artillery of the Union, to man the shore batteries at Fort McHenry. They prepared harbor obstructions, transported cannon, made wads for the guns, and exercised gun crews under the command of Capt. George Stiles, a veteran of the Quasi-War with France. Smith also ordered that signal stations be established between North Point and Fort McHenry to provide early notification of an approaching British force. On the possibility of an attack on the Maryland capital, Navy Secretary William Jones ordered Capt. Charles Morris to make the officers and crew of his blockaded frigate (corvette) *Adams,* 28 guns, immediately available at Annapolis to make up for the shortage of army artillerists. He was further to cooperate with the commanding military officer and would probably be given command of one or both forts. The alarms went out, but the attacks did not come.[28]

With Chesapeake heat and humidity at its height in mid-August, desertions and sickness spread through the British fleet. It was the time of the "sickly season," when the commanders made their departure to healthier climes, at Halifax or Bermuda. There they would rest, regroup, and refit the fleet. Not all the ships and sailors left, however. A small squadron, under the command of Capt. Robert Barrie, HMS *Dragon,* remained on station at Lynnhaven Roads throughout the fall and winter to maintain the blockade and harass American communications on the bay. For the defenders of the bay, however, it was a needed respite to train troops, strengthen fortifications, and build the Chesapeake Flotilla for the challenges to come.

Secretary of the Navy Jones corresponded with Master Commandant Barney during the winter of 1813–14, showing his concern that the Chesapeake Flotilla he had directed Barney to organize would be too weak to contend with the return of the British fleet. Jones increased by ten the number of second-class barges (50 feet) to be built and recommended that Barney contract for them to be built at St. Michaels. He also accepted Barney's recommendation that Solomon Frazier, a U.S. senator, be made a commander of one of the flotilla divisions. He described Frazier as a man of property and high standing who was very popular with local seamen and who would thus be useful not only in recruiting but also in supervising the construction of the barges.[29] Barney also selected Capt. Solomon Rutter to supervise the construction of barges at Baltimore. He had originally been assigned as a captain in charge of one of the companies of sailors in the First Marine Artillery, but he resigned that post to assume that of lieutenant in command of the flotilla division stationed at the Lazaretto.

The British, too, made preparations for the 1814 campaign. The war in Europe was coming to an end, with the defeat of Napoleon's armies in Spain and Russia. Soon, seasoned troops and more ships would be available to join the fight in America. The Admiralty had become disenchanted with Vice Admiral Warren's handling of his responsibilities. Too many privateers were escaping through the blockade, and even the U.S. Navy's frigates *President* and *Constitution* had slipped to sea without contest. He had failed to cut out the frigate *Constellation* from its well-defended berth at Norfolk. Too much effort had been spent in raiding the Chesapeake with no strategic result. The sloop of war *Argus* had played the devil with English shipping in the Channel and the Irish Sea. Warren would respond that he had too few ships to patrol the vast expanse of indented coastline and to oversee complexities of the operations under his control.

The new British commander of the Chesapeake campaign would be a younger, more active veteran of the European and earlier American wars, Vadm. Sir Alexander Cochrane. With a strong personality and a dislike for Americans, he had served as a lieutenant and commander during the American Revolutionary War and had been present at the taking of Philadelphia. At one time in command of the Leeward Island Station, he knew how dependent the United States was on these islands for their trading system. His brother had been killed at the Battle of Yorktown in the losing fight against the rebelling American colonies, and Admiral Cochrane had not forgotten. The Admiralty seemed in part to have accepted Warren's argument that his responsibilities were too broad. Other admirals were assigned to reduce the scope of Cochrane's command on the North Atlantic Station; they would report directly to London. Cochrane's mission was to prosecute the war on the mid-Atlantic states. Rear Admiral Cockburn now had to report to Cochrane, but they were both strong personalities, and differences of opinion would emerge.[30] Cockburn did not hesitate to give his recommendation to Cochrane on the target of future operations. On June 25, 1814, he wrote: "I am decidedly of the opinion that about the seat of Government and in the upper parts of the Chesapeake is where your operations may be commenced with most effect, but the country in general is in a horrible state; it only requires a little firm and steady conduct to have it completely at our mercy."[31]

Despite a general awareness that the renewal of fighting in the Chesapeake could bring new threats to Washington, D.C., Secretary of War John Armstrong persistently ignored this possibility and insisted that the main British thrust would probably be toward Baltimore. Other cabinet members, such as Secretary of State James Monroe, distrusted Armstrong and were thoroughly alarmed by the reappearance of the British fleet in the bay with greater numbers of more powerful ships than in the previous year. Rear Admiral Cockburn returned to the Chesapeake in February and Vice Admiral Cochrane made his appearance in March. They immediately set to work establishing a base of operations on Tangier Island, in the southern part of Chesapeake Bay, a few miles from the Eastern Shore of Virginia. Further reinforcements, in the form of troop transports carrying 3,000 veterans from the Peninsular War, arrived in late July. The U.S. Congress during the winter session increased the authorized strength of the army to 62,500 and had recruited

45,000 by early 1814. Yet, with Secretary Armstrong's eyes fixed firmly on further operations at Niagara, these troops went north as they became available. Maryland and Virginia, the obvious targets of further British operations, were left to their own devices. Thus, as the spring of 1814 came to life, Commodore Joshua Barney pushed the preparations of his Chesapeake Flotilla.

Despite difficulties in recruiting men and in correcting deficiencies in the newly constructed barges, Barney ordered his flotilla on a shakedown cruise on April 28. All told, he had fifteen vessels, including the cutter *Scorpion* (his flagship), two gunboats, and twelve barges. His ultimate objective was to arrive in Tangier Sound, where he could engage the enemy. Once under way, however, the squadron met with the unexpected. Arriving at the Patuxent on May 1, one of the barges had lost a mast, and the smaller barges shipped much water under way and rode too low in the water. Barney had to lighten them considerably to make them at all seaworthy and would have had to install washboards to keep out the seawater. Barney complained about his old navy gunboats (*No. 137* and *No. 138*) having leaky decks, which spoiled the provisions he was carrying for the barge crews. He needed a proper vessel to carry provisions and the sick, as well as the doctor and his medicines. It was clear that the flotilla could not operate well to windward in any kind of a blow. This would greatly hinder fighting the enemy in any condition other than light winds and smooth water. Jones promoted Barney to captain in the Chesapeake Flotilla as of April 25, but Congress took until October 18 to approve the act.[32]

On June 1 Barney led his squadron out of the Patuxent River and rounded Cedar Point as the sails of a British squadron came in view. Backed by a north wind, the flotilla headed south toward a British schooner and the division of armed boats, fired their guns, and were answered by guns and Congreve rockets, although this exchange was at too great a range to have effect. The wind shifted into the south. This put Barney's boats on the defensive, and he retreated to the mouth of the Patuxent River. Radm. George Cockburn ordered Capt. Robert Barrie (HMS *Dragon*) to blockade Barney in the Patuxent, informing him that he was sending reinforcements.[33] As the British squadron gathered in strength in the Patuxent, Barney ordered his flotilla to retreat farther up into St. Leonard's Creek, on the eastern shore of the river. There he fought two pitched battles with the British boats as they attempted to bottle him up in the creek, on June 10 and again on June 26. On the latter occasion, with the assistance of an army artillery battery and a calm wind, Barney beat back the British, broke out of the creek, and headed north up the Patuxent, where, for about a month and a half, his flotilla would be safe. Meanwhile, the British, awaiting the arrival of troop transports from Bermuda, employed their ships' boats and marines in marauding unopposed through the countryside on both sides of the Patuxent River, seizing food supplies, animals, and tobacco and searching for slaves willing to leave their masters.

Vice Admiral Cochrane's transports arrived in the bay under the command of Radm. Pulteney Malcolm between August 14 and 16. At that time, the British naval and military leaders finally determined on an attack on Washington. Admiral Cochrane had entertained doubts about the expedition to Washington. Maj. Gen. Robert Ross, commanding the British Army units sent from Europe to support Cochrane and Cockburn, reflected Cochrane's vacillation. It took Rear Admiral Cockburn's self-confident persuasive powers to convince Ross that it was a risk worth taking. After all, he argued, he had spent much time ashore with the marines the previous year and had found no concerted opposition. With that decision, the British fleet proceeded into the Patuxent and commenced landing their troops and equipment at Benedict while Admiral Cockburn, with the Royal Navy's launches and tenders, proceeded up the Patuxent, in parallel with the line of march. The farther they went the narrower and shallower the Patuxent became. As they approached Upper Marlborough, they discovered Barney's vessels moored along the river's banks.

Navy Secretary Jones had ordered the destruction of the flotilla vessels while salvaging as much of their equipment as possible. One after another the powder trains set by Barney's men exploded the vessels, many burning to the water's edge. Yet, even after a day on the march, Ross received a note from Cochrane, who had had a change of mind, warning him not to continue with the raid. Once again, Cockburn had to reassure the general of their probable success, assuring him that the vice admiral would relent when they returned. Barney retreated with his men in good order to the Washington Navy Yard. From there, Barney's sailors and marines hauled their cannon to the rise overlooking the bridge at Bladensburg, the next logical place for the British to cross the Eastern Branch of the Potomac (Anacostia) River. On August 24, 1814, they were the staunchest of the American troops who confronted the British at the Battle of Bladensburg.[34]

To defend the capital, on July 5 President Madison had appointed Brig. Gen. William Winder to command the American regular and militia forces. Winder, a lawyer without a military background, was a nephew of Levin Winder, the governor of Maryland, and had good political connections. He had volunteered earlier in the war and served in a capacity too great for his abilities, ending up captured at the battle of Beaver Dams in Canada after the landing at Fort George. Once again, now in charge of the defense of the nation's capital, he was out of his depth. Secretary of War Armstrong neglected to give Winder a capable staff. With huge responsibilities and no senior military officer to advise him, Winder spent his time making personal tours of inspection that should have been delegated to others and failed to collect sufficient numbers of Maryland and District of Columbia militia who had been called up. His counterpart in the District of Columbia was Maj. Gen. John Van Ness, another wealthy amateur, who was no more successful in getting support from Secretary Armstrong than was Winder. When, on August 19, Van Ness informed the secretary that the British had landed at Benedict and that immediate steps should be taken, Armstrong is said to have blustered, "Oh yes, By God, they would not come with such a fleet without meaning to strike somewhere, but they certainly will not come here; what the devil will they do here?"[35]

Van Ness and Winder met to discuss coordination of their militias but had a dispute over which of them was senior and in overall command. Armstrong ducked the decision and passed it to Madison, who nodded in Winder's favor. At that point Van Ness resigned his appointment but offered his assistance to Winder.[36] Winder, unsure of his enemy's true destination and where to confront him, finally assembled a force of approximately 2,500 militia, U.S. Marines, and regular army troops and marched them into Prince George's County, where they pitched camp at Woodyard (the Darnall plantation), a few miles west of Upper Marlborough. The nervous Winder ordered his troops to backtrack toward Washington, just a few miles ahead of the advancing British. He returned to Washington concerned about the Eastern Branch bridge and whether it should be destroyed. It was typical of the confusion of the day that, although officers attached to the Navy Yard had made preparations, they received no orders to destroy the bridge until after the Battle of Bladensburg, when it was a useless act.

On the morning of August 24 General Winder and President Madison's cabinet learned that the British were marching toward Bladensburg rather than Fort Washington or directly to the capital city. Winder had given orders for Maryland and District of Columbia militia units to gather there. At first, he directed Barney to place his artillery in a position to defend the bridge over the Eastern Branch. But when he heard that the British were proceeding directly for Bladensburg, he hastily ordered Barney's sailors and a company of U.S. Marines under Capt. Samuel Miller to march posthaste for Bladensburg along with their artillery: a battery of three 12-pounders and two 18-pounder long guns. Among the last units to arrive on the field, Barney placed his marine artillery and naval infantry across the Bladensburg-Washington road. Most of the militia had deployed to the left of this position. These included Maj. Gen. Samuel Smith's Third Division of the Maryland Volunteer Militia, including Col. William Beall's 700-man unit from Annapolis; Gen. Tobias Stansbury's Fifth Brigade of 2,200 men from Baltimore; Lt. Col. Joseph Sterrett's 800 riflemen and artillery men; and from Washington, Gen. Walter Smith's First Columbian Brigade of 1,000 volunteers and militia. Absent, however, was the Sixtieth Regiment of Virginia militia, under Col. George Minor, 600 strong, with 100 cavalry. They had arrived in Washington the evening before, but thanks to Armstrong's refusal to open the armory at night and provide weapons in a timely manner, the battle was over before the Virginia militia could leave the city for Bladensburg.

The British troops, 4,500 strong, had marched from Benedict over five days, with no serious opposition or obstructions, and arrived at the Bladensburg bridge on the morning of August 24, expecting a fight. It is notable that they had neither cavalry nor artillery to support their attack. The American militia had both but in short supply, and they had never trained in cooperation with other units for concerted action. In numbers, the Americans were roughly equal to the British, but not in quality or combat experience. The only truly seasoned, fully trained troops among them were Commodore Barney's sailors and marines, numbering just over 500 men. Held back until the last hour, Barney's troops marched rapidly over the six miles to Bladensburg and arrived just as the firing commenced. Barney tells what happened next:

> The day was hot, and my men very much crippled from the severe marches we had experienced the preceding days before, many of them being without shoes, which I had replaced that morning. I preceded the men and when I arrived at the line which sepa-

rates the District from Maryland the Battle began, I sent an officer back to hurry on my men, they came up in a *trot,* we took our position on the rising ground, put the pieces in Battery, posted the *Marines* under *Capt. Miller* and the flotilla men who were to act as Infantry under their own officers, on my right to support the pieces, and waited the approach of the Enemy.

During this period the engagement continued the enemy advancing—our own Army retreating before them apparently in much disorder, at length the enemy made his appearance on the main road, in force, and in front of my Battery, and on seeing us made a halt, I reserved our fire, in a few minutes the enemy again advanced, when I ordered an 18 lb. to be fired, which compleatly cleared the road, shortly after a second and a third attempt was made by the enemy to come forward but all were distroyed, The enemy then crossed over into an Open field and attempted to flank our right, he was there met by three twelve pounders, the Marines under Capt. *Miller* and my men acting as Infantry, and again was totally cut up, by this time not a Vestige of the American Army remained except a body of 5 or 600 posted on a height on my right from whom I expected much support, from their fine situation.

The Enemy from this period never appeared in force in *front* of us, they pushed forward their *sharp shooters,* one of which shot my horse under me, who fell dead between two of my Guns; The enemy who had been kept in check by our fire for nearly half an hour now began to out flank us on the right, our guns were turned that way, he pushed *up* the Hill, about 2 or 300 towards the Corps of Americans station'd as above described, who, to my great mortification made no resistance, giving a fire or two and retired, in this situation we had the whole army of the Enemy to contend with. Our Ammunition was expended, and unfortunately the drivers of my Ammunition Waggons had gone off in the General Panic, at this time I received a severe wound in my thigh, Capt. *Miller,* was Wounded, Sailing Master *Warner* Killed, *actg.* Sailing Master *Martin* Killed, & sailing Master *Martin* wounded, but to the honour of my officers & men, as fast as their Companions & mess mates fell at the guns they were instantly replaced from the Infantry, Finding the enemy now compleatly in our rear, and no means of defence I gave orders to my officers and men to retire.[37]

The remainder of the story concerns the flight of the militia from the battlefield, some toward Baltimore, others toward Georgetown and Washington. The actual number of killed and wounded Americans was fewer than some would believe, though more British fell than is commonly accepted. British losses were 64 dead and 185 wounded, while the Americans suffered 26 dead, 51 wounded, and at least 100 captured. The events of the British march to Washington, their brief occupation, the burning of the capitol (including the Library of Congress), the White House, and the Navy Yard, as well as the flight of President Madison, his wife, and the cabinet, have been well told by others.[38]

The British Army left Washington quietly during the evening of August 25. A violent storm had passed through the capital the night before, as if to show nature's unhappiness with the sad scene of the humiliated, smoke-filled city. General Ross ordered that the soldiers leave campfires burning and spread rumors that their next target would be Annapolis, to throw off any would-be pursuers. He commandeered all available horses and wagons to carry the sick and wounded and began the march back to Benedict. They passed through Bladensburg again, retracing their steps through farmlands and extensive forests to Upper Marlborough, and thence southward along the right bank of the Patuxent River. They marched by Dr. William Beanes's handsome home, where General Ross and Admiral Cockburn had chosen to spend the night on their way to Washington. Dr. Beanes, an elderly physician of Scottish birth, had played the gentleman, offering such hospitality as he could. They had departed well satisfied that at least one American had treated them with the respect they deserved. There was no stopping by on the return to Benedict; however, some soldiers straggled behind the rest to loot houses in the neighborhood. Former governor Robert Bowie, a neighbor of Beanes's, found these miscreants on his property and went to Beanes for help. They and others arrested and jailed the soldiers, but one escaped and returned to the fleet to tell his story about the Americans who had captured them. General Ross sent cavalry back to seize Dr. Beanes and two others and bring them to Benedict, where they were confined on board ship. Beanes's conduct angered General Ross, who had, mistakenly, thought him a friend and now felt betrayed. Ross held him as a hostile, the civilian equivalent of a prisoner of war, and did not release him from confinement for two weeks. Even the pleas of Maryland governor Levin Winder, who had gained the release of the other Marylanders, had no effect on General Ross.[39]

This minor incident during the British retreat from Washington was to have a major impact on American cultural history. It was on behalf of Dr. Beanes that Georgetown lawyer Francis Scott Key and his friend John S. Skinner visited the British fleet before its attack on Baltimore, hoping to obtain Beanes's release. Following the British cavalry's seizure of Dr. Beanes, it was Richard E. West, Key's brother-in-law and owner of the Woodyard (Darnall) plantation, who contacted Key and Skinner, another resident of Prince George's County, to seek out Beanes's captors and gain his release. Skinner was an important go-between in this transaction; he was the American agent for release of prisoners of war. Key applied to President Madison for permission to go on this mission and to use the flag of truce (cartel) sloop *President* to approach the British fleet.[40] Key then visited hospitals taking care of British wounded and requested letters of support from the wounded, testifying to the excellent care they had received. When, on September 7, the sloop delivered Key and Skinner to HMS *Tonnant,* Admiral Cochrane's flagship, he invited the pair to stay for dinner. On hearing their request for Beanes's release, Cochrane, Cockburn, and Ross expressed their unhappiness with Beanes's behavior and threatened to take him to Bermuda to be tried for treason, as a former subject of the British Crown. The situation looked grim for the good doctor, but Key then displayed a letter from a British sergeant who had written about his gratitude for good medical treatment after Bladensburg. After consideration, General Ross relented and freed Beanes from confinement but ordered that the three be kept under guard. They were transferred to HMS *Surprise,* commanded by Capt. Thomas Cockburn, the rear admiral's son, until the fleet went to the Patapsco. When Cochrane shifted his flag to *Surprise,* on September 12, the better to observe the battle from a position nearer Fort McHenry, he sent Key, Skinner, and Beanes back to their cartel, tied off astern of *Surprise*. From the deck of the cartel sloop *President*, Key and his companions observed the battle off Fort McHenry, and during the long, spectacular bombardment, worried whether the fort would be forced to surrender. When, at dawn on September 14, Key's telescope enabled him to see the American colors floating above the fort, he rejoiced and was so moved that he jotted down the first words of the inspiring poem that eventually, set to the melody of the popular song "To Anacreon in Heaven," became the United States' national anthem.[41]

After the Battle of Bladensburg and the British attack on Washington, the question was: Where would the British turn next? The answer: Admiral Cochrane had already laid plans for simultaneous efforts to mislead and confuse his American opponents. Capt. James Alexander Gordon, a battle-scarred veteran of the Royal Navy's battles with the French, was proceeding up the Potomac in his frigate HMS *Seahorse*, with a squadron of six vessels, toward Alexandria. Their orders were to cover a possible escape route for the British army, should they unexpectedly fail in the attempt on Washington. But the primary mission was to destroy the defenses of Fort Warburton (Washington) and lay Alexandria "under contribution"; in other words, remove the valuable goods and cargoes stored on the waterfront and threaten to destroy the city if opposed. Gordon had with him the frigate HMS *Euryalus*, a rocket ship, four bomb vessels, and a dispatch schooner—not an overwhelming force but one equipped to do enough damage to accomplish the mission. While Gordon was on his way, Cochrane deployed Capt. Sir Peter Parker in the frigate HMS *Menelaus* to patrol the upper bay opposite the Patapsco to gather information, divert attention, and intercept any reinforcements that might be sent to Baltimore or Washington by sea. The young Parker was a stiff disciplinarian who admired Admiral Cockburn's aggressive spirit. He sailed *Menelaus* to the Severn, sent officers to reconnoiter Annapolis harbor, then looked into the Patapsco, where he took the risk of sailing in a tender up the river near Fort McHenry and the Lazaretto. He reported seeing a frigate, two sloops of war, several gunboats, and a brig before he was hailed and mistaken for friendly by a boat patrolling the river.

That same day, August 30, Parker witnessed militia activities on the Eastern Shore opposite Pools Island and determined to raid the militia's camp that night. Upon landing with 100 sailors and marines, Parker encountered a black man who informed him that the militia were camped only one-half mile inland, but the camp had moved farther inland. All told, Parker's scouting party may have marched four or five miles, only to find a large body of militia drawn up ready for battle. This gives every indication that the militia had deliberately withdrawn inland to induce the British to commit themselves on unfamiliar ground on the night of a full moon. The battle joined, Parker stood out, "animating his men in a most heroic manner," when a charge of buckshot brought him down. The British withdrew under the direction of Lt. Henry Crease, *Menelaus's* first lieutenant, who reported that his crew had suffered fourteen killed and twenty-five wounded, a large proportion (nearly 40%) of the landing party. He claimed the militia had five hundred infantry plus cavalry and five pieces of artillery. This action, the Battle of Caulk's Field, near Fairlee in Kent County, was an unexpected and costly setback for the British on the eve of their attack on Baltimore. It must have been very painful for Admiral Cochrane to learn of Parker's death; not only was Parker a valuable officer but his father was the late Adm. Sir Peter Parker, whose squadron had attempted and failed to take Charleston in 1776. His mother was the daughter of Adm. the Honorable John "Foul Weather Jack" Byron, who briefly commanded on the North American Station during the American Revolution.[42]

Maj. Gen. Samuel Smith, Maryland Militia, ordered advance preparations for Baltimore's defenses, and merchant leaders formed a Committee of Vigilance and Safety to mobilize the community. Major General Smith, backed by this committee, persuaded Governor Winder to support him as the commander of the city's defense, rather than Brig. Gen. (Regular Army) William Winder, the governor's nephew, who had so utterly failed in the defense of the nation's capital. This decision, taken on September 11, was crucial to the defense of the city, as the British were preparing to attack. Smith had already put plans into effect, called on militias from neighboring states to send units to defend Baltimore, and persuaded the Committee of Vigilance and Safety to issue calls for all able-bodied men to bring wheelbarrows, pickaxes, and shovels to help reinforce and build the city's defenses. They constructed earthworks on the eastern side of the city, stretching from Bel Air Road in the north to Harris Creek on the Patapsco River, centered on a strong redoubt on Hampstead Hill. This came to be known as Rodgers's Bastion, after Commodore John Rodgers, a native son of Maryland, who arrived to lend his considerable military experience and the men at his command to the defenders' efforts.

The U.S. Navy, by coincidence, was able to provide several contingents of veteran officers, seamen, and marines to reinforce the lines in Baltimore and to aid in punishing the enemy after the ruin of Washington. On August 19, Secretary Jones had ordered Commodores Rodgers, David Porter, and Oliver Hazard Perry to come to Washington with all their men as soon as possible. At the time, Rodgers was stationed in the USS *Guerrière* in Philadelphia, Porter was in New York undergoing a court of inquiry on his recent arrival from the Pacific, where he had lost the frigate *Essex* in battle, and Perry was stationed at Baltimore, supervising the construction of his new command, the frigate USS *Java,* 44 guns. Rodgers arrived with his complement on August 25 and Porter came in the next day. Their presence was a tonic to the frightened people of Baltimore, who knew not what to expect in the wake of the defeat at Bladensburg. Acting in concert with General Smith, who had overall command, Rodgers issued general orders to all those who were part of the Baltimore naval station. By these, he created a brigade divided into two divisions or regiments. The first included the officers, seamen, and marines of the frigate *Guerrière* and those of the late frigate *Essex.* The second division comprised the officers and seamen of the Chesapeake Flotilla and all other volunteers. He assigned Captain Porter to command of the first division and Captain Perry, the second. As for the U.S. Marines, Capt. Alfred Grayson, the senior officer in Baltimore, wrote to Commandant Franklin Wharton: "I have this morning tendered [the Marines'] services with my own to Commodore Rodgers and he accepted them. In all there will be about 170 Marines, the whole force, sailors and Marines will be tonight about one thousand."[43]

No sooner had Commodore Rodgers arrived and begun to organize the naval

forces than he received orders from Secretary Jones, on August 29, that took prece-
dence over those of General Smith. The Royal Navy squadron under Captain Gordon's command had arrived off Alexandria on August 27. Jones saw an opportunity
to attack Gordon's ships before they departed and wanted Rodgers and his men to
come to Washington as soon as possible. Rodgers lost no time in obeying the secretary's wishes, although his response showed some reluctance at leaving Baltimore in
the lurch. He sent Captain Porter away with 100 sailors and marines and promised
to come himself with even more men. It is doubtful that Jones had considered the
effect his orders would have on General Smith's plans for Baltimore's defense. The
navy's detaching of nearly half of the force that Smith was counting on to man the
batteries on Hampstead Heights and improve harbor defenses caused him great
concern. He immediately wrote to Rodgers demanding his return and at the same
time wrote to James Monroe, who had become acting secretary of war. He told
Monroe, "their departure will damp the ardor of the troops and create an excitement more easily to conceive than describe. The absence of Commodore Rodgers's
men has stopped the preparations for a defense for that point we are most exposed."[44] Smith drove his argument home in a note to Rodgers on September 2,
commenting that setting fire to two frigates was hardly commensurate with the
defense of Baltimore, and "although you come at the time the British are before us,
your Station is not assigned & in the meantime the sloops of war [*Erie* and *Ontario*]
intended to defend the Western Branch [of the Patapsco] are not prepared. If we are
attacked on that side, we are not defended. It is our Weak Point. I am persuaded you
can do no good where you are—you may cause the burning of Alexandria."[45]

On reconsideration, Rodgers partially countermanded orders he had given
and told marine lieutenant Gamble to return to Baltimore with a good portion of
Guerrière's sailors and flotilla men. Jones, a few days later, realized the situation in
which he had placed Rodgers, writing, "I have received your note this morning, and
really am embarrassed between the desire of affording you an opportunity of destruction or injury to the enemy and the dread of an attack on Baltimore before
you shall have reached that place.... You will therefore use your discretion for two
or three days and in the interim should the state of things at Baltimore become
more alarming you shall be instantly informed. I have sent to the Navy yard to
hurry off the fire vessel."[46]

Rodgers made three attempts to injure the British squadron as it departed Alexandria. The first was the employment of three escorted fire vessels, loaded with
combustibles, manned until the last minute, to be sailed and then set on fire just
before they reached the British ships anchored below Alexandria. This was unsuccessful. The enemy was alert to the possibility and had stationed ships' launches
above the anchorage to fend off such vessels and to drive away the U.S. Navy boats
that accompanied them. The second effort was more successful. Capt. David Porter
set up a powerful battery on the Virginia shore at White House Point (near present-
day Fort Belvoir). Porter, with assistance from Captain Grayson, USMC, Gen. John
Hungerford, Virginia Militia, Captain Spencer, U.S. Army (Artillery), and the men
under their commands, placed guns, built gun carriages, and delivered musket fire
on the British ships and their prizes as they passed. The enemy anchored in front

of the battery and delivered a heavy fire in response. Porter's strength, in the guns at his disposal, was two 12-pounders, six 6-pounders, two 4-pounders, and a furnace for hot shot. He had two mortars and several 32-pounders, all without carriages. He estimated the enemy's strength at 173 guns from all ships: two frigates, 96 guns, three bomb ships, 30 guns, one sloop-ship fitted as a rocket ship, 26 guns, one brig of 18 guns, one schooner, 1 gun, and two barges, 2 guns. As for American casualties, Porter reported: "The number we have had killed and wounded on this occasion I cannot ascertain exactly. I am induced to believe, however, it does not exceed thirty, and we consider the constant fire which had been kept up by the enemy for the four days preceding their passage by the fort we should esteem ourselves very fortunate. His damage can never be known by us, some of his ships were much crippled, and I should suppose his loss considerable."[47]

Captain Perry set up his battery at Indian Head, on September 5, some miles down the Potomac, where the British squadron had to pass close to the Maryland shore. Militia artillerists from Georgetown and Washington assisted his men in positioning and serving the cannon. But, as Perry noted in his report, he had too few guns of too small a caliber and lacked sufficient ammunition to hold up the enemy ships for long or do them much damage. Likewise, Perry claimed that his battery received no punishment owing to its placement on a promontory overlooking the river, which made it difficult for the enemy ships' guns to elevate sufficiently. Captain Gordon's report to Admiral Cochrane contradicted Perry, maintaining that his bomb ships' mortars had a precise and decisive effect so that Perry's battery fire halted completely. However, this could also have been due to Perry's shortage of ammunition. Gordon's ships proceeded downriver the next morning without further molestation.[48]

Federal army and navy units rallied to Baltimore's defense, as did Commodore Barney's flotilla men, Pennsylvania and Virginia militias, and ordinary citizens. By the time the British fleet appeared before North Point, on September 11, the city had 16,400 armed men crowded into its fixed and improvised defenses, sunken vessels blocked the Patapsco River channel, and entrenchments lined roads on the North Point peninsula. The British fleet anchored in Old Roads Bay just to the west of North Point and disembarked the troops on the twelfth. Cochrane then advanced his frigates and bomb vessels as far as he could toward Fort McHenry, but the river's shoals prevented deeper-draft frigates from approaching nearer than four miles, putting the fort out of range of their 18- and 24-pounders. The bomb vessels had shallower drafts and were able to kedge over the shoals by having their launches carry anchors ahead and let them go, and then the crew would wind the ship ahead using their capstans. Each of these ships' mortars could fire a 13-inch, 190-pound cast-iron spherical exploding shell two miles. Once they had reached their optimum range, the bomb vessels' mortars, fired in high trajectory, could land many shells on target.

In Baltimore signal guns roared to tell the citizens that the long-feared British fleet had arrived. Under orders from General Smith to advance, Brig. Gen. John Stricker pushed eastward on the eleventh with his troops along the road to North Point. He had with him 3,185 soldiers in five regiments. On the following day, holding one regiment in reserve, Stricker followed his carefully laid plan of confronting the British near where the heads of Bear Creek and Bread and Cheese Creek converge. There the narrowing of the North Point peninsula would force the British to use the same road to reach Baltimore. He posted riflemen in a wood west of the Gorsuch Farm, where Ross and Cockburn had paused to take breakfast. Ross had been told that the American lines were still eleven miles away, so without knowing that Stricker's men were within four miles, he struck out on horseback with Cockburn and the skirmishers. Suddenly, firing broke out. Ross hastened to the front to investigate but was immediately struck down by a musket ball, which pierced his arm and entered his chest. He died from loss of blood only two hours later. This struck a heavy blow to British morale. Until this moment, there had been few losses, and none of their very senior officers had fallen. Nonetheless, they were there to fight and Colonel Arthur Brooke came up, quickly having learned the bad news from Ross's aide-de-camp. From that moment, there was a stiff fight, with both small armies engaged for two or more hours. Gradually, the British pushed around the left flank of the American lines, and the militia began to retreat in fairly good order—not a repeat of the "Bladensburg Races." The British troops, by now exhausted, camped on the battlefield and used the nearby Methodist Meeting House as a hospital. They were on the road at dawn, but it was a bad day for marching; rain fell in a deluge, and the British found that the Americans had felled trees to slow their march. It took the better part of the thirteenth for them to reach the lines of the entrenched defenders of Baltimore on Hampstead Hill.

While the march was in progress and despite the weather, the bomb vessels HMS *Aetna, Devastation, Meteor, Terror,* and *Volcano* opened up on Fort McHenry. The fort's batteries, including the French 36-pounders, waited until the bomb vessels were at a range of three thousand yards and then replied in kind. Barney's flotilla men, now under the command of Lt. Solomon Rutter, went to work sinking merchant ships as obstructions in the channel between the Lazaretto and the fort. He also had at his disposal eight gun barges, thirty-four men to a barge, four having long 8-pounder cannon fore and aft and four with long 12-pounders. Simultaneously, Lieutenant Frazier let loose with the three 18-pounders from the Lazaretto Battery. Other sailors were ready at Battery Babcock, on the Ferry Branch, with six 18-pounders under the command of Sailing Master Webster of the flotilla. At the fort's Water Battery, Sailing Master Solomon Rodman had prepared his eighteen 18-pounders. The sloop of war *Erie* had anchored in the basin with her short-handed gun crew ready, in case the British tried to enter in a boat attack. Young Midshipman George Hollins, a Baltimorean, was acting commander of the sloop.

The naval bombardment of Fort McHenry continued all day of the thirteenth and into the early morning of the fourteenth. With mortar shells arching up and exploding in and around Fort McHenry and the enemy's rocket boats firing off their Congreve rockets, it must have been a fearsome sight for the ordinary citizens who had left their homes and workplaces to take up arms and be on the receiving end of this bombardment. According to Major Armistead, the fort's commander, the British ships fired between 1,500 and 1,800 mortar shells, with some 400 landing and exploding within the ramparts. By a marvelous stroke of luck, however, one that landed in the powder magazine did not explode.[49]

Colonel Brooke and Admiral Cockburn arrived at the defensive lines with their troops in front of Hampstead Hill and surveyed the situation. Thinking they might be able to outflank the lines to their right, they sent troops in that direction, but the Maryland militia moved to preclude that possibility. The two commanders reconsidered, and Cockburn suggested to Admiral Cochrane that if their navy could assist by closing on and rushing the fort, the British troops could outflank the American defenses from that quarter after bombarding their lines. Cochrane's reply was devastating. "My dear Admiral, It is impossible for the ships to render you any assistance—the town is so far retired within the forts. It is for Colonel Brooke to consider under such circumstances whether he has Force sufficient to defeat so large a number as it [is] said the Enemy has collected: say 20,000 strong or even a less number & to take the town without this can be done only by throwing the men's lives away and prevent us from going on other services—At any rate, a very considerable loss let it be ever so great cannot be equally felt." In this message, Cochrane effectively told Cockburn that he was on his own if he encouraged further attempts on Baltimore. What the vice admiral also had in mind in referring to "other services" were operations on the Gulf Coast, where he would have great need of his land forces. Colonel Brooke responded about midnight: "Dear Sir—from your letter to Admiral Cockburn this evening I call'd a Council of War, though I had made all my arrangements for attacking the Enemy at three in the morning, the result of which was that from the situation I was placed in they advised I should retire. I have therefore ordered the Retreat to take place tomorrow Morning and hope to be at my destination the day after tomorrow—that is, the place we disembarked from."[50]

Thus, the British reluctantly retreated when Admiral Cochrane refused to make further efforts to assault Fort McHenry from the sea. He recognized the danger of their situation. Enough blood had been shed, and the odds were very much against them for the first time. The admiral had lost a fine general and valued friend, and he had orders to proceed against objectives in the American South (Mobile and New Orleans) that were strategically more important. As a result, Baltimore successfully resisted the major British bombardment and assault of the War of 1812. All told, it was the extraordinary efforts of all, military, navy, and citizens alike, working under the determined leadership of Gen. Samuel Smith that saved Baltimore.[51]

Following the battle, the British squadron sailed down the bay and gradually reduced its presence in the Chesapeake. The larger ships, with the transports, sailed to Bermuda and the Caribbean, where they refitted, restored their troops to health, and prepared for the final attacks of the war at Mobile, New Orleans, and Cumberland Island, Georgia. The American victory at the Battle of Lake Champlain (and Plattsburg) occurred just days before the defeat of the British at Baltimore. The news of both events arrived simultaneously in Britain, undermining the resistance of the British peace commissioners and creating brighter prospects for the American negotiators. Meanwhile, in Vienna, the conference that would settle the peace in Europe for two generations was under negotiation. This, for the British government, was the more important of the two conclaves, and they sent their principal diplomats to see that the results were favorable to Great Britain. The Treaty of Ghent was signed on December 24, 1814, but the news of its ratification was slow to arrive, and fighting continued into 1815 on both land and sea. The Battle for New Orleans, a three-weeks-long struggle, ended in January with a resounding victory for Gen. Andrew Jackson, Commodore Patterson, and their allies. The last skirmish of the war in Maryland was that of the "Ice Mound," off James Island on February 7, 1815, when the Maryland militia marched out on the bay ice and seized the British tender *Dauntless,* which had been stranded with its crew of nineteen.[52]

~~~

Chapter Four

The Surge of Maritime Baltimore under Sail and Steam

~~~~~~~~~~~~~~~~~~~~~~~~~~~~~~~~~~~~~

THE CITY OF BALTIMORE was a principal beneficiary of the War of 1812. Many of its merchants had gambled and won in the high stakes of privateering, and the city had enhanced its reputation for competent leadership and stout patriotism in resisting the British onslaught of 1814. With British harassment fading, the way was clear for Baltimore's merchant and seagoing community to seek profits on foreign seas. The war had come to an end, but some Baltimoreans who had profited from war were not yet prepared to adjust to peaceful trade while there were other wars to fight. Spain's American colonies had been exposed to the struggle for independence in the United States, and in Spain, anti-French guerrillas rose up against Napoleonic usurpers in support of the Cortes and King Ferdinand VII. The war against Napoleon provided the pretext for the proclamation of "republics" in Mexico and in Central and South America between 1810 and 1825.

Some of Baltimore's unemployed privateersmen exploited their next opportunity by obtaining letters of marque from the new republics to capture Spanish prizes. The nations most open to these entrepreneurs were Colombia and Venezuela, where Francisco de Miranda and Simon Bolivar had sparked revolutions. Also willing were the nations that sprang up in the Rio de La Plata viceroyalty—Argentina and the Banda Oriental (Uruguay). Merchants such as Henry Didier Jr. exported arms to these countries, and Capts. Joseph Almeda, J. D. Danels, William J. Stafford, Francis Jenkins, Hugh Davey, Daniel Chaytor, James Taylor, James Barnes, and John Chase were among those who participated in this new war.[1] It must be admitted, however, that these activities were illegal, since the United States was not at war with Spain, and Americans who engaged in this business had to do so surreptitiously.

The slave trade, too, though illegal, was still attractive to former privateersmen and shipbuilders of Baltimore.[2] Vessels "sold to foreigners" and some owned and sailed by Baltimoreans were valued for the speed with which they could evade the antislavery patrols of Great Britain and the United States. Despite the death penalty authorized by Congress for slavers in 1820, the trade continued for decades because of the demand for slaves in the southern United States, the Caribbean, and South America. As long as there were those who would buy, slavers continued to operate, although public opinion soon turned against this activity, and those who valued their reputations and ability to obtain credit sought other ways of turning a dollar.

Transatlantic commerce revived after the end of the Napoleonic Wars and the War of 1812. During the years 1815–60, the American merchant marine reached its zenith in terms of the percentage of American trade it carried. American shipowners possessed a price advantage that enabled them to undercut the European carrying trade for most of the period. Maryland shipowners, captains, and crew were to participate in this rapid expansion, but the day of the "Baltimore clipper" schooner had passed by the late 1830s.[3] These vessels were undoubtedly swift, but they could not carry cargo in bulk, being relatively narrow and shallow in the hold. They would continue to serve in the coastal trade and in local waters for use as pilot vessels. Passenger- and freight-carrying ships would largely abandon these schooners for square-rigged ships of greater length, beam, and draught.

While Chesapeake Bay is better known for its famous schooners, the ubiquitous sloop preceded the development of schooners and ships in many countries and cultures. The origin of the word *sloop* was originally European, derived from the Dutch *sloep;* in Sweden it was *slup,* in France, *chaloup,* in Germany, *schlup,* and in England, *shallop.* The word in the American colonies was variously *shallop, shaloop,* and *sloop* and was used to describe a one-masted two-sail rig. In a census of vessels built in Maryland, taken in 1697, sloops and shallops were the most numerous types, reported as follows: sixty-six sloops, fifty-five shallops, thirteen ships, twelve brigantines, and six pinks.[4] Though the sloop may have evolved from small fishing craft, the sloop-rigged vessel became common as a coastal transport during the eighteenth century, and when the American Revolution broke out in 1775, patriotic shipwrights constructed armed sloops for war as large as 60 to 80 tons, mounting 8 to 12 guns. In 1783, some 40 percent of all registered American vessels were sloops. With the end of the Revolutionary War, American merchants sought trade everywhere, and a few sloop-rigged vessels of greater than 50 tons were transiting to China via the Cape of Good Hope.

The origins of the evolved American sloop design had come perhaps from Jamaica via Bermuda. These sloops had a large mainsail, reaching jibs, raked mast, long bowsprit, deep drag in keel, low freeboard, and considerable sheer. The oceangoing sloops of late-eighteenth-century origin fell into disuse on Chesapeake Bay during the early nineteenth century, giving way to the fast-sailing Chesapeake Bay schooner, with which the sloop shared some design features. The deep keels of the oceangoing sloops were not well suited for work in the bay, but smaller versions were adapted to its shallow waters. Even though there were some shallow-draft, open sloops, skiffs, and log canoes that could carry produce, they were not adequate to the quantities needed.

During the 1820s, sloop design advanced to involve a larger, shallow, round-bottom hull with a fair amount of beam and a centerboard trunk. The first official record of these was made in 1839 as a 6.5-ton vessel of no name; a second, called *Amphibious,* was registered in Richmond. She was much larger, at 39 tons, and was presumably a buyboat or tobacco transport on the James River. The number of these fair-sized sloops was small, but after the Civil War, the number exploded. Their captains used them to tow dredges (drogues) to scrape the oyster grounds, as was done in other locations, such as Long Island Sound and Delaware Bay. Watermen from these regions brought their vessels into the Chesapeake and competed with the Chesapeake watermen for the available oystering grounds. This predictably led to strife over who had the right to work the oyster beds. The most capable and easily handled vessels were beamy, round-bottomed sloops with large sails that could drag the dredge through the heavy sediment of the oyster beds. The number of sloops jumped dramatically in the immediate post–Civil War years. The dredge sloops were of 6 to 12 tons, whereas the buyboats were of 25 to 40 tons.

The number of sloops registered increased threefold between 1865 and 1870. Sloop builders were active in both Maryland and Virginia and on the Eastern and Western shores. The greatest number of documented sloops appeared between 1880 and 1885, when 122 were built. Some examples of these are *William Wesley,* built at Crisfield in 1870, and the scow sloop (square-bowed) *Elsie,* built in Philadelphia in 1874. Most of these sloops were under 20 gross tons, but the largest were *Annie,* built in 1865, at 26 gross tons; *Charles O. Milbourn,* built in 1862 in Somerset County, 24 tons; *Charles W. S. Banks,* built in Cambridge in 1882, 24 tons; and the *Effie A. Chase,* built in 1881 in Crisfield, 22 tons. The largest Maryland-built working sloop on record was *Carrie,* built in Havre de Grace, at 41 tons, in 1882.[5]

The number of sloops built dropped suddenly between 1890 and 1895. Probably the last Chesapeake Bay working sloop was *J. T. Leonard,* 10 tons, built by Moses Geohegan on Taylor Island in 1882. She was kept at the Chesapeake Bay Maritime Museum in St. Michaels in the 1960s but was beyond repair by the 1970s.[6] Competition from steamboats and railroads had made inroads at a time when keeping costs low was critical, and more simply built vessels were gaining in popularity.

The schooner, one of the most characteristic historic sailing crafts of Chesapeake Bay, ascended to prominence in the early nineteenth century as the "Baltimore clipper."[7] Naval architects and maritime historians often argue about the origins of this uniquely swift vessel, but there is no doubt that, in the United States, its reputation will always be closely associated with maritime activities on the bay. While Sweden, Holland, France, and Bermuda provided fertile ground for other versions of this swift-sailing craft, the design and rig of the clipper schooner were of Chesapeake origin. Footner does not point to a definitive statement by an earlier expert but draws his conclusion from a variety of sources: newspaper advertisements, government ledgers and licenses, court records, and images from prints, drawings, models, and old photographs. Although the two-masted fore-and-aft rig is recorded as having early use in England and Holland, the schooner in its mature and most successful form is probably derived from the Chesapeake pilot schooner of the eighteenth century.[8]

To understand why this is so, consider the geographical factors of the Chesapeake Bay region: the elongated structure of the bay, its many tributaries, its generally shallow water, and the prevailing winds. To the planters and merchants whose vessels carried produce to and from distant markets, these factors underscored the need for swift, maneuverable sailing craft that could negotiate the sometimes tortuous and narrow channels of Chesapeake rivers. The first schooners appeared in Chesapeake waters in 1730, at about the same time that Maryland's tobacco-bound

Pilot schooner *Commerce of Baltimore,* with house flag hoisted on the mainmast. Courtesy, Maryland Historical Society, M1977.5.1.

economy began to diversify and grain shipments gained in importance. In those distant colonial days, the American colonies were the breadbasket of a North Atlantic economy that was increasingly interrupted by maritime warfare in the Caribbean. The Chesapeake pilot schooner evolved in the 1750s. Its characteristics were a double-ended shallow hull with significant deadrise (vee-bottomed) that sat low in the water, driven by two gaff-rigged fore-and-aft sails on raked masts, a gentle turn of bilge, and a long run. A schooner might also carry a square topsail and topsail yard or gaff-rig topsails. At the bow, the schooner's bowsprit allowed the use of a forestaysail. Its relatively broad, shallow hull made for speed but restricted its cargo-carrying capacity. The pilot schooner of the eighteenth century was relatively small compared to her mature cousin, sometimes called the "Baltimore schooner" as the type evolved after 1792. This was the schooner-type used as privateers that grew to exceed 300 tons, carried several guns, and required a large crew to facilitate the taking of prizes. The term *Baltimore clipper* should be used to describe the largest-size Chesapeake schooner, which evolved after 1830 and which was used to carry heavier commercial cargoes and, sometimes, slaves. As the search for speed under sail commenced in the 1840s, schooner-rigged vessels found themselves outclassed by larger, longer, square-rigged ships with three masts, ships that could better compete in the interocean carrying trade.

During the American Revolution, Eastern Shore and Baltimore shipwrights built schooners that carried flour, grain, bread, and livestock to the Dutch, French, Swedish, and Danish Caribbean islands and returned with firearms and gunpowder for the Continental Army and troops of the Maryland Line. After the end of the Revolutionary War, pilot schooners were widely used within Chesapeake Bay. In the 1790s, as war broke out between revolutionary France and the European monarchies, French planters and merchants in the Caribbean saw much utility in purchasing a larger type of pilot schooner for offshore trading and blockade running. The French did not design and build these schooners, but they did purchase them, and some were extremely effective at evading the British blockade of the American coast and the Caribbean.[9]

The U.S. Navy sought out pilot schooners when, with the outbreak of the Quasi-War with France, it became clear that it had few vessels of the fast and maneuverable type that could pursue and capture French schooners in the tricky island passages of the Caribbean. In 1799, Secretary of the Navy Benjamin Stoddert requested that Fells Point Navy Agent Jeremiah Yellott order the construction of one fast vessel for service against the French. Yellott selected William Price of Fells Point to construct a schooner, along commercial lines, with less rake than usual in stem and stern. The vessel was named *Experiment.* Soon afterward, Stoddert wrote asking Yellott to order the building of a second schooner. This time Yellott went to the Spencer family of boatbuilders at St. Michaels, on the Eastern Shore. This second schooner became *Enterprize,* one of the most famous names in the navy's history. While no original drawings for either vessel are known to exist, *Enterprize* underwent extensive repairs at the Arsenal in Venice, Italy, where the naval architect Andrea Salvini took down her lines. While the drawing has no name for the vessel, the similarity of the lines to those of the Baltimore pilot schooners suggests that this draft is that of *Enterprize,* found in an unlikely place.[10] Her lines seem to differ somewhat from those of the schooners *Superior* and *Nautilus* of that period. The question is, Was she built more for stability as a gun platform than the others? Her stern and stempost have less rake and there is less drag to the keel, indicating that logical adjustment had been made. At any rate, both *Experiment* and *Enterprize* had numerous successes in the naval service and lived up to their Chesapeake builders' expectations.

In 1803, under orders from Secretary of the Navy Robert Smith, the navy soon purchased another fast-sailing schooner, *Nautilus,* built in Talbot County. Very swift sailing and larger than other Baltimore schooners, *Nautilus* had a fine record in the Mediterranean but was rerigged as a brig and was captured by the British early in the War of 1812. Unfortunately, some naval officers seem to have been uneasy with the schooner rig, preferring the square-rigged brig. These included some well-known figures of the time, Capt. William Bainbridge and naval constructor Josiah Fox, among others. This did not, however, quench the enthusiasm of Baltimore sailors for armed schooners, for the merchants of Baltimore fitted out about 130 large pilot schooners as privateers or letters of marque (armed) traders, which bedeviled British merchantmen during the War of 1812. These private men of war captured some 550 enemy ships. The Fells Point shipwrights constructed about 75 large Baltimore pilot schooners, while Talbot County builders launched 36. Dorchester County, Queen Anne's County, and Somerset County accounted for most of the rest.[11]

As soon as the War of 1812 ended, with the ratification of the Treaty of Ghent in early 1815, privateer owners either sold their vessels or converted them to trade. Baltimore increasingly flourished, based on manufacturing as well as the seaborne trade of agricultural goods. The privateering vessels, however, were not well suited for trade. Fast, sleek, and sharp-built, they lacked the cargo-carrying space that burgeoning coastal and overseas trade now required. Baltimore's trade was oriented in a north-south direction and was less well adapted for the North Atlantic trade than for the Caribbean and for South America. The year 1815 also saw the conclusion of treaties with the Barbary States coerced by the threat of bombardment by the U.S. Navy's Mediterranean Squadron.[12] Trading schooners that reached Smyrna, in Turkey, could obtain opium, which was in demand in China. Although few Baltimore merchants traded in China, they did exchange goods such as opium with Philadelphia and New York merchants who were involved in the China trade. The McKim family of Baltimore had become wealthy and powerful in the course of flour and grain trade in exchange for Chilean copper through the port of Valparaiso. Two of Maryland's more famous schooner constructors of this period were George Gardner, a former partner of Thomas Kemp, and James Beacham, both of Fells Point. Gardner's schooners *Yellott* (1823) and *Dart* (1844) and Beacham's *Greyhound* (1826) were somewhat larger and heavier than previous generations of Baltimore schooners owing to their long-distance trading missions. *Greyhound* was known for her voyaging in China and involvement in the opium trade, so she came to be known as an "opium clipper," even though she was not, technically speaking, a clipper.[13]

In this same period, the young John Robb (1773–1867), a Scotsman who emigrated to Halifax and later to New York, arrived in Baltimore to work with James Beacham. Robb had been apprenticed to the renowned New York shipbuilder Henry Eckford in the days when Isaac Webb, David Brown, and Jacob Bell became shipbuilders as well. Eckford came to trust Robb's work and sent him to work with Beacham on a warship contract obtained from Brazil. Beacham completed this frigate, named *Baltimore,* in 1826. Lieut. Franklin Buchanan, USN, received temporary command of *Baltimore* and made delivery to the Brazilian government on Christmas Day 1826, after a passage of fifty-two days.[14]

The schooner clipper was born in the late 1830s. In those days, while schooners were still heavily engaged in trade, the brig rig was more numerous in terms of foreign ships. Baltimore was losing trade to New York. At this time, the slave trade, although illegal, was flourishing, particularly in the Spanish and Portuguese colonies. Merchants involved in the slave trade sought out Fells Point ship constructors because they needed a hull and rig that could provide maximum capacity but could still outrun British or American naval vessels on antislavery patrol. Although many schooners were slavers, the brig rig was preferred as being more stable on the east to west run from Africa with human cargo on board.[15] In constructing the single-decked brig *Elizabeth,* William Price experimented with a larger hull, measured at

300 tons. The clipper brig came to have increased breadth with short sharp ends, less deadrise, and a shallower depth of hold than her pilot schooner cousins.[16] Of all the builders from Baltimore or the Eastern Shore, William Price was probably the most prolific and timely with his schooner and brig designs, matching the trends, whether for war or peace, and speed or cargo capacity. His productive years ranged from 1794 to 1829. He died in 1832 and has received less attention than he deserves, for his beautiful and swift designs characterize an entire era of Baltimore pilot schooner construction.

The Cuban schooner *Amistad* was one that followed the offshore Baltimore pilot schooner style of construction. She was built in either Chesapeake Bay or Cuba about 1833. The dimensions were 64 feet in length, 19 feet 9 inches of beam, and 6 feet 6 inches depth of hold. A relatively small vessel for her type, she was engaged in carrying fifty-three slaves from Havana to another Cuban port. The African slaves broke their manacles and violently took control of the vessel on June 26, 1839. The slaves wanted the course set for Africa, but the Cuban owners at the helm managed to deceive them and kept sailing farther north and closer to the United States. A U.S. Navy warship halted and boarded *Amistad* near Sag Harbor, Long Island. She was taken to New London, where a federal magistrate placed the schooner in the charge of the U.S. marshal and ordered the slaves thrown into jail, on August 26. After many hearings, the case ended in the U.S. Supreme Court, where the court ordered that the slaves be freed, as they had been illegally taken and transported from their native land. Had this case been tried in a southern state, it might not have reached the highest court in the land. In any event, the schooner *Amistad* had played a part in the rise of dramatic tensions between northern and southern states that would end in civil war two decades later.

A few years after the *Amistad* incident and its related trials, the schooner *Pearl*, a Chesapeake Bay trading vessel based in Philadelphia, played a leading role in another attempted escape from slavery.[17] To set the scene, the city of Washington was, in April 1848, in an uproar over news of revolutions in central Europe, which had cropped up in response to a series of repressive measures against university students who were advocating universal manhood suffrage in France and national unification in Germany and Italy. In the midst of these public debates, people speculated as to what effect this news would have on the United States. Some took these exciting developments as harbingers of a new era of democracy, while others saw them as a threat to the established order. One of the major issues of the day in the United States was the concern both over whether slavery would be extended into new territories as they became states and over calls for the abolition of slavery that were spreading in the northern states. Nat Turner's slave uprising of 1831 in southern Virginia had shocked legislators in the slave states, all of whom passed laws (the "Black Codes") tightening restrictions on slaves and slave owners, restricting the mobility of slaves, curtailing their education, restricting manumissions, and curbing freed blacks. In the north, antislavery societies sprang up in New England, New York, and Ohio. Abolitionists such as William Lloyd Garrison, Theodore Weld, and Frederick Douglass, an escaped slave from the Eastern Shore, began speaking out and publishing on the evils of slavery. The "underground railroad," a loose, secret network of hiding places for fugitive slaves, had come into existence after the War of 1812 but began to flourish in the years after Nat Turner's rebellion. At the same time, the expansion of cotton production in the lower South made slaves an even more valuable commodity there. Slave traders in the Washington area were constantly looking for slaves to buy and ship to dealers for auction in New Orleans. In antipathy to these developments, several northern states passed "personal liberty laws" to obstruct enforcement of the federal fugitive slave law of 1793.

By 1848, the ferment over slavery and abolitionism was increasing, and hundreds of slaves were seeking new ways of finding freedom. One of these was to escape by sea. This required fugitive slaves, or their surrogates, to find a sea captain willing to take them north. Daniel Drayton, a mariner from New Jersey, was one of these. He recorded in his memoirs that it was apparently not an uncommon event on Chesapeake Bay in the 1840s for local slaves to approach anchored boats that happened to be passing by and to ask for passage to a free state.[18] On April 15, a group of seventy-six slaves, many from Washington households, gathered and slipped down to the Potomac River waterfront, while crowds of Washingtonians in Lafayette Park mall were listening to speeches about events in Europe. This same Daniel Drayton had arranged with Capt. Edward Sayres, owner of the 150-ton schooner *Pearl*,[19] to charter the vessel for delivery of these individuals to New Jersey, a state where slavery was illegal. Drayton would accompany the vessel as supercargo in charge of the passengers. Sayres's plan was to sail down the Potomac and into Chesapeake Bay, and then to shape a course northward for the Chesapeake and Delaware Canal. Having transited the canal, the *Pearl* would enter the Delaware River and make her way to the free state of New Jersey, whose river ports were familiar to Drayton. This would be a trip of at least three hundred miles as the crow flies, but of course sailboats are subject to the whims of the weather, and adverse winds might have lengthened the voyage considerably. As it happened, after the *Pearl* departed, her progress was at first delayed by fluky winds on the Potomac, but she then made good progress until reaching Point Lookout. Captain Sayres anchored in nearby Cornfield Harbor because a northwesterly gale had come up on the bay and he feared for the safety of the vessel and her many passengers. Captain Drayton, who had hired the vessel and was on board, argued strongly that Sayres should take advantage of the wind and head south for the Atlantic to make an outside passage to the north. This would have made sense, because any pursing vessels might logically have turned north toward the C&D Canal.

Unfortunately for *Pearl* and her passengers, the word of their escape had spread quickly through Washington and neighboring Virginia. A local freedman named Judson Diggs (or Digges), who knew of the secret escape plans, had a grudge against one of the female passengers and gave away the information to the authorities. They obtained the steamer *Salem* from Alexandria and caught up with the Sayres's *Pearl* at her anchorage. All the slaves were recaptured, along with Captain Sayres, Captain Drayton, and the vessel's cook, Chester English. *Salem* towed the *Pearl* back to Washington with the fugitives, who were immediately put in chains and led to the city jail.

The escape of the *Pearl* had caused great commotion among slave owners in

Washington, Georgetown, and Alexandria. Fire bells spread the alarm of a mass slave escape, and authorities immediately moved to police the local roads and waterways. Most of the fugitives, now prisoners, had been domestic servants, who worked in local homes, hotels, and boardinghouses. The local slave traders made quick work of buying the fugitives from their owners and prepared to send them south to New Orleans, where they would be resold. Proslavery agitators attempted to close down the *New National Era,* a local abolitionist newspaper whose editor, Gamaliel Bailey, they believed to have been involved in the *Pearl* escape plan. The resulting uproar became known as the Washington Riot of 1848. The failure of the escape caused much grief in the families of the fugitives, who were torn from their midst, sold and distributed they knew not where.

Washington lawyer Philip Barton Key, son of Francis Scott Key, was the U.S. attorney who prosecuted Sayres and Drayton for attempting to execute the escape on the *Pearl.* They were convicted for aiding slaves to escape, a crime akin to theft in the south, despite the efforts of Horace Mann, the educator and lawyer who served as their defense counsel. Sayres and Drayton spent the next four years in prison. The sympathetic senator Charles Sumner persuaded Attorney General John J. Crittenden that President Millard Fillmore had the authority to pardon them, which he did, on August 12, 1852. The entire episode brings to light the little-known event of the *Pearl*'s attempted escape and suggests that Chesapeake Bay and its tributaries may have played a much larger role than is usually acknowledged in providing a watery highway to freedom.[20]

Baltimore schooners also sailed in the opium trade of the Far East during the 1820s and 1830s. Among those built in the Chesapeake region and taking part in the trade were *Black Joke, Psyche, Nymph, Red Rover,* and *Frolic* (brig), and English adaptations of the Baltimore schooner hull and rig, such as *Omega, Delia,* and *Wild Darrell,* earned riches for their owners in the early-nineteenth-century opium trade. In order to contend with drug and slave traders, the U.S. Navy had to purchase, charter, or construct similar vessels. For his campaign against pirates in the Caribbean, the navy authorized Commodore David Porter to purchase several small Chesapeake pilot schooners, including *Greyhound, Jackal, Beagle, Wildcat, Terrier,* and *Ferret.* During the twenty years after the War of 1812, the navy constructed the schooners USS *Alligator,* USS *Porpoise,* USS *Shark,* and USS *Dolphin,* designed along Baltimore pilot schooner lines by William Doughty at the Washington Navy Yard, and USS *Grampus,* designed by Henry Eckford of New York. The navy constructed three more schooners in the early 1830s: USS *Boxer,* USS *Experiment,* and USS *Enterprize.*[21]

On the question of French influence on the design of pilot schooners, it was really the other way around. French naval architects imitated the Chesapeake pilot schooner designs in their work. There were many "French connections" between France and the Chesapeake region, including French immigrants from Nova Scotia during the colonial period, French soldiers and sailors during the American Revolution who passed through the Chesapeake region to combat British forces in Virginia, and French exporters who kept in close touch with their Baltimore counterparts in the 1790s. As war broke out again in Europe at the beginning of Napoleon's

69

The Surge of Maritime Baltimore under Sail and Steam

rise to power, French agents purchased Baltimore pilot schooners for use in their *guerre de course* against British shipping in the Caribbean. The French government sent Jean-Baptiste Marestier, a naval architect/engineer, to Baltimore in 1820 for the specific purpose of obtaining American designs for steamboats. But Marestier also took down the lines of schooners in Fells Point, acting in effect as "an industrial spy, climbing over ships in the water or on ways."[22] This explains numerous drafts for American-style Chesapeake Bay pilot schooners to be found in the French marine archives. Great Britain's Royal Navy also coveted the design of the swift-sailing Chesapeake pilot schooner. The French had purchased the Baltimore schooner *Superior* and renamed it *La Supérieure.* The British captured her in 1803 and took her into the Royal Navy, as they had *La Poissant Volant,* the American schooner *Flying Fish.* Both of these Chesapeake-built vessels served for several years. Their intermediate nationality has confused the issue, leading some to believe, erroneously, that they were built in France.

British naval constructors also took inspiration from the Chesapeake pilot schooner. Draftsmen in Portsmouth dockyard took the lines off the Chesapeake pilot schooner *Swift* in 1794 and then made plans for this vessel to be the model for several dispatch schooners to be built in Bermuda. In the process, however, the Bermuda builder altered the plans, and the resulting schooners were physically dissimilar to *Swift.* He shortened the bow, made it fuller, and deepened the keel, thereby adding many more tons to its displacement. Based on this, the Admiralty constructed more than a dozen schooners. One of them, *Haddock,* served as the model for a second group of Royal Navy schooners built between 1806 and 1808. One of these, named *Ballahou,* became famous because its name was used to generally describe the "American" schooner design of West Indian or Bermuda origin. Thus the archives of the French Service Historique de la Marine contain the "Plan d'un balaou Americain." Another curiosity to be found in the National Maritime Museum at Greenwich is the American design for a three-masted schooner from which the Admiralty produced six three-masted schooners from yards in Bermuda in 1808 and 1809. These were supposedly based on an original plan of William Flannigain of Fells Point, who constructed three three-masted schooners in 1805, *Revenge, Luna,* and *Orestes.*[23] Even after the War of 1812, the Royal Navy had a lively interest in Chesapeake schooner designs; Lieut. Frederick Fitzgerald de Roos traveled in the United States in the 1820s, visiting shipyards, and wrote that he tried to bribe the foreman of a yard for a book of "the fastest sailing schooners of Baltimore."[24]

The phrase *clipper ship* generally describes a square-rigged cargo vessel of three masts, with a sharp bow leading a hull that gradually widens. The first of these vessels constructed in Maryland was probably Baltimore's *Ann McKim,* built at Fells Point in 1832 for Isaac McKim.[25] She was a ship-rigged "Baltimore Clipper" and slightly smaller, at 400 tons, than the legendary clipper ships. Other ships approaching her size were *Splendid,* 473 tons, in 1832; *Napier,* 470 tons, in 1833; *Tweed,* 307 tons, in 1834; *Valparaiso,* 402 tons, in 1836; *Venus,* 465 tons, in 1838; and *Inca,* 377 tons, in 1840. One excellent run was made by *Splendid,* 102 days from Canton to

Baltimore, in 1843.[26] In the 1850s, Maryland-built ships had grown to more than three or four times their earlier tonnage, yet they still lagged behind New York and Boston ships in speed and carrying capacity. Baltimore faced the disadvantage of being from one to four days' voyage farther from European ports than the northern cities but was closer to the grain- and coal-producing states and had easy access to southern ports. Merchants concerned with bulk shipments and market timing preferred to operate out of New York and Boston. This led to a concentration of major shipwrights and chandleries in the northern cities.

Some of the larger Maryland clipper ships during their heyday were *Mary Whitridge,* 978 tons; *Atalanta,* 1,289 tons, built by Gardner and Palmer in Baltimore in 1856; *Carrier Dove,* 1,694 tons, built by James Abraham in 1855; and the largest, *Flora Temple,* 1,916 tons, built by James Abraham in 1853. By the 1860s the day of the ocean-going, cargo-carrying Maryland-built clipper ship had passed. Merchants must have had a premonition of this with the arrival in New York of two British steam-driven side-wheel passenger ships, *Sirius* and *Great Western,* within a few hours of each other on April 22, 1833.

Baltimore's shipping industry flourished because of the agricultural products processed in and around the city. Its merchants also made the most of their proximity to Latin American markets and raw materials. In the 1820s, western grain and southern cotton were processed into flour and fabrics to be exchanged for precious metals, such as raw copper, from Chile on the west coast of South America. From the eastern side of South America came the sugar, coffee, cacao, and indigo of Venezuela, the Guianas, and Brazil and salt beef and hides from Uruguay and Argentina. Baltimore exported more flour to Brazil than to all other ports in the

Sailors' Bethel, *William Penn*. Interior view of worshipers, 1846. Courtesy, Maryland Historical Society, Z24.625.

United States combined, and it sent it out in Baltimore ships. In 1858, 94 percent of Baltimore's exports to Brazil were sent in Maryland ships. In return, Baltimore ships brought back cargoes of Brazilian coffee. Between 1841 and 1845, Baltimore imported 80 percent as much coffee as did New York. With the completion of the B&O Railroad to Wheeling, West Virginia, the western markets increased demand for coffee through Baltimore. By 1850, 20 percent of all the coffee sent to the United States went through Baltimore. Such was the demand for this commodity that, between 1825 and 1860, coffee was the most important element of Baltimore's import trade. Sugar and molasses imported from the West Indies ran a close second.[27]

Another commodity that came into prominence in Baltimore before the Civil War was guano, composted bird droppings, accumulated over centuries on islands off the Peruvian coast. This was the first commercial fertilizer used in large quantities by American farmers. The first regular shipment to the United States entered Baltimore in 1844. Factors shipped it south to tobacco and cotton plantations suffering from soil exhaustion. The only problem was the limited supply, guano being a monopoly of the Peruvian government. When the Maryland legislature demanded inspections of these cargoes, Peru objected and moved its agency to New York. Still, Baltimore remained the best guano market in the United States until the Civil War. Other ports in Maryland benefited from the fertilizer trade, even after the trade in guano diminished. Booming agricultural production on the Eastern Shore in the late nineteenth century attracted dealers in fertilizer, and mixing plants sprang up in Cambridge, Salisbury, Pocomoke City, and Snow Hill, Maryland, and in Seaford, Delaware. Shipped in bags to prevent loss of cargo, the fertilizer came in by way of the Choptank, Wicomico, and Pocomoke rivers carried by ram schooners, the most economical mode of hauling such freight until World War II. The schooners *Edwin and Maud, Edward R. Baird Jr.,* and *Jennie D. Bell* were the workhorses of the fleet that served the Worcester Fertilizer Company in Snow Hill.[28]

~~~

THE AGE OF STEAM DAWNED EARLY on Chesapeake Bay. Capt. Edward Trippe of Dorchester County introduced steam-powered vessels to the region in the second decade of the nineteenth century.[29] He had formed a partnership with William McDonald and Andrew F. Henderson to establish the Union Line, a sailing packet service from Baltimore to Philadelphia, via Frenchtown, in 1806. They soon invested in construction of a steamer at William Flannigain's yard on McElderry's wharf in Baltimore. Trippe supervised the work, which was completed in 1813. They named the new steamer *Chesapeake,* for the waters she would ply.

Maryland's first steamer was 137 feet in length, 21 feet in beam, and drew 6 feet 8 inches, with a burden of 183 tons. She was driven by two paddle wheels ten feet in diameter. Her engine was a crosshead with 4½-foot stroke, revolving a cogwheel that worked in teeth on a cast-iron shaft. She had a smokestack amidships behind the engine. There was a mast and sail on the foredeck to use with fair winds and as motive power in case of an engine breakdown. *Chesapeake's* first voyage took place on Sunday, June 13, advertised in advance as an excursion to Annapolis, for a round-

trip fare of two dollars. These were not the best of times for a pleasure cruise on the bay, as the British navy was very much in charge of who went where, at least in the lower bay. Chesapeake made voyages to Rock Hall and to Frenchtown when the enemy was not in sight. It must have been exciting to be a passenger on these occasional cruises on a radically new vessel, with possibilities of engine breakdown or boiler explosion and the danger of an enemy attack. When the enemy was in the vicinity, however, *Chesapeake* kept within harbor and local waters with the result that, fortunately, she was not captured.

As soon as the war was over, steam competition on the bay increased apace. In 1815, the Briscoe & Partridge Line brought the steamer *Eagle* down from the Delaware River to offer competition on the Baltimore-Elkton run. In 1816, Trippe, McDonald, and Henderson bought two additional steamers for the Union Line, *Baltimore* and *Washington* (built at New York), which inaugurated steamer service on the Potomac. Competition from Virginia appeared in the person of Benjamin Ferguson, who built the steamer *Virginia* for his Norfolk-Baltimore line; he already had the *Powhatan* engaged on the Richmond-Norfolk run.[30] Maryland's George Weems inaugurated a new shipping line in 1817 with *Surprise,* which he commanded between Baltimore, Annapolis, and Easton.[31] Weems purchased *Eagle* as her replacement in 1821. As for *Chesapeake,* little is known after 1815, but she was listed as "broken up" in 1820. Thus arrived the maritime technology that would revolutionize transportation on Chesapeake Bay in the nineteenth century.[32]

Model of the steamboat *Chesapeake,* the first commercial steamer on Chesapeake Bay, constructed in 1813. Date of model unknown. Courtesy, Maryland Historical Society, Z24.635.

An integral part of the story of the steamboat industry is the development of the machinery that drove these vessels in their daily voyages to all parts of the Chesapeake. Although the *Chesapeake* was Baltimore's first steamboat, the technology of steamboat engines was known in the United States for many years before 1813. Newspapers told of experiments by Americans such as William Henry, John Fitch, James Rumsey, Robert Livingstone, Robert Fulton, and John Stevens, men who were in touch with the advancing Industrial Revolution in England and whose vision informed them that there was money to be made when steam technology could take hold in the United States. In England, steam was first applied to move large amounts of water, first to pump floodwater out of coal and copper mines and then to pump water into the spreading system of canals.

Technology transfer with respect to steam engines as applied to water transport first occurred when American gunsmith William Henry of Lancaster, Pennsylvania, visited England in the early 1760s. Impressed by the early use of steam engines there, he returned to begin developing a steamboat engine. The engine worked, but the boat sank. The inventor John Fitch and he were well acquainted, so it is likely that Fitch based his more practical steamboat and engine on Henry's early efforts. Other influences arrived in the minds of British immigrants, who came to America in the late eighteenth century, having worked in the factory of Matthew Boulton and James Watt in Birmingham, England. After Henry and Fitch, other experiments with steam-propelled boats in the United States took place on the Delaware and Hudson rivers, with Philadelphia and New York being the cities where both capital and industry flourished. In New York, the wealthy Livingstone and the inventive Fulton combined to attempt a monopoly of steamboat transportation in the United States. Fulton's *Clermont,* with an imported Boulton and Watt engine, made its maiden voyage in 1807 on the Hudson; however, John Stevens of Philadelphia challenged him on the Hudson in 1808 with the steamboat *Phoenix,* powered with a modified Boulton and Watt engine. Stevens then bravely brought *Phoenix* to Philadelphia in an unprecedented steamboat voyage down the New Jersey coast from New York and to the Delaware Bay and River.

Two men whose names are indelibly connected to the coming of the steam engine to Baltimore are Daniel Large and Charles Reeder. Of the two, Large is the one who links the Baltimore steamboat industry to developments in England and Philadelphia. Large, who had been the youngest apprentice of Boulton and Watt, emigrated from England in 1807 and established his own engine workshop in Philadelphia. At this point, the history of the steamboat *Chesapeake* intervenes. Edward Trippe, who had learned of Large's talents from Benjamin Latrobe, contracted with him to build an engine to be installed in the *Chesapeake,* then under construction in Flanagan's boatyard on the Patapsco. Charles Reeder, Large's apprentice, assisted in assembling the engine, which Large had shipped to Baltimore. Reeder had been born in Bucks County, Pennsylvania, was trained as a millwright and carpenter, and then moved to Philadelphia, where he found employment in Large's foundry. It was in the midst of the War of 1812 that Large selected Reeder to move to Baltimore to work on the *Chesapeake*'s engine. This was but the first step for Reeder in the establishment of his own engine-building shop in Baltimore, in Honey Alley on Federal Hill.[33]

Reeder's mechanical talents and skill in providing a dependable steam engine for Trippe's *Chesapeake* enabled him to gain an early lead over others in Baltimore's nascent steamboat industry. In doing so, he had to manufacture in his own shop many of the machine tools needed to build his engines and he had to train the men who came to work there. The engines he and his competitors built from 1813 into the 1820s were called crosshead, or steeple, engines. They were supported by a double A-frame, which suspended the up-and-down action of a piston rod attached to an athwartships bar or beam. This transmitted the vertical motion of the engine's single large piston to the shaft that turned the paddle wheels via the crankshafts. Also, the *Chesapeake* steamboat engines were of the low-pressure, condensing type, which made very little noise compared to the loudly pulsating noncondensing engines of steamboats on the western rivers. These low-pressure engines made an efficient use of steam coming from the boilers. The steam entered the piston chamber, pushed the cylinder, and then escaped into a condenser. Jets of water pumped from the bay cooled the steam back to water, which then replenished the boiler. This was an engine that endured much hard use without frequent breakdowns.[34] Reeder's competition was not long in coming. Two British engineers, Watchman and Bratt, set up their engine shop in 1816 near Reeder's on the Patapsco below Federal Hill. They were soon placing their engines in Flanagan's steamboats as well as others'. But competition came and went. Reeder would outlast them all, founding an engineering dynasty that flourished throughout the nineteenth century.[35]

The Watchman & Bratt steam engine firm, first located at Hughes and William streets on Federal Hill, was in business from 1816 to 1845. Over the years, Watchman's company expanded its lines of work as well as the area covered by its buildings. The company manufactured all manner of iron goods, steamboat engines, marine boilers, dredges, mill machinery, railway passenger and freight cars, bridges, and other heavy industrial goods. This diversified activity assisted the firm as it competed against the Reeder company in the manufacture of marine engines. In all, Watchman & Bratt built engines for thirty-five steamboats during its twenty-nine-year tenure; rarely a year went by without an engine being built at their plant, and sometimes, as many as three (in 1833 and in 1835). Watchman employed about two hundred fifty men in his factory, a great number for the time and certainly more than Reeder's firm, whose employees numbered about two hundred.

Although very successful in its engine-building business, Watchman & Bratt is also remembered for what has been called the greatest steamboat disaster of Chesapeake Bay. The *Medora,* built at the neighboring shipyard of John S. Brown & Company, had just received her engine from Watchman in April 1842 and was to depart on her sea trial. Many local dignitaries were on board and alongside on the pier at William Street and Battery Avenue. Gideon Brown, the boiler designer of Watchman & Bratt, had designed the ship's huge boiler, supposedly the last word in power and safety. *Medora*'s master gave the engine room the signal to reverse and back out of the slip. The paddle wheels had revolved three times, pushing *Medora* back about thirty feet from the pier, when an enormous explosion rocked basin and all of downtown Baltimore. *Medora*'s boiler exploded and sent ragged bits of metal and wood planking soaring in all directions. The steamboat sank in twelve feet of water, but the human cost was enormous: twenty-five dead and forty injured, some scalded or maimed for life. The entire city went into mourning, as almost everyone seemed to know someone who had been killed or hurt. Among the dead were Andrew Henderson, president of the Baltimore Steam Packet Company, John C. Moale, the company's general agent, and his son, others associated with the steamboat business, and of course, the men who worked the *Medora*'s steam plant. John Watchman testified at the coroner's inquest that in his opinion there had been too many visitors in the engine room and fire room and that someone had held down the safety valve so that it did not function properly. Two others testified that they could not see the dial of the pressure gauge. Benjamin Latrobe believed that the boiler design was flawed: the huge boiler's quarter-inch-thick metal casing was too weak to withstand the immense pressure to which it was subjected. John S. Brown & Company raised the *Medora,* rebuilt her, and changed her name to *Herald.* Charles Reeder provided the renewed engine and boiler, much to the dismay of John Watchman. She spent many more years in service, some in the Chesapeake and later in New York waters, where she ended her career as a towboat on the Hudson River.[36]

The shocking result of the *Medora* explosion gave impetus to federal legislation regarding the growing dangers of unregulated steamboat navigation. The primary causes of steamboat disasters at that early date were boiler explosions, fires, and collisions. Congress had already enacted a law in 1838 to "provide better security of the lives of passengers on board vessels propelled in whole or in part by steam." The persistence of these disasters gave rise to the Steamboat Act of May 30, 1852. This act required the organization of a federal inspection service placed under the administration of the Treasury Department. Among other things this law required that boilers be tested, safety valves be put in place, and pilots and engineers be licensed. Earlier attempts to pass strict inspection laws had been blocked by steamboat industry champions who argued that it would be too costly for the owners and operators trying to expand service and still make a profit. Further advances in steamboat safety would have to wait until 1871, when a more sweeping law codified existing regulations, required the licensing of masters and chief mates, gave a Board of Supervisory Inspectors the authority to issue rules of the road, and created the Steamboat Inspection Service. Later this agency was combined with the Bureau of Navigation, and it became part of the U.S. Coast Guard in 1942.[37]

From 1831 to 1843, ten steamship companies were formed in Baltimore. They linked Baltimore's trade with the lower bay, plantations in southern Maryland, the Eastern Shore, and the Norfolk region. Other lines replaced sailing vessels on the New York, Philadelphia, and New Orleans coastal routes. Of the internal bay steamship companies, the Weems line became a leading shipper between 1817 and 1904. *Eagle* suffered an explosion in 1824 while en route from Annapolis to Baltimore, killing one passenger and injuring Weems. He recovered and placed *Patuxent* in service in 1827. This steamer was long-lived, commencing her career on the run from Baltimore to Fredericksburg on the Rappahannock, with intermediate stops

at Herring Bay and on the lower Patuxent River. By the time Weems died in 1853, his four sons were serving on the line as captains or engineers, and the vessels *Planter Mary Washington* and *George Weems* had joined the line.[38]

The Maryland and Virginia Steamboat Company (M&V), established in March 1828, linked Baltimore, Richmond, and Norfolk for nearly a dozen years. This company was formed by the consolidation of several individually owned vessels that competed on the Baltimore-Norfolk run. Steamboat travel was becoming popular, with notable increases in the number and tonnage of steamboats. The line

Dixon's Letter describing the explosion of the steamboat *Medora* in the Baltimore Harbor, April 14, 1842. Courtesy, Chesapeake Bay Maritime Museum, 462–5.

began to attract rivalry from other lines with faster vessels, so the M&V simply purchased the faster vessels from the competition. Finally, however, the M&V and other steamship lines had to compete with the railroad companies, which were rapidly cutting into their traffic. In doing so, the M&V probably spent too heavily and was forced to liquidate. It was from the sale of M&V assets that the Baltimore Steam Packet Company obtained its first vessels. Edward Trippe's former partners, Henderson and McDonald, organized the Baltimore Steam Packet Company in 1839, popularly known as "the Bay Line." The origins of the line's nickname are found in the rise of its competitor the Leary Line of Norfolk in the late 1860s, which called itself the "New Line." In response, the owners of the "Bay Line" then referred to themselves as the "Old Bay Line," a company that lasted until the mid-twentieth century.[39]

A major development for the improvement of interstate trade and communications was the completion of the Chesapeake and Delaware Canal on October 17, 1829. It had been a subject of discussions and plans since the 1760s, but for lack of coordination and funding, nothing was done.[40] Previously, travelers and their goods had to disembark at Elkton and take a stagecoach to Newcastle, on the Delaware River. After railroads began to develop, the Frenchtown & Newcastle Railroad, thought by some to be the first railroad in the country, was built to replace the stagecoach. With the opening of the canal, an inexpensive and relatively fast transit of the "Delmarva" neck was made via horse-towed barges. An advertisement for service by the People's Line from Baltimore to Philadelphia read as follows: "*Kentucky* will leave the company's wharf, Light Street, every morning at 6 a.m. The Chesapeake & Delaware Canal, through which the passengers will be conveyed in splendid and commodious barges, affords, particularly to the ladies, the most comfortable route to Delaware City, where they will take the *Ohio* and arrive in Philadelphia the same afternoon at an early hour."[41]

Competition developed, though, when the Baltimore & Philadelphia Steamship Line was established in 1844, by John Shriver of Baltimore. He shared ownership with the Cadwalader family of Philadelphia and took the name Ericsson Line, after John Ericsson, who had developed the screw propeller for a ship of this line. The Ericsson line enjoyed eighty years of service on this route. The early vessels were narrow and small, since they had to pass through three sets of locks, and the canal was only twenty-four feet wide. In the last years before the Civil War, Chesapeake Bay steamboats took a step forward, with some companies purchasing larger vessels, over 230 feet in length, 31 feet in the beam, and an 11-foot-deep hold, with a burden of 1,100 tons each. The Bay Line's *North Carolina* and *Louisiana* fitted these dimensions. *Louisiana,* at 266 feet overall, was the largest vessel that ever sailed for the Bay Line, commencing in 1854. It was possible to buy through tickets from New York to Wilmington, North Carolina, by rail and steamboats on connecting schedules. *North Carolina* made her record run from Baltimore to Norfolk in ten hours and five minutes, at an average speed of eighteen knots. Unfortunately, *North Carolina* suffered a fire in January 1859 and burned to the water's edge in the mouth of the Potomac River.

On the eve of the Civil War, Maryland-owned steamboat passenger and cargo

Early photograph (daguerreotype) of side-wheel paddle steamers alongside Federal Hill piers, ca. 1850. Courtesy, Maryland Historical Society, MC 711.4.

traffic reached all but the minor tributaries of Chesapeake Bay. The major steamboat companies were the Union Line, the Weems Line, the Old Bay Line, and the Ericsson Line. The Eastern Shore Steamboat Company served Annapolis, West River, and the Choptank River. The Washington, Alexandria & Georgetown Steam Packet line had been making voyages from Baltimore to Potomac River ports as early as 1832. Although the nonstop distance from Baltimore to Washington was 174 miles, on a typical forty-eight-hour voyage from Baltimore to Washington, a steamer would travel about 320 miles, stopping briefly at as many as twenty-five landings on the Maryland and Virginia sides of the Potomac.[42]

Other Maryland companies, such as the Baltimore and Rappahannock Steam Packet Company, established in 1830, sent vessels into ports on Virginia's Western Shore. The Powhatan Steamboat Company, later called the Chesapeake Steamship Company, initiated service in 1841 from Baltimore down the bay. Its vessels operated to Richmond and Petersburg via the James River. There were also independently owned steamboats, such as *Monmouth,* running from Baltimore to Walkerton, on the Mattaponi River, and to Pungoteague, on the Eastern Shore of Virginia. Another independent, *Sea Bird,* operated on the York River, serving landings such as Allmonds, Claybank, Gloucester Point, and Yorktown in 1859. In this way, an extraordinary network of steamboat lines and independently owned vessels provided regular and efficient service from densely populated ports to boat landings in isolated locations on Chesapeake Bay.

As if to punctuate the end of one era and the beginning of the next, the world's largest steamship, the *Great Eastern,* made her appearance on Chesapeake Bay during the summer of 1860. This unexpected event galvanized the American public from New York to Norfolk, and all who could possibly do so made expeditions to visit the ship. The ship was the creation of Isambard Kingdom Brunel, a British designer, engineer, and builder whose ambition knew no limits. This vessel, 679 feet in length and 120 feet in the beam, drew 31.6 feet, displacing 22,500 tons. Her propulsion machinery combined one engine, which drove a gigantic propeller 24 feet in diameter, and another, which turned two huge sidewheels 58 feet in diameter— and in case all this failed, she carried 6,500 square feet of sails on six masts. According to James Dugan, she was built to dominate trade with the Far East, to carry enough coal to power a 22,000-mile round trip to Ceylon.[43] Brunel had designed the ship to carry 4,000 passengers, but on her first transatlantic cruise she carried only 43 first-class passengers and 418 crew members. The passage to New York was made in a half gale, and though she pitched and rolled, none of the predicted disasters occurred. Owing to her deep draft, the ship avoided the Sandy Hook passage and arrived at New York via Long Island Sound, Hell Gate, and the East River. As might be imagined, the ship's arrival in New York created great excitement, and thousands came to visit the ship. In her four-week stay at New York, the ship sold 143,764 tickets to visitors waiting to board.[44] A group of Baltimore businessmen saw the opportunity to attract the ship to their port and made sure that Baltimore was on *Great Eastern*'s visiting list.

To attract even more attention, in late July the ship's owners advertised a cruise down the coast as far as Cape May for ten dollars a person. To their delight some two thousand would-be passengers showed up, and the ship departed. Perhaps to the passengers' dismay, they discovered that the ship was not prepared to provide sleeping cabins for more than three hundred. However, unable to escape, the crowd somehow managed, sleeping in parlors or on deck, and when they awoke the next day they found themselves anchored off Old Point Comfort, in Chesapeake Bay. Here, too, the ship provoked a sensation and stimulated great interest. She returned to New York with many unhappy customers on board, deprived of their nights' sleep and given unappetizing food service. Some disgruntled passengers who could afford rail travel had jumped ship and returned to New York by train. In early August the ship returned to the Chesapeake, this time with only a hundred paid passengers, intending to anchor off Annapolis in order to draw visitors from Baltimore. Presumably, the deep draft of the *Great Eastern* made it too risky to attempt passage up the relatively shallow Patapsco River.

On her way up the bay, the "leviathan," as some called her, passed many steamboats crowded with passengers anxious to get their first view. One of the first vessels was the *George Peabody,* one of the newest and fastest vessels of her class, carrying the welcoming committee. Due to a miscommunication, the *Great Eastern*'s captain was unaware of her local importance and steamed on by at fifteen knots, without a signal, leaving the welcoming committee in her wake and far behind. She remained anchored in Annapolis Roads for five days and enjoyed much attention. The Baltimore and Ohio Railroad sponsored three trains a day from Baltimore to Annapolis, offering passengers from as far away as Wheeling, Virginia, tickets at one-half the usual round-trip fare. Steamboat companies from Baltimore brought thousands of visitors in steamers such as *Lancaster, Pocahontas, Juniata, Star,* and *St. Michaels.* The Baltimore Steam Packet ("The Old Bay Line") Company sent its vessels *Adelaide, Louisiana, Philadelphia,* and *Georgeanna,* charging its passengers $1.50 for the round trip and an opportunity to board the ship.

Great Eastern's master, Capt. J. Vine Hall, paid a call on President James Buchanan at Washington with an invitation to visit the ship. The president and his staff accepted gladly, traveling on August 9 by special train to Annapolis, where they met the president of the B&O Railroad. They boarded the steamboat *Anacostia* at the Naval Academy pier and headed for the *Great Eastern,* where Governor Hicks of Maryland greeted the party. Captain Hall treated his important guests to a two-hour tour of the ship. Hoping to entice the ship to visit, the City of Baltimore and the B&O Railroad provided 2,500 tons of coal, but the ship's captain declined the opportunity to bring the ship up the Patapsco. He weighed anchor and departed the Chesapeake on August 11, never to return. The *Great Eastern* continued her storied career and became the first ship to successfully lay the Atlantic cable and five others. No ship was to exceed her size for almost fifty years; she had made a memorable impression in the United States, achieving accolades like "Great Maritime Wonder of the Deep" and "Marvel of an Era Never to be Equalled." In the Chesapeake Bay region, her visit would long be remembered.[45]

Only a few months later, in November 1860, Abraham Lincoln won election to the presidency of the United States, an event that presaged the outbreak of a long-smoldering sectional conflict, as one Southern state after another seceded from the Union. The breaking of long-established social, economic, and political ties brought suspicion, doubt, and confusion as people sought to decide on future courses of action. Chesapeake Bay, the estuary that had for some two hundred fifty years linked northern and southern ports, soon became a battleground. Those who earned their living on the bay from fishing, transportation, and commerce of all sorts felt the brunt once hostilities broke out at Charleston, with the firing on Fort Sumter on April 12, 1861.

Suffice it to say, Maryland steamboats and their owners suffered during the Civil War. Under the threat of confiscation, several steamboat companies were forced to contract their steamboats to the federal government. The U.S. Navy took over a number of commercial steamboats and converted them to river gunboats, while the U.S. Army needed steamboats for transportation of troops, weapons, munitions, uniforms, and provisions. Many of these steamboats provided an essential service in moving troops from point to point as military operations required, as in the massive effort to move the Army of the Potomac to the York Peninsula as part of General McClellan's plan to find a shortcut to Richmond in 1862. Ultimately, this plan failed, and the troops, horses, mules, and all the military equipment they would require were returned to the defenses of Washington in August 1862. The navy used other steamboats to keep open the Potomac, Rappahannock, and other rivers of Virginia in order to enhance federal military communications in the seesaw struggle for control of Virginia's battlefields. Hard usage and little maintenance took a toll on these steamboats; when returned to their owners in 1865, their useful lives were nearly exhausted.

The war brought profits as well as difficult times to the shipbuilders of Baltimore. One example, drawn from many, was the Fardy & Auld Yard. John T. Fardy was an English shipwright who joined in business with Hugh Auld, of the Talbot County shipbuilding family. They set up their yard on Federal Hill near the intersection of Covington and Hughes streets in 1847 and built a wide variety of vessels before the Civil War. Of sailing vessels, they constructed twenty-four schooners, nine brigs, and eight barks. The schooners were mostly intended for the bay trade, although some went into coastal work. Most of the barks were intended for the South American trade, two brigs became government light ships, and four schooners went to the U.S. Coastal Survey. When Auld left the firm in 1854, John took his brother Matthew into the business. From then on it was known as John T. Fardy & Brother. They must have made profits, for they were known to have the largest steam marine railway in the city of Baltimore as well as enough land to build three ships at a time. During the Civil War, the firm essentially shifted from sailing- to steam-vessel production. From 1862 to 1865, it built the propeller steamers *New Jersey, United States, Monitor* (tug), *Arctic* (tug), *Atlantic* (tug), *Gladiator* (tug), *Wenonah* (paddle), and *Wayanda* (propeller). The federal government was a demanding customer, and it had no need of sailing vessels. As William Kelley wrote, "the need was for speed and mobility during the war which sailing vessels could not offer. Repairs during the war were mostly to steam vessels; at least, these obtained the publicity as they were utilized in the war effort of the Federal Government. Privately operated sailing vessels were rendered unglamorous during the war. Sitting ducks could not be utilized by either antagonist during the war."[46]

Another characteristic of the Baltimore shipbuilding industry during the war was labor unrest. Fardy's workers were not the only ones involved. On April 1, 1864, the *Baltimore American* reported that ship carpenters on the south side of the basin (Federal Hill) went on strike, demanding a 20 percent increase of pay. This would then pay them $3.00 per day, up from the $2.50 a day they had been receiving. They were saying that men in the metalworking trades had already had such an increase, so the carpenters needed a raise, too. The ship caulkers followed suit. The strike went on for two weeks, being complicated by the shipyards starting to hire men who did not belong to the association. When the caulkers stopped work, the yards began to lay off carpenters, whose work could not continue until the caulkers went back on the job. The navy's agent threatened to issue an order prohibiting strikers from working on U.S. vessels. This apparently persuaded the workers to return to work.[47]

The end of the war was not far off, and of course, this meant that commerce and shipbuilding could return to normal, but the reconversion to peacetime com-

merce required a period of adjustment during which no new steamboats were built, although there was repair work. Meanwhile, John Fardy died in 1867. His widow, Emily J. Fardy, formed a partnership with William E. Woodall, who had been foreman of the yard after Auld's departure in 1854. The yard continued its work under the new name Fardy & Woodall until 1873, when Mrs. Fardy decided to get out of the business. Woodall continued the work of the yard and moved it to Locust Point in 1876. It had been a restless postwar era, with many steamboats coming in for repairs, following which they might be sold or transferred and renamed. With renewed prosperity, steamboat excursions again became a popular pastime, and the yards returned to building steamboats with improvements in size, power, and elegance.

View of Baltimore Basin (Inner Harbor) from Federal Hill, with steamboats alongside their piers, ca. 1872. Courtesy, Maryland Historical Society, MC 2910.

Along with the industrialization of commerce on the nation's waterways during the nineteenth century, there was a simultaneous movement toward improvements of aids to navigation and safety at sea. These were reflected in the building of lighthouses on Chesapeake Bay and the establishment of lifesaving stations along Maryland's Atlantic seacoast. One of the earliest statutes passed by the first Congress under the Constitution, on August 7, 1789, was to turn all twelve existing lighthouses over to the federal government, to be administered by the Department of the Treasury. By 1800, the nation had twenty-four lighthouses, all located along the Atlantic coast, but only one was located on Chesapeake Bay—the Cape Henry light, on the south side of the entrance to the bay, opposite Cape Charles, Virginia. Considering the incredibly indented, complex Chesapeake shoreline and the high volume of trade on the bay, this was an anomalous condition begging for improvement. The government rectified the situation, steadily if not swiftly. By 1850, the bay had twenty-one lighthouses and nine lightships, located at critical locations. In the latter half of the century, the Lighthouse Board built and manned forty-nine more lights and replaced all the lightships.[48]

The types of lighthouses installed were at first solid brick or stone towers, interspersed with some wooden towers or keepers' houses with small towers fixed on their roofs. This soon changed, with the recognition that the bay's sandy or muddy bottom sediments might better support a new type of lighthouse structure called screwpile. This type first found favor in England, near the mouth of the Thames River. Engineer Alexander Mitchell developed the screwpile for better holding in a soft or sandy seabed. It featured a central support of iron shaped in a helical or spiral form, with a point that would dig its way to a certain depth without disturbing the ground through which it passed. On the extremities of the hexagonal platform, six other hollow iron pilings were sunk ten feet into the bottom and rose ten feet above the surface of the water. This platform supported a nine-foot-high house, which in turn supported a tower, which contained a lantern with a Fresnel lens fifty feet above the water. Supporting the screwpile platform was a system of braces and cross braces of cast and rolled iron. Though less costly to build and erect, the screwpile lighthouses were vulnerable to damaging ice floes. Additional structures were added to divert the ice from directly impacting the platforms. The first screwpile light, installed on the Pungoteague River on Virginia's Eastern Shore in 1854, lasted only a few months more than a year—a poor start for this new design—but the government built forty-two screwpile lights in the ensuing fifty years. The alternative was to erect the far more massive and expensive caisson, constructed in the shape of a huge cylinder, which had to be towed out and sunk in a dredged location. But, once in place, the caisson lighthouses were sturdier and less costly to maintain.[49]

The lamps used in the Chesapeake lighthouses underwent an interesting transition during the mid-nineteenth century. In the eighteenth century, lighthouse keepers used tallow candles and lamps that burned whale and fish oil. These were used in combination with an Argand burner, developed by the Swiss engineer Aime Argand, whose device used a hollow cylindrical wick and a glass chimney to increase the draft and brightness of the flame. In the early nineteenth century, sea captain Winslow Lewis invented an improved Argand system, which utilized parabolic reflectors and less oil, thereby improving conditions for the keepers. The previous system had produced stinging fumes, which prevented keepers from spending much time tending to the flame. In 1822, the French physicist Augustin Fresnel developed a much more effective method of projecting light by means of prisms and magnifying lenses, which revolutionized lighthouses worldwide. But in the United States, the system was not quickly adopted for use. It took the proverbial act of Congress to push bureaucrats into a sweeping change that not only put the Fresnel lens into widespread use but also changed the system of lighthouse administration.

From 1852 on, the Treasury Department's Lighthouse Board, composed of two naval officers, two army officers, and a civilian scientist, ran the lighthouses through a system of districts. More administrative changes came in the early twentieth century, when the Commerce Department replaced Treasury and established a Bureau of Lighthouses, which operated through a Commissioner of Lighthouses. In 1939, the U.S. Coast Guard, operating under the Treasury Department, took over from Commerce and has retained responsibility until the present day, although it took many of the older lighthouses out of service and replaced the keepers with automated lights. As of 2003, the newly created Department of Homeland Security became the administrative manager of the U.S. Coast Guard, which still has overall responsibility for the lighthouses and other aids to navigation in the United States.

The Lighthouse Board, in addition to maintaining lighthouses and hiring lighthouse keepers, also had the responsibility for establishing a buoyage system for coastal and inland waterways. From the colonial era to the mid-nineteenth century, local jurisdictions took care of placing and maintaining the buoys that guided vessels in the sounds, bays, rivers, and harbors of the United States. It cannot be said that this was a system; each locality had its own way of marking shoals, usually with spars, juniper poles, or casks. These would vary in color, size, and shape, and usually only local pilots and mariners understood their meaning. Thus, shipmasters from different U.S. and foreign ports had trouble interpreting them. Congress, commencing in 1848, finally took notice and ordered the Treasury Department to set up a lateral system of buoys in the nation's waterways. Essentially, this meant that buoys of certain shapes and colors would be anchored at the edges of shoals to keep mariners in safe channels. As it evolved, red-colored shapes and lights would be kept on the right-hand, or starboard, side of the vessel when heading up rivers or into ports, while black shapes and green lights would be kept to the left-hand, or port, side. In the twentieth century, green was substituted for black on buoys because it could better be seen from a distance. This popularized among mariners the sayings "red right returning" and "green to port on entering." When standing out of port and downriver, the vessel's master would have to keep green to starboard and red to port. Although there are variations on this system, it is still the basic one for mariners in the United States, and as with the nation's lighthouses, the buoyage system and its upkeep have evolved as a task for the United States Coast Guard.[50]

Although many of Maryland's surviving lighthouses are no longer operational, they do possess unique historic and aesthetic value. They represent the navigational needs and methods of a bygone era and can be used to teach a younger generation about seafaring and its safety requirements. Some lighthouses have been converted into museum exhibits while others have been transferred to private hands, but with the obligation to maintain and preserve their characteristics. Those historic lighthouses that are still active as aids to navigation are the Baltimore Light, built in 1908, at the south entrance to the Craighill Channel; the Bloody Point Bar Light (1882), at the south end of Kent Island; the Cove Point Light (1828), at the entrance to the Patuxent River; the Craighill Channel Lower Range Lights (1873), at the Patapsco River's mouth, and the Cut-off Channel Range Lights (1886 and 1938), leading to the Patapsco River; the Hooper Island Light (1902), at Middle Hooper Island; the Point No Point Light in Chesapeake Bay, north of the entrance to the

Potomac River; the Sandy Point Shoal Light (1883), north of the Chesapeake Bay Bridge; the Sharps Island Light (1882), southwest of Tilghman Island; the Solomons Lump Light (1895), in Kedges Straits north of Smith Island; and the Thomas Point Shoal Light (1875), near the entrance to the South River. The Thomas Point Shoal Light is the last screwpile lighthouse still operational in its original location. The Coast Guard transferred management of the lighthouse to the City of Annapolis, the Chesapeake Chapter of the U.S. Lighthouse Society, and Anne Arundel County in 2005. The Annapolis Maritime Museum sponsors periodic tours to the lighthouse in good weather during the summer months.

Those light stations and lighthouses that are now historic sites and museum exhibits are the Concord Point Light (1827), at Havre de Grace, marking the entrance to the Susquehanna River; the Drum Point Light (1883), a screwpile light that has been moved to the Calvert Marine Museum at Solomons Island; the Hooper Strait Light (1879), which was moved to the Navy Point campus of the Chesapeake Bay Maritime Museum in St. Michaels; the Piney Point Light, on the Potomac River, now a museum in conjunction with the St. Clement's Island–Potomac River Museum; the Point Lookout Light (1830), a historic site in Point Lookout State Park; and the Seven Foot Knoll Light (1855), which was moved to Baltimore's Inner Harbor and is now part of the National Historic Seaport of Baltimore (formerly Baltimore Maritime Museum), under the aegis of the Living Classrooms Foundation.[51]

The rising importance of maritime coastal trade as the nation was expanding in the nineteenth century brought attention to the frequency of shipwrecks all along the Atlantic Coast of the United States, and the coast of Maryland on the Delaware, Maryland, and Virginia peninsula (Delmarva) was no exception. These wrecks and the sensational publicity they attracted awakened public concern, so by the 1840s Congress began to enact laws requiring the establishment of lifesaving stations along the coast. At first these were but shelters or boathouses at which shipwrecked passengers and crews could find some comfort after surviving a shipwreck by luck or by the efforts of volunteers along the coast. The first states to have these facilities were Massachusetts, New Jersey, New York, Rhode Island, and the Carolinas; soon thereafter, the Great Lakes shores had some lifesaving boathouses and equipment, under the establishment of the Revenue Marine. No significant improvements occurred until after the Civil War, when the Revenue Marine finally offered pay to surfmen, those brave enough to challenge the waves in small boats.

In 1871, the fortunate appointment of Sumner I. Kimball to the post of the head of the Revenue Marine Bureau changed everything. His first step was to order an inspection of all lifesaving stations, their personnel, and equipment. When the disappointing results came in, with poorly trained surfmen and missing equipment at the top of the list, Kimball instituted sweeping reforms. He stiffened uniform procedures, established lifesaving drills, fired incompetent keepers, and with the help of Congress, gained funds to improve stations and equipment. During the later 1870s, the Revenue Marine built a number of new lifesaving stations from Maine to Florida, including those in Maryland at Green Run and Assateague Beach in 1875 and one at Ocean City three years later.[52]

Perhaps it is hard to imagine Ocean City, with its towering hotels, condominium buildings, restaurants, bars, and other amusements stretching along the beach for miles north of the Ocean City Inlet, as a barrier island. But one has only to look a little farther south, to Assateague, a barrier island that, thanks to federal legislation, has been preserved in primitive condition, to see what the Ocean City area may have looked like a century and a half ago. It had been inhabited and used by Indians, and a few whites used it for grazing cattle and fishing. It was a barren stretch of windblown sand and dunes constantly moved about by the ocean waves and currents without manmade obstructions of any kind. There were no bridges connecting it with the mainland. It was not possible to visit the barrier beaches without transferring from wagon to boat for the short voyage across Sinepuxent Bay. Back in colonial times and in the early Federal period, an inlet through Assateague to Sinepuxent Bay allowed ocean and coastal trading vessels access to the landings and roads leading from the bay up to Snow Hill, where the Pocomoke River permitted transfer of cargo to baycraft with destinations on Chesapeake Bay. This trade ceased after a hurricane in 1818 closed the inlet and destroyed the village of Sinepuxent, on Sinepuxent neck, which had provided a transfer station for imported and exported goods.

For Ocean City, this began to change in the early 1870s, when, thanks to the Wicomico and Pocomoke Railroad, which ran from Salisbury to the Sinepuxent Bay, a group of men calling themselves the Atlantic Hotel Corporation bought some land to build that hotel and sell additional lots at $25 each. Then came the building of a railroad trestle bridge to the barrier island, and this was soon converted to a toll bridge for visitors coming by bicycle and automobile as well as train. In 1893, a modern train powered by coal, instead of wood, huffed and puffed its way into Ocean City all the way from Claiborne on the bay, carrying steamboat passengers from Baltimore and beyond. This was the beginning of the settlement that became Ocean City.[53]

It was in these days of American westward expansion and industrial growth that increased coastal traffic sent ships sailing close to the Delmarva coast toward either the Delaware River's mouth at Cape Henlopen or the Virginia Capes, which were the entrance to Chesapeake Bay. Most ships passed by this coast without incident, but when fog or northeasterly gales blew on shore, ships unsure of their position or unable to maneuver would often ground on the shoals off Fenwick or Assateague Island. This was when the surfmen of the Life Saving Service earned their keep. The schooner *Sallie W. Kaye* of Somers Point, New Jersey, was on its way from Baltimore to Boston with a cargo of coal and a crew of seven on January 10, 1883, when she was caught in a ferocious, blinding snowstorm as she was passing Ocean City. She struck bottom at six in the morning and was immediately smothered with heavy seas, which pounded her against the hard sand. Her location was about five miles north of the Ocean City Life Saving Station and two hundred fifty yards from shore. The crew had taken refuge on the mast to escape the seas that swept the vessel, but fearing that the mast would snap, they hastened down and climbed on the bowsprit and jib boom to await rescue. None having arrived after three hours, one of the crew decided to swim to shore to get help. The captain tried to dissuade him, but the sailor, a German named Anton, insisted on making the effort. He jumped into the icy sea and swam for shore, all the while buffeted by the breaking waves. Each time he neared the beach, he was swept back by the undertow and the along-shore currents. He never made it, and when last seen, he was still struggling toward the beach as the surge carried him southward.

A surfman of the Ocean City Life Saving Station was on duty that morning and had started out on his patrol, but the deep snow, swirling winds, and high tides forced him back. He reluctantly stood his watch on the lookout platform of the station. When the snowstorm abated, the surfmen finally got a glimpse of the embattled vessel and began their attempt to haul the thousand-pound wagon and rescuing apparatus the six miles up the coast. They soon realized that they would need oxen to do the job, so one of their number walked across the railroad bridge to a nearby farm to borrow the oxen. Four or five hours later, they arrived opposite the wreck and could still see the sailors clinging to the rigging. With their Lyle gun they fired a line over the schooner. This enabled the exhausted sailors to laboriously pull in the messenger line, to which was attached a heavier rope. This they set up as high as possible in the rigging. Once that had been done, a breeches buoy was sent out from shore, and in separate trips each survivor was hauled back to the beach. From there the surfmen carried the sailors back in a wagon to the Life Saving Station, where warmth, food, and beverages awaited them. Several days later the body of the gallant sailor who had attempted to swim to land washed ashore. The survivors must have considered themselves lucky not to have shared his fate.

This is but one example of the acts of bravery by the Life Saving Service along the Maryland Shore. Only one week later the three-masted schooner *Wyoming* foundered off Green Run Inlet in a similar storm. She had been on her way from San Domingo to New York with a cargo of sugar and lignum vitae, a valuable hard wood used in making ships' blocks. The surfmen of the Green Run Life Saving Station responded as soon as their patrol brought back the news. They hauled their surfboat a distance of three miles and then launched when they were too fatigued to push on. They rescued the six-man crew and brought them ashore to the small village of North Beach, where the settlers cared for them and nursed them back to health. Thrice more that terrible month, ships foundered (*Elizabeth M. Buebler, Julia Grace,* and the Spanish steamship *Alpin*), and the Green Run surfmen went to the rescue. All told, they rescued fifty people within a two-week period. The surfmen of the North Beach Life Saving Station, also on Assateague Island, rescued passengers and crew from the schooner *Margaret A. May* in December 1884. Their ship was not a total loss, and a tug came from Philadelphia to pull her off and return her to port for repairs. The North Beach crew made rescues from eight major shipwrecks during their tenure.[54] These and later employees of the Revenue Marine Life Saving Service contributed greatly to the traditions of the Maryland surfmen, who were willing to risk lives to rescue shipwreck victims along the Atlantic beaches of the Eastern Shore. After many years of debate as to whether the Revenue Cutter Service and the Life-Saving Service should continue as separate entities, be merged with the navy, or be subsumed under a new and separate service, Congress finally decided, in 1915, to create the United States Coast Guard, under the Treasury Department. Twenty-four years later, in 1939, that organization also added the Lighthouse Service and the Bureau of Marine Inspection and Navigation to the Coast Guard's already manifold duties.[55]

FROM THE CIVIL WAR UNTIL WORLD WAR II, maritime commerce flourished on Chesapeake Bay. This was epitomized by the dominance of the steamboat, linking communities not yet visited by railroads, transporting agricultural products to market, mail to isolated communities, and finished goods to rural homes, and bringing recreation to jaded city folk who longed for the delight of a moonlight cruise on the bay or an easy voyage to a bayside resort, such as Betterton, Tolchester, and Bay Ridge. The popularity of these locations increased during the latter part of the nineteenth century, when prosperity spread through members of the middle class and enabled them to have leisure time activities. Southeast of Annapolis, local entrepreneur James Vansant bought land and built a large hotel at Tolly Point on Bay Ridge, overlooking the Chesapeake Bay, in 1879. After he arranged for the extension of a rail line from Annapolis to Bay Ridge, it was not long before thousands of city dwellers from Washington and Baltimore came to spend their vacations at the "Queen Resort of the Chesapeake." Steamboats such as *Theodore Weems, Louise, Excelsior,* and *Samuel J. Pentz* soon made daily stops at the long pier extending into the bay from in front of the Bay Ridge Hotel. The list of steamboats from Baltimore and the Eastern Shore grew longer and longer in the mid-1880s with the popularity of the voyage and the resort. The famous *Emma Giles* called in on her way to regular stops on the South, West, and Rhode rivers. The huge steamboat *Columbia,* which could carry as many as four thousand passengers, made the trip from Baltimore frequently during the years 1888 to 1899, and for a time Bay Ridge became the terminal of the Baltimore and Eastern Shore steamer *Tockwogh* on her runs to Claiborne, where she connected with trains running to Ocean City.

The Bay Ridge hotel, however, began to suffer from the competition of the Cape May and Ocean City beaches after the turn of the century. With fewer visitors, the services offered gradually began to decline, and the electric rail line to Annapolis stopped running. The *Columbia* no longer called at the pier, and workmen at the hotel went on strike in 1899. The resort continued on, fitfully, for another few years under the management of George R. Buffham. The great Bay Ridge resort came to a climactic end in a tragic fire, which burned its grand hotel on March 4, 1915.[56] A few miles to the south, in Calvert County, the resort of Chesapeake Beach came into existence around 1900 as the dream of developers who saw it as a vacation destination for Washington, D.C., city dwellers. The Chesapeake Beach Railway Company completed the Washington and Chesapeake Beach railway and constructed a long pier with casino and bandstand out into the bay, as well as an amusement park. Soon, excursion steamboats, such as *Dreamland* and *Dixie* from Baltimore, and trains from Washington were coming regularly to this beach resort. In 1935, the railroad went into bankruptcy. Nonetheless, Chesapeake Beach and its sister community, North Beach, thrived on the new access to the bay that extension of steamboat and rail transportation had made possible.

The steamboat *Love Point* approaching the steamboat *Joppa* at the Light Street pier, ca. 1930s. Courtesy, Chesapeake Bay Maritime Museum, 453–3.

The steamboats kept regular schedules, made frequent stops, and were dependable. There were several types: double-ended ferries, overnight freight and passenger steamers serving landings on Maryland's many rivers and creeks, large packets running from Baltimore to the bay's other major ports, and excursion boats. Homeported in Baltimore, hundreds of steamboats, belonging to dozens of lines, made it their business to serve Maryland's bayside communities and distant urban centers, such as Washington, Norfolk, Wilmington, and Philadelphia. They traveled at an average of twelve knots, though many were capable of top speeds in excess of fifteen knots. A typical overnight passage from Baltimore could carry a businessman to Norfolk in time for a full day's work. Some of the steamers were so familiar that they became part of the landscape—an institution—such as the venerable *Joppa,* built in 1885, which worked on the bay for forty-four years; the *B. S. Ford,* steaming on the Chester River for forty-six years; the *Emma Giles,* which carried passengers to Tolchester, Annapolis, and St. Michaels, as well as West River and Little Choptank ports, for forty-nine years; and *Tred Avon,* built in 1883, serving Claiborne and Love Point, Kent Island, for an impressive fifty-six years.[57]

The *B. S. Ford,* a side-wheel steamer built in 1877 in Wilmington, Delaware, became a legend on the Baltimore-Chestertown run. She was part of a small fleet of boats run by the Chester River Steamboat Company that included the side-wheeler *Emma A. Ford, Gratitude, Corsica,* and *Endeavor,* the last two both propeller-driven steamers. The steamers *Ford* were named for husband and wife, Colonel B. S. Ford, who was once president of the line, and his wife, Emma, who survived him by several

The Tolchester line steamboat *Emma Giles* at the Chalk Point Landing, Shady Side, ca. 1920s. Courtesy, Chesapeake Bay Maritime Museum, 152–1.

years. It is a charming remembrance that the two namesake steamers would often start from opposite ends of the route, Baltimore to Chestertown on the Chester River, and either meet or pass each other en route. The *Corsica,* used as a freight boat for most of her career, ran up the river to Crumpton, taking on livestock and produce. One of the great exports of the region was the peach crop, which produced over a million baskets in good years. All the steamboats made stops at numerous boat landings along the way, always including Queenstown, to take on or drop off passengers and cargo. The *Gratitude* ran between Baltimore and Rock Hall and made a stop in Swan Creek, at Deep Landing Wharf. In later years, the steamboat's name was used as the name of the landing at Gratitude, Maryland. The *B. S. Ford* lasted longer than the other boats of the line, which gradually went out of service due to fires (*Emma A. Ford*), being sold off (*Gratitude*), and conversion to barges. The *B. S. Ford* continued to run on the Chester River until 1929, when Capt. George Curlett bought her and converted her to a cargo-carrying barge under the same name. He abandoned her as a wreck in 1960.[58]

In the early twentieth century, wealthy railroad companies bought up steamboat lines in order to supplement their transport services and to support their own competition with the burgeoning trucking industry. The Pennsylvania Railroad's steamboat lines came to include lines that normally serviced the Eastern Shore in competition with the Pennsylvania's rail service to those points. Through subsidiaries in 1894, the railroad bought the Choptank Steamboat and the Maryland Steamboat companies and named the new company the Baltimore, Chesapeake, and Atlantic Railway Company, sometimes called "Black Cinders and Ashes" by detractors.[59] In 1905, the Pennsylvania Railroad purchased the Weems Creek Steamboat Company, the Chester River Steamboat Company, and the Queen Anne's Railroad Company, thereby acquiring a new rail link to the Delaware seacoast at Lewes and Rehoboth. The new entity was called the Maryland, Delaware,

Stevedores loading livestock on board the steamboat *Anne Arundel,* ca. 1920s. H. Graham Wood Collection, Courtesy, Chesapeake Bay Maritime Museum, 462–11.

and Virginia Railway Company (MD&V). After these purchases, MD&V management modified steamboat routes and changed the steamers that served those routes. In the 1920s, there was a noticeable decline in the profits of steamboat companies as motor trucks and automobiles began to provide alternate means of transportation to urban centers and resort areas. When the Pennsylvania Railroad sold off the MD&V in 1923, a new entity, the Baltimore & Virginia Steamboat Company, also owned by the Pennsylvania Railroad, bought a portion of the MD&V properties, essentially those serving the Potomac and Rappahannock rivers.

As the Great Depression grew after the New York stock market crash of 1929, almost all businesses were affected, but particularly steamboats. Freight shipments dropped off because of lack of demand, hitting the steamboat business hard. Steamers were already losing business to the trucking industry, but this made it worse. On top of that, the U.S. Congress passed legislation requiring installation of sprinkler systems, fire doors, and fire alarms that could be heard by all in steam vessels, owing to the *Morro Castle* disaster, when a cruise liner caught fire off the New Jersey coast in September 1934 and killed 137 passengers and crew. In July 1937, the steamboat *City of Baltimore,* having just set out for Norfolk, erupted in flames at the mouth of the Patapsco near Seven Foot Knoll. The ship burned down to the water's edge. While there were only four casualties, two missing and two dead, the result brought the same message to Chesapeake residents. The Bureau of Marine Inspection and Engineering stepped up the pace of their inspections based on the Safety at Sea Regulations instituted by Congress in 1936. Some steamboat owners could scarcely afford the expense of retrofitting sprinkler systems and installing fireproof bulkheads. The venerable steamboat *Anne Arundel* was one of the victims. She made one last sentimental voyage from Baltimore to Fredericksburg, with excursionists as passengers wanting to relive one more time their memories of the old steamboat days. The Western Shore Steamboat Company ceased operations at the end of October 1937. They sold *Anne Arundel* to a company that modified her and operated her as an excursion boat under the name *Mohawk*.

Eventually, she and vessels like her were sold off to be used as barges or to be broken up for scrap.[60]

During the Great Depression, the Pennsylvania Railroad cut its steamboat business to the bone and in 1932 closed down the Baltimore and Virginia line's services, except the ferry run to Love Point on Kent Island.[61] Other steamboat companies took over the runs abandoned by the Pennsylvania Railroad's lines. The leading example is the Western Shore Steamboat Company, formed by produce dealers in Baltimore to bring Eastern Shore agricultural and fisheries' products to market. This brave effort lasted another five years but ended in 1937. The Old Bay Line maintained its services throughout the 1930s and even survived World War II, when the War Shipping Administration took over four ships of the company for conversion to troop transports. The bay steamers *President Warfield, Yorktown, State of Maryland,* and *State of Virginia* were sent to England with others, under naval convoy. During an excruciating passage of the Atlantic in September 1942, *Yorktown* was sunk by a torpedo, as were a destroyer and two steamers from the New York to Boston run. The other steamboats made the passage safely and saw service in European waters.[62] *President Warfield,* however, had an exceptional career in the aftermath of World War II. Jewish refugees from many parts of Europe who had somehow survived the terrible German concentration camps had a dream of escaping Europe to reside in their historic biblical homeland, Israel. That land was the British mandate territory of Palestine. Jewish organizations purchased *President Warfield* to ferry the refugees to the near East. Renamed *Exodus 1947,* this vessel took thousands of refugees to Palestine in 1947 under bizarre conditions, which captured the imagination of many in Western Europe and the United States. She finally arrived at Haifa, but the British were not ready to allow these holocaust survivors to land in Palestine, and took the extreme step of forcibly

Passengers awaiting steamboat at Booker's Wharf, Chester River. Frank A. Moorshead Collection. Courtesy, Chesapeake Bay Maritime Museum, 462–2.

Steamboats *Annapolis* and *Emma Giles* at Light Street wharf, July 1935. Photo by R. L. Graham. Courtesy, Chesapeake Bay Maritime Museum, 152–4.

removing the passengers from their ship, placing them in other ships, and returning them to internment camps in eastern Germany. There they remained until international protests forced the British to reconsider. Many of those refugees who managed to survive this outrage eventually found a way to arrive at their long-sought Jewish homeland. Meanwhile, *Exodus 1947* remained tethered to a breakwater at Haifa until she burned in 1952. She had become the most famous of the twentieth-century Chesapeake Bay steamboats.[63]

In the immediate postwar years, ship fires, collisions, and labor strikes took their toll on Old Bay Line operations. Gradually, management curtailed passenger services to Norfolk. By 1960, the line sent out its ships only on weekdays, and in 1961 and 1962 they carried only freight. The Old Bay Line halted its operations in April 1962, after 122 years of service on Chesapeake Bay. The steamboat era thus did not end entirely with World War II, though by the end of the war it was a dying industry. The union movement and the vagaries of federal subsidies to the maritime industry both added their impacts. By 1960, steamboats were no longer competitive because of higher costs of doing business, competition from other modes of transportation, and the faster pace of American life.

One of the major developments that accelerated the rate of change and the disappearance of steamboats from the bay was the completion of the Chesapeake Bay Bridge in 1952, linking Sandy Point and Kent Island. The bridge greatly en-

hanced the accessibility of the Eastern Shore beaches for the urban populations of Baltimore and Washington and their suburbs. Instead of driving the lengthy route around the head of the bay and then south to places like Salisbury and Ocean City, drivers could cut their travel time in half by using the bridge. This would affect the bay region in many ways far into the future. According to Scott M. Kozel, with the opening of the first two-lane bridge span, traffic increased annually, nearly doubling in the first decade of its use. During the 1960s the state constructed a second parallel bridge, with three lanes. It opened in 1973 and enabled the Maryland Transportation Authority to alternate lane openings to allow for traffic surges on weekends and during twice-a-day rush hours. Needless to say, there was no further need for ferry traffic to facilitate commerce or tourism.[64]

Once again, however, in the first decade of the twenty-first century, complaints about bridge gridlock and the danger of bad accidents blocking the bridges for hours or days have brought forth suggestions for a new bridge as well as cross-bay ferries. In 2005, the state established a Task Force on Traffic Capacity across the Bay, also known as the Chesapeake Bay Crossing Study. The Maryland Transportation Authority estimated that during the previous fiscal year, some 25.9 million vehicles had crossed the bay bridge. The task force considered four different construction locations, from Baltimore to Kent Island, Sandy Point to Kent Island

The steamboat *President Warfield,* launched in 1928, was one of the Old Bay Line's finest. One of several Chesapeake steamboats to be requisitioned as a troop transport in 1942, she carried troops for the Normandy D-Day invasion. After the war, new owners named her *Exodus 1947.* She then carried refugees from war-torn Europe to Palestine, only to be turned back. Courtesy, Maryland Historical Society, MCZ24.645.

(adding a third span to the existing Sandy Point bridges), from Anne Arundel or Calvert County to Talbot County, and from Calvert County to Dorchester County. Aside from the immense cost of these structures, each of these options poses other formidable problems, primarily the upgrading of existing roads and small bridges on the Eastern Shore to accommodate the new traffic load. If the option were to link Calvert to Talbot or Dorchester counties, the bridge across the bay would have to be not much longer than the crossing from Sandy Point to Kent Island, although the Chesapeake Bay Crossing Study states for some unexplained reason that the bridge would have to be from ten to twelve miles long.

The task force also looked at the possibility of a new cross-bay ferry. This would probably require high-speed catamaran or hydrofoil designs and bring an entirely new dimension of maritime activity to the bay. To adequately complement and ease the burden on the existing bridges, the ferries would have to carry cars and trucks, but the task force found that the longer passage time, small vehicle capacity, and higher transit fees involved would make the ferries impractical. It estimated that the ferry fees would range between $25 and $45 per vehicle and that ferry service could handle only a fraction of the millions of vehicles that cross the bridges. Thus, the ferry-crossing option seems ill fated, but the building of new bridges would also face public opposition on the basis of high costs, small local benefits, and adverse environmental impact on sensitive wetlands on both the Eastern and Western shores.[65]

Chapter Five

Civil War on Chesapeake Bay

∽∽∽∽∽∽∽∽∽∽∽∽∽∽∽∽∽∽∽∽∽∽∽∽

Tʜᴇ ᴀᴅᴠᴇɴᴛ ᴏꜰ ᴛʜᴇ ᴄɪᴠɪʟ ᴡᴀʀ in the spring of 1861 severely disturbed
the thriving maritime industries that had developed in Maryland's Chesapeake
Bay over the previous forty-five years. The control and use of the waters of Chesapeake Bay were strategically essential for both sides, but the Confederacy lacked a
navy of sufficient force to challenge Union control. What Confederates were able
to do, however, was to conduct maritime guerrilla raids along creeks and rivers and
at times on the bay, a primary artery for the transport of U.S. (Union) troops, provisions, and munitions. With its Western Shore tributaries, the James, York, and
Rappahannock rivers, the bay's reach stretched deep into Confederate territory, even
to Richmond, its capital. Railroads, the Chesapeake and Delaware Canal, and the
bay linked the industries of the North to Baltimore, where Locust Point served as
a depot and principal port for supply of the Union armies.

The war brought the interruption of regular commerce to Norfolk and to Virginia's many river landings, as well as the federal commandeering of commercial
steamboats and tugs, Confederate destruction of federal lighthouses and lightships
in the lower bay, the activities of Southern sympathizers on the Eastern Shore, and
treasonous smuggling across the Virginia border on both the Eastern and Western
shores. The federal government's need of shipping to transport troops and supplies
provided ideal opportunities for government contracts and profiteering. But the
U.S. Army's Quartermaster Department also seized many steamers and forced owners to accept a lease contract with the federal government. The army ran the steamers fast, long, and hard without paying much attention to maintenance. At the end
of the war, if and when the steamboats were returned to their owners, these vessels
were in much need of overhaul and repair. The steamboats of the Baltimore Steam
Packet Company, the Eastern Shore Steamboat Company, the Weems Line, the
Slaughter Line, the Individual Enterprise Company, and others all felt the long arm
of the Quartermaster Department.[1]

After South Carolina seceded on December 20, 1860, deep concern arose in
Washington because military posts and naval bases in the South had come under
attack by state militias. If this were to happen in the Washington area, the nation's
capital would be imperiled. On January 5, 1861, even before the war started in earnest, the navy garrisoned Fort Washington, on the Maryland side of the Potomac,

with forty marines from the Washington Navy Yard to protect public property. On January 9, more marines were sent to garrison Fort McHenry, at Baltimore.

Only forty-two ships were in commission in the U.S. Navy. Twelve of these were assigned to duty with the Home Squadron, four of which were in Northern waters. The Navy Department recalled ships from foreign stations to meet the national crisis. One of the first problems arose at the Norfolk Navy Yard, the navy's major base on the East Coast. The commandant's staff included many Southern officers, and a large number of the navy's vessels lay in varying states of repair in the Norfolk yard. In early April 1861, the major crisis point was Fort Sumter in Charleston Harbor, but if Virginia voted for secession, the fate of the Norfolk yard would be in question. Whatever happened at Norfolk would affect navigation throughout the bay.

Secretary of the Navy Gideon Welles prepared to bolster loyal sailors and employees in the yard and to remove as many ships as possible before the yard could fall into rebel hands. On March 31, he sent 250 men from New York Navy Yard to Norfolk. On April 10, Welles warned Capt. Charles S. McCauley, Norfolk's commandant, to prepare USS *Merrimack* to be removed to a northern shipyard but advised him also to "take no steps that would give needless alarm." McCauley was a loyal, brave, elderly officer who was by nature cautious; such a warning made him doubly so. The navy's chief engineer, Benjamin Isherwood, arrived from Washington on April 10 to reassemble *Merrimack*'s engines and put them in working order in the shortest possible time.[2]

Confederate guns opened fire on Fort Sumter on April 12, and on the next day the fort surrendered. The onset of hostilities increased the sense of urgency at Norfolk. On April 16, Secretary Welles ordered USS *Cumberland*'s commanding officer to assist in preparing vessels in the Norfolk yard, to load ordnance and ordnance stores, suppress violence, and repel assault. Meanwhile, Confederates placed obstructions in the water to prevent vessels from departing through the Norfolk channel. These measures later proved to be ineffective. Chief Engineer Isherwood reported *Merrimack* ready for sea, and on April 18, Welles ordered Capt. Hiram Paulding to Norfolk to take command and to destroy the yard and its contents rather than allow it to fall into Confederate hands.

All the hasty attempts to prepare an evacuation were insufficient. On April 20, events overtook McCauley, Isherwood, and Paulding, and instead of taking the ships from the yard, they burned most where they lay moored or in ordinary. The yard buildings were partially destroyed, along with some of the oldest ships in the navy, including the frigate *United States*. *Merrimack* burned to the water's edge, but her hull was still viable. The Confederates moved in and took possession of the dry dock and the industrial plant, where they could manufacture urgently needed naval ordnance and other equipment. Most of the guns and fortifications erected by the Confederacy along their coasts and rivers in the early days came from the Norfolk Navy Yard.

Meanwhile, at Annapolis, the U.S. Naval Academy was teeming with activity. Maryland was a state with a divided populace. Officially, the state stayed with the Union, but its citizens included many would-be secessionists and Confederate sympathizers. The Navy Department worried that batteries set up on the left bank of the Severn River could damage the venerable frigate USS *Constitution,* which had been moored at the academy as a training ship. On April 19, when a train carrying the troops of the Massachusetts Sixth Regiment off-loaded the troops at Baltimore's President Street station to march through the city to entrain again at Camden Yards, angry crowds of secessionist Baltimoreans obstructed their way and fighting broke out. On 20 April, the steamer *Maryland* arrived at Annapolis, bringing a contingent of federal troops that had left their trains at Perryville on the Susque-hanna and boarded the steamer to avoid the riotous situation in Baltimore. *Maryland* towed "Old Ironsides" into Chesapeake Bay to prevent her damage or capture by Confederate guerrillas, but both steamer and frigate ran aground, and two other steamers came to their rescue. The steamer *R. R. Cuyler* freed the frigate, and the gunboat *Harriet Lane* escorted them down the bay. *R. R. Cuyler* towed *Constitution,* with the remaining loyal midshipmen on board, to Newport, Rhode Island, where they were to spend the next four years in a makeshift Naval Academy building.[3]

The first "federalizing" of the Chesapeake steamboat fleet took place on April 21, as Col. Charles S. Smith, USA, seized the steamers *Baltimore, Mount Vernon, Philadelphia,* and *Powhatan* in the Potomac near Washington. He ordered them to be fitted out to defend the capital's river approaches. Aquia Creek, on the Virginia side of the Potomac, was the first location chosen by Confederates for a battery to interdict communications on the Potomac. Capt. Franklin Buchanan, a Mary-lander and Commandant of the Washington Navy Yard, resigned on April 22 from the U.S. Navy to join the Confederate States Navy. Capt. John Dahlgren succeeded him in command.

Simultaneously, more federal troops arrived at Annapolis by steamboat after having embarked above Baltimore. The mob of Southern sympathizers that attacked the Sixth Massachusetts had begun destroying the railroad bridges that traversed Baltimore. These federal troops were commanded by Gen. Benjamin Butler. He ordered them to repair the railroad tracks that had been sabotaged between Annapolis and Washington. At about the same time, Cdr. James H. Ward of the USS *North Carolina* recommended to Secretary of the Navy Welles the formation of a "flying flotilla," later officially referred to as the Potomac Flotilla, for the protection of Chesapeake Bay and its tributaries. Welles approved his proposal, and Ward purchased and fitted out these vessels in New York, arriving at Washington Navy Yard on May 20.

Potomac River steamers, refitted as improvised gunboats, took part in the raid on Alexandria mounted from the Washington Navy Yard under Commander Stephen Rowan's command on May 24. This was the first landing of Northern troops on Virginia's shores. Commander Ward's improvised Potomac Flotilla went into action, joined later by Commander Rowan's USS *Pawnee,* and engaged Confederate batteries at Aquia Creek, on the Virginia bank of the Potomac. On Chesapeake Bay, the steamers of the Bay Line continued to operate, carrying passengers and the mail from Baltimore to Hampton Roads, but the navy required the line to terminate voyages at Old Point Comfort. The navy chartered the line's *Adelaide* for use as a transport attached to the North Atlantic Blockading Squadron. She was useful in towing the "stone fleet," nineteen schooners loaded with huge stones that were sunk in the inlets of the Outer Banks. This was intended to assist in bottling up Confederate access to the sea and to prevent blockade runners from carrying goods, including munitions, from Europe to the Confederacy.[4] *Adelaide* and the steamer *George Peabody* carried hundreds of federal troops in operation against Forts Hatteras and Clark on August 28–29, 1861. As a result of this successful operation, the federal government was able to exercise control of the North Carolina sounds.

In one of the earliest Confederate guerrilla actions of the war, Capt. George Hollins, Confederate States Navy (formerly USN), seized command of the steamer *St. Nicholas* in company with the famous Richard "Zarvona" Thomas, an Eastern Shore youth who had fought with Garibaldi in Italy. With funds provided by the governor of Virginia, Hollins arranged for Zarvona to purchase weapons, obtain the assistance of about sixteen men, and take passage from Baltimore on board the ship as she headed south. Hollins boarded at Point Lookout and gave Zarvona, who was disguised as a "French lady," the signal to break out small arms. This they did, and soon Hollins took charge of the vessel. His original intent had been to use *St. Nicholas* as a means of capturing the U.S. Navy gunboat *Pawnee*, but that night *Pawnee* had gone upriver to Washington. Shifting to secondary targets, Hollins took two prizes, schooners, one carrying ice and the other, coal. Hollins sent the prize schooners to Fredericksburg, where their cargoes were much appreciated. Confederate Secretary of the Navy Stephen Mallory rewarded Hollins with promotion to the rank of commodore.[5]

There were two major trouble spots for the Union along the shores of Chesapeake Bay: that part of Maryland forming the left bank of the Potomac, made up of Charles and St. Mary's counties, and the Eastern shores of Maryland and Virginia. Both areas were rife with smugglers, who usually crossed the river or the bay at night. The smugglers on the Eastern Shore took their contraband from Maryland to Accomac County, Virginia, and then came in the Onancock, Pungoteague, or Cherrystone inlets, and from there across the bay to the York or Rappahannock rivers. There were also those in the North who "traded with the enemy" by sending their supplies south on the Atlantic coast and off-loading them at Chincoteague. The Virginia smugglers met them and loaded the provisions in wagons to cross the Virginia Eastern Shore and then loaded them into bay-crossing boats. Of this, Capt. Thomas T. Craven, USN, commanding USS *Yankee* on Potomac River patrol, stated: "I am convinced that all these persons are active participators in the rebellion and are constantly engaged in traitorous acts."[6] Union officials were also gathering information provided by escaped slaves and other sources, indicating that a rebel force was massing on the Eastern Shore. Gov. Thomas Hicks of Maryland, an Eastern Shore man, warned Secretary of War Simon Cameron and recommended that the Potomac Flotilla be strengthened. Maj. Gen. John A. Dix, commanding troops in the Department of Maryland, had foreseen the necessity of crushing secessionist elements on the Virginia Eastern Shore as early as July 23, 1861. The moment arrived in November, when General Dix in Baltimore ordered elements of the Wisconsin Fourth Volunteer Regiment and the Massachusetts Light Artillery, as well as cavalry, to embark for Newtown, Maryland, near the Virginia border. Then a larger force of 4,500 men boarded the steamer *Pocahontas* for Newtown. Dix ordered Brig. Gen. Henry H. Lockwood to disperse the rebel force, to reestablish the sabotaged Cape Charles lighthouse, and to persuade the wayward Virginians to swear allegiance to the Union. This impressive demonstration of force frightened them into submission. Col. Charles Smith, the erstwhile leader of this untrained rebel band, fled with a few hundred followers to Norfolk. The results of this expedition were important. Union troops had succeeded, without bloodshed, in expelling the troublesome element and in obtaining the cooperation of the remaining citizenry. As a result, the Virginia Eastern Shore was quiet for the remainder of the war.[7]

∽∽∽

ALTHOUGH THE FAMOUS DUEL between USS *Monitor* and CSS *Virginia* (formerly USS *Merrimack*) on March 9, 1862, did not take place in Maryland waters, the impact of that battle confirmed Union control of the bay. Had the armor-plated *Virginia* defeated *Monitor,* U.S. naval forces would have been unable to control shipping in the lower bay and the Hampton Roads area would have fallen under Confederate dominance. For a while, at least, there might also have been a Confederate blockade of access to the bay from the Atlantic. But *Monitor*'s surprising maneuverability and her revolutionary revolving turret, with its 11-inch Dahlgren guns, neutralized the South's only ironclad on the Chesapeake. This event opened the way for the U.S. Army's Peninsula Campaign and the actions of navy gunboats in support of the military on the York and James rivers.

The Union Army, in its failure at the first battle of Bull Run (Manassas), had shown several weaknesses: inexperience, lack of coordinated leadership, and inadequate intelligence. In the aftermath, new officers rose to the top. During the winter of 1861–62, Maj. Gen. George B. McClellan, General-in-Chief of the U.S. Army, had gathered and trained an army of 135,000 men to contend with the Army of Northern Virginia, commanded by Confederate general Joseph E. Johnston. In fact, Johnston's army numbered not much more than 55,000, but federal spies, under Allan Pinkerton's direction, overestimated the numbers by about half, so McClellan believed that he was facing an army of 115,000. Being a cautious man who hated to move his army until it was a perfectly ready, overwhelming force, he procrastinated in advancing against Johnston. Thus, he managed to annoy President Lincoln and to infuriate members of Congress, who were impatient for good news.[8]

Instead of confronting the Confederate army, McClellan decided he would outflank it, move his army south by water, and dramatically shorten the distance over which he would have to fight before besieging Richmond. While this plan made good strategic sense, the president, concerned for the safety of the capital, insisted that a force be left to cover the defenses of Washington while the Army of the Potomac was in the field. McClellan developed two versions of the plan. The first proposed to deliver the army to Urbana, on the Rappahannock River, outflanking Johnston's army and placing the Union army on the shortest possible line of march to Richmond, thereby cutting off Confederate troops on the peninsula between the York and James rivers. In the event, General Johnston anticipated Mc-Clellan's move and withdrew his troops toward Richmond, leaving the Union general free to exercise the other alternative, an advance up the peninsula from Fort Monroe. Although initially opposed to this plan, the president yielded, but on March 9, 1862, he ordered that sufficient troops be posted to the defense of Washington, that Confederate batteries be cleared from the right bank of the Potomac, and that McClellan accept the title of Commander of the Army of the Potomac, a reassignment that was, in effect, a demotion. As a result of his truculent and disrespectful attitude toward the president and the secretary of war, McClellan was no longer in charge of the entire U.S. Army.[9]

On March 17, the first elements of McClellan's Army of the Potomac left from Alexandria on board a multitude of steamboats, tugs, and towed schooners and barges for a joint operation, based at Fort Monroe, to capture Richmond by marching up the peninsula. The initial movement of the troops required 324 vessels, including steam ferries and propeller and side-wheel steam tugs. Some of these vessels departed from Perryville and others from Baltimore. They carried 54,828 men, 11,416 animals, 1,200 wagons, and 24 ambulances. In addition, the flotilla carried teamsters, horses, gun batteries, food rations, beef on the hoof, thousands of gallons of water, and coal on board each steamer. Subsequent shipments provided another 60,000 troops, 3,000 more animals, pontoon bridges, telegraphic materials, and much other equipment needed for supplying and moving the army.[10]

On April 2, General McClellan and his staff arrived at Fort Monroe on board the steamboat *Commodore,* with naval vessels standing by to provide gunfire support on both the James and York rivers as the troops moved westward toward the Confederate capital. McClellan's peninsular campaign (April to August 1862) foundered on the unexpectedly stiff Confederate resistance at Yorktown and Williamsburg, made more difficult by the flooding Chickahominy River and Confederate skill at deceptive maneuvering. The Confederates fought well at the battles of Fair Oaks, Gaines's Mill, Malvern Hill, and the Seven Days. McClellan, on the other hand, continued to believe the exaggerated estimates of Confederate strength and was loath to push forward when he could have done so. As he said in a letter to his wife, "I dare not risk this army. . . . I must make a sure thing of it."[11]

While McClelland dallied, Gen. Robert E. Lee, who had replaced Joseph Johnston in command of the Army of Northern Virginia, urgently ordered General Jackson to quick-march his troops from the Shenandoah Valley to assist in the defense of Richmond. The battle of Malvern Hill brought heavy losses to both sides, and McClellan decided to retreat to Harrison's Landing, on the James River, where navy gunboats could provide protection. In the end, however, Lee defeated McClellan's offensive, and General Halleck ordered him to reembark his troops and return to the nation's capital. On August 22, Secretary of the Navy Welles ordered Radm. Louis Goldsborough to assist the army by embarking troops at Fort Monroe and Newport News and returning them to Alexandria. This marked the end of the campaign on the York Peninsula.[12]

As the 1862 campaign season progressed, General-in-Chief Halleck ordered General McClellan to counter new Confederate movements that threatened Gen.

John Pope's small covering force. Lee, learning that McClellan would withdraw from the York Peninsula, decided to move against Pope before he could be reinforced. McClellan, however, resented Halleck's order and regretted his own failure; he was in no hurry to elevate General Pope's reputation. His delay allowed the Army of Northern Virginia, with Generals Lee, Jackson, and Longstreet combined, to outmaneuver and defeat Pope's army at the second Battle of Manassas from August 28 to 30. Meanwhile, Secretary of the Navy Welles ordered gunboats from the James River to Washington and Baltimore, paralleling the northward march of the contending armies. With the disbanding of the James River flotilla, the Navy Department reinforced the Potomac Flotilla and divided its command. Lt. Cdr. S. R. Franklin commanded the First Division, patrolling the lower Potomac, and Lt. Cdr. Samuel Magaw was in charge of the Second Division, patrolling the upper Potomac as far as Washington. There were still many smugglers who traveled between St. Inigoe's and Smith creeks, near St. Mary's City and the Virginia side of the Potomac. The smugglers often used oystering as a convenient cover for their smuggling activities.

During the early morning hours of October 7, the intrepid Confederate naval officer Lieut. John Taylor Wood, using small boats borne on army wagons, launched them in the Potomac and then captured, looted, and burned the trading schooner *Frances Elmor* near Popes Creek. On October 28, he seized, looted, and burned the merchant ship *Alleghanian,* 1,400 tons burden, bound for London and carrying a load of guano fertilizer, at anchor off the mouth of the Rappahannock River.[13]

After Second Manassas, General Lee moved his army northwestward toward the Potomac. Having finally gained the initiative, he wanted to keep it. He hoped to gather new support for his cause by invading Maryland. As for the Union army, General Pope's debacle led to his own disgrace as well as that of General McDowell. President Lincoln, despite his anger at General McClellan's selfish delaying tactics, decided that he needed McClellan and the general's popularity within the army to counter Lee's next move.[14] Thinking that he could raise Southern sympathies and recruit more troops in Maryland, Lee marched his armies across the Potomac toward Hagerstown while General Jackson moved north through the Shenandoah Valley. McClellan followed Lee into Maryland with a much larger army during early September. Jackson's army struck hard at Harper's Ferry, a Union strong point, and captured that place with its huge arsenal and tons of supplies. Within days, however, the armies clashed near Sharpsburg on Antietam Creek, September 15–17, in one of the bloodiest battles of the war. The result has been described as a stalemate, with severe losses on both sides. Strategically, Lee lost the initiative and had to retreat. Actually, he was allowed to retreat because McClellan refused to pursue, pleading fatigue and exhaustion. McClellan's delaying tactics finally persuaded Lincoln to remove him as commander of the Army of the Potomac. Gen. Ambrose E. Burnside, his replacement, took the offensive, and by December 11 had led his corps to attack Fredericksburg on the Rappahannock River.

Meanwhile, on the Chesapeake, a joint U.S. amphibious force under the command of Capt. Foxhall Parker on board USS *General Putnam* destroyed Confederate vessels and buildings used by smugglers in the vicinity of Mobjack Bay. As the preparations for the battle for Fredericksburg mounted, *Currituck, Anacostia, Jacob Bell,* and *Coeur de Lion,* vessels of the Potomac Flotilla on the Rappahannock, came under harassing fire from Maj. Gen. D. H. Hill's batteries at Port Royal. General Burnside's army engineers were having a great deal of trouble completing the pontoon bridge across the river because of sniping and interdiction from the guns of the battery at Pratts Bluff. He asked Parker's gunboats to create a diversion. The resulting naval bombardment caused the evacuation of the Confederate batteries. Burnside's effort at Fredericksburg came to naught, with severe loss of life, as the Confederates mounted a stout defense of the town from high ground.[15]

The smuggling conflict on the Chesapeake continued as the Civil War entered its third year, in January 1863. For example, Commodore Harwood of the Potomac Flotilla informed Secretary of the Navy Gideon Welles, "I enclose for the information of the department a certificate of capture of a sloop and nine canoes, with thirteen prisoners and a quantity of contraband goods, by the *Currituck,* I have this day placed them in the hands of the civil authorities. All captures have been made between the mouth of the Potomac and the Piankatank Rivers . . . these canoes were full of freight which has been brought to the Washington Navy Yard."[16] Radm. Samuel P. Lee was hard put to support a blockade of a coast that was so indented with rivers and creeks as the lower Chesapeake Bay. The Potomac Flotilla fought this riverine war with little-known vessels such as the converted steamboats *Commodore Barney, Commodore Morris, Delaware, Mount Washington,* and *Stepping Stones* on the York, Pamunkey, Nansemond, and Ware rivers. Meanwhile, shortages of food were plaguing Lee's army near Fredericksburg. During the winter of 1862–63, he sent Gen. James Longstreet and his corps south of Richmond to collect supplies in the Suffolk area until they were recalled to join other Confederate forces gathering near Chancellorsville.[17]

After the Confederate victory at the battle of Chancellorsville, May 1–4, 1863, and despite the death of Gen. Stonewall Jackson, Lee again decided to take his army north into Maryland. President Lincoln entrusted the Army of the Potomac to Gen. George Gordon Meade, the fifth general officer in charge of that army in a year's time. The resulting battle at Gettysburg, a turning point in the war, reinforced the Lincoln administration's reputation at home and abroad. The battle's military results were, like those at Antietam and Fredericksburg, a great bloodletting and the capture of many Confederate prisoners of war. Many of these soon found themselves incarcerated at a new POW camp built at Point Lookout, Maryland, a narrow point of land marking the separation of the Potomac from Chesapeake Bay on the Maryland side. This brought new responsibilities for the navy as well as the army.[18]

Built to accommodate ten thousand prisoners, the Point Lookout POW Camp ended the war with twenty thousand Southern soldiers living in unhealthy, miserable conditions. Secretary of the Navy Gideon Welles ordered Commodore Harwood's Potomac Flotilla always to keep an adequate naval force in close vicinity of Point Lookout and to be in close communication with the senior army officer in charge. And with good reason, for rebel seaborne guerrilla warfare continued to be a threat. On August 22, 1863, Lieutenant Wood took another "boats on wheels" raiding party toward the mouth of the Rappahannock. They boarded and captured two anchored Union gunboats, USS *Reliance* and USS *Satellite,* during an evening thunderstorm. Biding his time, Wood soon steamed out, with the U.S. ensign hoisted, and captured three Union merchant vessels. He towed them as prizes up the Rappahannock to Urbanna, where they were stripped of everything useful. By this time, the alarm had spread over the bay, and Union troops and gunboats were on the lookout for Wood and his men, so he scuttled his vessels.

The notorious "pirate" John Yates Beall, an acting master in the Confederate Navy, followed in Wood's footsteps and led Yankee gunboats a merry chase in the southern parts of the bay. Based on Mobjack Bay, in July 1863, with ten men under his command, he captured two small boats, *Swan* and *Raven,* and crossed the bay. On the way, they cut the telegraph cable connecting Fort Monroe with Washington and destroyed the Smith Island lighthouse. Then they crossed over Virginia's Eastern Shore and operated among the shoals and islands on the Atlantic Coast. According to federal reports, in company with Acting Master Edward McGuire, CSN, Beall captured the schooner *Alliance* and its cargo of sutlers' stores on September 19, 1863.[19] During the next two days, they captured three more schooners, *J. J. Housman, Samuel Pearsall,* and *Alexandria.* Beall cast these schooners adrift off Wachapreague Inlet. He put to sea in *Alliance,* picked up a pilot off Cobb Island, and ran into the Chesapeake. Attempting to bring the ship into Milford Haven on the Piankatank River, he ran aground, but slippery as ever, he escaped again. The Union navy went on the alert, as it was obvious that their blockade at Cape Charles had not been effective.[20] Union forces finally captured Beall in November 1863, on the Eastern Shore near Chesconnessex Creek, after he had destroyed several lighthouses, undoubtedly making navigation difficult for Maryland vessels headed down the bay.[21]

Annapolis was the principal point of exchange for prisoners of war in the East. The old Naval Academy grounds had been converted to a series of hospital buildings for former federal prisoners released from Southern POW camps. It was called USA General Hospital, Division No. 1, and the grounds of St. John's College were covered with tents and barracks known as USA General Hospital, Division No. 2. The flag of truce steamer *New York* plied the waters of the Chesapeake from Annapolis to Aitkens Landing or City Point on the James River carrying paroled Confederate prisoners. Returning, she carried tens of thousands of recently freed Union soldiers back to the Annapolis hospitals. Many were in dire need, with unattended wounds or sores and wasting away in a starving condition. The army sent former prisoners not in need of hospitalization to a camp three miles west called Camp Parole, where they awaited processing and back pay. That part of Annapolis, now developed into shopping malls, still bears the name *Parole.*

As 1864 hove into view, the situation of the Confederacy became desperate. Lincoln had ordered Gen. Ulysses S. Grant to replace General Meade as the head of the Army of the Potomac, whose ranks had been swelled by conscription in an effort to replace its thousands of casualties. By the same token, the Confederate Army of Northern Virginia had suffered irreplaceable losses through battlefield deaths, wounds, and desertion. Their loss in capable commanders at the rank of colonel and brigadier was crippling. Grant's principal strategy aimed to move directly on Richmond and to grind down Lee's army through battles of attrition. Thus, the opening battles of 1864 were those of the Wilderness, Spotsylvania, North Anna, and Cold Harbor, from May 5 to June 3. With Union military pressure ever more threatening to Richmond and Petersburg, General Lee conceived a plan that would endanger Washington and Baltimore and distract Grant from tightening the noose around the Confederate capital.

In early June 1864, Union general David Hunter proceeded down the Shenandoah Valley toward Lynchburg, in south central Virginia. Grant had instructed him to do all possible damage to the James River and the Kanawha Canal, a vital supply artery to Richmond. Lee sensed the danger Hunter posed and sent Gen. Jubal Early to confront him. This he did, saving Lynchburg and the canal and forcing Hunter's army to retreat toward western Virginia.[22] Lee then saw his opportunity. He provided secret orders to Early, giving him latitude to return to Richmond if the situation warranted, but he also ordered him, if possible, to march north through the valley, east along the Potomac, attack Washington, and then send cavalry to cut telegraph lines and burn bridges near Baltimore. In the event, Maj. Gen. Lew Wallace delayed Early's advance at the Battle of the Monocacy on July 9. This allowed time for the startled War Department to recover its wits and deploy troops north of the capital. Early intended to send his cavalry circling to the east of Washington into southern Maryland to liberate the prisoners at Point Lookout. Jefferson Davis planned to send, simultaneously, a naval force under Cdr. (formerly Lt.) John Taylor Wood to bring arms to Southern prisoners at the Point Lookout POW camp. The increasing numbers of prisoners held there had planted the thought that, if armed and organized, these men would be tantamount to a twenty-thousand-man army in President Lincoln's back yard.[23]

This plan was bold but risky, with Brig. Gen. Bradley Tyler Johnson and Maj. Harry Gilmor's First Maryland Cavalry sweeping east and south to meet Commander Wood at Point Lookout. His landing at Point Lookout with a gunboat carrying twenty thousand rifles, supplies, and ordnance would be the signal to attack the POW camp and to arm the prisoners.[24] But word of the raid leaked out, and Confederate president Jefferson Davis advised Wood (his nephew) to reconsider. In addition, General Johnson's advance arrangements for remounts in southern Maryland had become known. The Point Lookout commandant, Brig. Gen. James Barnes, made strenuous efforts to strengthen his defenses. How Wood could have successfully brought a steamer through the Union blockade with enough arms and men through Hampton Roads to Point Lookout is a mystery, but possibly he had in mind using the former blockade runner CSS *Tallahassee,* which he actually did use in breaking through the Wilmington blockade in August.[25] How thousands of sick and malnourished prisoners could have formed an army to march against Washington is another big question.

Despite the failure of the scheme to come to fruition, enough information about enemy troops moving in their direction caused apprehension in Annapolis. On July 12, Lieutenant Commander Braine of USS *Vicksburg* sent a boat expedition into the South River to destroy all means of crossing the river in order to protect gun emplacements around Annapolis. Reinforcements sped to the bay from Wilmington to Havre de Grace to defend the Susquehanna railroad bridges. The Navy Department sent ships of the Potomac Flotilla to defend the bridges over the Bush and Gunpowder rivers, north of Baltimore, but they arrived too late. USS *Minnesota* and other vessels steamed at top speed to protect Washington, Point Lookout, and Annapolis.

General Grant's ability to send several divisions north by steamboat via the Potomac in less time than General Early's troops could march on Washington put an end to all speculation. Grant had earlier sent General James B. Rickett's division of the Sixth Corps from City Point, Virginia, to Baltimore, arriving on July 8, in time to take part in the battle. One day later, he expedited transport of the First and Second Divisions of the Sixth Corps and then sent the Advanced Army Division, Nineteenth Corps, just arrived from New Orleans, in all about nine thousand men by steamboat.[26] They disembarked at Washington just in time to reinforce the capital's thinly spread troops and deflect an attack on its defenses. Such were the advantages of Union sea power on Chesapeake Bay.[27]

In recent years, Maryland's assistant underwater archaeologist, Bruce Thompson, uncovered the aftermath of a tragic episode of Civil War history on the Potomac that occurred in November 1864. At that time, the Potomac Flotilla's USS *Tulip,* a small propeller-driven steamer "gunboat" under the command of Acting Master William H. Smith, was under orders to patrol the lower Potomac and Northern Neck bays and creeks for evidence of Confederate activity in support of smuggling and attempts to attack Union shipping to and from Washington, along the right bank of the Potomac. *Tulip* had been assigned to this duty since August 1863 and had some success in capturing or destroying enemy small craft and covering amphibious landings by Union soldiers in the Rappahannock River area. As of November 11, Acting Master Smith knew that he was many months overdue to return to the Washington Navy Yard for a cleaning and repair of machinery. One of his two boilers had been acting up, unable to produce the required steam pressure. Smith got under way at 2 p.m. from St. Inigoe's Creek, where the Potomac Flotilla was stationed, and headed upstream for Washington. Despite being warned not to use both boilers, Smith insisted they be put online so as to make a rapid passage up the Potomac. Four hours and twenty minutes later, a terrific blast blew out the starboard side of the gunboat as the defective boiler exploded. All was chaos on board, as men, officers, machinery, and hull went in all directions. The death toll was very high. Of a crew of fifty-seven men, only eight survived, but later two of them died from their wounds. Forty-seven died of drowning or severe lacerations and other physical trauma. Both the master and the pilot, James Jackson, were lost in the explosion or sinking of the vessel. Several bodies drifted onto the Virginia shore, where they were later collected near Ragged Point. Eight of the dead sailors could not be identified. They were buried on the grounds of Cross Manor on the left bank of St. Inigoe's Creek, where a later owner of the estate erected a monument to the *Tulip* crew in 1929.

Historians now have a much more complete record of what happened to the ship and crew. Thompson located and interviewed men who as teenagers in the

1950s and 1960s had dived on *Tulip* with SCUBA gear and picked up a large number of artifacts. He also led teams of divers to survey and document the remains of the wreck. According to law, the remains of *Tulip* and all artifacts associated with the ship still belong to the U.S. Navy. The Naval Historical Center cooperated with the Maryland Historical Trust in supporting the survey and the eventual recovery of many of the artifacts that had been hidden away for years in garages and attics. This was a truly remarkable event, in which happenstance, wreck-looting, historical research, nautical archaeology, and state and federal cooperation resulted in a beneficial reconstruction of the past.[28]

THE FINAL EPISODE IN THE PART the bay played in the Civil War occurred during the crisis that followed the assassination of President Lincoln. Actor John Wilkes Booth hatched a bold plot, which included attempts on the lives of Vice President Andrew Johnson, Secretary of War Edward Stanton, and Secretary of State William Seward. Booth carried out his part with the murder of Lincoln in Ford's Theater on April 14. This event galvanized the Secret Service, the army, and the navy in pursuit of Booth, who fled Washington on horseback despite a broken ankle. Secretary of the Navy Welles turned the energies of the Navy Department toward Booth's capture. His order of April 16 put the Potomac Flotilla on notice: "To prevent the escape of the assassin who killed the President and attempted the life of the Secretary of State, search every vessel that arrives down the bay." When five of the suspects were captured the next day, Welles repeated his orders, adding, "Detain all suspicious persons. Guard against all crossing of the river and touching of vessels or boats on the Virginia shore." To Radm. Samuel P. Lee at Hampton Roads, he ordered: "Send any vessels that may be unemployed to blockade eastern shore of Virginia and Maryland coast from Point Lookout to Baltimore."[29]

Booth and his friend David E. Herold fled southward along the left bank of the Potomac River. They found medical assistance at the home of Dr. John Mudd in Charles County. Then Booth and Herold got help from Thomas Jones, the head of a Confederate spy network in Maryland. He obtained the use of a skiff and helped them set off across the Potomac River near Mathias Point. Theirs was not an easy crossing. Contrary currents sent the skiff back to the Maryland shore on the first effort, and it was not until April 22 that the pair reached the Virginia shore. With some assistance they crossed the Northern Neck and the Rappahannock River, and they hid in a tobacco barn on John Garrett's farm near Port Royal, where federal troops found them four days later. When Booth refused to surrender, the troops set fire to the barn and shot him as he attempted to escape. Herold and Booth's body were brought to the Washington Navy Yard to be incarcerated in the hold of USS *Montauk,* where the surgeon Dr. William F. May positively identified Booth's body. Herold and the other suspects (with the exception of John Surratt) in the assassination conspiracy were tried and sentenced at the Arsenal Penitentiary (now Fort McNair) on June 30. Four of them, including Herold, were hanged on July 7, 1865.

At the war's end, the navy reduced the Potomac Flotilla to half strength, on May 3, 1865, and on July 31 Cdr. Foxhall Parker sent the following message to his men:

> My heart is filled with Pride when I reflect upon the past and remember the taking up of the torpedoes from the Rappahannock with the destruction or capture of the whole rebel force engaged in placing them there, thereby making Fredericksburg a secure base of supplies for General Grant's vast army, the burning of the schooners at Mattox Creek under severe musketry fire of the enemy and almost daily expeditions up the rivers, in the creeks, and through the marshes of the northern neck of Virginia all requiring skill and nerve—I can truly say "the Potomac Flotilla has not been unmindful of the traditional honor and glory of the Navy."[30]

Chapter Six

Oysters, Crabs, Fish, and Watermen

≈≈≈≈≈≈≈≈≈≈≈≈≈≈≈≈≈≈≈≈≈≈≈≈≈≈≈≈≈≈≈

Oysters have been a primary food source in the Maryland Chesapeake since prehistoric times. Seventeenth-century documents point to Indians harvesting Chesapeake Bay oysters the size of dinner plates. They grew in huge clusters so large on the seabed of the bay and its rivers that they formed reefs and were a danger to navigation. But oysters were not then considered the delicacy they have become in recent times. Baltimore city directories, in references to oystermen, oyster houses, and taverns offering oysters in the early 1800s, show that many were familiar with them, but there were no wholesale dealers, packers, canners, or shippers. At the same time, in New England, oysters, particularly those from Connecticut, were very popular. The catch of oysters in New Haven in 1811 was nearly half a million bushels.[1]

Even before the Civil War, Maryland's small oystering industry had been under pressure to accommodate increased demand and competition from other states in obtaining their product. Oyster boats hauling dredges across the oyster beds could produce many more bushels per day than could tonging methods. Both Maryland and Virginia legislatures passed laws prohibiting the dredging of oysters; Maryland went further and forbade shipments of oysters out of state, except by Marylanders. These laws were difficult to enforce, though some arrests were made. Despite this, Connecticut and New York watermen from Long Island Sound brought dredges to the Chesapeake in the 1830s, and New York and New England packinghouses soon established oyster packinghouses in Baltimore. The growth of railroads linking the East Coast to midwestern cities provided new markets for Chesapeake oysters during the 1840s and 1850s.

The first Baltimore oyster packer was Edward Wright from Kent County, on the Eastern Shore, who established his plant in 1831. In 1842, he first advertised his firm as a "preparer of oysters for export," at about the time the heat-processing method of canning had become commercially viable. The first financially successful oyster packing and shipping firm in Baltimore was that of Daniel Holt and Caleb Maltby, both Connecticut men, who shipped their oysters on the Baltimore and Ohio Railroad to Pittsburgh and points beyond as "The Western Oyster Line." Another who followed this pattern was Abiathar Field, from Massachusetts, who may have originated the term *cove oysters,* and his brand name "A. Field's Cove Oysters" became a standard in the field. William B. Burke, an immigrant Irishman who once drove wagons for Holt and Burke, set up his own firm, with agencies stretching from North Carolina to Tennessee. William Numsen and Sons became another successful packer, adopting the "hermetically sealed" commercial canning process made popular by Thomas Kensett II (1814–77), who arrived in Baltimore from New York in 1849. He pioneered using tin cans instead of wide-mouthed jars in the canning process. Soon afterward, can manufacturing became a basic industry in Baltimore, as others followed Kensett's example. He came to dominate the industry and bought out Abiathar Field's business in 1866 for $50,000.

During the 1860s, oyster canning went through several phases of improvement as the canners experimented with methods to heat the contents more rapidly and sterilize them more effectively. The discovery of gold in California and the Civil War were major developments, both of which dislocated the industry at first and then stimulated increased demand. At the onset of the Civil War, there were more than sixty oyster-packing firms on Baltimore city wharves.[2] In 1865, the Assembly enacted a new oystering law that permitted dredging from September 1 to June 1 in certain areas, primarily along Chesapeake's main channel. Thus, the central part of the bay was opened up for extensive harvesting, while shoreline areas were protected for tonging. The state also tried to encourage the planting of seed oysters ("bedding") in barren shoreline areas.[3]

After the Civil War, a depression pushed prices down and prompted some packers to short the process, offering far less than 16 ounces of oysters in a 16-ounce can. It was in opposition to this tendency that the Union Oyster Company organized in New England and the Middle Atlantic states in 1878. They reformed and organized the oyster-packing industry and gained members with an emphasis on honesty in labeling. Another industry leader arrived in Baltimore during the mid-1870s. Alfred E. Booth and son came from Chicago after the "Great Fire" and set up an oyster-canning business that set high standards in weight and quality. Raw shucked oysters became very popular within the city and raw oyster bars flourished, giving work to more than three thousand black oyster shuckers. The 1870s and 1880s saw a high total volume in the oystering, shucking, and packing businesses, with the years 1873–74 and 1885 showing the highest production of oysters, at 14 million and 15 million bushels, respectively. Entire trains with millions of oyster cans steamed westward on a daily basis. But this could not last forever. The overharvesting of the bay's oysters soon took its toll. By 1890, production had dropped to 10 million bushels per year, and by the 1900s, production ranged between 5 and 6 million bushels.

Despite this precipitous decline, Maryland, at the turn of the century, led all other states in the canning of oysters and provided half the United States' total of canned oysters. Oysters and other seafood products were in great demand not only in the United States but also in China, Japan, and Europe. On Chesapeake Bay, the most visible result of the demand for Maryland seafood had been the growth of major processing centers at Crisfield, Deal's Island, Cambridge, Rock Hall, Solomons, Annapolis, and Baltimore. The extension of railroads down the Eastern and Western shores to almost all the major steamboat and fishing ports opened new sources of supply to meet the growing demand for seafood of all varieties. John Crisfield, president of the Eastern Shore Railroad, had the vision to sense a bonanza in the demand for oysters and acquired rights of way to the town of Somer's Cove. Crisfield's line, for example, opened up in 1866, enabling the more rapid transit of oysters and crabs from the Chesapeake to regional and national markets. By 1872, Somer's Cove had become the town of Crisfield, with the largest oyster trade in Maryland, servicing some six hundred oyster vessels.[4]

There were social consequences of prosperity, competition, and greed in the oystering fields. One of the most famous events of Maryland's maritime heritage was the outbreak of the "oyster wars" in the 1870s. The oyster dredgers on the Eastern Shore were an unruly and lawless band that had its own sense of vigilante justice. In the entire business there were perhaps fifty-six hundred men in some seven hundred boats. To control the situation, the state established in 1868 what became known as the oyster police. A Kent Island man named Hunter Davidson, a former officer in the Confederate States Navy, was in charge. Davidson's flagship was a side-wheel steamer, while his deputies sailed on board twelve sloops and patrolled local creeks, straits, and points. He sought his nemesis, a pirate named Gus Rice, who always seemed to escape when he had to. The oystermen largely kept ahead of the game. The oyster police were a relatively harmless political entity, but in the early 1870s, fights broke out between oystermen from Maryland and Virginia in Pocomoke Sound and on the Potomac, where the boundary between the states was on the Virginia side of the Potomac. In other words, Maryland owned the river and the oyster beds beneath. A joint bistate commission took five years to come to an agreement in 1877 about a line to be drawn, from Smith's Point on the lower Potomac and to Watkins Point on the Pocomoke.

In 1883 shooting again broke out on the bay when Marylanders saw that the Virginia police were not enforcing the laws on their competitors. Maryland oystermen shot up the Virginia police schooner *Tangier* at Smith Island. Virginia, in retaliation, strengthened its maritime patrol force and put stiff penalties into effect. Finally, in 1894, the U.S. Supreme Court ordered a division of Pocomoke Sound between the two states. Still, violence broke out from time to time. Meanwhile, severe dredging in the bay had taken its toll. The wonderful oyster harvests of the 1870s were not to be repeated. Instead of 15 million bushels per year, the oystermen were reaping but 10 million in 1890. At the same time, a dwindling supply of oysters made competition even fiercer, and it was reported that several men a week were killed as dredgers fought pitched battles with the marine police. New laws were passed after 1900 to punish oyster poachers and increase the number of marine police. The Maryland Assembly passed a law in 1906 to establish a Shellfish Commission to govern oyster seedbeds in the Chesapeake and to survey areas most useful for oystering. Thus began a trend toward the scientific management of the oyster industry in the twentieth century. The commission embarked on a six-year survey of the natural oyster bars of the state in cooperation with the U.S. Coast and Geodetic Survey. The *Maryland Oyster Survey* was implemented under the control of C. C. Yates, who later published a series of important, extensive reports on the distribution of oyster beds in different regions of the bay. This

work supplemented earlier work done by an Oyster Commission in 1882–84 and that completed by F. Winslow in 1884, entitled "Present Condition and Future Prospects of the Oyster Industry." The *Maryland Oyster Survey* was the last extensive study of the Maryland oyster bars until the 1970s. While a recent report attributes the recovery of a portion of the economic strength of the oyster industry to the Yates Survey, the authors describe these efforts as "sporadic and under funded" because of the "socio-political resistance by oystermen and legislators."

The steep decline of the Maryland oyster fishery that began in the late 1880s spawned a great deal of debate, controversy, and research over the methods to be used in revitalizing the oyster industry. The oyster commissioners recommended conservation measures and a system of private oyster culture. They also recommended an annual surveying and marking of oyster grounds, the closure of oyster beds when necessary to allow for rehabilitation and growth, and the return of oyster shells to the beds to serve as culch, to which the oysters' offspring, or spat, would attach for its period of growth. These ideas were not new, having been used in other regions, such as New England, to stimulate rebirth of declining oyster harvests. Yet watermen and their political allies in the Maryland legislature over many years have

Watermen tonging in log canoe, ca. 1900. Courtesy, Chesapeake Bay Maritime Museum, Z6.509.PP8.547.

The motorized log canoe *Flo-Mar* moored to the footbridge on Cherry Street, St. Michaels. The bugeye *Bride* is on the right, with oystermen's canoes in the background. Photo by Thomas H. Sewell, 1910. Courtesy, Chesapeake Bay Maritime Museum, 709–2.

distrusted and derided scientific approaches to the problem. Oystermen in Maryland have traditionally opposed private oyster culture, even though in other areas it has proven to be more productive. They also are wary of the monopolistic control of oyster beds that might occur if oyster-packing corporations gained control of private oystering beds. Further, oystermen opposed the planting of spat on anything but natural oyster bars, as they did not believe spat would be productive on barren ground. If oysters did result somehow from such a practice, then, they would argue, the ground was probably not barren in the first place and should not have been restricted to private cultivation.[5] In the intervening seventy years since the Yates Commission report, some efforts have been made to lease oyster grounds, but the acreage under cultivation is minimal; in 1983, for example, 651 leaseholders controlled 9,000 acres of bay bottom, or about 3 percent of the 279,000 acres of the oyster ground reserved for private or public use, thanks to "the political influence of oystermen and tidewater politicians."[6]

There was evident tension between the scientific community and the watermen and their allies in the Maryland legislature, but scientific research continued in the 1930s with the construction of the Chesapeake Biological Laboratory and the establishment of a 1,000-acre oyster farm in the Honga River, on the Eastern Shore. Dr. R. V. Truitt's experimentation with oyster larvae in a badly overharvested area demonstrated the utility of properly managed shell planting. Yet, despite Truitt's recommendations that the experimentation continue, the state turned the area over to public use as a tonging bar, to the detriment of the seed program and the potential of the area for rehabilitation.[7]

During the post–World War II era, as oyster harvests continued to decline, increased emphasis on experimentation with cultivation on state or private grounds yielded improved production of about sixty bushels per acre, whereas oysters taken

Oystermen selling their catch to the schooner *Kate McNamara* off Ashcroft Point, near St. Michaels, in 1905. Photo by Thomas H. Sewell. Courtesy, Chesapeake Bay Maritime Museum, 708–18.

from public grounds were averaging only six bushels per acre. This represents progress, but increased cooperation has also resulted from increased alarm over the continued diminution of the oyster population due to diseases. By the 1980s, an annual shell-planting program was put in place whereby the state contracted with oystermen for transporting fresh spat-carrying shell from seed areas and replanting on public oyster grounds. This arrangement has evolved over several decades, as a result of improved interaction between oystermen, politicians, state bureaucrats, and marine biologists.

In an article written for the *Washington Post* in 1998, Cheryl Lyn Dybas reviewed the oyster industry, particularly from the watermen's point of view. She touched upon the life of the oyster from conception through the dredging process on board the skipjack *Kathryn,* owned by Capt. Russell Dize. She quoted Dize as saying that in the late 1970s he and his crew normally harvested about one hundred fifty bushels per day, which was the limit. Now, in the late 1990s, Dize said they would be lucky to reach one hundred thirty bushels per day, which would bring $23 per bushel. Dybas also quoted Dorothy Leonard, a former director of fisheries at the Maryland Department of Natural Resources, now at the University of Maryland's Horn Point Environmental Laboratory near Cambridge. There, scientists hoped to increase the oyster catches by working through the Oyster Roundtable, whose members include representatives of state regulatory agencies, watermen, environmentalists, and marine biologists who collaborate to restock the bay with spat. Each year millions of spat have been introduced to the bay's major tributaries, such as the Patuxent, the Choptank, and the Severn rivers. The main enemies of these young oysters are the diseases MSX and "Dermo." MSX is a parasite that prevails in the more saline stretches of the bay. Dermo is a bacterium that is nearly always present but does not affect the oysters unless they are stressed. Yet, Dermo can operate in

Tonger on a deadrise workboat peering at the ice he will have to work against as he probes for oysters. Photo by Robert de Gast, 1970. Courtesy, Chesapeake Bay Maritime Museum, 975–7004–5T.

waters with low salinity, so it is more prevalent than MSX. The oysters generally do better in the northern part of the bay and its tributaries, where the water is less salty. It would take an optimist to say things are getting better for the oystermen, but the state is making major efforts to improve the health of the bay and its oysters, although it has been, and will be, a long, difficult battle.

The big question facing those who would increase oyster production is whether the introduction of a non-native Asian species (*Crassostrea ariakensis*) to the Chesapeake Bay would save the oyster industry or create more problems in the marine environment. This Asian species could conceivably bring with it undesirable consequences. To give an idea of how urgent the situation is, Maryland's production of oysters in 1987–88 dropped to 363,000 bushels, and then things got worse. The harvest amounted to an average of only 104,000 bushels per year from 2002 to 2006.

This crisis has awakened national attention. In 2000, the states of Maryland and Virginia, the District of Columbia, the Chesapeake Bay Commission, and the U.S. Environmental Protection Agency signed an agreement that called for an effort to produce a tenfold increase in native oysters in the bay by 2010, measured from a 1994 baseline. The goal is to create a strategy to restore the bay's oyster population to a level that would support harvests comparable to those of the period 1920–69, when watermen were reaping upwards of 2.5 million bushels per year, and to the period 1970–2002, when harvests averaged 1.3 million bushels.[8] The methods to be used include improvement in water quality, reduction of oyster harvesting in certain areas, continued depositing of shells to rebuild reef structures, and experimentation with non-native oysters to see if they could not just survive, but thrive, in the waters of Chesapeake Bay. In fact, this last seems to have become the preferred approach with Maryland and Virginia policy makers. But the scientists did

not agree. To resolve the issue, Congress responded to a National Research Council (National Academy of Sciences) report, entitled Non-native Oysters in the Chesapeake Bay, by requesting that the U.S. Army Corps of Engineers develop an Environmental Impact Statement (EIS) on the proposal to introduce non-native oysters and create a scientific advisory body to review the sufficiency of the EIS. Congress instructed the corps also to study all the alternatives, including restoration of native oyster species.[9]

Watermen culling their oyster catch, ca. 1970. Photo by Robert de Gast. Courtesy, Chesapeake Bay Maritime Museum, 975–70004–2–23.

The introduction of a fast-growing, disease-resistant East Asian oyster might lead to a restored Chesapeake oyster industry and a cleaner bay, but there are potential risks. The non-native species could bring with them new shellfish diseases, which could spread through and outside of the region. They could also outcompete the native Chesapeake oyster, bringing the ultimate deathblow to the *Crassostrea virginica*. Thus, there are no guarantees that this particular strategy will work, so scientists are working very deliberately to test the Asian oyster's ability to grow in laboratories. As of late 2005, the Department of Natural Resources cautiously predicted that scientists would soon have the results of their experiments so that policy makers could make a decision by the end of 2006.[10] But, according to researcher Dr. Mark Luckenbach, of the Virginia Institute of Marine Science, there is still a great deal of uncertainty about species identification, competitive interactions, the introduction of new diseases, and reef-building capabilities. As of 2007, he stated, "current knowledge suggests that the most likely outcome of a large-scale introduction [of Asian oysters] would be neither panacea nor Pandora."[11] Thus, for Maryland and Virginia policy makers and watermen, the long period of waiting continues, as scientists try to make sure their recommendations are scientifically defensible. The complexity of the issues regarding the introduction of non-native species and the disagreement of many scientists with the main thrust of the EIS have led to continued postponements of the final report.[12]

The oyster buyboat *Island Star* at Crisfield, 1989. Photo by Richard Dodds. Courtesy, Chesapeake Bay Maritime Museum, 760–40.

Meanwhile, the State of Maryland is working to increase the number of native oysters that can be harvested. The University of Maryland's Horn Point Center for Environmental Science Laboratory rears oysters in a hatchery that, since 2000, has resulted in the planting of an estimated 1.4 billion oysters on 1,100 acres of formerly productive oyster reefs. Gov. Martin O'Malley announced, in September 2008, that the state had developed a pilot program involving a partnership with waterfront property owners living along the Tred Avon River to assist in growing the oysters. The idea is that each of 250 property owners will place four oyster cages off their piers, and then, after nine to twelve months, the oysters will be placed in a protected sanctuary in the river. The organizations involved in this experiment are the University of Maryland Center for Environmental Science, the Maryland Department of Natural Resources, Talbot County, the Oyster Recovery Partnership of the Maryland Department of Public Safety and Correctional Services, and the Chesapeake Bay Trust, which provided the funding. To be effective, of course, this effort will have to be accompanied by a rigorous drive to eradicate oyster disease and sources of pollution in the bay.[13]

On the Western Shore, the Chesapeake Bay Foundation (CBF) has established a Maryland Oyster Restoration Center, located at Discovery Village in Shady Side, Maryland. Their scientists are conducting experiments with oyster gardening, and they provide educational outreach to explain the value of oyster reefs as water filters and fish habitats. Their oyster restoration vessel *Patricia Campbell* is a state-of-the-art seeding vessel, which, in one deployment, transferred 3.1 million oysters to a sanctuary reef north of Broome's Island in the Patuxent River. The CBF also has a branch on Virginia's Lynnhaven River, where it has restored the river to 30 percent of its former production levels and where it has ex-

perimented in the growing of sterile oysters, which put energy into growth rather than reproduction.[14]

≈≈≈

NEXT TO OYSTERS, the Chesapeake blue crab is Maryland's most famous product. The Maryland part of the Chesapeake is almost perfect for the crab's breeding ground. From the time of Chesapeake explorer Capt. John Smith until our own times, the crab has been included along with culinary seafood specialties. Yet it was not a commercial enterprise until the nineteenth century. As William Warner has said, "catching crabs was but an occasional or leisure time activity, something to keep the pot full in idle summer months, and only the unregenerate would do it on Sundays."[15] The reason for this is that crabs were too perishable to be shipped out of the local area. In the latter half of the nineteenth century, as the industrial revolution arrived on the Eastern Shore, this began to change. Regular steamboat traffic crisscrossed Chesapeake Bay and extended up Maryland's many winding rivers, and in 1866 a railroad magnate, John Crisfield, extended a rail link into the richest crabbing grounds on Chesapeake Bay at Somers Cove, whose name was changed to Crisfield. Finally, development of the ice machine enabled packers and shippers to ship crabs in nearly fresh condition to distant locations.[16]

In the Chesapeake, crabs sought for personal consumption are often caught

Smith Island crabbing skiff getting a washdown at Oxford, 1925. Howard I. Chapelle Collection, Courtesy, Chesapeake Bay Maritime Museum, 901253.

with a mesh dipping net on a long pole while the crabber is fishing from a pier or working his way slowly along the marshes in a small boat. The oldest commercial method of catching crabs was to use the trotline. These are made from strong cotton or nylon line ranging from 1,000 feet to nearly a mile long. The lines are baited with pieces of salted eel about five inches long that are tied with slipknots from every one to five feet along the trotline. The waterman lays down his trotline in the early morning, marking each end with distinctively colored plastic milk jugs or bleach bottles, which can be easily recognized. He then returns and lifts the opposite end of the line with a dip net and places it on a roller attached to a washboard on his boat. As the boat proceeds, the trotline runs over the roller while the waterman stands ready with a wire dip net to catch crabs as they come to the surface clinging to the bait. The waterman runs the length of the line several times, as long as the bait lasts. He then collects the line and heads for home, where he will rebait the line for the next day. Most recreational boaters have learned to avoid crossing in front of a waterman running his trotline.

When Benjamin Lewis, a Virginia waterman, invented and patented a wire crab pot in 1938, he made life easier for those who could earn a living crabbing. This "pot" was really a trap, and it allowed watermen to dispense with dipping nets and tending trotlines. This invention was major factor in the development of commercial crabbing in the bay. For more than twenty years, from 1938 to 1959, Daniel Barrett Sr. ran a "crab house" on Hellen Creek off the Patuxent River. In 1946, he also patented a design for a crab steamer, which allowed the sale of cooked "steam crabs" with a spicy seasoning. With fifty crab pickers, Barrett's firm processed nearly

a million pounds of crabmeat per season. An experienced picker could process sixty to seventy pounds of crabmeat per day, but it was exploitive work. While the price of crabmeat had tripled between 1920 and 1940, the picker's wages remained very low, at five cents per pound, only two cents per pound more than it had been in 1890. When the navy began construction of the Patuxent River Naval Air Station in 1942, the day-labor wages offered outbid by far the meager wages offered at crab-picking houses. Many young people, especially blacks who labored in the low-paying crab-picking industry, left southern Maryland to find better jobs.[17]

Marylanders extended efforts to expand soft-shell harvests by building crab pounds. In these underwater structures, the hard crabs would shed their shells for a period of three to four days. Wooden lath cages that allowed water to circulate while not overly disturbing the molting crabs within were constructed. Still, this method proved rather too tedious for some, and a fellow named L. Cooper Dize, from Crisfield, developed the "crab scrape." It resembles a lightweight oyster dredge, with a submersible frame for a long bag made of twine and a smooth bottom bar. Use of the crab scrape is frequent, particularly in the shallower reaches of the bay, as are found on the lower Eastern Shore. It is similar to an oyster dredge although smaller and lighter. Typically, it is constructed using a welded-iron bar shaped into a triangle, so that the upper and lower bars hold open a light nylon mesh net. The waterman lowers the scrape into the water and then drags it over the bot-

"Pot pie" style deadrise skiff built by George Jackson on the marine railway at Jackson's former boatyard in St. Michaels in 1987. Photo by Richard Dodds, Courtesy, Chesapeake Bay Maritime Museum, 723–3.

tom. Instead of biting in, it slides over the seabed, and the lower, smooth bar tips up the crabs and scoops them into the net trailing behind. This method is especially good for finding soft crabs hiding in eelgrass.

The most widespread device for catching hard crabs is the crab "pot." The name may have descended from the Cornish (England) pots, bent willow and hazel stick baskets that resemble flowerpots. At any rate, the American version is a far cry from that and is designed to trap the agile and clear-sighted blue crab. Chesapeake crab pots measure about 24 inches square and are made from 2¼-inch wire mesh anchored to one side of an iron frame, which keeps the pot upright in the water. It also contains a bait box, approximately 10 inches by 4 inches, to hold alewives, which lure the crab in and lead it into a church, or lower area, from which escape is difficult. The pot is attached to a forty-foot line attached to a float or buoy, which is scooped up from the waterman's workboat as he makes his early morning run to check his crab pots. The most valued crabs are the soft crabs. Hard crabs that have begun the process of shedding their shells as they grow are called *peelers*. Crabs that are entering this stage seek out marsh grass or eelgrass for protection, and different techniques must be used to catch them. Soft crabs can be caught with dip nets or scrapes. Peelers caught by the usual means must be transferred to crab floats tied alongside piers until they become soft. Then they should be harvested quickly, lest they spoil.

A difference emerged between Maryland and Virginia as to which state's crabs were the most sought after. Crabs flourished in the saltier waters of the lower bay, and Virginia's watermen went after the hard crabs, while Maryland's crabbers invested most of their efforts in the more difficult-to-market soft-shelled crabs. The first crab cannery on Chesapeake Bay was James McMenamin's, established in Norfolk in 1878, while the first crab cannery in Maryland was set up in Oxford in 1900. As the oyster fishery diminished in the 1920s, many Chesapeake watermen shifted their attention to commercial crabbing. Patuxent River packinghouses, such as Warren Denton & Company, handled 12,000 to 24,000 crabs per day, packing them in ice and sending them on steamboats to Norfolk and Baltimore. Another Patuxent River firm, J. C. Lore & Sons, located at Solomons Island, began packing fresh crabmeat in 1922 and continued through World War II. Crabbing became more lucrative in the late 1930s, as the Depression eased and prices rose to triple those of the 1920s.

The Chesapeake Bay crabbing industry has been under increasing pressure in recent years. The bay's crab population has declined greatly. Mick Blackistone, a professional waterman who became a nationally known spokesman for watermen, has sounded a pessimistic warning that crabs may become an endangered species. He reported that throughout the 1990s, the Chesapeake catch averaged 42 million pounds per year. This includes the difficult-to-estimate harvest by noncommercial crabbers (chicken neckers).[18] Seven years later, watermen were having even more trouble making a living because of higher gasoline costs, the rising price of bait, and government restrictions. With warmer waters to contend with, the crabbers have to follow the migration as crabs move north to cooler locations, such as the Sassafras River. The rising cost of steel wire for making crab pots is another factor that is

driving higher the price of crabmeat for the public, whether in restaurants or in seafood markets. In an interview reported in the *Annapolis Sunday Capital,* Bob Evans, president of the Anne Arundel Waterman's Association, said that crabbing has gotten to the point where it doesn't pay. He has to gross $160,000 annually to obtain a net profit of $30,000, after taking care of his overhead, fuel, and bait expenses. Scientists expected that crabbers should have been able to harvest 28 million pounds of crabs in 2007, but the total was only 21.8 million pounds. That sounds like a lot, but it's not enough to meet the public demand for the popular blue crab. At Buddy's Crabs and Ribs restaurant in Annapolis, customers consume from fifty to eighty bushels of crabs per week in the summer months.[19] To help protect the crab population, the Maryland Department of Natural Resources limits the number of crabbing permits issued each year, insists that watermen must take one day off per week, and allows them to put out nine hundred pots per boat, but these must have cull rings to allow smaller crabs (those less than five inches long) to escape.[20]

Smith Island crab scrape *Margaret H.* at Ewell, Smith Island, July 1991. Photo by Richard Dodds. Courtesy, Chesapeake Bay Maritime Museum, 785–17.

≈≈≈

THE GREAT VALUE OF CHESAPEAKE BAY has been its various uses as a means of transportation, a source of food for local and regional populations, a location for water-borne recreation, and a source of earnings by those who work it and those who provide related services, such as marketers of its products. The essential problem in tracing the history of the Chesapeake finfisheries is a paucity of historical information regarding the health of the many species that used to be abundant in the bay. Thanks to action by the governors of Maryland, Pennsylvania, and Virginia, the situation has improved during the past twenty years with the publication of reports of tristate regional commissions established in the early 1980s. Helpful, too, are the reports of the U.S. Fish and Wildlife Service. More than two hundred species of fish have been reported in Chesapeake Bay over the years. Among the most prolific are shad, alewife, menhaden, blueback herring, white perch, striped bass, bluefish, butterfish spot, croaker, weakfish, flounder, and sturgeon. Early English settlers observed Native Americans using weirs made of reeds, wooden spears, and hooks fashioned out of bone to catch the fish they needed. The colonists brought seines from England but were inexpert in their use and generally copied the Indians' style of catching fish in quantity. Other methods they developed were trolling, casting nets, setting nets, hand fishing, and using long lines. By the use of haul seines, they dragged huge quantities of herring to shore. They salted the catch and in this way provided dependable food for many weeks and months.[21]

Commercial pound net fishing was well known along the Atlantic coast before it arrived in Maryland in 1858, but it did not prove successful until the 1870s. According to local lore, the critical year was 1875, when New Englander George Snediker arrived in the bay and chose to set the first pound of its type in Virginia's Mobjack Bay. Using long sharpened stakes made of young spruce, Snediker worked them into the deep bay sediment in a line perpendicular to the shore and then by stages set other stakes at angles to the first line, creating a fish trap. After fishnets were draped on the stakes, the fish would swim toward the center of an elaborate maze from which they were unable to escape. This method was so successful that the local farmers, who also fished part-time but less successfully, became jealous and proprietary about their fishing grounds. To make their point, they cut down Snediker's carefully constructed pound nets and made it clear that his sort was unwelcome in Mobjack Bay. Snediker left for the Eastern Shore, but not before selling the remainder of his stakes and nets to a local farmer. Before long, pound nets were in use throughout the Chesapeake.[22] It is estimated that, by 1888, there were about six hundred pound nets in Maryland, trapping many different species. Pound nets, by 1920, accounted for 68 percent of fish harvested in the Maryland Chesapeake.[23]

Maryland fishermen traditionally, from colonial times, have also used haul seining as way to catch large numbers of fish. Although little used commercially in recent years, haul seining was popular in the 1940s and 1950s, particularly in the Patuxent River area. The fishermen used vast lengths of netting with weights on the bottom and floats on the top of the nets, usually operating from shore, with one end fixed and the other attached to a boat, moving out, around, and back toward shore to surround the fish. The men then hauled the net, by either hand or power winch, in toward shore. The bunt, or baggy midsection, of the net would then contain most of the haul of fish. The men would then use dip nets to transfer the fish into boxes or another boat for shipment to a packing plant. It is estimated that more than five million pounds of fish were harvested by this method in the Patuxent River from

1944 to 1950. Although all types of fish could be harvested in this way, certainly rockfish (striped bass) were one of the most profitable catches.[24]

An alternative to haul seining was the gill-net method of fishing. Although less important from the commercial perspective, gill nets are being used more widely because they are less costly to purchase and maintain and, because they involve less massive netting, they can be worked by one person. The gill net is set across the predicted path of schools of fish. The gill nets are normally 6 to 10 feet in height and 100 yards long. The size of the mesh is critical to the type and size of fish being caught, the purpose being to entrap the fish by the gills in the mesh, not allowing the body to pass through. The preferred type of line used in the netting is twisted nylon, which the fish cannot detect. The finer nylon monofilament netting is prohibited for use in the Chesapeake. Gill-net operations can be done using stationary stakes, anchored nets in deeper waters, or drifting nets, which can be pulled behind a boat. The practical side of the gill net is that it can be adjusted for the type and size of fish wanted; the smaller fish can swim through without being trapped.

A variant of net fishing in Maryland is use of the fyke net, made to be cylindrical, with round hoops about three to four feet in diameter and funnel-shaped netting about ten to twelve feet long. The fyke is attached to a leader net that runs perhaps fifty yards to shore. Thus, the fish will swim along the shore and along the leader into the fyke net's funnels, where they are trapped in the chamber. The fisherman will put a bait of menhaden or crushed clams along the leader, to whet the appetite of the targeted fish, and also deep in the chamber. Usually, these nets are not in use during the summer, when they would attract crabs as well as fish. Fyke netting is a favorite business on the Sassafras River of the northern Eastern Shore, whose fishermen are likely harvesting catfish live for shipment to the midwestern states, where farmers need them to stock their ponds.[25]

One of the historic mysteries of the Chesapeake fisheries has been the virtual disappearance of the famous shad as a commercial catch. This once prolific fish used to run in great numbers in Maryland's rivers, but now the shad population is but a shadow of its former dominance in the fishery. In the early twentieth century, fishermen landed close to 50 million pounds along the Atlantic coast. By 1980 that catch had declined to 3.8 million pounds, with Maryland taking only 25,000 pounds, and it was in that year that the state declared a moratorium on shad fishing. It took Virginia another four years to make a similar decision. Since that time the Atlantic States Marine Fisheries Commission (ASMFC) has made a major effort to urge collective action by states in restocking shad and in limiting the commercial ocean fishing of shad. The states that shape the Chesapeake drainage basin—Pennsylvania, Virginia, Delaware, and Maryland—launched hatchery operations to produce shad for release in their rivers. After much persuasion and argument, the utilities that control the Conowingo Dam built fish lifts at a cost of $10 million to facilitate the migration of shad and other species up the Susquehanna to their spawning grounds. However, in the most recent survey (2008), only 19,912 shad were counted at the dam, the lowest number since 1997. There are also three other dams on the Susquehanna that the fish had to pass before reaching free waters. This made it extremely difficult for the shad to reach the quality nursery and spawning

Oysters, Crabs, Fish, and Watermen

habitat of the upper reaches of the river; only twenty-one shad were able to get past the fourth dam, at York Haven. Even the fish hatcheries in other states are having problems getting the fish to produce enough eggs to reproduce in great numbers for the Susquehanna hatchery. This is true of the Hudson and the Delaware rivers, and the shad runs in Virginia's James and York rivers are trending down, despite that state's efforts to stock shad.

The one bright spot seems to be the Potomac, where there has been a small but notable increase in shad runs in the last fifteen years. According to the Interstate Commission on the Potomac River, this may be the result of their efforts to clean up the Potomac, allowing underwater grasses to flourish, and to open a fish way at the Little Falls dam, which allows shad to reach a protected spawning area, away from natural predators. The Potomac, during the nineteenth century, was the scene of tremendous shad runs; the catches ran as high as 20 million fish per year at their peak in the 1880s. This makes the shad runs of recent years look paltry indeed. Fisheries experts at the ASMFC and the Chesapeake Bay Foundation have speculated that the rebounding of the striped bass (rockfish) population may be in part due to their feeding on shad small fry as well as menhaden. Also, the degree to which shad in the Atlantic have been diminished as bycatch in other fisheries could be a factor, but the degree to which this is so is unknown.[26]

The strange-looking Atlantic sturgeon is another rare fish, a throwback to those that swam in the bays and oceans during the ice ages. Bony plates cover its head, and thick, armor-like scales protect its body. Sturgeon are known to have grown to enormous sizes, as long as fifteen feet and weighing eight hundred pounds, but they are now rarely found in Chesapeake Bay. They prefer fresh water for spawning and stay in the rivers until late fall. Their young do not start to migrate, and then singly, until about five years old. Generally bottom dwellers, they use a soft mouth without teeth to bottom feed for worms, crustaceans, and small fish. Their only enemies seem to be sharks and humans. Gourmets of the world prize the sturgeon not only for its meat but especially for its eggs, prepared as caviar and preferably consumed with a fine champagne. When sturgeons were plentiful they were sought in the Hudson, Susquehanna, and Delaware rivers, as well as the major Western Shore rivers of Chesapeake Bay. Fishermen captured them using gill nets 1,500 feet long, 21 feet deep, and with mesh gaps measuring 13 inches. At their most successful in the late nineteenth century, sturgeon fishermen, on a national basis, landed up to 7 million pounds per year. But by the 1920s, the catch was down to 22,000 pounds. In Chesapeake Bay, similarly, sturgeon landings in the 1890s came to 700,000 pounds, but in the 1990s, only 2,200 pounds were caught. In 1998, the Atlantic States Marine Fisheries Commission took drastic action and, in a desperate move to save the fishery, forbade sturgeon fishing for the next forty years. Beyond this, hatcheries are at work to try to restore the Chesapeake sturgeon, releasing thousands of infant sturgeon in the Nanticoke River.[27]

One of the most popular fish in home kitchens and restaurants along the East Coast is the striped bass (called *rockfish* in the Chesapeake region), so-called because of the seven or eight dark stripes that run from head to tail along its silvery body. These fish spawn in fresh water at the heads of the streams and rivers that flow into

Chesapeake Bay, the Delaware River, the Hudson River, and the North Carolina rivers and then migrate to salt water. Known for their strength and fighting ability, striped bass are prized by recreational fishermen. So popular was this fish that in the 1970s the record commercial catch was 14.7 million pounds; ten years later, that catch had diminished to 1.7 million pounds. This shocking statistic, a decline of almost 90 percent, prompted Congress to call for the study that resulted in passage of the Emergency Striped Bass Act in 1979. The findings of this study pointed to toxic pollution at spawning locations, which was killing bass in the larval stage and degrading the habitat where the bass like to spawn. Their larvae like to feed on zooplankton, but this microscopic animal was suffering from high levels of chlorination found near sewage treatment and electric power plants. The food source of the striped bass was thus being contaminated. To allow this fish a chance to recover, the scientists of the U.S. Fish and Wildlife Service recommended setting limits on the size and weight of striped bass that could be caught. The State of Maryland, however, went even further and in 1985 imposed a total moratorium on fishing for striped bass. Virginia followed suit in 1989, but even this was not enough to reverse the situation. The U.S. Fish and Wildlife Service took the lead in evaluating ways to measure the health of the striped bass population. They recommended the establishment of a coastwide hatchery program and, with help from state agencies and universities, began a tagging program to determine migratory patterns. They established a database to help analyze these data for decision makers. The hatchery-reared striped bass provided managers with information about population dynamics, growth, and migratory patterns. In 1988, hatchery fish comprised nearly half of Maryland juvenile striped bass in some rivers, for example, the Patuxent. By 1989, the Maryland Department of Natural Resources recommended removal of the moratorium.

These restrictions and hatcheries measures proved highly successful. As of 2007, wild stripers far outnumber hatchery fish, but scientists will continue to evaluate the potential contribution of hatchery fish to depleted stocks. They may even have been too successful. Striped bass as predators may be a factor in the reduction of other bay species, such as the shad, which is hovering near the endangered species level.[28] According to the DNR, the striped bass population is still not clear of contamination from mycobacteriosis, an infectious wasting disease that progresses slowly and is often not visible to the naked eye.[29] Scientists first diagnosed this disease in 1977, and recent surveys have found it in as many as 60 percent of the bay's striped bass but have not detected it in other bay species. This disease, when it is transmitted to humans, is called "fish handlers' disease." The DNR website informs readers that if the bass have no outward signs of lesions, hemorrhage, or dark patches on the filets, they can be safely eaten as long as they are carefully prepared and cooked. However, anglers and fish processors should normally be wearing heavy gloves to avoid puncture wounds and should be ready to use antibiotics if persistent bumps or nodules appear under their skin.

The blueback herring and alewife are, likewise, other once-prolific Chesapeake Bay fish now suffering from environmental degradation and population decline. In colonial times, these fish were easily caught with dip nets as they made their annual spawning runs up the Potomac, Susquehanna, and other rivers. They usually returned as adults to the waters where they were born, during the spring months of April and May. The herring prefer to spawn in swift water, whereas the alewives do better in slow-moving currents. Once hatched, the juveniles move downstream until the summer months bring on more saline waters, when they move back upstream. In the fall, they swim downstream toward the sea and remain in coastal waters for three to six years, when they reach maturity. These fish are taken for a variety of reasons. In earlier times, they were salted and stored for food during the winter, and their oily backbones were used as lamp wicks. They are reputedly good for eating: pickled and smoked herring are considered a delicacy in some countries. Commercial fishermen ordinarily catch herring and resell them as crab and eel bait or fishmeal.

The species are in decline for many of the same reasons other species are in decline: overfishing, especially by foreign offshore commercial fleets, pollution in the rivers, manmade obstructions on the way to spawning grounds, and natural predators, fish as well as birds. The first decade of the twentieth century marked the high point of herring catches. In 1908, commercial landings of herring in the bay amounted to 66 million pounds. By the 1970s, the catch had declined by nearly 80 percent. To reverse the situation, state agencies must make greater efforts to clean up the waterways that serve as channels to spawning grounds, create more and better fish lifts around dams, and restock the rivers with juvenile fish from hatcheries and other rivers. This will have to be a continuous effort, not a one-time event.[30]

On Maryland's Atlantic shore, in the late 1800s, the commercial fishing business operated entirely differently than it does today. On Assateague Island there were seven fishing camps along the beach near the location of what would become Ocean City. From these camps, groups of six to eight fishermen launched surf boats to gather fish from pounds that they had built in the ocean. They went out in all sorts of weather to empty the pound nets into 35- to 40-foot boats. With their catch filling the boats, they returned to shore, beached the boats, and unloaded the fish. Thereafter, they salted the fish, to be taken by rail to cities for further processing. At the south end of Assateague Island, there was a fish factory. Fishermen in that location were near an inlet, and with sail-equipped workboats they brought in their catches to be crushed for fertilizer and oil. The workers there had crude living quarters and a dining room, but all this was swept away by the hurricane of 1933.[31]

Commercial fishing has rebounded and played an important role in Ocean City's economy ever since the hurricane surge opened the inlet from the Atlantic into Sinepuxent Bay. Rather than let nature take its course, local officials appealed to Congress for the U.S. Army Corps of Engineers to stabilize the inlet for the benefit of commercial and sports fisherman in the Ocean City, Worcester County, area. The result has been a growth in all kinds of fishing—sea scallop and ocean clam dredging, lobster and sea bass long-line fishing, and, inshore, harvesting of hard clams and blue crabs. Ocean fishing is highly regulated by both the state and the federal governments. Scallop fishermen before 2004 regularly visited a rich scalloping area about fifty miles east of Delmarva, known as Elephant Trunk because of the shape of the seabed beneath. In 2007, a report from the New England Fisheries Management Council stated that the U.S. scallop fishery is one of the most

Table 1. Recreational and commercial fish landings: United States

	Weight in Pounds	
	Recreational	Commercial
1998		
Striped bass	13,379,000	6,715,000
Bluefish	12,534,000	8,299,000
King and cero mackerel	8,305,000	5,204,000
Summer flounder	12,567,000	1,211,000
Atlantic croaker	8,120,000	25,401,000
2007		
Striped bass	22,910,000	7,147,000
Bluefish	21,558,000	7,539,000
King and cero mackerel	9,697,000	6,088,000
Summer flounder	9,810,000	9,778,000
Atlantic croaker	8,843,000	19,677,000

Table 2. Recreational and commercial fish landings: Maryland

	Weight in Pounds	
	Recreational	Commercial
1998		
Striped bass	1,908,344	43,486
Bluefish	841,921	276,009
Atlantic mackerel	13,792	—
Summer flounder	298,979	205,100
Atlantic croaker	1,150,459	89,173
2007		
Striped bass	3,178,237	991,258*
Bluefish	1,045,765	120,240
Atlantic mackerel	736[†]	16[†]
Summer flounder	312,864	176,352
Atlantic croaker	1,056,471	474,388

* Data for 2008.   [†] Data for 2003.

valuable, with landings in excess of 50 million pounds yearly and revenues in excess of $300 million per year. But because of evidence that the area was being overfished, the National Marine Fisheries Service closed down Elephant Trunk to scallopers. Their alternative is to fish inshore of the Elephant Trunk Access Area, a site not as productive, while the ETAA scallops are given a chance to recover. Hard times have arrived. The scallop fishermen do not know when the Elephant's Trunk will reopen. This poses a problem for commercial fishermen, whose operating costs have mounted with the rise in fuel prices and with the inflation of property values along the shores where they have traditionally docked their boats, landed catches, and stowed their equipment. As in Chesapeake Bay, the working watermen are being shoved aside as dockage costs rise and preferred berths are converted to recreational yacht usage. Thus, there are real questions as to whether the commercial fishermen, especially those who dredge, will be able to survive as favorite fishery areas are closed down for environmental reasons.[32]

Recreational fishing is also a very important activity on Chesapeake Bay and its tributaries, and it has had a certain impact on the bay's commercial fishermen, a concern that recreational fishermen reciprocate. The Department of Commerce's Marine Recreational Fisheries Statistics Surveys of 1998 and 2007 highlight the impact of marine angling on the fisheries (tables 1 and 2).[33] Not only have recreational and commercial harvests become smaller in recent years, but recreational fishing has a far greater impact on the commercial fishing industry than one might expect, and it contributes significantly to the income and tax base of local and state governments. These recreational anglers have influence in the state legislature and on the Department of Natural Resources regulators, and this has at times had negative effects on the income of Maryland watermen, whose livelihoods are at stake.[34]

THE WATERMEN AND THEIR FAMILIES have always been dependent on the whims of the weather, the luck of the catch, the skill of the watermen, and the health of the bay. Numerous writers have described the hard times these folk have endured and how the seasons vary, with some years bringing a fruitful harvest and others barely putting food on the table. Sometimes, the waterman down on his luck will have to go ashore to earn a living for at least part of the year. Usually, though, a waterman will shift his seafood harvesting from species to species as the seasons change, from crabs in the spring to oysters as summer blends to fall. Perhaps he will try the pound fisheries, as well. In his introduction to *Working the Bay,* Jack Greer, of the Maryland Sea Grant Program, aptly characterized the situation:

> Watermen often work alone or in small groups, spending hours, days, years, on the open water, far from the comforts of office or home. Sometimes likened to frontiersmen who roamed the American West, they are in some sense range rovers, living by their wits, and their range is the Chesapeake Bay. One should be careful not to push the comparison too far, after all, watermen generally descend from the very families that did not go west, but it is true that like the ranch hands, trappers, and buffalo hunters of the frontier, watermen have developed a rough wisdom, shaped as their skin is shaped by wind and sun, ice and rain. No wonder that as modern life becomes increasingly complicated we watch the Chesapeake's watermen with a wistful curiosity. Still using the tools of their grandfathers, products of an old ingenuity, these watermen represent, in some way, our cultural past.[35]

In *Bringing Back the Bay,* Marion Warren and his daughter, Mame Warren, an oral historian, brought to fruition a ten-year project in the images and words of the watermen, their families, and other people whose work impacts and reflects the life of the bay region. Traveling widely through Chesapeake hamlets and waterside villages, visiting with watermen in their own environments, Mame Warren elicited their thoughts even as her father photographed them at work and at rest. Some of their quotations are worth considering as one thinks about their hardy lives in the midst of the alluring yet unforgiving element on which they spend most of their time. Warren quotes Bobby McKay of St. Jerome, Maryland, a second-generation waterman: "When you go on the water it's not like farming a field. A field is yours. The water out here belongs to everybody so you can't have your own little place. So it's not much good worrying about it. You just have to get what you get." Here one senses the self-reliance and yet also the resignation with which the waterman accepts the cards that nature deals him.[36]

The watermen's families, too, are affected by the weather and the state of the catch, as Virginia Evans shows in her description of the long absences and the joyful homecomings. She was born in 1907 on Smith Island and refers to dredging for oysters in the second decade of the twentieth century in the following comment:

> Way back when my father was a'dredging, when they would leave in the fall, they wouldn't come home until Thanksgiving if it was pretty weather. If it was bad weather, they'd have to stay until Christmas. . . . Thanksgiving wasn't anything special. But Christmas, oh my! When they're expecting all the men home there's four and five cakes,

chickens and ducks—you name it, they had it. Everything was decorated, lit up like I don't know what. They'd always stay 'til after New Year's and then they'd go back and stay out until March.[37]

Watermen are very aware of the dangers out on the water. Chesapeake weather can change quickly and can wreak havoc with those who are not prepared. Watermen often operate miles from their homeports—or any port, for that matter. It can take hours to retreat to a secure, protected anchorage and ride out a storm. Larry Marsh, a Smith Islander who runs a boatyard, has also been a waterman and knows whereof he speaks:

> Every day these watermen are out you wonder if you're gonna get back. We've had some lost. It's bad. It's a tragedy around here, something like that happens. We've had two young ones get drowned that I knew in my time. Way back they'd had several drowned. Makes you wonder when you hear 'em on the radio, "Wonder if he's gonna get back today." You know if it's a real bad storm, they won't leave in it. But when you get out there and get caught in it, then that's when you've got to wonder.[38]

Large numbers of African Americans have been watermen since before the end of slavery in the United States. If a plantation was near the water, then slaves who worked the water had another way of putting food on the table. After abolition, former slaves often lacked a way to make a living in the disturbed economy of the times. For many, oystering, crabbing, and fishing was to be their way of life for an indefinite period. In the middle years of the nineteenth century, there were racially restrictive laws to prevent black watermen from competing on an equal basis with white watermen. They were, for example, forbidden to own or captain vessels large enough to have been registered. Nevertheless, whether through subterfuge or with the protection of whites, blacks continued to work the water. The historian Kay McKelvey, a specialist in African American history on the Eastern Shore, observed that with high demand for oysters and at small expense, individuals could make a reasonable living even though the big seafood-packing companies were competing. She remarked that "oystering was one of the highest paying jobs for black men."[39]

Harold Anderson, an anthropologist, provides three examples of the black waterman's experience. He interviewed Capt. Sam Turner, an eighty-five-year-old waterman from Bellevue, a community across the Tred Avon River from Oxford. Both Turner's father and grandfather followed the water. They captured oysters and crabs and hauled freight on their boat to and from Baltimore. Turner and his father established a shucking and packing business, Bellevue Seafood Company, in 1939. They bought oysters, mostly from white watermen, processed them, and sold them in Baltimore. Turner served in Europe in World War II and returned to Bellevue to expand the business into clamming. He remembers the turbulence caused by the white reaction to the *Brown v. Board of Education* decision in 1954, but he believes that the racial attitudes among watermen were less pronounced than in land-oriented businesses. Anderson quotes him as saying, "There wasn't no friction down here amongst the watermen. There ain't no color line out there on that river."[40] When Hurricane Agnes hit the Chesapeake region in 1972, it ruined the clamming industry. Turner managed to survive, but even though the business was successful, he discouraged his two sons from becoming watermen. They were able to go away to college but eventually came back to help out in the family business, and now they run it.

Not far away, in St. Michaels, on the Miles River, Wilson Cannon made a life for himself as a waterman. Born in Crisfield in the 1930s, he left in the 1950s because he did not know any black watermen, although blacks did work in the packinghouses. His timing was good because not long afterward, the oyster and crab catches began to decline, and soon there were but two or three packinghouses where once there had been more then twenty. At St. Michaels, where his brother-in-law lived, there was a well-established black watermen's community. Cannon arrived in the late 1950s and began tonging for oysters and crabbing to make a living. In the late 1980s he stopped tonging because of the shortage of oysters. Looking back, he said that when he arrived in St. Michaels, "there were so many black watermen, you could not count them. Today there are only three." Asked about race relations on the water, he said that both races endure the same hardships and that in the early days there were differences in the way that white buyers treated the black watermen, paying white watermen more for their oysters than they paid blacks. He said that "there used to be a little bit of that, but not a lot." Cannon remembered that life began to change for the worse for both white and black watermen in the late 1970s. One year the river froze up during Christmas and didn't thaw until the first week in March, leaving them idle. What little credit they had was gone, and times were tough. Their business has been slowing ever since. "Most of the young people are not getting into the water business anymore. It used to be a pretty good living but not anymore. You might only have a couple of months of the year that you might do well. Young people are looking for a better job with more security."[41]

The Rev. William Wallace is another African American from the Eastern Shore, who, as a young man from Deal Island, began his working life in the oystering trade. Most of the men of his family had been watermen, including his father and grandfather. He gave up the waterman's life and entered the ministry in his twenties, and by the 1990s was the pastor of the Waugh United Methodist Church, in Cambridge. His memories of working the water are clear and riveting. His father, he said, never thought of doing anything but working the water. He had tried some "inland jobs," but wasn't satisfied. He went back to the water, and Wallace commented, "I think it's the freedom, the freedom of being able to determine your own fate. If you went out there and worked hard, then you made money. If you went out there and didn't do anything, then you didn't make money. You determined that— no one else." He also talked about the challenges of working on the water.

On a skipjack, you have to know where to find the oysters and at the same time you have to know the wind and current and the force of that current and know when to pull them in. Then, there is the physical challenge and the danger. Dredging for oysters meant living on a boat during the winter, without the comforts of home. It meant sleeping on a berth the size of a table and not being able to take a bath because the boat would be away from home for five days at a time. You only get the day off if it's too windy . . . if it's rain, you're out there; if it's hail or snow as long it's not blinding, you're out there.

He recalled the painful memory of when he lost his father, brother, and several other male relatives when the skipjack they were on went down in a sudden March storm in 1975. Their push boat's batteries gave out, and they had to sail through Hooper's Straits in wind, rain, lightning, and fog. Their boat took on water and eventually foundered. Lacking radio communication, they could not call for rescue and fog prevented them from being seen. Six family members died of hypothermia within sight of home.[42]

One of the best-known African American watermen on Chesapeake Bay was Earl White, a native of Dames Quarter, near Deal Island. Born in 1918, he too came from a multigenerational waterman's family. He worked on a deadrise work-boat tonging for oysters on Tangier Sound as a teenager. During his sixty-year-long career, he worked in the Atlantic Ocean commercial fisheries as well as in most of the Chesapeake Bay fisheries. He capped his career as the first mate of the Chesapeake Bay Foundation's skipjack *Stanley Norman*. In recollecting scenes from his life as a waterman, White referred to the skipjack *Ralph T. Webster* from Tilghman Island:

> We worked the middle deck of the boat handling the dredges and tending jib sail out on the bowsprit . . . we loaded her twice a day, 400 bushels each time. We really used to get a lot of oysters off the Hanes oyster bed off of Deal Island. . . . Back then, you had to help unload every bushel that went off the boat at the oyster packinghouses. You shoveled the oysters into a big tub and you had to really be careful because those heavy buckets and booms would swing all over your heads.

White echoed what some other watermen have said about race relations on the bay. According to him there was no class system and everyone worked hard. "Everyone got paid the same. You take out for the expenses, take a share for the boat and then 'whack up' the remaining money with the crew. Out on the bay if you were the best at your trade, it didn't matter whether you were black or white, old or young. Race was never a big deal on the water, but once you came back to land, that was another matter." In work for the Chesapeake Bay Foundation, White took school children out on the bay to learn about its history, aquatic life, and conservation. In 1996, in recognition of Earl White's great knowledge, skill, and dedication to the Chesapeake Bay, Governor Parris Glendenning commissioned him an "Admiral of Chesapeake Bay."[43]

In 1910 the Annapolis city directory showed that over 70 percent of the black population were laborers, servants, or waiters. But, according to Annapolis author Philip Brown, "the other major occupation was in the local seafood industry, mainly as oystermen or shuckers." One of the best known of several canneries in the Annapolis area was McNasby's Seafood Company, located in the Eastport district, at the foot of Second Street and Back Creek, where generations of African Americans, women as well as men, found employment as shuckers.[44] William J. McNasby founded the seafood company in the 1885, after having moved the business from New Jersey. He marketed some of the catch locally as "Pearl Oysters," named for his wife. He shipped most of his canned oysters to Akron, Ohio, where his son, William McNasby Jr., handled national distribution. The original McNasby's was located on the Annapolis side of Spa Creek on Compromise Street, near the Eastport bridge. In 1919, McNasby moved the business to the Eastport side of Spa Creek, at a time when there were eighteen other seafood companies working in Annapolis. Here he employed as many as thirty-two shuckers, paying them twenty to thirty cents per gallon of oysters. After his father's death in 1941, William Jr. came to Annapolis and continued the business. At least two generations of African American residents who lived in Eastport can remember working at McNasby's.[45]

"Mr. Mac," as his employees called him, outlasted the competition, but when he died in the 1970s, he bequeathed his business to his longtime partner, John Turner, who ran it for another fifteen years before selling it to a local developer, in 1985. The property lay idle for two years, until the City of Annapolis bought it and helped create a Waterman's Cooperative, where local watermen brought in their oyster catches to be shucked, packed, and sold to retailers. In 1994, new city health regulations requiring changes, combined with the declining harvests of oysters and crabs, brought an end to the seafood business. This, however, was not the end of the story. Under the leadership of Eastport historian Peg Wallace, the old McNasby's plant and its companion building, the Barge House, which used to house some of the workers, became the home of the Eastport Historical Committee and future site of the Annapolis Maritime Museum (AMM). The new museum's leadership successfully urged the city to lease the property to them in 2001. The museum was renovating the McNasby's structure in 2003, when Hurricane Isabel struck a devastating blow, with wind-blown waves from the Severn River pounding holes in the walls and flooding the buildings to a height of more than five feet.

The rebuilding effort began anew, with many eager volunteers, and the AMM completed its work in 2009, renovating its original building in the quest to become accredited by the American Association of Museums. One of the AMM's many outreach projects is to collect the oral histories of the watermen and oyster shuckers who lived in Eastport at a time when that community had a largely African American population.[46] It has been said that only when we realize that a way of life or a culture is in the process of dying do we recognize its real value. If this is true, it is a pleasant irony that the once-vibrant McNasby's Oyster Company is now becoming a museum to convey an understanding of what it meant to be a waterman.[47]

Chapter Seven

Maritime Commerce
after the Civil War

~~~~~~~~~~~~~~~~~~~~~~~~~~~~~~~~~~

MARYLAND'S INTERNATIONAL TRADE after the Civil War reflected the growth of the state's industrialization. Until 1915, grain exports (corn and wheat) did well. Gradually, though, exports shifted from raw materials to manufactured food products. The outbreak of World War I in Europe in 1914 caused an increased demand for agricultural and manufactured products from the United States. This included cigarettes and tobacco suited for that commodity. As agriculture became more attractive, the catches of the oyster fishery declined. By 1917, the year the United States entered the war, oyster harvests reached their lowest level since the Civil War.

Baltimore usually had a competitive advantage over other cities in providing a market and trans-shipment point for midwestern grains: it was closer to the source of supply. Of the foreign customers, Great Britain led the way, followed by Germany, Holland, Denmark, and Belgium. This was particularly true during periods of poor European harvests, as in the late 1890s. Baltimore remained an important flour exporter to the West Indies and Brazil. By 1910, however, European demand had dropped off and the coffee trade with Brazil had diminished. But cotton finally returned as an export, with Liverpool and Bremen as important recipients. Tobacco exports remained important, with exports from Ohio, Kentucky, North Carolina, and Virginia, as well as Maryland, leaving Baltimore.[1] As an importer, however, Baltimore was losing her customers to New York. Baltimore's shippers had held too long to shipping by sailing vessel, whereas New York had shifted largely to steam by 1910. Baltimore until 1914 remained fifth in shipping capacity in the nation.[2]

The spread of railroad lines through Maryland enhanced the port of Baltimore. The B&O developed the largest port terminal on the East Coast at Locust Point, covering a mile of waterfront and funneling hundreds of thousands of immigrants and millions of tons of freight each year. The growing Pennsylvania Railroad took over the Baltimore and Potomac steamship terminal at Canton. Canal transportation continued to be important. The Chesapeake and Ohio Canal, from Alexandria and Georgetown to Cumberland, ran two hundred miles and carried mainly coal. The Chesapeake and Delaware Canal had been improved over the years and carried mainly lumber to northern ports. By 1896, there were nineteen miles of dredged ship channel 600 feet wide by 27 feet deep. A number of ocean

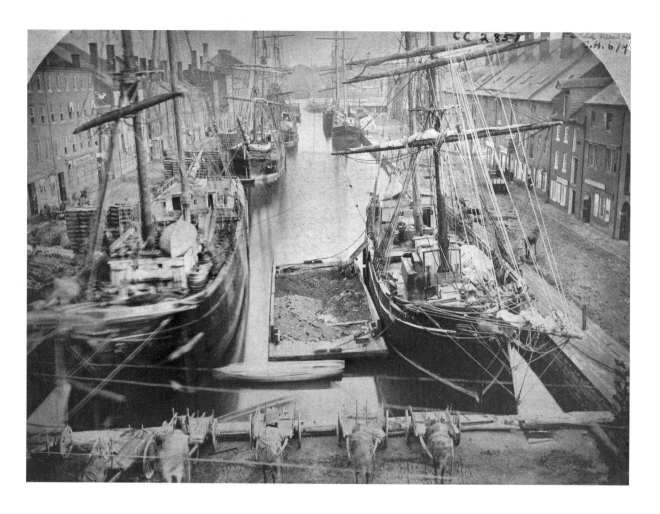

Merchant ships unloading cargo on Pratt Street wharfs, 1875. Courtesy, Maryland Historical Society, CC2851.

liners had regular service between Baltimore and Copenhagen, Hamburg, Bremen, Antwerp, Rotterdam, Le Havre, and British ports. There had been a significant increase in competition since the early 1880s, when there were thirteen shipping lines in coastal traffic; six ran to Europe, of which the North German Lloyd was the oldest. By 1914, thirty-four lines, both domestic and foreign, were in operation.[3]

The many projects of the Army Corps of Engineers contributed to port and channel improvements throughout the Maryland Chesapeake.[4] They made a major effort to improve the Chesapeake and Delaware Canal. In 1919, the federal government purchased the C&D Canal, and by 1927 had deepened and widened it, eliminating the need for locks. This allowed larger, swifter classes of vessels to pass through.[5] During the ninety years during which the C&D Canal was operated privately, 57 million tons passed through the locks. Since 1919, an estimated 565 million tons of shipping used the canal, averaging in excess of 8 million tons per year.

A modernization project completed in 1969 dredged the canal to a depth of 35 feet and widened it to 450 feet. By the 1980s, it could accommodate ocean-going vessels to a length of 650 feet. Ships bound from Baltimore to New York could save ten hours by making passage north through the canal and then down the Delaware

River around Cape May and up to New York. To make the voyage out the Chesa-peake capes and around Delmarva Peninsula to New York would take twenty-eight hours; a ship steaming via the C&D Canal takes but eighteen hours, saving both time and fuel.[6]

Baltimore's position in coastal shipping during the post–Civil War period showed considerable activity. In 1890, Maryland's coastal tonnage was 3.4 million tons, as compared with 2 million tons for foreign commerce. But while foreign trade was relatively lower in tonnage, it was higher in value than coastal trade. Still, the value of coastal shipping as a whole was higher than foreign trade. In 1914, the coastal trade was worth $240 million, compared with $144 million in foreign trade. The most important items in Baltimore's coastal trade were general merchandise, boots and shoes, tobacco, coal, fertilizer, cotton manufactures, whiskey, lumber, canned goods, and raw cotton. By 1896, Baltimore had the second-largest bay and coastal fleet on the eastern seaboard. Raw cotton arrived in Baltimore from Nor-folk, Charleston, and Savannah by steamer, though by rail from Cincinnati and St. Louis. Most of the product was exported, and Baltimore mills consumed only a small portion.

The growth of shipping from Baltimore encouraged shipbuilding and re-lated industries—the production of iron and steel. The end of the Civil War had witnessed the rapid decline of the U.S. Navy. Perceiving no hostile naval threat, the United States poured its energies into westward expansion. Shipbuilding went into a national decline as shipping companies used foreign-flag vessels to carry their goods. Still, Maryland shipbuilding had a life of its own, and in 1880 Balti-more had seventeen shipyards building and repairing wooden bay and river vessels. The construction of iron ships resumed in 1872, and by the 1890s, shipbuilding had become a branch of the steel industry.[7]

In 1884, the Pennsylvania Steel Company had purchased land for a large plant on Sparrows Point on Chesapeake Bay, six miles from Baltimore. Sparrows Point built the first American oil tanker in 1890. Hit hard by the ill effects of the depres-sion of 1893, the Pennsylvania Steel Company reorganized and increased its produc-tion of pig iron and steel for ships and bridge construction. By 1900, Maryland had forty-seven shipyards, of which four built iron and steel vessels, as compared with thirty-four such establishments in 1890. Pennsylvania Steel soon had a formidable competitor. The Bethlehem Steel Corporation appeared and, by 1905, was not only producing iron and steel but also constructing and repairing ships and marine en-gines. The navy became a major customer of the Bethlehem shipbuilding and repair yards, purchasing armor plate, ordnance, and ammunition as well. Through the shrewd management of magnate Charles Schwab, Bethlehem Steel acquired Penn-sylvania Steel and its Sparrows Point Ship Yard in February 1916.[8] In the years be-fore World War I, the Maryland Steel Company and its successor, Bethlehem Steel, built more than 120 vessels of all types, most of them intended for commercial use. They included tugboats, barges, railroad lighters, colliers, dredges for the Isthmian Canal Commission and the U.S. Army, cargo ships, ferries, car floats for railroad companies, tank barges for the Standard Oil Company, coastal passenger ships, dump scows, the steam yacht *Dungeness* for Mrs. L. C. Carnegie, three destroyers

Three-masted schooner alongside Gay Street Pier, 1898. Courtesy, Maryland Historical Society, CC 110.

(USS *Truxtun,* USS *Whipple,* and USS *Worden*), and three fleet colliers (USS *Mars,* USS *Hector,* and USS *Vulcan*).[9]

World War I stimulated the construction of wooden as well as steel ships. To replace the coasting vessels used in convoys to Europe, a number of large three-masted schooners of wood construction were built. These could carry more cargo than the traditional two-masted schooner, being of greater length, and with additional though smaller sails, they could be more easily handled by reduced crew and were, consequently, cheaper to operate. Several were built on the Eastern Shore at yards in Pocomoke City, Sharptown, and Seaford, Delaware. The increased demand for coal in northern ports pushed owners of sailing cargo ships to the next step, the four-masted schooner. Eight hundred tons was the maximum practical size for three-masted schooners, so more cargo could be carried in a four-master, and the larger the vessel, the more economical she could be. Among them were *Charles M. Struven,* in 1917, *Purnell T. White,* in 1917, *Alexander H. Erickson,* in 1918, and the *Anandale,* in 1919.

These schooners were to make their way in the world by hauling coal, lumber,

Gray's Inn Creek Shipyard, off the Chester River, ca. 1750. The overpanel comes from Spencer Hall, Kent County, and shows colonial-era vessels of all types. Oil on wood panel by unknown artist. Courtesy, Maryland Historical Society, 1900.5.1.

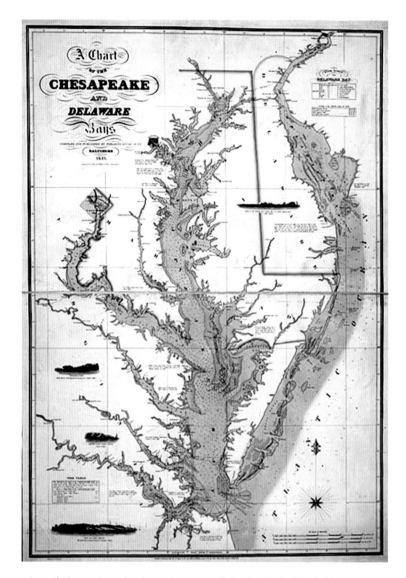

Chart of Chesapeake and Delaware bays, compiled and published by Fielding Lucas Jr.; corrected 1840; engraved by John and William Warr, Philadelphia. From David Rumsey Map Collection. Courtesy, Maryland State Archives.

Maryland ship *Defence,* the first vessel of the Maryland State Navy, 1776. Work on paper by Melbourne Smith, 1978. Courtesy, Maryland Historical Society, M1978.3.1.

View of Baltimore Basin and Federal Hill. Oil on canvas by Francis Guy, 1803. Courtesy, Maryland Historical Society, MA8148.

Baltimore clipper ship *Ann McKim,* built in 1833 at Kennard and Williamson's shipyard and registered at 493 tons. She sailed in the China and South American trade. Lithograph by Armitage McCann. Courtesy, Maryland Historical Society, Z24.2966.

Sailors' Bethel, a floating shiphouse chapel built on board the ship *William Penn,* near Federal Hill. Oil on canvas by Samuel Kramer, 1846. Courtesy, Maryland Historical Society, Z24.637.

Commodore Joshua Barney, commander of the Chesapeake Flotilla and hero of the Battle of Bladensburg. Portrait displaying his medal from the Society of Cincinnati. Oil on canvas by Rembrandt Peale, ca. 1815. Courtesy, Maryland Historical Society, CA682.

Privateer schooner *Patapsco* in battle, making escape from an enemy brig, September 21, 1814. Watercolor on paper, unknown artist. Courtesy, Maryland Historical Society, M1986.88.

Privateer schooner *Patapsco* entering the Bay of Naples, all sails set, 1813–14. Watercolor on paper, unknown artist. Courtesy, Maryland Historical Society, M1986.87.

Fardy and Auld shipyard, Federal Hill, beneath the signal tower that announced ship arrivals by hoisting the house flag. Oil on canvas by William Hare, ca. 1854. Courtesy, Maryland Historical Society, CA866.

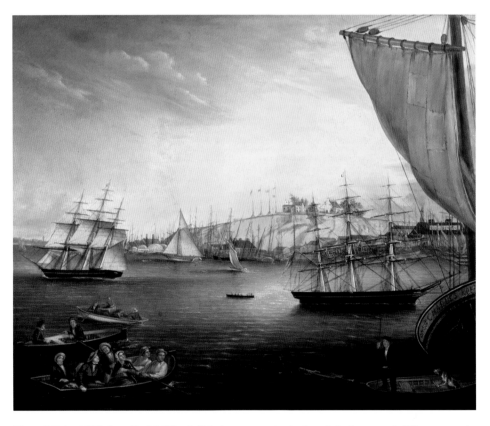

View of Federal Hill from Bayly's Wharf. Ships' passengers in the launch in foreground. Oil on canvas by Charles Koehl, 1851. Courtesy, Maryland Historical Society, MA3456.

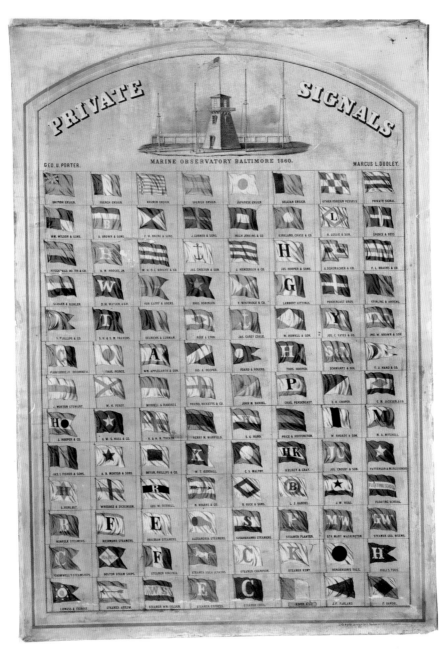

Private signals used by ships departing and arriving at Baltimore and relayed to the marine observatory tower on Federal Hill, 1860. Lithograph by E. Sachse & Company. Courtesy, Maryland Historical Society, E33.

Vane Brothers Company tugboat *Nanticoke* on the Patapsco River passing the containership wharves at Fairfield. Photo by Lindsay Staton. Courtesy, Vane Brothers Company.

U.S. Sailboat Show, Annapolis city dock, October 1991. Replica of Revolutionary War–era sloop *Providence* is moored in foreground, lower right. Photo by Jeff Holland. Courtesy, Annapolis Maritime Museum.

Deadrise workboat, skipjack, and buyboat moored at Annapolis city dock, with spire of St. Anne's Church and the Maryland State House dome in distance, 1991. Photo by Jeff Holland. Courtesy, Annapolis Maritime Museum.

Liberty Ship *John W. Brown,* a World War II veteran, passing down the Patapsco River under her own power, 2008. The ship, maintained by veterans, makes cruises down to the Chesapeake several times a year on patriotic occasions. Photo by and courtesy of John D. Bernard.

Chesapeake 20 one-design sloops, just after the start of a race on the Severn River, sponsored by the Annapolis Maritime Museum in June 2008. Many came from the West River, where the class originated, at Hartge's Yacht Yard in 1936. Photo by Jeff Holland. Courtesy, Annapolis Maritime Museum.

The Whitbread Round the World Race of 1997–98 featured several Whitbread 60 designs developed by Bruce Farr of Annapolis and New Zealand. Shown here is *Chessie Racing,* owned by George J. Collins, passing beneath the Chesapeake Bay Bridge in April 1998. Photo by and courtesy of Jack Hardway.

The schooner *Pride of Baltimore II,* an updated War of 1812 replica of the privateer *Chasseur,* approaches Annapolis harbor in October 2003. *Pride* represents the city of Baltimore during coastal and international port visits. Photo by and courtesy of Jack Hardway.

The 12-meter America's Cup defender *Freedom* passing the Thomas Point Shoal Light on a visit to the Chesapeake Bay in April 2003. Photo by and courtesy of Jack Hardway.

The Great Chesapeake Bay Schooner Race is held each year in October, with contestants racing from Baltimore to Norfolk. In the race of 2006, boats were becalmed for several hours just south of the Chesapeake Bay Bridge. Photo by and courtesy of Jack Hardway.

In the Volvo (formerly Whitbread) Round the World race of 2005–6, the racers (now Volvo 70s) visited the bay in May 2006. Shown in the foreground is the American entry *Pirates of the Caribbean,* skippered by Paul Cayard, challenging the Netherlands boat *ABN-AMRO I,* the eventual winner. Photo by and courtesy of Jack Hardway.

Chesapeake Bay is the scene of many yacht races by dozens of yacht clubs every season. In this photo, two national offshore one-design boats have a close call in a stiff breeze off Tolley Point, May 2005. Photo by and courtesy of Jack Hardway.

The sloop of war *Constellation* under way to witness the commissioning of USS *Sterrett* in Baltimore harbor, assisted by a Vane Brothers tugboat, in August 2008. *Constellation,* built in 1854, was the last sailing man-of-war constructed by the U.S. Navy. Photo by Lindsay Staton. Courtesy, Vane Brothers Company.

The colonial schooner *Sultana,* a replica of the American-built revenue schooner that patrolled the Chesapeake in 1768–70. The replica was built in Chestertown, 1994–95, based on plans found in National Maritime Museum, Greenwich, UK. Photo by and courtesy of Drew McMullen, Sultana Projects.

pulpwood, and guano. The *White* was a four-masted schooner whose history has been recorded by Robert H. Burgess.[10] Her port of record was listed as Salisbury, Maryland, though she sailed mostly from Baltimore for fourteen years, making for southern U.S. and Caribbean ports to deliver or pick up lumber, coal, salt, fish, scrap, cement, and logwood. A frequent run was from Baltimore to Georgetown, South Carolina, for lumber. Indeed, it was on such a run in 1934, during a winter voyage, that the *White* met her fate, foundering off the Virginia Capes, with a loss of four men, including the captain. While the *White* was recovered, she had been damaged and dismasted and her owners deemed her not worth repairing. She ended her days at a Baltimore landfill area off Hawkins Point. The *White*'s useful though sad ending was not unlike those of other four-masted cargo schooners of the time. Among those were *G. A. Kohler, Doris Hamlin, Albert F. Paul, Anna R. Heidritter,* and the *Herbert L. Rawding.* In their later days, the 1930s and 1940s, these schooners were frequently employed in the logwood trade from Haiti and Jamaica to Baltimore. They were a dying breed, but many admired their beautiful appearance while they lasted.[11]

The final incarnation of the large cargo-carrying schooner on the Chesapeake was the homely schooner barge, of which the *Ruxton,* launched in Baltimore in 1920, was an example. These vessels were designed to be towed, with the sails acting to increase the efficiency and ease of the tow. Chesapeake builders constructed approximately seventy of these vessels between 1899 and 1922, with widely varying capacities. The largest appears to have been the *Hermitage,* with five masts, of 2,111 gross tons, measuring 306 feet in length and 50 feet in the beam. Some were cut down conversions of full-rigged ships that were no longer economical for operation under sail alone.[12]

The onset of World War I stimulated the economy of Maryland, and the maritime trades enjoyed flush times. Between 1916 and 1919, the shipyards increased their tonnage of steel ships launched from 14,883 to 131,012—more than 800 percent. In 1919, the Sparrows Point yards launched sixteen ships, and Baltimore's other yards provided ten, most of them intended for naval service. Beyond this, maritime activity had increased with the opening of the Panama Canal in 1914, which strengthened Maryland's traditional ties with South American, West Coast, and Asian ports. With the deepening of the Chesapeake and Delaware Canal, Baltimore's connections with northern ports were expanded. By 1939, the city ranked seventh in the nation industrially, was second to New York in terms of foreign trade tonnage, and was second in the United States for total volume of imports. A total of sixty-five different shipping lines made Baltimore a port of call, and in 1940, Baltimore was the third-ranking port in the country in total waterborne commerce.[13]

Bethlehem Steel's Sparrows Point shipbuilding intensified during World War II. From 1938 the plant's workers built 127 vessels ranging from freighters (Types C1 to C3) to tankers (T2 to T3) for private firms as well as the U.S. Maritime Commission. Many of the larger C3 freighters were later converted to U.S. Navy cargo ships (AKs) or troopships (APAs) to deliver soldiers overseas. Others saw service as light-escort carriers or submarine, seaplane, and destroyer tenders. The navy converted the larger T3 tanker hulls to either U.S. Navy oilers (AOs) or hulls for escort aircraft carriers (CVEs). Smaller than the navy's Essex class aircraft carriers, these ships measured 525 feet in length, 75 feet of beam, and had a draft of $30\frac{1}{2}$ feet. Equipped with boilers able to produce 4,450 pounds of steam pressure per square inch and two propeller shafts, the engines developed 13,500 horsepower and drove the ships at 18 knots. This was a relatively high speed for the time and was essential for ships assigned to the fast-carrier task forces of World War II.

After World War II, Bethlehem Steel returned to building ships for commercial use. Out of 214 vessels constructed from 1948 to 1986, there were 89 oil tankers, 19 crude carriers, 23 break-bulk cargo ships, 11 tank barges, 7 tunnel tubes, 7 ammunition ships (USS *Nitro, Pyro, Haleakala, Suribachi, Mauna Kea, Santa Barbara,* and *Mount Hood*), 2 container ships, and 27 barges of various types. Bethlehem Steel abandoned new construction at Sparrows Point in 1986, after losing the competition for the T-AO program second-source contract, but continued in the ship-repair business, moving a large floating dock from its Key Highway yard to Sparrows Point for this purpose. Uncompetitive in the repair business because of its high-cost structure, Bethlehem sold the shipyard to Veritas Capital in 1997, which renamed it Baltimore Marine Industries (BMI).[14]

From the 1950s through the mid-1970s, Maryland stood out well in the competition with other North Atlantic ports in foreign trade. New York, Philadelphia, Norfolk, and New Orleans offered stiff competition, but Baltimore usually stood third or fourth, nationally, in terms of the total tonnage and value of foreign commerce that entered and cleared the port during this period. Quantities of exports and imports rose steadily at Baltimore as the port authorities worked to modernize the port, with containership loading and unloading docks and distribution networks receiving most of the attention. During the mid-1940s, there was a near equality of volume in imports and exports, but in 1947, imports surged ahead of exports, with Baltimore importing more than twice as much tonnage as she exported. In the

mid-1970s, imports hit a plateau, while exports rose to nearly equal volume. Certainly, the sinking value of the dollar with respect to foreign currencies stimulated U.S. exports as a whole during this period, but so too did certain fluctuations in the oil market. Oil shortages and higher prices in the mid-1970s produced a 30–40 percent increase in U.S. coal exports, a trend that definitely benefited coal-exporting ports like Baltimore.

With the weaker buying power of the dollar in the early 1980s, Baltimore's imports showed signs of faltering in the foreign commerce market.[15] Total foreign commerce (exports and imports combined) for the port of Baltimore fluctuated during the 1980s. Over ten years, Baltimore's share of the commerce enjoyed by U.S. ports dropped from 4.1 percent to 3.2 percent. This is a trend that Baltimore will have to struggle to reverse. The total of exports from Baltimore dropped considerably during the period, from 5.4 percent of U.S. exports to 3.3 percent, while the city's share of imports remained essentially the same in 1989 as it had been in

The SS *Patrick Henry,* shown sliding down the ways at the Bethlehem-Fairfield shipyard, was the first Liberty Ship launched, September 27, 1941. She and many other Liberty Ships carried much of the cargo that helped the Allies win World War II. Courtesy, Maryland Historical Society, MC 2179.

1980—3 percent. While Baltimore maintained a relatively strong position among other North Atlantic ports—and with continued channel dredging and port improvements could improve its competitive position—the main challenge, in terms of tonnage, now comes from southern ports, such as Houston, New Orleans, Norfolk, Corpus Christie, and Baton Rouge, rather than the older northeastern ports of Philadelphia and Boston, although New York still ranked higher in both tonnage and dollar value as of 1990. As for dollar value of exports and imports, the West Coast ports were at the top of the ladder in 1989, as Los Angeles, Long Beach, Seattle, and Tacoma all ranked higher than Baltimore, probably because of the surge of Pacific Rim shipping ports in recent years.[16]

Since the early 1990s, the Maryland Port Authority and the Port of Baltimore have made major improvements by expanding cargo-handling facilities and road and rail access to the major harbor shipping points, Seagirt Marine Terminal, Dundalk Marine Terminal, and the Fairfield and Masonville terminals. Currently Baltimore is only one of two East Coast ports where the shipping channel reaches the depth of fifty feet required for the largest containerships. It is notable, however, that most of the terminal berths can only accommodate vessels with draft of up to about forty-two feet. As foreign-built container ships are increasing in size and capacity, dredging more berths to fifty-foot draft will soon be essential. As of 2007, the general cargo handled through the public marine terminals reached an all-time high of 8.7 million tons, the sixth consecutive year of tonnage increase. The port is ranked twelfth in the nation for total dollar value of cargo and thirteenth for the total of foreign cargo handled. In exports, the port's volume was 11.3 million tons, 35 percent higher than the previous year and the highest in exports since 1996. Sharing widespread concern for the safety of American seaports in an era of global terrorism, the Maryland Port Authority is working closely with the Department of Homeland Security and local law enforcement to improve port security with high-tech surveillance of cargo and transporters. The Port of Baltimore was one of the first in the nation to check all imported containers for radiation.[17]

~~~

ONE OF THE FIRMS that has epitomized the entrepreneurial spirit of maritime Baltimore is Vane Brothers, originally a Fells Point ship chandlery established in 1898 by Capt. William Burke Vane and his brother, Capt. Allan P. Vane. The Vanes hailed from Church Creek in Dorchester County, five miles southwest of Cambridge on Maryland's Eastern Shore. Their grandfather, Joseph T. Vane, was a slave-owning farmer and miller and their father, William A. Vane, had been active in politics, serving as local postmaster, county commissioner, and judge of the orphans' court. Burke Vane made his living at sea, shipping out on vessels bringing produce from Eastern Shore farms to Baltimore and in the Atlantic coastal trade between Baltimore, the West Indies, and Nova Scotia. Allan, also a seafaring man, went to work in Baltimore for a shipping firm and at times helped his brother's interests. After some twenty years at sea, Captain Vane came ashore and in 1898 joined his brother in founding a ships' chandlery, on Thames Street in Fells Point. This was a perfect location. Fells Point was a famous shipbuilding area and offered deep water for piers and docks, a very busy place in the 1890s. Ships' chandleries had originated in the distant past as sources for candles, hence the name *chandlery,* but had evolved into stores where shipowners and masters could obtain all manner of implements needed uniquely on board ships as well as ordinary staples for long voyages. Thus, in getting his ship ready for sea, a master could find anchors, chain, bilge pumps, kerosene lanterns, shackles, belaying pins, mast hoops, life jackets, cordage in the form of line and rope, sou'westers and oilskins, rubber boots, ships' running lights, ship carpenters' tools, bunk mattresses, oaken barrels for water storage, and many other necessities. Beyond these, chandlers found it profitable to offer canned goods, sacks of coffee, dried beans, barrels of molasses, large rounds of cheese, salted eggs, salt cod, salt pork, bacon, and hindquarters of beef—in short, almost everything needed in a ship's galley. This is also where seagoing men would gather for comradeship and to obtain the latest harbor gossip. The Vane brothers found success in Fells Point, but by 1910 there was more shipping activity and commerce in the Inner Harbor, so they moved to 602–604 Pratt Street, near Pier 4, the "Long Dock." Here, they were close by the ships' agents, the Customs House, and other piers, where ships unloaded farm produce, coal for the East Baltimore steam plant, and lumber for the construction businesses in town.[18]

The chandlery business flourished during the 1910s, particularly as maritime commerce expanded in the halcyon days leading to World War I. When the war broke out in 1914, the United States proclaimed its neutrality and continued its trade while the European powers struggled for dominance on land and at sea. The Germans waged U-boat war against British shipping while the Royal Navy blockaded German ports and awaited the moment when the Grand Fleet would meet the German High Seas Fleet in the North Sea, as it ultimately did at the Battle of Jutland, in 1916. The United States maintained a formal neutrality until 1917, but public opinion favored Great Britain heavily after a German U-boat sank the passenger liner *Lusitania* on May 7, 1915, with the loss of 1,198 passengers, including 124 Americans.

Meanwhile, Baltimore and other U.S. ports continued busier than ever, with the anticipation that eventually the United States would be drawn into the war on the side of the British, French, and Russian allies.[19] During the immediate prewar years, Vane Brothers expanded and diversified its business into shipbuilding. They purchased J. S. Beacham and Brothers Shipyard and the Maryland Block and Pump Company, both located on Federal Hill. To help in this work, they gained a partner in the person of John Carroll Redman, another seafarer from the Eastern Shore. The new name of their firm was the Redman-Vane Shipbuilding Company, specializing in the repair of sailing vessels but servicing steamboats as well. According to Morris Kemp, the treasurer of Redman-Vane, the yard worked on all types of bay craft—barges, scows, steamboats, yachts, sailing vessels, tugs, revenue cutters, and lighthouse vessels. It was equipped with two electrically powered marine railways and could lift vessels up to 1,200 tons. The yard did extensive caulking work on some of the three-masted ram schooners and possessed a large supply of lignum vitae, an especially hard and durable wood used in making shives in pulley blocks and steamboat paddle wheel bushings.[20] In a foreshadowing of future operations, Captain

Vane, in 1919, purchased a small wooden vessel containing a tank for the delivery of fuel oil, kerosene, gasoline, and fresh water, as well as for the delivery on board of the usual ships' stores that the chandlery provides to its afloat customers. At about this time a new partner came to the firm.

Capt. Claude V. Hughes, a scion of the Charles Venables Hughes family of Salisbury, in Wicomico County, joined Vane Brothers in 1919. The Hugheses were distant cousins of the Vanes. The brothers Claude V. and Charles F. Hughes grew up on their father's farm near Salisbury but found seafaring to their liking. It happened that their father was a part owner of the schooner *R. E. Powell,* and Claude had often sailed on the *Powell* with his father. In 1910, Claude bought Capt. Thomas White's quarter share, and soon his father gave him command. For nearly ten years, Captain Claude sailed the bay carrying all manner of cargos, including timber, coal, fertilizer, shells, and farm produce. He did well during this time and took over full ownership of the *R. E. Powell.* His arrival at Vane Brothers is told in a charming anecdote that he related in his memoirs. He was at the time courting a young woman. When he asked her to marry him, she replied, "What's the use in marrying, you're never home." This set him back on his heels, so he went to his cousin Capt. Burke Vane, in the ship chandlery, to ask for advice. At the same time, he asked Vane if there was any way he could work at the chandlery. Burke responded by saying that if that was what he wanted, he would sell him a half ownership in the chandlery. This was exactly what Claude wanted to hear, so he sold his schooner and his farm and within six months he was married and living in Baltimore.[21]

Within a year, Claude's brother Charles joined the Vane Brothers firm. He had served in the army air service during World War I and was planning to study law, but Claude persuaded him to try the chandlery business. Before long, a mariner friend from the Eastern Shore visited and asked if he'd like to buy a share in a two-masted schooner, the *John R. P. Moore.* He said he would but lacked the cash; however, Captain Burke said that if he would apply for a loan, he would cosign for him. Charles did so and soon found that co-owning a trading schooner could be a profitable enterprise. In the 1920s, the Vane Brothers continued to expand their work and became co-owners in a number of trading vessels that plied the bay and coastal waters. These included the schooners *Brownstone, Lydia Middleton, Thomas J. Shyrock, Esther Melbourne, G. A. Kohler,* and the *Doris Hamlin.* In the case of the *Doris Hamlin,* Capt. George Hopkins, her master, a highly capable seaman, had invited Robert Burgess, the son of a marine engineer, to accompany them in 1936 on a three-month voyage. This impressionable young man, stimulated by the experience, eventually devoted his life to preserving the memory of the sailing vessels of the Chesapeake. Likewise, the Baltimore-based photographer Aubrey Bodine sailed in *Doris Hamlin* along with Burgess and took some of his famous photos of *Hamlin* on that voyage.[22]

The onset of World War II brought a relief of the watch at the Vane Brothers' chandlery. The Depression years had been difficult, with little income and businesses failing right and left, but as war clouds formed on the horizon, the nation's economy regained momentum. The chandlery's galley fuel supply boats, *Charles Wright* and *Melvin,* kept busy, and in 1938, Vane Brothers commissioned a specially constructed steel-hulled tanker, *Charles Wright II,* with a 6,000-gallon capacity, to increase deliveries. In 1941, the U.S. Coast Guard requisitioned her for its own use, so the firm immediately ordered another, the *Hughes Brothers* (later renamed *Vane Brothers*), to be built. Gradually the demand for this service grew to include "picket boats," private yachts commissioned to complement the nation's shortage of sub-chasers and destroyers. Capt. Allan Vane died that year, and shortly thereafter, Capt. Burke Vane sold his share of the business to the Hughes brothers. The war years were busy ones, with new customers, among them Esso and Texaco tankers, as well as the Liberty ships being produced by the Baltimore shipyards. The U.S. government demanded ever more land for the expansion of the Bethlehem Steel Company and, unfortunately, the Redman-Vane Shipbuilding Company's property stood in the way. Shipyard researcher William Kelley put it this way:

> Without warning, on January 20, 1942, the Navy Department issued condemnation proceedings calling for immediate acquisition of the three long-established and adjoining ship-repair firms. They were Redman & Vane, Booz Brothers and the Baltimore Marine Repair Shops, Inc. (formerly McIntyre & Henderson and afterwards Baltimore Ship Repair Co., Inc.). They comprised a total of about ten acres and were on the north side of the Bethlehem Shipbuilding Corporation, ship repair plant, and were required for Navy work to be contracted for by Bethlehem. They had a water frontage of approximately 1000 feet. The owners of these three plants received their first intimation of the proceedings when the sheriff posted notices upon their respective plants. Booz Brothers and the Baltimore Ship Repair Company resumed operations adjoining the former site of William E. Woodall & Company, shipbuilders, at Key Highway between Woodall and Lawrence Streets, several blocks southeastward, but Redman & Vane discontinued business.[23]

By 1946, Charles Hughes had worked in the chandlery business for nearly thirty-one years. He became ill, and, luckily, his son Charles V. Hughes Jr., who had served in the navy and was a student at the Johns Hopkins University, agreed, if reluctantly, to come on board to assist his Uncle Claude. In 1951, Charles Sr., having regained his health, returned to the business, and his son completed his degree work at Hopkins and rejoined the firm. Soon Claude retired, agreeing that Charles Jr. could now share control of the business with his father. In the 1950s, changes for the worse had taken place in the Inner Harbor, working schooners were seldom seen, and the old steamboat piers were decaying. It was time to move the Vane Brothers' firm to a new location, where they would have more space and be closer to the shipping they serviced. They chose to go to 916 South Broadway in Fells Point, to the old Immigration Building, where they would have their pier across the water from the Recreation Pier.

In the 1960s, the Hugheses began to diversify the company beyond the chandlery business by expanding the tanker trade. Ten years later they added a 42,000-gallon tanker, christened *Duff,* after Charles Duff Hughes, the son of Charles Jr., for use in supplying gas oil (No. 2 marine diesel fuel) to all types and sizes of ships. In addition, they invited Capt. Russi Makujina to join the firm to bring his international seafaring background and expertise to this highly competitive business. Makujina had been master of the Pakistani ship *Ohrmazd,* a passenger liner, when it was suddenly stalled at the Bethlehem Steel pier because of a longshoreman strike in 1967. During this prolonged period ashore, he and his family got well acquainted with the Hughes family and a few years later, when Pakistan nationalized its shipping lines, he immigrated to the United States and became a valuable and trusted member of the Vane Brothers firm. He was to become Vane Brothers' senior port captain, the company's fleet manager. With the assistance of this master mariner, Vane added more sophisticated tankers to the fleet to deliver the three basic types of fuel needed on board large ships: gas oil, No. 6 (Bunker C) oil, and marine lubricants used in the many different kinds of machinery that operate in ships. They also delivered a large supply of fresh water to these thirsty vessels. Beyond this, there was an opportunity to enter the market for land delivery of diesel fuel in the form of a new subsidiary, Vane Line Fuel. In 1986, the firm acquired the Marine Launch Company, the vehicle for providing marine lubricants and a property in Fells Point for storing the 55-gallon drums and 500-gallon totes of lube oil for the delivery launches.

From the late 1980s into the 1990s, Vane Brothers continued to expand its services and to enter new geographical markets. As Fells Point became more developed, the area was less desirable for a marine service company's operations. The Hugheses decided to move farther east on the Patapsco, into Canton (so named for the nineteenth-century China trade) at Pier 11, the former site of United States Lines, with 3,600 feet of deep-water berthing and 160,000 square feet of warehousing space. It could then afford to take on tenants, one of which was the U.S. Navy's hospital ship USNS *Comfort,* a converted oil tanker. The navy's Military Sealift Command keeps a small permanent crew stationed on board for emergency situations. This ship is kept in constant readiness for immediate wartime deployment, as at the outbreak of the Gulf War in 1990–91, or for humanitarian operations, such as the Haitian immigrant crisis in 1994. Internally, Vane Brothers underwent reorganization, with Charles Hughes Jr. moving to chairman of the board and son Duff stepping into the presidency. With ties to the major oil companies, Vane was positioned to move into areas of greater responsibility and soon stepped into the bunkering business, at the invitation of the Shell, Hess, British Petroleum, and Chevron oil companies.

In 1987 Vane added its first double-hulled 15,000-barrel black oil bunker barge and in 1988 purchased its second. This in turn required the hiring or purchase of powerful tugboats to move these barges promptly from source to customer. As the more rational choice was to purchase, the company bought a rebuilt 60-foot-long, 800-horsepower tug christened *Elizabeth Ann,* for the company's vice president, the wife of Charles Hughes Jr. The company searched for areas where its services would be needed. Philadelphia, with its vast refineries and storage fields in close proximity, was one, and Norfolk, blessed with near access to the sea and major shipbuilding companies, also beckoned. In both places, Vane Brothers went into business and eventually bought out the competition. In addition to transferring fuels to shipping in these busy ports, Vane also provides lightering services and transports fuel oil by barge and tug to other ports of the Chesapeake Bay, such as

Salisbury, Maryland, and Seaford, Delaware, as well as ports along the Atlantic coast, such as Plymouth, North Carolina. In recent years the company has further diversified into marine safety equipment sales, repair, and maintenance of twenty-five-man inflatable emergency life rafts and other equipment for both working and recreational vessels.[24]

The story of Vane Brothers is a fascinating tale of one Baltimore-based family-owned firm making the best of challenges during more than a century in the chandlery and ship-services industry. Each generation of entrepreneurs took the firm a few steps further and modernized when the times were right. As Vane Brothers, under the Hughes family's direction, entered the twenty-first century, these processes were still at work. The firm moved again, this time to Fairfield, an industrial area on the right bank of the Patapsco, where it constructed five new buildings and was in full operation as of 2003. It has five hundred employees and a state-of-the-art electronic operations center, with the ability to instantly locate and communicate with its fleet units, advising of changed weather conditions and new business opportunities or problems that can arise suddenly. At last count, the fleet numbered seventy-eight, with thirty-two tugs, forty-three barges, one motor tanker, and two launches.

Chapter Eight

The Decline of Working Sail

~~~~~~~~~~~~~~~~~~~~~~~~~~~~~~~~~~~~~

THE GRADUAL DISAPPEARANCE OF WORKING SAIL, that is, of the wind-driven vessels that performed the bulk of the carrying trade and bay harvesting of oysters, crabs, and fish, began in the nineteenth century and lasted until nearly the middle of the twentieth century. The Industrial Revolution had gone to sea in the early 1800s, bringing steam engines to propel ships and do the work on deck that otherwise would have been done by human hands. With the arrival of steam, the economics of seafaring fit in with the increasing pace of life ashore—information moved faster with telegraphy, and the spread of railroads opened new markets in the West and created demand for the seafood products that the Chesapeake could produce in abundance. Steamboats proliferated on Chesapeake Bay, enabling passengers and cargo to transit from rural piers to city docks on schedule. Entrepreneurs developed methods to preserve and can the Chesapeake region's seafood, vegetables, and fruit, enabling their shipment to areas hitherto unable to enjoy them. For several years, fortunes could be made in the seafood industry, but along with this trend, the cycles of financial boom and bust affected virtually everybody.

Soon after the peak oyster-producing years came the depression of 1893. In a search for lower costs, watermen moved from building or purchasing bugeyes to the less expensive, more practical skipjacks. Soon the application of the gasoline combustion engine to smaller vessels brought into being the power-driven deadrise workboat, introducing lower costs and reducing the need for so many hands to work nets and drogues. More efficient oyster dredging meant that, sooner or later, the supply of marketable oysters began to decline, bringing on competition and hostility between oyster tongers and dredgers. The shift from sail to power took many years—close to a century—but during this lengthy process, some remarkable shipbuilding took place, much of it on the Eastern Shore.

Those who lament the passing of the characteristic log canoes, brogans, bay-built sloops, schooners, bugeyes, and skipjacks are primarily those who admire the aesthetics of sailing vessels, with their beautiful sheer lines and shapely sails. The pilot-schooner design held sway well into the late nineteenth century in the form of the pungy schooner, used for transporting oysters and farm produce. Many of the schooners so produced came from yards in Somerset and Talbot counties on Maryland's Eastern Shore. Some 590 pungy schooners were con-

structed on the Chesapeake between 1841 and 1855. It is worth mentioning the stories of three nineteenth-century boat builders, Robert Lambdin, Thomas H. Kirby, and Joseph W. Brooks, all of whom worked primarily on the Eastern Shore.

Robert Lambdin (1799–1885) was a scion of boat builders dating from the early eighteenth century in Talbot County.[1] He began working in his stepfather's yard on San Domingo Creek at age fifteen, and after five years he went to Baltimore to work as a journeyman shipwright. Soon Lambdin was starting up his own business with partner Samuel Butler, with whom he did piecework for other yards, but he built at least four clipper schooners and one brig between 1836 and 1839. Lambdin returned to St. Michaels, built a house, and leased land at the foot of Mulberry Street, where he put up a shipyard and launched a sloop, his first vessel since returning from Baltimore in 1841. From then on, for a period of forty-five years, he built an average of three vessels a year, ranging from oyster-tonging skiffs and sloops to pungy schooners and bugeyes. As the years passed, the sharp-built pilot schooners and clippers yielded to the more practical, shallow-draft pungy schooners, which were handy for oyster dredging in shoal waters. What was unique about Lambdin's bugeyes was his plank-on-frame method of construction; rather than carving the hulls from logs, he shaped them with round or square sterns, as opposed to the sharp stern that had been customary in these craft, to afford more

The bay's watermelon fleet of sailing workboats, pungies, and skipjacks at the Long Wharf. A buyboat can be discerned in their midst, ca. 1931. Photo by Aubrey Bodine. Courtesy, Maryland Historical Society, B478–3.

Three schooners and a bugeye at Kirby's marine railway in St. Michaels, Maryland, 1907. Photo by Thomas H. Sewell. Courtesy, Chesapeake Bay Maritime Museum, 704-8.

working room aft. Lambdin and his wife Ann Goodwin had ten children; the five boys all apprenticed in their father's yard, along with other lads from the area. Thomas Kirby, who later became a well-known St. Michael's shipwright, was one of these. In 1869, Lambdin renamed his yard Robert Lambdin and Sons. George Lambdin and Robert D. Lambdin took up log canoe construction, and Robert became prolific in this, building several canoes that were frequent winners in locally held races. The Lambdin boat-building dynasty ended with the death of Robert D. Lambdin in 1938. Fortunately for the rest of us, he left a memoir that illumines this family's history.[2]

Thomas H. Kirby (1824–1915) established his boatyard on his own property in St. Michaels, at the foot of East Chestnut Street. He began his work as proprietor by taking on repair jobs in the 1840s, and he also worked in the Baltimore shipyards during the Civil War. It was not until the war's end that he began to build vessels from the keel up at his own yard. He specialized in schooners, pungies, and centerboard sloops, with partners and later with his boys, under the name of Thomas H. Kirby & Sons. In conjunction with his partner, Frederick Lang, Kirby built the first

The yawl *Vesta* on Thomas H. Kirby's marine railway at St. Michaels. In the picture is Kirby with his sons and other workers, 1910. Photo by Thomas H. Sewell. Courtesy, Chesapeake Bay Maritime Museum, 708–18.

marine railway in the St. Michaels vicinity. Naturally, this brought him more business and enabled repairs to be done in less time with lower labor costs. Kirby never bothered to construct skipjacks, and in his later days turned from construction to maintenance and repair work. He was over eighty when he launched his last vessel, the *Emma K. Reed,* a powerboat, in 1904. This was also the last vessel built in St. Michaels.[3]

Joseph W. Brooks (1832–1915) was another Eastern Shore shipbuilder, made famous by the quantity as well as the quality of his vessels. Based in Dorchester County, Brooks had a diversified business, which included a marine railway and more than one sawmill; at one time he had as many as twenty men in his employ. He at first apprenticed with his uncle, the ship carpenter George Brooks, and by the time he was twenty-one, Joseph had built his own yard on Parson's Creek, near Madison, off the Little Choptank River. He was a self-taught shipwright but was well read and is known to have used John W. Griffith's *Marine and Naval Architecture,* which gave him a theoretical grounding in ship design. Brooks's design method commenced with the carving of a half model from which the lines would be lofted to full scale. His earliest vessels were pungy schooners, used in the Chesapeake Bay carrying trade and in oyster dredging during the winter months, once that became legal after the Civil War.[4] The characteristic that enabled Brooks to survive the economic cycles was his ability to change with the times. His yard built numerous schooners, pungies, sloops, and bugeyes as clients requested, but proved adept at building steam tugs and gasoline-powered vessels as demand increased. By 1893, Brooks had built twenty-one shallow-draft versions of schooners with centerboard for those who needed to navigate shoaling waters. He built one extremely shallow-draft scow schooner for use on the Susquehanna flats, at the head of the bay.

In building bugeyes for the oyster fishery, Brooks built plank-on-frame as opposed to the customary method of carving out logs, and he also experimented with round- and square-transom sterns, but after 1889, his bugeyes carried the usual sharp sterns, probably because his customers preferred them at less cost. While the depression of 1893 discouraged the building of many more sailing vessels, he continued to build bugeyes until 1903. In addition, Brooks's yard constructed two Chesapeake three-masted schooner "rams," *Margret H. Vane* and *Phillips M. Brooks*. These lengthy, narrow, shallow-draft vessels required few hands and were economical for long-haul cargoes. Brooks's last sailing vessels contained auxiliary gasoline engines and may have been among the first to accommodate the sailing rig to power. Interestingly, Brooks avoided building skipjacks, which were in their ascendancy after the turn of the century, perhaps because he considered their deadrise construction an inferior type of boat. Brooks's integration of sawmills into his shipbuilding operations put him in an advantageous position, but he did contract out the ironwork and engine manufacture to others. He lived and worked where forests of pine and white oak were once extensive. His workboats were remembered for their durability and beauty, with carved and painted trailboards and small figureheads. Some of his best-known vessels were the pungy *Amanda F. Lewis,* the bugeye *Thomas M. Freeman,* and the schooner *Mattie F. Dean.*[5]

The masters of these vessels purchased oysters from tongers and carried them to packinghouses in Baltimore. Another use of the pungy schooners was to haul oysters from Chesapeake Bay to reseed the exhausted oyster beds of New England. The opening of the Chesapeake and Delaware Canal in 1829 sped these developments along, greatly facilitating traffic between Baltimore, Wilmington, Philadelphia, New York, and New England. The coming of railroads to the Chesapeake region stimulated the taking of oysters and the off-loading by schooners of their cargoes of oysters at Seaford, Delaware, and Crisfield, Maryland, for delivery to market. While pungy schooners were somewhat greater in length and shallower in draft (less drag) than the pilot schooners of the late eighteenth and early nineteenth centuries, their proportions remained nearly the same, as did their rig, which was modified only by replacing the overlapping foresail with a boomed foresail and eliminating the square topsails. The pungy schooner owed its longevity to its stable design, low rate of repair, and minimal crew wages. All this changed with World War II, when motorized land transport took over from the Chesapeake Bay cargo schooner.

Chesapeake Bay has seen a rich diversity of sailing craft, and for most of Maryland's history these vessels have been used in commercial ventures. Only since the end of World War I have the sails on the bay become predominantly those of pleasure craft: yachts cruising, day sailing, or racing in regattas. Until the advent of the

Pungy schooners on marine railways at Crisfield, ca. 1930s. Howard I. Chapelle Collection. Courtesy, Chesapeake Bay Maritime Museum, #901–372.

powerboat, trade within the bay, as opposed to the coastal trade, had been the province of sloops and two-masted schooners. The schooners, particularly, carried the bulk of bay cargoes. They were full-bodied, shallower, slower, and often smaller than their oceangoing sisters, and by the mid-nineteenth century most were equipped with centerboards to compensate for their lack of draft. Such vessels maintained scheduled voyages between bay ports, carrying passengers, mail, and commercial cargo. Steamboats eventually replaced cargo-carrying schooners, but they continued to operate into the 1930s. Few new schooners were constructed, and as time went by, Baltimore firms occasionally purchased New England–built schooners to replace older ones that were native to Chesapeake Bay. Mostly, they hauled lumber and continued to ply their trade until after World War II, when some were converted to power or were sold in the Caribbean.

Among other traditional Maryland sailing vessels were the log canoe, bugeye, pungy, skipjack, and ram. The log canoe evolved into the brogan, which was built like a canoe but was 40 to 50 feet long, with a bowsprit, a cabin aft the foremast, bulkheads, and standing rigging on the foremast. The bugeye emerged in the 1860s as an evolved variant of the log canoe. Varying between 35 and 45 feet in length, this craft was originally fashioned from logs that were fastened together, and it served as an oyster-gathering vessel into which the oysters were lifted by tongs and scrapes. The sails carried on these two-masted vessels were a jib, a triangular leg-of-mutton foresail, and a mainsail of similar design. As the demand for oysters grew, so did the need for larger vessels.[6]

The legalization of the oyster dredge at about the end of the Civil War fostered

Unidentified bugeye outward bound from Baltimore, ca. 1920s. Courtesy, Maryland Historical Society, Z24.812.

another increase in size, including the addition of two more logs for greater beam, a deck, and larger sails. Thus, the brogan evolved into the schooner-rigged bugeye, which became the favorite craft of the oystermen, with its peak popularity being the 1880s. Bugeyes varied from 51 to 65 feet in length, 13 to 15 feet in beam, and 2.5 to 5 feet in draft. The records of builder John Branford indicate he charged $1,183.58 for the construction of the bugeye *Coronet* in 1888. As catches declined, however, smaller and cheaper oystering vessels began to appear, carrying but one mast, with a jib and single leg-of-mutton mainsail. The general financial panic of 1893 and the depression it produced caused a reduction in new boat orders. As prosperity slowly returned, watermen turned to a sloop-rigged bateau called a skipjack, which could be built at roughly half the cost of a bugeye. Branford charged from $600 to $800 for five skipjacks that he built in 1899.[7]

At the same time, the gasoline-powered internal combustion engine was adapted from its use on early automobiles, and numerous bugeyes suffered the conversion to power. This usually involved the removal of bowsprit and mainmast, with shortening of the foremast. A cabin pilothouse was then built near the stern, above the engine. To retard the decline of the oyster beds, and perhaps of working sail as well, the Maryland Assembly about 1865 passed a law prohibiting dredging by any but sail-powered vessels. A rough count of a list provided by Marion Brewington indicates that more than 580 bugeyes were built in Maryland, and about 30 more built in Virginia.[8] None was constructed after 1918, so it is not surprising that only two sailing bugeyes remained afloat in the 1970s: *Edna Lockwood,* in the care of the Chesapeake Bay Maritime Museum, and *Little Jennie* (converted to a yacht).

Bugeye *Edna C. Lockwood* drying her sails, May 1973. Photo by C. C. Harris. Courtesy, Chesapeake Bay Maritime Museum, 302–2.

John Branford over a span of twenty-three years (1887–1911) built at least twenty-five bugeyes. The only builder that produced more bugeyes was M. M. Davis and his son Clarence, who constructed thirty at their yard in Solomons, Maryland, between 1883 and 1912.[9]

The ram was a variant of the Chesapeake schooner. She was a large and unattractive vessel by comparison with those previously described. Rams were bluff-bowed, slab-sided vessels with high freeboard, carrying a "bald-headed" rig (i.e., no topsails). The man credited with building the first ram was J. M. C. Moore of Lewisville, later Bethel, Delaware, on the Nanticoke River. Moore was an innovative shipwright who put up the design for the ram as a way of fitting a large cargo-carrying schooner through the C&D Canal instead of relying on canal barges. The rams averaged about 123 feet overall, measured less than 24 feet in the beam, and drew about 8 feet. They evolved from the larger three-masted, shoal draft, centerboard schooners of the post–Civil War period. They could carry more cargo than the two-masted schooner, and with smaller sails, and a smaller crew could manage them. The three-masted schooners thrived from the late 1860s to the 1890s. They averaged about 140 feet in length, 32 feet in beam, with a depth of hull of 13 feet. The cargoes they carried were mostly lumber, coal, fertilizer, and ice.[10]

Most of the Chesapeake rams were built in the 1890s and early 1900s on the Eastern Shore at Bethel, Delaware, and on Broad Creek, which empties into the upper Nanticoke River. Others were built at Sharptown, two at Madison, and one at Pocomoke City, Maryland. While some were designed for the practical purpose of carrying cargo through the C&D Canal, their use was not limited to this route, and many would be found in the bay trade and in coastal traffic. These early rams were "inside" rams, intended for carrying cargo inside Chesapeake and Delaware bays. Their beam measured between 22.5 feet and 23.9 feet, enabling them to pass through the 24-foot-wide canal. Their draft was about 8 feet, likewise limited by the depth of the canal and the shallow rivers up which they had to pass. "Outside" rams had a beam of over 30 feet and a length proportionately longer (about 130 feet) than the inside ram. The rams' economical functions allowed them to endure during the depression years. They were cheaper to operate than engine-powered vessels, carrying bulk cargos of grain, lumber, coal, and fertilizer.

The largest three-masted outside ram was *Joseph P. Cooper,* which measured 150 feet in length, 28.2 feet in beam, and had a 10.2-foot draft.[11] Another example was the ram *Edward R. Baird Jr.* G. K. Phillips constructed her in Bethel in 1903. She made many passages to New England, bringing stone from Sullivan, Maine, to New York City. In 1907 she ran afoul of the Nantucket lightship and had to be beached to avoid sinking. A salvage tug towed her safely off, and after repairs she returned to her trading voyages. During World War I, a U-boat surfaced near the Virginia Capes and ordered her abandoned. The U-boat skipper used gunfire to try to destroy her and submerged, but the ram did not sink. After repairs in Norfolk, *Edward R. Baird* continued sailing, carrying fertilizer for C. C. Paul & Company between Baltimore and Snow Hill without any auxiliary power except her yawl boat. She lasted until the 1950s but sank as she was being towed to Baltimore for repairs in 1955.[12] As many as thirteen rams were still sailing in Chesapeake Bay in 1933, but the numbers had diminished sharply by the 1940s. Some owners extended the lives of their rams by converting them to passenger cruise vessels. One of the last rams commercially active in the bay was the *Jennie D. Bell,* which made her final voyage in 1954. The ram *Edwin and Maud,* however, still carries passengers out of Rockland, Maine, under the name *Victory Chimes.*[13]

As fewer and fewer schooners were being built during the early years of the twentieth century, their numbers were in absolute decline because many were going out of service. Some were converted to power, others were used for a time as barges, and as they neared the end of their useful lives, their owners hauled them to various watercraft graveyards, such as Curtis Bay on the Patapsco River, and abandoned them. Robert Burgess has written that as of the 1930s "the sails or spars of the schooners could be seen at almost any point on the Chesapeake. They were still playing an important part in the commerce of tidewater Maryland, Delaware, and Virginia." But, beyond ordinary hard use, on August 23, 1933, a devastating storm, considered the worst hurricane to hit Virginia and Maryland since 1821, took a toll of vessels on the bay and on the Delmarva coast. It swept ashore in North Carolina after skirting northwestward south of Bermuda and then tore a path northward through tidewater Virginia and the Western Shore of Chesapeake Bay. The hurricane took many by surprise with its tremendous winds and high tides, driving schooners ashore to be pounded by surf until damaged beyond repair. Others met their fates in dismastings and groundings, and a large number were listed as abandoned in the 1941 Register of Merchant Vessels of the United States. Perhaps, with the onset of World War II, the influx of men into the armed services made it difficult for masters to find able men for crew. After the war, some schooners were sold out of the bay to new owners in Philadelphia and New York. One in particular, *Australia,* gained a long and useful life as a coastal trade exhibit in Connecticut at the Mystic Seaport Museum.[14]

THE RENOWNED MARYLAND SKIPJACK, perhaps named for the skipjack tuna, was a boat whose design came to the Chesapeake Bay region from New England in the 1880s. She was a less expensive alternative to the schooner-rigged bugeye at the turn of the twentieth century. Simple to build, a typical decked skipjack was about 45 to 50 feet in length, with a deadrise, or V-shaped hull, a centerboard, and a single raked mast with a leg-of-mutton mainsail. The work on deck was physically demanding—the crew had repeatedly to wind by hand the large cranked drums that brought in the heavy dredges. The largest skipjack, 60 feet in length and measured at 35 tons, was *Robert L. Webster,* built near Deal Island. Later, many adopted power-driven winders. Watermen living on the lower Eastern Shore of Maryland (Dorchester and Somerset counties) often referred to skipjacks with the French term *bateaux,* while in Virginia, watermen called them *Crisfield flatties* or *sharpies.*[15] There were smaller open skipjacks, as well, which measured 24 to 31 feet in length. When ably sailed, they were fast, powerful, and easily suited to the hard work of an oyster-catching waterman. Skipjack captains obtained their catches by hauling dredges over the oyster grounds and were protected by Maryland law against competition from motor-powered dredges.

One of the better-known later skipjack builders was Bronza Parks, of Wingate in Dorchester County, who built his first skipjack, *Wilma Lee,* in 1940. In 1955, he laid down the keels for *Rosie Parks, Lady Katie,* and *Martha Lewis.*[16] Mark Jacoby's description of a day in the life of the skipjack *Helen Virginia,* operating out of Chance, Deal Island, demonstrates the hard life of the dredging waterman of the 1980s.[17] The few remaining working skipjacks operate under regulations that permit dredging, but only from skipjacks without auxiliary power, except for their powerful yawl (push) boats with their 350 horsepower engines, which the skipjack captains are allowed to use as propulsion two days a week. This had to be, originally, on Mondays and Tuesdays, but any two days can now be selected. When not in use these boats hang from davits at the stern of the skipjacks. Their extinction may be only a matter of time, but enough remained in use to be seen sailing in the annual skipjack races held during Chesapeake Bay Appreciation Days, until the late 1990s

Stevedores unloading a "banana boat" freighter from Central America at a Baltimore wharf, ca. 1930s. Courtesy, Maryland Historical Society, B477.

off Sandy Point (at Cambridge); at Deal's Island, Tangier Sound, on Labor Day; and at Tilghman, during Tilghman's Island Days.[18]

An excellent source of basic information about the history of skipjacks as a type and of life on board is Pat Vojtech's well-illustrated *Chesapeake Bay Skipjacks.* Particularly useful is its list of skipjacks, including their size, when and where they were built, and their builders.[19] It is notable that as of April 1994, the National Park Service proclaimed the *Hilda M. Willing,* the oldest working skipjack, to be a National Historic Landmark on the National Register of Historic Places. Actually, both the *Kathryn* (1901) and the *Fannie L. Daugherty* (1904) were a year or two

senior and were still on the job at that time. The *Hilda M. Willing* was built in 1905 at Oriole, Maryland, in Somerset County. She is 40 feet in length, 14 feet in the beam, and she draws 3 feet 1 inch. As a traditional flush decker, with single jib–headed mainsail, she has a motorized pushboat hanging from davits at the stern. The *Willing* was equipped with two dredges, one on each side, with the winders and their motor just forward of midships. Owner Peter Sweitzer had upgraded her over more than fifty years to ensure that she remained an active and safe working vessel, and his son Barry has operated her since 2000.[20]

A remnant of the Maryland oyster dredging fleet still survives. Twenty-six skipjacks were still afloat as of May 30, 2008, the oldest being the *Rebecca T. Ruark,* built at Taylor's Island in 1886. Most of them were built before 1956, and the most recent, *Nathan of Dorchester* and *Sigsbee,* were constructed in 1994. Eleven skipjacks are now preserved in land exhibits or are under restoration in either Maryland or Virginia, and eight have sunk, burned, or been broken up since 1994.[21]

~~~

THE SHIPYARDS OF ANNE ARUNDEL COUNTY have provided an important link between the decline of working sail and the rise of recreational sailing as an important industrial and mercantile activity of that small maritime community. In the middle of the eighteenth century, Annapolis shipyards were alive with activity. Shipowners and captains preferred Annapolis above other Chesapeake ports for fitting out and ship repairs. After the Revolutionary War, Annapolis lost its preference as a port to Baltimore, which, although it was not the state capital, had at-

The ram schooner *Edwin & Maud* in Curtis Creek off the Patapsco River, 1940. Converted to a passenger cruising vessel, with her name changed to *Victory Chimes* (1947), she still cruises off the coast of Maine. Photo by Robert H. Burgess, Louis J. Feuchter Collection. Courtesy, Chesapeake Bay Maritime Museum, 977–144.

Skipjack *Hilda M. Willing,* dredging for oysters on the Choptank River, November 1990. Photo by Richard Dodds. Courtesy, Chesapeake Bay Maritime Museum, 776–10.

tracted industrial and commercial entrepreneurs by virtue of its location near the fall line and the main north-south transportation roads from Washington, Wilmington, Philadelphia, and New York. Fells Point came into its own as a deepwater port and ship construction locale as early as the 1780s, and by 1800 its waterfront was thriving, building pilot schooners for the cargo and passenger carriage on Chesapeake Bay as well as for coastal and transoceanic operations. After the development of the steam engine and the appearance of steamboats on the bay, Federal Hill shipyards also began to flourish in competition with Fells Point. These two areas attracted talented shipwrights from the Eastern Shore yards, which had a long history of boatbuilding. Annapolis shipping and its commerce on the Severn River disappeared in the shadow of the maritime activity of Baltimore on the Patapsco. Still, in the gradual recovery from these doldrums, Annapolis received a shot of adrenalin in the establishment of the U.S. Naval Academy on the site of old Fort Severn in 1845.

The advent of the Civil War in 1861 brought Annapolis under martial law because of its vulnerable position in a pro-secessionist part of the state. With troops

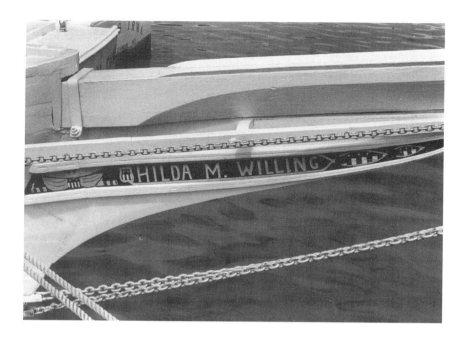

Trailboard and bow of the skipjack
Hilda M. Willing, August 1990. Photo
by Richard Dodds. Courtesy, Chesapeake Bay Maritime Museum, #759–17.

arriving in April and May 1861 on their way to defend Washington, supplies and
ordnance stores would come to support them. The departure of the midshipmen
for Newport in the old frigate USS *Constitution* paved the way for new usage of the
Naval Academy buildings and grounds. Before long, hospital tents were set up on
the campus to care for wounded soldiers. Supply ships came and went, as did cartel
(flag of truce) steamboats carrying federal soldiers released on parole from Confederate prisoner of war camps. Annapolis's population grew during the war, as did her
mercantile waterfront.

   Very few publications illumine the maritime life of Annapolis in this period,
but thanks to Mike Miron's research, we now know a good deal about Annapolis's
late-nineteenth- and twentieth-century boatyards. One of the most important,
called Hallis-Maddison's, was equipped with a marine railway on Horn Point, at
the mouth of Spa Creek. That is near where Wilhelm Heller built a house and
shipyard in 1868. Heller, a German immigrant born in Oldenberg, in 1834, had
learned the fine art of shipbuilding in the old country. After settling with his wife
in Annapolis, he prospered, and by 1880 he expanded his yard, adding a second
marine railway and three shops for paint, lumber, and machines. His yard became
a byword in the boating community, well known for the quality of its building
and repair business. In the Barrie brothers' book, *Cruises, Mainly on the Bay of the
Chesapeake,* there are several references to the Heller yard, one of which states:
"There are many other railways on the Bay, but I doubt if any one of them has a
repair trade like Heller's. One could spend several days there, and on no two would
there be the same collection of vessels."[22] Wilhelm's son, Henry, learned the business at his father's side and continued the yard's work on the local skipjacks,
bugeyes, and pungy schooners. When Wilhelm died in 1916 Henry continued the
tradition, but when Henry died in 1936, there were no more Hellers willing or able
to operate the yard.[23]

Harry E. Lewis, another Annapolitan boatyard owner of this era, started his working life as a waterman in the 1880s and by the time he married in 1899 had accumulated enough savings to buy a property in Eastport, on Spa Creek, between Third and Fourth streets. He and his brother, Will, built a boatyard and marine railway and developed a unique way of doing business. They built workboats and leased them out to watermen who could not afford to buy their own. The Lewis brothers did well in this business, and Harry accumulated some twenty properties in Eastport. In time, he transferred the yard to his two sons-in-law, who operated the yard as Miller & Speaks. They finally sold the property to Harry Bureau, the last person to operate the Lewis yard. Developers bought the land in 1963 and built a waterfront condominium project (the Tecumseh)—the fate of many traditional boatyards.

The Sarles boatyard on Spa Creek is, as of 2007, about a century old. Ben Sarles hailed from Connecticut and came down to the Eastern Shore to participate in a boxing match. Afterward, entranced with the Chesapeake, he became an oyster tonger. In the off seasons, he worked at the Oxford Boatyard. In 1907 he relocated to Annapolis, where he established the boatyard where he built and serviced workboats on the Annapolis side of Spa Creek. By 1924, he could afford to buy a property on the Eastport side, and he reestablished his yard on Boucher Avenue. He was a skilled boat designer who built scale models before constructing the full-size boat. One of his sons, Benjamin R. Sarles, joined him as an engine mechanic, so there was a good balance in the family team. His son, Benjamin O. Sarles, became adept at both engine mechanics and wooden-boat carpentry. He was also a good businessman, and in 2007, in its hundredth year, the family business was still flourishing as Sarles Boat and Engine Shop.

During the pre–World War I years, the James Chance family owned and operated the Chance Marine Construction Company, also located on Spa Creek, between Second and Third streets. Over time the Chance yard became the largest on Spa Creek. Catering to wealthy yachtsmen, the Chances, father and sons, built beautifully finished motor yachts in the 36- to 85-foot range. In 1917–18, the U.S. Navy awarded Chance Marine Construction contracts to build four 110-foot subchasers. They completed two, commissioned in 1918; the third was completed but not commissioned, and the fourth was only 40 percent complete when canceled because of the Armistice in November 1918. Returning to the yacht building and repair business, the Chances did well until the Great Depression. In the 1930s, they defaulted on a loan they had taken out with the Reconstruction Finance Corporation to buy land next to the Annapolis Yacht Club, and the federal government seized their properties on both sides of Spa Creek. After its sale, the former Chance property next to the Yacht Club became the site of the Annapolis Yacht Basin Company. The Chance sons and their former employees joined the shipwrights who worked for the Annapolis Yacht Yard and John Trumpy & Sons.

Mason and Sons was another family firm in the Annapolis boatbuilding business. Harvey Mason, originally from Deale, established his boatyard in 1918 on Spa Creek, where he constructed small sailboats while his wife Grace cut and sewed the sails. By 1933, Mason's family had grown, and Harvey's sons were able to join the business. They shifted construction from sailboats to powerboats. Wife Grace and daughter Mildred now helped out by fabricating the yachts' interiors. World War II brought more changes; two sons went overseas, though son Bill stayed home to help the family business. In the late 1940s, Harvey bought a property at the foot of Fourth Street and Spa Creek, near where the old Spa Creek bridge had been located. Though the firm built a few more luxury yachts, Bill Mason also built speedboats and raced them successfully. He took the helm of *Sally II* in 1946 and reportedly won the President's Cup race in the stock cruiser category at Washington, D.C.[24]

In the 1920s, electrical engineer Charles C. Owens arrived in Annapolis after having worked for General Electric and Henry Ford and Horace Dodge as an efficiency expert. Owens had a passion for yacht design and boatbuilding. He and his three sons set up a business building powerboats on Creek Drive, in Eastport. Owens also designed a sailboat for his sons to use on Spa Creek. This soon led to a contract to build the first "Knockabout" sailboats for the U.S. Naval Academy sailing program and to a partnership with Mason and Sons to build the boats. When the Depression hit, the Owens Yacht Company felt the pain and was unable to sell several completed boats. Although Charles Owens died in 1933, the Owens boys and their sister carried on with a new design for mass production powerboats that caught the public's imagination. Soon they needed more land to produce the boats, so they moved the plant to Dundalk, Maryland, where they found continued success with a 30-footer called the Deluxe Sedan Convertible in 1937. The company went on to develop a national reputation building lines of both sailing and powerboats. To cope with the crush of business, the company employed up to a thousand persons at the Dundalk plant. The 40-foot Owens Cutter was a very popular cruising boat from the 1940s to the 1960s. The Owens brothers sold their company in the 1960s, at about the time boatbuilders were converting to fiberglass production.

After the Chance family company folded, another boatbuilding company took its place. Chris Nelson and Erik Almen were a pair of entrepreneurs from the New York firm of Nelson-Reid, where they been naval architect and yacht broker, respectively. They purchased the Chance Marine property and buildings in 1937 and called it the Annapolis Yacht Yard. The men commenced business by designing and producing the "Annapolis Cruiser," but as soon as war broke out in Europe in 1939, Chris Nelson traveled to England and secured the rights to build a 70-foot Vosper PT (Patrol Boat, Torpedo) Boat for the Royal Navy. This was so successful that they obtained many more contracts, with some variances in design, from Britain, the U.S. Navy, and the USSR.[25] All told, the partners Nelson and Almen built 25 luxury yachts, 13 sub-chasers, and 128 PT boats for the U.S. and Allied navies. These fast patrol boats were designed to be very maneuverable and well armed, carrying little or no armor. Typical of the ordnance the PTs carried late in the war was the following: two to four Mk-VIII torpedoes, two dual 50-caliber machine guns in the turrets, a 40mm Bofors cannon mounted aft, a 37mm cannon far forward, flanked by two 20mm cannons and an assortment of other weapons, such as deck-mounted mortars and additional 30- and 50-caliber machine guns, including two multiple 5-foot rocket launchers. They operated at high speeds, usually in excess of 40 knots, and were used in the Baltic Sea, the English Channel, the Solomon Islands, and the

Philippine Islands. The German Navy used a comparable vessel designated the E-Boat (*Schnellboot*). After World War II, the partners returned to designing and building the Annapolis Cruiser. Unfortunately, Nelson died of a heart attack in 1947, and Almen sold the Annapolis Yacht Yard to naval architect and shipwright John Trumpy Sr., of Camden, New Jersey.

John Trumpy was a Norwegian immigrant who arrived in the United States in 1902, equipped with training in naval architecture he had received in Germany. He found his earliest employment at New York Shipbuilding in Philadelphia and then with Mathis Yacht Building Company, across the Delaware River in Camden. His clients were among the wealthiest in America. By 1917 he had designed 47 sleek, beautifully furnished yachts; thirty years later this number had reached 250 yachts. The only trouble was that the Delaware River's pollution had reached the point that it was wreaking havoc on the hulls of Trumpy's berthed yachts. He and his sons Donald and John Jr. paid a visit to Annapolis in 1947 and liked what they saw at the Annapolis Yacht Yard's former site on the Eastport waterfront. Here they crafted more of the finely finished luxury yachts for which the firm became famous. But in 1962, disaster hit in the form of a fire that destroyed half the yard, and a year later John Sr. died, at age eighty-four. John Trumpy Jr. took over, but conditions had changed in the boatbuilding world with the advent of fiberglass as the primary building material. To work with this new material no longer required the fine woodworking skills of the older generation of shipwrights and yacht carpenters. Then, in the 1970s, labor strikes crippled production, and the men, complaining that wages were too low, began to leave Trumpy's yard in search of other work. The closure of the yard in 1974 brought the end of an era for the building of luxury power yachts in Eastport.[26]

Chapter Nine

The Growth of Recreational Boating

KENNETH GRAHAME, IN HIS CLASSIC *The Wind in the Willows,* uttered some universal truths; one of them was stated as follows, "There is nothing—absolutely nothing—half so much worth doing as simply messing about in boats . . . or with boats . . . in or out of 'em it doesn't matter."[1] There almost certainly have been people "messing about in boats" on Chesapeake Bay since well before European settlement. We have dealt so far with people who, over three centuries, used the Chesapeake waters for personal profit as well as corporate gain, to fight, transport supplies, and simply earn a subsistence-level living. Since the early twentieth century, a more common phenomenon has been the growth of sailing or power-boating in the bay for pleasure. It is difficult to document recreational boating in Chesapeake Bay much before 1900. Popular yachting, by sail or motor, was a product of the upper- and middle-class affluence that burgeoned during the late nineteenth century. The playgrounds of wealthy yachtsmen were largely located near New York and Boston, with Long Island Sound and Massachusetts Bay being their centers of activity.

Those who discovered Chesapeake Bay as a cruising ground in the late nineteenth century owe a debt to authors Robert Barrie and George Barrie Jr., who wrote a charming book about their summertime cruises in the 42-foot plumb stem sloop *Mona.* They brought her to the Chesapeake from Long Island Sound in the late 1890s, entering from Delaware Bay via the Chesapeake and Delaware Canal when the canal had locks. To stem the tide they hired a tug to bring them down to the Elk River, and from there they took a leisurely sail, exploring the bay with a hired hand who took care of the boat when the brothers were off visiting friends or searching for supplies. In later years on other boats, they explored virtually the entire bay at a time when there were no marinas, and they frequently had to depend on the kindness of farmers for chickens and eggs and walk into villages to find ice. They went to Heller's Boatyard in Annapolis for repairs on several occasions. Written in a light-hearted vein, the Barries' careful descriptions give us a vision of the bay at a time when the pace of life was simpler and slower. *Cruises, Mainly in the Bay of Chesapeake* provides an attractive picture of sailing adventures in the Chesapeake when it was a place still relatively unknown to sailors from the northeastern states.[2]

The yacht clubs to which Chesapeake sailors belonged in those early days were few. Among them were the Baltimore Yacht Club (1880), the Chesapeake Bay Yacht Club (Easton, 1885), the Severn Boat Club (Annapolis, 1886, which later became the Annapolis Yacht Club), the Capital Yacht Club (1892), and the famous Gibson Island Club, which came into existence in 1921. Farther down the bay, in Virginia, the earliest clubs were the Hampton Roads Yacht Club (1896) and the Virginia Yacht Club (1907). The most popular boats of those days for class racing were the R, P, and Q class boats designed according to the Universal Rule, and the 6-, 8-, 10-, and 12-meter boats under the International Rule. Six years after World War I began, the newly developed Star class made its debut on the Chesapeake, sponsored at the Gibson Island Club. The class originated in 1911 and raced first on Long Island Sound. At 22 feet, with a large main, small jib, fin keel, and a crew of two, she was an ideal training boat for several generations of sailors, who would end up in the larger sloops, ketches, and yawls. The International Star Class Yacht Racing Association granted the Gibson Island Club a charter for the Chesapeake Bay Star fleet in 1924.[3]

As Geoffrey Footner states, "Reviewing the contents of newspapers and journals of the period between 1880 and 1910, one is struck by the dearth of yachting news outside of New York and New England."[4] Yet in quiet ways, Chesapeake Bay shipwrights made a significant contribution to yachting in general. For example, the two-masted bugeye schooner was a very influential craft. Several of these work-oriented boats became models for yachts in later years. James T. Marsh, a New York shipbuilder who had come south to Solomons in the decade after the Civil War, built the 56-foot schooner *Leatha,* one of the first sailing yachts to emerge from Maryland waters. She was sent north as a possible America's Cup contender but never entered competition.[5] Other Maryland-built yachts during this period included Lucy Carnegie's 120-foot steam yacht *Dungeness* and *Bretagne,* perhaps the largest of that time, the 240-foot bark-rigged steam-powered yacht owned by Leon Say. William O'Sullivan Dimpfel commissioned the Baltimore Yard of Malster and Reaney to build *Chronometer* during the 1880s. Dimpfel was a Philadelphian active in yachting circles and a charter member of the Baltimore Yacht Club in 1880. He later moved to Maryland's Eastern Shore, where he founded the Chesapeake Bay Yacht Club in 1885. This is now considered the oldest surviving yacht club in Maryland.[6]

The Chesapeake Bay bugeye, descended from the log canoe and the brogan, had a strong impact on northern yacht builders. Yachtsmen who saw the bugeye in action purchased and converted some of them into yachts. The Solomons Island boatbuilding firm of M. M. Davis built one of them, *Blue Wing,* in 1893; several were converted to pleasure yachts, among them *E. F. Terpie* and *Retsilla.* The graceful bugeye design caught the eye of other northern yachtsmen, and in particular Philip Rhodes, who provided many popular designs derived from the bugeye. Among shipwrights of the period who built yachts at Solomons Island were James T. Marsh, Thomas W. Elliott, J. J. Saunders, and Robert T. Allinson. John Henry Davis moved his shipbuilding family from Cambridge to Solomons Island in 1879. When John Henry died in 1882, his son Marcellus "Cell" Mitchell Davis took over the family business. His son Clarence E. apprenticed at his side. From that point on, for the next forty years, the Davises were predominant among shipwrights of the Solomons Island area, outlasting most of the others from the early days. In the 1880s, M. M. Davis and Company concentrated their efforts on building oyster sloops and bugeyes; then, when the oyster trade declined in the 1890s, the company branched out into the construction of steam tugs, motor yachts, trawlers, and even barges and freighters for service during World War I. After the war, the Davises found it lucrative to build for yachtsmen. At first, there was interest in converting working bugeyes into schooner yachts, but as northern yachtsmen became more curious, naval architect Philip L. Rhodes in 1929 asked Clarence Davis to collaborate in building his bugeye-based yacht designs.

Other northern yacht builders discovered the Chesapeake, such as Leonard J. Nilson, whose Nilson Yacht Building Company set up shop in Baltimore in 1899. He built a number of yachts, both sail and steam, for members of the New York Yacht Club. According to Footner, Nilson claimed to have built some two hundred vessels at his yard at Ferry Bar on the Patapsco over a thirty-year period.[7] Another early Chesapeake yacht builder was Otis Lloyd, who established the Salisbury Marine Construction Company in Salisbury, Maryland. He built bugeyes until 1910 and then shifted his efforts to yachts, for which there was more demand. This yard built yachts primarily for Philadelphia clients of J. Murray Watts and Thomas Bowes until the mid-1930s. John Smith and Norman Williams, of Sharptown, on the Nanticoke River, took over the Salisbury Marine Construction Company and renamed it Smith and Williams. They operated this yard, building mostly schooner yachts, until the Great Depression hit in 1929 and forced them into bankruptcy. Few boatbuilders survived this crisis, but Clarence Davis succeeded because he had diversified his boatbuilding into commercial construction and repair as well as into yacht building. The Solomons Island location was especially fortunate as it was a main refuge and reprovisioning port on the north-south inside route (later, the Intracoastal Waterway) from New England to Florida, the Bahamas, and the Leeward Islands.

In 1925, the Davis yard received an order to build six 22-foot Star-class sloops for the Gibson Island Club. This would be an important step toward building small, economical racing-class boats for the growing number of yacht clubs in the upper Chesapeake. The man who connected constructor Clarence Davis with yacht designer Philip Rhodes was Donald Sherwood, a wealthy midwestern sportsman who, in the 1920s, was determined to find a competent yacht builder on the Chesapeake. Sherwood scouted out Davis through his connection to the Gibson Island Yacht Club and its growing Star-class fleet. He wanted Davis to build a yacht designed by Philip Rhodes of New York. When Davis saw the plans and the many pages of specifications, he hesitated, fearing he would be taken advantage of by this very particular designer and his client. However, with their reassurance and the prospect of a steady flow of contracts if successful, Davis finally agreed. The result was the launch in 1926 of the gaff-rigged yawl *Seawitch,* a beautiful and successful racer that set up the reputations of both Rhodes and Davis in the East Coast yachting community. In 1932, the owner altered *Seawitch*'s rig from gaff to Marconi and sailed her successfully for many years as a racer and a cruiser. She ended her days as a charter boat in the Virgin Islands in the 1980s.

Many other successful racing cutters, ketches, and yawls were built at the Davis yard over the years, despite Clarence Davis's death in 1936. These included twelve designed by Rhodes, six designed by Sparkman and Stephens, and a couple by John Alden, a yacht designer popular in New England. If the Rhodes-designed *Seawitch* was important for Davis's yachts breaking into racing circles, then his building of *Lord Jim,* a 62-foot gaff-rigged cruising schooner designed by John Alden, and *High Tide,* an Alden-designed schooner of 70 feet, put Davis among the finest yacht builders in the United States in the early 1930s. Originally owned by J. Rulon Miller, an important member of the Gibson Island Club, *High Tide* raced successfully, and after Miller's untimely death in 1931, Eugene E. DuPont purchased and raced her. *High Tide* had a lengthy career, which included naval service under the Coast Guard on antisubmarine picket patrol in World War II. After the war, she changed hands and sailed on the Great Lakes, and the Seven Seas Sailing Club picked her up in rather sad shape, reconditioned her, and renamed her *Golden Eagle.* Later, under new ownership, *Golden Eagle* became *Mariah* and finally sank in a storm off Delaware Bay in 1980.[8]

Many of the other yachts built by Clarence Davis achieved not only local fame but also regional and national reputations, although this would only happen, as Footner states so well, "when an owner reaches a level of experience comparable to his boat's performance." A listing of these yachts' names reads like a Chesapeake Bay hall of fame: *Windward, Orithia, Mimi II, Lady Patty, Tidal Wave, Trivet, Narada, Aweigh, White Cloud,* and *Manitou.* In summing up the contributions of the successive generations of boatbuilding Davises, one must acknowledge the great sense of family tradition, of knowledge and skills passed down from father to sons. In the case of the last Davis generation, Clarence grew gradually into his role as a leading builder of sailing yachts, learning how to treat his wealthy customers and becoming the public relations officer as well as the director of his firm. The Davises were also fortunate to have a loyal and skilled pool of labor available, and they treated their men with respect. The key individual in the success of the yard under Clarence Davis was J. Barnes Lusby, a team leader and artisan of the first rank who was a member of a Solomons' family many of whose members had at one time worked at the Davis yard. It was Lusby who gathered the workers together to continue working under the new owner, George H. Townsend, after Clarence Davis's death in 1936.

As the Stars became more popular with the younger set, more experienced sailors began to purchase and race larger schooners and yawls. For example, in 1927 the Gibson Island Club sponsored an ocean race between New London, on Long Island Sound, and Gibson Island. This race attracted forty yachts, including some of the more famous yachts of that day, such as the Starling Burgess–designed schooner *Nina* and the John Alden–designed *Sachem,* as well as several 35-foot yawls, including William McMillan's *Merry Ann* and C. E. Henderson's *Kelpie.* Another race from New London to Gibson Island was held in 1933. It was won by Gibson Island's schooner *High Tide,* owned by Eugene DuPont. In 1937, a third

New London–Gibson Island race featured race winner *Aventi,* designed by Sparkman and Stephens, *Highland Light,* and *Narada,* designed by Philip Rhodes. The New London–Annapolis race of 1939 evolved into the Newport-Annapolis/ Annapolis-Newport race in 1957, sponsored by the Annapolis Yacht Club. In the 1930s, Chesapeake clubs participated in other big boat point-to-point races, such as the race to Cedar Point, the Rhode River, Poplar Island, Love Point, and Swan Point. When the Tred Avon Yacht Club was founded, in 1931, it and the Chesapeake Yacht Club established the Baltimore Light Regatta, from Gibson Island to Oxford. There was also the popular Hampton Race, in which boats raced from Baltimore Light to Hampton, Virginia, and the racers did not need to observe any buoys or channel markers.

As other clubs came into existence and grew in size and number, they felt a need to reestablish the dormant Chesapeake Bay Yacht Racing Association (CBYRA), originally founded in 1908, in order to coordinate interclub racing activities, standardize rules, and avoid conflicts of racing schedules. To accomplish this, representatives of seven yacht clubs—Chesapeake Bay, Hampton, Gibson Island, Miles River, Tred Avon, Havre de Grace, and the Corinthian Club of Philadelphia— met at Easton in 1934 and drafted the bylaws that gave life to the interclub organization, which still functions today. The Annapolis Yacht Club did not participate, as it was still the Severn Boat Club and was only reorganized as the Annapolis Yacht

Star-class boats racing in light air during a Corsica River Yacht Club regatta in 1951. Photo by Constance Stuart Larrabee. Courtesy, Chesapeake Bay Maritime Museum, 927–1091.

Narada, a 46-foot cutter designed by Philip Rhodes and built by M. M. Davis at Solomons Island in 1936. Owned by Corrin Strong, she often placed well in competition. Photo by Morris Rosenfeld, 1937. © Mystic Seaport, Rosenfeld Collection, Mystic, CT, USA, 81596F.

Club in 1937. After that, however, the AYC rapidly grew to become a dominant force in yacht racing in Chesapeake Bay. In 1939, the AYC ran a major regatta of 238 entries, which, at the time, was said to be the largest ever held on the bay.

~~~

THE U.S. NAVAL ACADEMYS'S sail training program has contributed many good sailors and some famous racing boats to Maryland's Chesapeake. But today's active Naval Academy sailing program, with many different classes of small and large sailboats represented, in no way represents a continuing tradition at this famous Chesapeake Bay institution. Traditional sail training in tall ships died in the early twentieth century and was reborn in the form of competitive sailing just before the outbreak of World War II. The schooner *America,* winner of the 100 Guinea Cup in 1851 in a race around the Isle of Wight, arrived at the Naval Academy after having briefly been used as a blockade runner during the Civil War.[9] During the years after the Civil War, the Naval Academy had at its disposal a number of vessels for summer training cruises, for example, in 1866, the sloops of war *Macedonian* and *Savannah,* the screw steamers *Sago* and *Winnepec,* the gunboat *Marblehead,* and the schooner *America.* The academy's commander, Richard Meade, head of the Department of Seamanship, led a crew of sailors and midshipmen in *America* to defend the cup in 1869. While she did not qualify as the defender, she performed respectably while giving the midshipmen a taste of racing seamanship. The sloop of war *Constellation* was available during the 1870s through the 1890s, and in the later years of the nineteenth century, the Naval Academy made use of sloop of war *Monongahela.*

The end of the summer sailing cruises came in 1909, with the use of the aging sloop of war *Hartford,* Admiral Farragut's flagship during the Civil War, and three other steam-driven warships. The midshipmen had no opportunity to perform sail training. From then on, the emphasis was on steam propulsion and electrical engineering. From 1910 to 1933, the discipline of sail training was notable for its absence from the Naval Academy's curriculum. There was a modicum of small-boat instruction in gaff-rigged centerboard sloops and catboats, and there was rowing practice in 26-foot "pulling cutters," but there was no sailing program worthy of the name. Indeed, according to Rear Admiral McNitt, "the attitude of the Academy toward getting midshipmen out on the water ranked from indifference to scarcely disguised anxiety." Commandant after commandant issued new regulations against boating outside of signaling distance, and they required full uniforms when going boating, effectively discouraging the use of small boats for recreation.

Still, from time to time wealthy yachtsmen donated vessels to the academy and occasionally midshipmen could use them, under strict supervision. A Mrs. Mary Ludlow donated the 60-foot cutter *Medusa* in 1895. She renamed it *Robert Center* in memory of her son. A future Chief of Naval Operations, Lt. Robert B. Carney, later recalled sailing her to the Eastern Shore, during the early 1920s. Dr. Charles Fitzgerald gave the 57-foot yawl *Argo* to the academy in 1906, and she was used until 1930. In the late 1920s, the Bureau of Construction and Repair purchased four Star-class sloops to replace the ancient catboats then in use, but when the commodore of the Miles River Yacht Club invited the commandant to permit the boats to compete in a regatta, Admiral Nulton refused, saying they were for use at the Naval Academy only.

Outside developments relating to intercollegiate sailing had much to do with an eventual change of heart at the Naval Academy. With the development of organized intercollegiate sailboat racing in the 1920s, and particularly with the establishment of the Intercollegiate Racing Association of North America in 1930, the scene was set. The navy's failure to produce good competitive sailors stimulated criticism from both outside and within the navy. In 1929, the navy's own Lt. Cdr. F. E. Whiting wrote in *Yachting* magazine that few officers left the Naval Academy with any interest in sailing and that some could not even steer a small boat safely or with any accuracy. The noted yachtsman Albert F. Loomis in 1932 wrote a letter that was published in the U.S. Naval Institute *Proceedings,* entitled "Are there any sailors in the Navy?" in which he stated that in the prior ten years of competitive ocean racing, there had been no entry from the U.S. Navy. Still the Naval Academy delayed, finally entering a team in intercollegiate competition in 1939, but its team did not win the championship until 1956. Likewise, the Naval Academy at last entered a boat in the Newport to Bermuda race in 1938 but did not win until 1992.[10] When the change of attitude came about, it reflected the thoughts of the academy's leadership and the midshipmen themselves.

The Star-class boats at the academy had not faired well. The maintenance department did not pay any attention to the special needs of these delicate racing craft. There were no boats suitable for overnight cruising. In 1935, a group of midshipmen approached the superintendent to request that the academy obtain large boats for overnight cruising and possibly racing on Chesapeake Bay. Rear Admiral David F. Sellars, who had enjoyed sail training in the class of 1894, obligingly requested the Bureau of Construction and Repair to convert four 50-foot motor launches into auxiliary ketches. When they finally arrived, they were not beautiful and, without centerboard or keel, could not sail well on a beat, but they were much better than nothing. Moreover, qualified midshipmen were allowed to sail these ketches to nearby Chesapeake harbors without officer supervision, and in doing so they had to master the basic skills required in handling these larger sailing craft. To encourage sailing as a recreation in the fleet, the navy assigned 30-foot, ketch-rigged sailing whaleboats to larger ships in the fleet. These led to competitions in various ports where the fleet units happened to be assigned. These open boats had centerboards and could be enjoyably sailed with a large crew.[11] The academy received its next major donated racing boat, *Vamarie,* from Vadim S. Makaroff, in Oyster Bay, New York, in 1936. A 72-foot wishbone ketch, she was a frequent ocean-racing winner. Despite their request, the sailing midshipmen were not allowed to race this vessel in the New London–Gibson Island Race of 1936, and unfortunately the rules were that the vessel should be maintained by the midshipmen, who did not have the experience, the skills, or the time do the job properly. This occasioned further complaints from civilians that the navy was not giving proper support to their new sailing program, a complaint that would have to be heard many more times before things improved.

Yet small steps were taken in the right direction. Before a summer training cruise in 1937, the midshipmen asked that the academy's Stars be carried on board the fleet units so that they could compete with their counterparts in European ports. The navy cooperated and the midshipmen competed against German naval cadets and those from the Britannia Royal Naval College at Dartmouth, England. In these two competitions, the Germans triumphed proudly over the Americans, but the U.S. midshipmen defeated their British opponents in a more enjoyable contest a few weeks later. Another definite step forward was the midshipmen's success in obtaining approval to enter *Vamarie* in the Newport-Bermuda Race of 1938. This took intense lobbying outside the chain of command, a method not pleasing to the Naval Academy's leading officers but one to which they had, perforce, to yield when an assistant secretary of the navy became involved. In the race, *Vamarie*'s rig

MARITIME MARYLAND

was damaged and she finished far back in the fleet. Still, the midshipmen had done well, considering it was their first effort, and they remembered the experience fondly many years later.

Meanwhile, the Navy Department had taken steps to provide much-improved competitive racing boats for the academy's sail-training program. Admiral Sellars had approved the purchase of ten International 14 dinghies for intercollegiate racing, paid for by the Naval Academy Athletic Association. On the offshore racing side, the navy contracted with the Luders Marine Construction Company to build three 44-foot yawls that could accommodate a crew of eight. These yawls, *Alert, Intrepid,* and *Resolute,* were very successful, and the academy ordered nine more for delivery in 1942–43. These held up so well that, twenty years later, the navy replaced them with fiberglass-constructed boats of the same design. According to Alf Loomis, *Yachting* magazine's editor, these boats enabled the midshipmen to compete against civilians on the most favorable terms both offshore and in the lighter winds of Chesapeake Bay.[12] The academy received three wonderful gifts in 1940 from individuals who wanted to strengthen the sail-training program. These were Wallace Lanahan's *Spindrift,* a 55-foot cutter, Dudley Wolfe's *Highland Light,* a 68-foot cutter, and Sterling Morton's *Freedom,* an 88-foot schooner. Of these, the most memorable and successful performer was *Highland Light,* built in 1931. Dudley Wolfe was a sportsman who lost his life in 1939 while attempting to climb the Himalayan mountain K-2. He left a bequest to the Naval Academy that included not only the gift of this vessel but also $100,000 to enhance the sailing program.

Yachting on Chesapeake Bay continued during World War II, although ocean racing ceased with the commencement of hostilities. Many competent young sailors joined the armed forces, but others took their places in the ranks of up-and-coming skippers and crews. The Naval Academy's *Highland Light* won the Chesapeake Bay Yacht Racing Association's High Point Trophy for two successive years, 1943 and 1944. From 1946 on, the Newport-Annapolis race occurred every two years on the odd year, alternating with the Newport-Bermuda Race. After a long, slow New London to Annapolis race in 1955, the course was reversed to become the Annapolis-Newport race, taking advantage of the prevailing southwesterlies, and thereafter the race was generally faster and more enjoyable.

During the 1960s, fiberglass yachts began to challenge the wooden hulls for dominance in the bay's club races, and the increase in the number of boats out on the bay became noticeable. To a lesser degree, some racers used aluminum hulls, among which were Gifford Pinchot's 45-foot yawl *Loon* and Clayton Ewing's 58-foot *Dyna.* In the 1970s the premier aluminum hull racer was Al Van Metre's *Running Tide,* which dominated Chesapeake racing for nearly a decade after she arrived in 1972. With a wide variety of classes to choose from it should not be surprising that long-distance single-handed sailing also found adherents in the Chesapeake area. In addition to transatlantic races, Gibson Island sailor George Stricker competed in the Around (the World) Alone competition. Monk Farnham of Preston, Maryland, made the record books as one of the oldest persons, at seventy-two, to sail across the Atlantic, in a 28-foot Shannon sloop.[13] Bill Homewood, an English-man now living in Annapolis, successfully completed two Observer Single-handed Transatlantic Races (OSTAR), in 1980 and 1984, in the trimaran *Third Turtle*. In 1975, another offspring of Chesapeake Bay sailboat racing was "the Great Ocean Race," a grandiose title for a race around the Delmarva peninsula, which can be challenging despite its relatively short course. St. Mary's College, having one of the nation's leading intercollegiate racing teams, in 1974 sponsored the first Governor's Cup race, which now has a big following. The course runs from Annapolis to St. Mary's City and is a seventy-mile overnight race, capped off with a festive party. South of Annapolis, the yachting center of Solomons Island, on the Patuxent River, has drawn many cruising and racing sailors. Two well-known races sponsored there are the Screwpile Regatta and the Solomons Race Week.

The Naval Academy's sailing program continued to have its ups and downs during the postwar years, but not for lack of talent or the will to compete. As out-side observers in the civilian sailing world were quick to point out, the academy's sailboats lacked an adequate yacht-maintenance program. There was no overall, centralized responsibility for the program, and the academy lacked a professional sailboat coaching staff. Well-known successful yacht racers such as Carleton Mitch-ell, Robert N. Bavier Jr., Sherman Hoyt, Rod Stephens, Cornelius Shields, and the commodore of the New York Yacht Club, DeCoursey Fales, offered to help with advice and influence. Adm. James L. Holloway Jr. helped greatly to turn the situation around. He appointed Commodore Fales to head a voluntary advisory group, which was invaluable in providing the impetus to obtain the changes needed to create a winning program. The Naval Academy Sailing Squadron has become a frequent winner on many levels of competition in Chesapeake Bay and beyond, thanks to the full commitment of the Naval Academy to sailing as a sport deserving of its attention.

Although there are a vast number of them, at least some mention should be made of Chesapeake-designed and Chesapeake-built yachts and of boats that, though not of Chesapeake inspiration, spent a good deal of time associated with the Maryland Chesapeake. Occasionally, traditional skipjacks, pungies, and bugeyes were converted to yachts. Such a one was the *Kessie C. Price,* a pungy schooner built in 1888 at Rock Creek, Maryland. After a lengthy career as a workboat, she was purchased and converted to a yacht. *Kessie C. Price* sailed the bay in one guise or another until 1954. Four bugeye yachts graced Gibson Island harbor for several years before World War II. These were *Applejack, Florence Northam, Bee,* and *Brown, Smith, and Jones,* the last a former member of the state's oyster patrol. To-day, the replica pungy *Lady Maryland,* designed by Thomas Gillmer, can be seen in Baltimore Harbor as part of the Living Classrooms fleet. The modernized re-creation schooner *Pride of Baltimore II,* also designed by Gillmer, sails as a vision of the past, as close a copy of the War of 1812 schooners as Coast Guard regulations will allow. The first *Pride of Baltimore,* an authentic replica, capsized and sank in a sudden squall near the Virgin Islands in 1986, with the loss of her captain and three crew. Like her historic forebears, the schooner probably sank owing to her lack of internal compartmentalization, which exacerbated the damage by allowing water to enter and flood the entire hull. The Chesapeake "Tancook" sloops, designed by Ralph Wiley on the Eastern Shore and Peter Van Dine on the Western Shore, were unique double-enders whose originals were developed at Tancook Island, Nova Scotia, in the nineteenth century. Wiley's sloops were cutter-rigged, with a self-tending staysail and a roller-furling genoa. They were easy to handle and sliced through choppy seas with ease. Van Dine's tended to be 25–35 feet in length, with considerably less freeboard and a shallow keel and centerboard.

The sailing log canoe is another recreational vessel that evolved from a working version from the earliest Chesapeake origins. Log canoes predated the arrival of European colonists. They provided the earliest means of local transportation on the bays and its rivers, later supplemented by European-designed small craft. By the mid-nineteenth century, the double-masted lateen-rigged log canoe with triangular leg-of-mutton sails was not an uncommon sight, as demonstrated on the Pocomoke canoe *Methodist,* built circa 1805.[14] This rig predominated until about 1870, when a sailor added a jib to the foremast. It was only after watermen observed log canoes racing with jibs that they added them to their working log canoe sailing rigs. The addition of sails to the log canoe led to the hull with a false keel. This provided a highly useful element of lateral resistance to the water, so the canoe could make forward progress rather than sideslipping, and provided more vertical stability. By the end of the nineteenth century, centerboards had replaced keels in most of the bay's sailing canoes.

It may be surprising to learn that organized Chesapeake log canoe racing began as early as the 1840s at St. Michaels. There was no club in the modern sense, merely a group of enthusiasts eager to try the canoes' speed in competition. The result was a kind of melee, which started from the beach with sails furled. At a given signal, all hands rushed for the boats, pushed them off, hoisted sail, and the devil take the hindmost. After the formation of the Chesapeake Bay Yacht Club in 1885, races became better organized, with prizes awarded to the winning canoe. The story goes that the first canoe won a cash prize and the last received a ham—so they could grease the bottom and do better next time. As competition heated up, clever owners planed the hulls to make them lighter and faster, but of course this meant a loss of stability in a breeze. They also added more sail area, notably a "kite," or small triangular sail hoisted to the top of the foremast. To compensate, log canoe sailors added movable ballast, and the most innovative added a "springboard," which enabled crew members to slide out to windward when the canoe heeled to counter the wind's pressure on the sails. As a measure of the popularity of these craft, whether as working or racing craft, authorities estimated that in Talbot County, Maryland, 50 canoes were being built per year. The U.S. Census of 1880 recorded 6,300 log canoes in use on the bay, with 175 being built around the bay as a whole.[15]

In the early years of the twentieth century, log canoe races faded with occasional comebacks, until the Miles River Yacht Club formed in 1924. The genuine interest at St. Michaels led to the formation of the Chesapeake Bay Log Canoe Association in 1933. It is remarkable that this organization is still racing canoes, albeit with some modifications, that were built a hundred years ago. Some of the older canoes still competing are *Island Bird, Island Blossom, Island Image, Island Lark,*

Log canoe sailing regatta off St. Michaels, on the Miles River, ca. 1910. Photo by Thomas H. Sewell.

Jay Dee, Magic, Mystery, Silver Heel, Daisy Belle, Billie P. Hall, Oliver's Gift, Sandy, S. C. Dobson, Persistence, Rover, Spirit of Wye Town, Edmee S., Tenacious, Flying Cloud, and *Faith P. Hanlon.* As of 2006, canoe races were being held at the Miles River, Chester River, Rock Hall, and Tred Avon yacht clubs.[16]

FROM THE 1940S TO THE 1960S, one of the most popular Chesapeake yacht designs was the Owens Cutter, a cruiser-racer produced by Owens Yacht Company of Dundalk, Maryland. These vessels measured 40.5 feet in length, with a waterline length of 28 feet and a draft of 5 feet 10 inches. They were successful not only in the bay but also across the nation, winning championships on the Great Lakes and on the West Coast. Competing with the Owens design was that of Robert Henry's Oxford 400, built of wood at the Oxford Boatyard. Henry began producing the 400 (named for its square feet of sail area) at the end of World War II. The boat's overall length was 28 feet, 10 inches; beam, 8 feet 4 inches; and draft, 4 feet 6 inches. She had a pronounced sheer, a short cabin, and ample deck space. The Henry 400's jaunty look and seaworthy lines earned her a write-up in *Yachting* magazine (April 1948). Annapolis-based naval architect Thomas C. Gillmer, already mentioned for his part in designing *Pride of Baltimore I* and *Pride of Baltimore II,* also designed a fair number of yachts for the cruising-racing market. His design of the fiberglass Seawind 30, produced by the Allied Boat Company, accounted for a number of unusually fast hulls. Her measurements were 30 feet 6 inches; beam, 9 feet 3 inches; and draft, 4 feet 4 inches. Another well-respected postwar boatbuilder was William C. Dickerson, who constructed both wood and fiberglass yachts at his Church Creek and later La Trappe Creek yards on the Eastern Shore. His best-known yachts were his Dickerson 35-, 37-, 40-, and 41-footers, designed by either Ted Graves or Ernest Tucker. After Dickerson retired in 1967, Thomas

Log canoe *Belle M. Crane,* with crew out on the springboard to hold her down in a gust of wind. Photo by H. Robin Hollyday. Courtesy, Chesapeake Bay Maritime Museum, 1234–17.

Lucke bought the company and continued to produce well-designed boats, including the Farr 37 into the early 1980s.

Bruce Farr, a transplanted New Zealander who came to Annapolis in the early 1980s, has revolutionized racing-yacht design by combining ultralight, very strong composite materials and light displacement hulls with fine bows and broad quarters. On Chesapeake Bay in the 1990s, Farr's most popular stock-racing designs were the Farr 33, 37, and 43. Farr's designs often win races, as can be seen in his success in designing America's Cup and Whitbread (now Volvo) challengers for many nations. The Whitbread Round the World Race began in 1976. It has become the world's best-known ocean race, held every four years. It sends a small fleet of the world's best sailors on a risky, challenging, exhausting race of some 31,000 miles, lasting nine months. Farr-designed boats have competed in every Whitbread/Volvo Race since 1981, and they won the 1986, 1990, 1994, 1998, and 2002 races. Perhaps the most famous design that emerged from Farr Yacht Designs was the Whitbread 60. For the 1997–98 race, Farr's firm designed eight of the ten competing boats. The one called *Chessie Racing* was created for George Collins, the CEO and president of the mutual fund firm T. Rowe Price, based in Baltimore. His was the only nonprofit syndicate, and it had the smallest budget. Despite Collins's valiant effort in this demanding round-the-world race, *Chessie Racing* ended up in sixth place out of a ten-boat field. Her competitors were boats representing the Netherlands, Sweden, Norway, Monaco, and England, as well as two others from the United States. This was the first round-the-world sailing competition in a "one-design" class designed specifically for the Whitbread Race.[17]

The Chesapeake, with its relatively sheltered waters, is home to small sailing classes as well as large. Lowndes Johnson of Easton designed the Star Junior (or "Baby Star") class called the Comet in the early 1930s. At 16 feet, with a centerboard and an outboard rudder, she is a fine boat for young sailors and is easily trailered and launched. From the southern bay in 1934 came the Hampton, an 18-foot one-design sloop, another small racer designed and built for Chesapeake racing. Like the Comet, the Hampton was originally designed to be built of wood but is now made of fiberglass; she is not as popular as the Comet, but she does well enough, numbering perhaps a thousand boats. Another import from the Virginia Chesapeake in 1954 was the Mobjack, an 18-foot one-design sloop that quickly found an audience.

Emile Hartge, who gained fame as a West River boatbuilder, was the scion of a German family that had settled near Baltimore and later moved to Shady Side and Galesville. He founded what became a boatyard dynasty on Whitestake Point, near the head of the West River. Beginning with log canoes and bugeyes, he later branched out into other vessels. During the 1930s, in Galesville, Maryland, his son Ernest H. (Dick) Hartge designed and built a double-ended 20-foot sloop named *Albatross*. As its popularity grew, he built thirteen more. He further developed a transom-sterned version called the *Sea Witch*. Both of these were centerboard sloops with a high rig, carrying lots of sail, which made them tender and easily capsized, but they were fast racers. His next design was the Chesapeake 20, very similar to the earlier versions but even more successful. The Hartge yard built an estimated seventy-five Chesapeake 20s between 1936 and 1948.[18] Finally, the Philip Rhodes–designed 11-foot Penguin class was commissioned by Chesapeake Bay sailors as a small training sloop for youngsters in 1938–39, and it soon gained national popularity. Many clubs have also adopted this class for wintertime "frostbite" sailing.[19]

≈≈≈

WHILE SAILBOAT RACING IS NOW WIDESPREAD, whole industries have grown to support the traditional but now increasingly popular mode of cruising the bay, in boats under both sail and power. From the late nineteenth century, vacationing in sailboats on Chesapeake Bay has been considered an exhilarating experience by those lucky enough to have the time and wherewithal to undertake the voyage. As mentioned earlier, Robert and George Barrie made the voyage from Philadelphia to the bay several times over a decade at the turn of the nineteenth century. The publication of their nostalgic memoir itself stimulated others to try their hand at bay cruising. A couple of passages will suffice to show the allure of the bay's many rivers and creeks to them in their time.

The bay would lose a large part of its fascination if there were no rivers to ex-

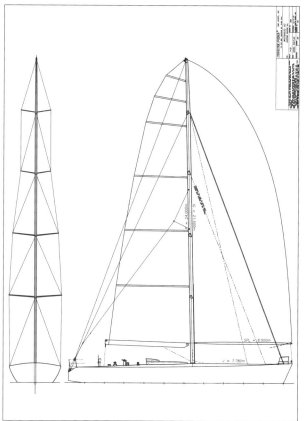

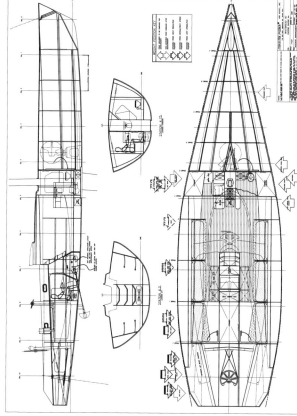

Chessie Racing is a Whitbread 60 (W60) design, a radical departure from earlier round-the-world racers. She was designed by the Farr Yacht Design firm in Annapolis in 1993–94 for the 1997–98 Whitbread Race. The concept projected a sloop constructed of lighter and stronger materials than the earlier Whitbread racers, which had differing designs, two masts, and measured more than 70 feet. While all W60s were of similar design, they were not identical but provided for variances within strict limits. The owners could tweak the design to create an edge that might allow them to win.

Sail plan: Chessie Racing measured 64 feet overall and 17.2 feet in breadth, and she had an L-shaped keel, with a depth of 12.3 feet to balance her large sail area. The mainsail measured 1,259 square feet, the jib 893 square feet, and the spinnaker, at 3,229 square feet, is

a huge sail used in downwind sailing. The boat carried sails of different sizes, shapes, and weights as spares and for all conceivable wind conditions. With this came a stronger mast rig to withstand the great velocities of wind, 50-plus knots, in the Southern Ocean. Courtesy, Farr Yacht Design, Ltd.

Hull plan: Chessie Racing and the other W60s had a unique water-ballast system, which could pump water as needed from one side to the other to compensate for their large sail area and advanced sail shapes. They had a longitudinal center of buoyancy farther forward, full around the mast, and a deep V-shape in the bow. The weight of the boat was nearly 15 tons; the keel bulb alone weighed 7 tons. The design shows the position of the helm and the compass pedestal, the winches for sail handling, and the navigation station belowdecks. Since any unnecessary weight could slow the boat, the twelve crew members had to live in primitive conditions, sleep on six simple pipe bunks, and bring a minimum of gear for a nine-month voyage. Courtesy, Farr Yacht Design, Ltd.

Comet-class racing on the Miles River, 1951. Photo by Constance Stuart Larrabee. Courtesy, Chesapeake Bay Maritime Museum, 927–1079.

plore, no bays to sail about in, no snug little creeks or coves in which to drop anchor at night. Providence must have made the Chesapeake early in the morning after a good night's rest and the Delaware late in the evening after a long hard day, as the latter is all mean, unpleasant, low, and aggravating, while the former is the direct antithesis. Gradually, more and more yachts are seen on the Chesapeake, especially since gas engines have become so popular. Few yachtsmen realize the beauties of this great bay—a perfect Paradise for the cruiser.[20]

In an account of an early spring sail, perhaps in 1906 or 1907, the Barries were sailing their custom-built skipjack *Omoo* in the middle bay area when they decided to run from St. Michaels across the bay to the West River. Here, off Parish Creek, they came upon Capt. Charles E. Leatherbury, a famed local boatbuilder who had in fact built *Omoo* two years before. He came on board for an "inspection," and after he departed, the brothers visited a friend who lived at Tulip Hill, the mansion that had belonged to merchant Samuel Galloway in the mid-eighteenth century. During the sail north to Annapolis the following day, the Barries observed that

the Bay was very attractive this afternoon; hardly a cloud in the sky, the water a deep blue with here and there white caps; vessels beating down looked all alive and full of motion, while others were lazily running wing and wing. Here and there were small sails which had left the fleets of gayly painted oyster canoes working the bars off each point. How the remembrance of an afternoon like this will linger with one through after years and create longing when sitting in some close stuffy office.[21]

Robert Gibson teaching racing tactics to sailors at the Tred Avon Yacht Club, Oxford, Maryland, ca. 1950s–60s. Courtesy, Collection of the Historical Society of Talbot County.

Another remarkable and even earlier account of bay cruising is contained in *Chesapeake Odysseys: An 1883 Cruise Revisited,* by Joseph T. and Jane C. Rothrock. Dr. Rothrock and his wife had found a published account of his great-grandfather's three-month cruise on Chesapeake Bay in 1883 and decided they would attempt a one-month re-creation of that cruise a century later.[22] The book they published on completion of their modern cruise contains passages of each stage of the voyage published side by side with the account of the first Dr. Joseph T. Rothrock's cruise. He had been a medical doctor, academic biologist, and naturalist with a love of sailing and a desire to shake off the year's academic dust by spending his entire vacation in a 30-foot "well fastened" sloop equipped with gaff-rigged main, jib, and bowsprit, and two powerful holding anchors. He brought with him a compatible sailor-friend—named, happily, Lewis Seaman—who did all the things that crew members do: keep their eyes open, track changes of direction of nearby boats, hoist and reef sail, set anchor, and help with navigation. With them they also brought a paid hand, a black sailor named Moses, who did the cooking and other chores as needed. Dr. Rothrock equipped their boat *Martha* with a barometer, compass, charts, leadline, navigational lights, and mosquito netting. He was also an avid amateur photographer, so he brought along a camera to record nature as he saw it.

Martha's cruise began at Delaware City, waiting many hours on a hot June day for a tug to haul her and other waiting vessels through the locks of the Chesapeake and Delaware Canal. Once through, the panorama of the Chesapeake gradually opened as they glided south along the Elk River, with the high bluffs of Turkey Point on the starboard hand and the wide mouth of the Bohemia River on the other. Well beyond, to the west, lay the expansive Susquehanna Flats, part of the delta of the Susquehanna River as it empties into northern Chesapeake Bay. Miles farther to the south, they passed the mouth of the Sassafras River, with its high forested banks and intriguing meanders, which lead all the way to Georgetown,

Downes Curtis and his brother Albert at work in their sail loft at Oxford, Maryland. They gained fame for the high quality of their sails, produced from 1940 to 1996 for all manner of sailboats, including skipjacks and racing log canoes. Courtesy, Collection of the Historical Society of Talbot County.

seven miles deep into the Eastern Shore. Their first secure anchorage was Still Pond Harbor, south of the Sassafras. There they caught fish for their dinner and observed the natural beauty of the place, with its many varieties of birds, particularly fish hawks (ospreys), that coursed overhead. They could even enjoy the predictable summer thunderstorm that made its nearly daily appearance in hot summer weather. The author did not neglect to point out how useful his barometer was in indicating the approach of the storms. And so it went, as *Martha*'s crew headed toward Annapolis, stopping for the night at Worton Creek, again on the Eastern Shore, before rounding Sandy Point and heading into Annapolis on the Severn River. During his voyage, Dr. Rothrock observed how well a distant bugeye moved—swiftly, stiff, and close-hauled—through the waves compared with his relatively short and beamy sloop, which was more adapted to Delaware Bay, as she labored through the Chesapeake chop.

After a brief stay at Annapolis, where a naval officer gave them a tour of the Naval Academy, Rothrock and crew, anxious to reach Virginia waters, took *Martha* out and plunged south. They were blessed by passage of a cold front and the arrival of fresh northerly breezes, which pushed *Martha* rapidly south, logging ninety miles in one day. They bypassed the Patuxent River, rounded Point Lookout, and anchored in Smith Creek, just inside the mouth of the Potomac River. At Smith Creek, Rothrock made the observation that, as well watered as the shores of the Chesapeake were, this may have retarded their development, rather than enhancing it. He argued that water transportation made it too easy to get from place to place, removing the necessity of having good roads. Perhaps true, though native residents of that area would probably not have agreed. There are many reasons for an area not having good roads—scant population, small tax base, distance from big commercial centers, and so forth. Nor did they linger here; a full day's sail brought them to Milford Haven, on the Piankatank River. They found a safe anchorage after some effort but later made the complaint that the chart makers had neglected to sound the approaches to some of the small bays off the Chesapeake. The next day they were again in motion, toward New Point Comfort, but they made the mistake of anchoring downwind from a fish mill, a plant where fish (perhaps bunkers or menhaden) were processed into fertilizer. Rothrock's real objective, it seems, was the James River, for there the pace becomes more leisurely. He writes of the Civil War military operations that took place along the James and of the Union base at City Point during the long siege of Richmond only about twenty years earlier—which to Rothrock must have seemed like recent times. Aside from the ruined wharves, Rothrock found little that reminded him of the war except the six U.S. Navy monitors that lay anchored in the channel, their black hulls covered with canvas awnings spread over the decks to protect their crews from the hot June sun. He remarked on the growing shortage of timberlands in the north when he saw how much timber was being shipped down the James, and he predicted that there would be a time when a forest might have as much value as a silver mine.

When it came time to reverse course and descend the river, Rothrock showed his appreciation of the colonial history of the region by visiting the plantation manors of Berkeley and Lower Brandon, where he toured and took photographs. He found delight in the natural history and geology of the Chickahominy River and visited the site of "Old Jamestown." From there, *Martha* cruised to Newport News, through Hampton Roads, to the York River, and made anchorage in a beautiful, virtually landlocked portion of Antepoison Creek, where thunderstorms would not be a threat. Hoping to arrive at the Patuxent River, with forty-five miles to go, Rothrock and crew found themselves becalmed at the mouth of the Potomac River, which, from Smith Point to Point Lookout, measures an impressive seven miles and has a reputation for nasty seas when tide, current, and wind are opposed. Wisely, when he saw the barometer dropping and unsettled storm clouds dotting the sky, he steered *Martha* for the Great Wicomico River when the wind finally arose. They anchored safely just before darkness and the predicted storm arrived.

From early morning the next day, they swiftly crossed into Maryland waters with a following breeze, anchoring, as so many cruisers do, in the backwaters of Solomons Island in the Patuxent River. "Solomons," as it is called, is one of the best-sheltered harbors in the bay and convenient as well, being just off the main north-south route, with plenty of water for deeper draft vessels. From there, *Martha* sailed up the stem of the bay until reaching the mouth of the Choptank River, guarded by the Sharp Island Light, on the Eastern Shore. After two days at Cambridge, Rothrock's party spent most of the following day sailing westward into the bay and then to Poplar Island, just off the Eastern Shore, where he anchored in an evening gale—somewhat unusual for Chesapeake Bay. Crisscrossing the bay as she worked north, *Martha* anchored in Annapolis, where Rothrock enjoyed a rare visit to the dome of the State House, after which he sailed eastward to the Chester River for an evening in Queenstown harbor. As *Martha* departed the Chester River, with light breezes, her crew saw the gathering of dark storm clouds in the west. With no way rapidly to escape the onslaught, they hoped at least to find safety in the Magothy River on the Western Shore. Unfortunately, this was impossible in the nearly flat calm that preceded the squall. They stowed the jib and double-reefed the mainsail, all the while watching the crew of a nearby schooner drop all her sails. When the wind struck, its force was such that they could not keep *Martha* head to wind to enter the Magothy. Failing that, they dropped the main and ran before the wind under bare poles, as did all the other sailing vessels in their vicinity. The worst was over in twenty minutes, but they still had to keep clear of other vessels fleeing before the storm. When able to hoist sail again, they made for Annapolis harbor to take stock of their situation, and finding nothing terribly amiss, Rothrock and company headed north by stages to complete their cruise without further incident. In conclusion, the author summarizes his view of the experience, no doubt shared by many fellow cruisers: "In spite of its storms and its calms, its overdreaded mosquitos, and its alleged malaria, I have come to think of the Chesapeake as my sanitarium. I know that I come back from my trips stronger than when I start on them. It is a soul expanding process simply to gaze out on the water, to study the features of the headlands, and to conjecture in what time and by what agencies they were formed."

One hundred years later, Dr. Rothrock's great-grandson and namesake decided, with his wife Jane, to replicate the doctor's cruise in the *Response,* a 26-foot fiberglass British-built sloop. They did not deny themselves modern conveniences but did study the area to be cruised and, being good students of history, learned as much as possible about the area. They brought with them a VHF radio, an electronic depth finder, a battery-operated television and radio set, as well as roller furling jib and plenty of books, a camera, and many rolls of film; however, they had no Global Positioning System (GPS) device because, although it had been invented, it had not yet been manufactured and marketed as a handheld instrument for the ordinary cruising sailor. Starting from their base at the Higgins Boat Yard in St. Michaels, they sailed north to the Chesapeake and Delaware Canal and visited its museum to gain a better appreciation of the development of this valuable transportation artery, where great-grandfather Rothrock had begun his cruise. The locks through which he had passed are long gone, and the canal has been widened and deepened to allow passage of containerships transiting the bays to move to Wilmington, Philadelphia, or Baltimore without having to take the outside ocean passage, which would cost both time and money.

The Rothrocks sailed *Response* to many of the same anchorages and ports: Still Pond, and then Worton Creek, bypassing Annapolis on their way south. They noticed that accommodations for cruisers at Worton Creek had blossomed, with several marinas and their modern accoutrements—fuel dock, showers, convenience stores—but they anchored out to experience a more natural environment. Off Annapolis, they tried out their spinnaker, a sail that draws the boat ahead, before the wind, a sail that Dr. Rothrock did not have in his inventory but one that definitely helps the modern sailor cover ground more quickly. Passing a deadrise workboat, the authors discuss its antecedents, the log canoe used for tonging, and its evolution to a racing craft on the Eastern Shore, especially on the Miles River.

Instead of trying to sail all the way from Worton Creek to Smith Creek in one day, they broke their voyage at Solomons, where they were treated to a sudden, thunderous flyby of navy jet fighters from the Patuxent River Naval Air Station, a thrilling if not frightening event. From Solomons, *Response* went on to a quiet anchorage at Smith Creek and then to Milford Haven, where marinas had also sprung up in the hundred years since *Martha* had passed this way. Following an exciting ride south in twenty- to twenty-five-knot winds, the Rothrocks made a point of anchoring at Norfolk, where they attended the annual Harborfest, with its many exhibits and evening fireworks display. Proceeding toward the James River, they paid a visit at Newport News and the Warwick Yacht Club for the purpose of visiting the Mariners Museum, one of the nation's finest, which they heartily recommended to other boaters. Cruising the James River, they passed the Reserve Fleet of "mothballed" ships maintained in case of national emergency and stopped to visit the same plantations that great-grandfather had visited so many years before. On telling their story, they were introduced to the owners of Berkeley and the hostess of Lower Brandon, who delighted in showing off their mansions and relating the history that had taken place there in colonial times.

As they reversed course and headed for home, the Rothrocks paid visits to the other planned sites of interest, but they deviated from the great-grandfather's voyage by heading for Tangier Sound and Crisfield, on the Eastern Shore, one of their favorite ports, and taking a slip at Somer's Cove Marina for a meal of crab cakes at a local restaurant. For the remainder of the voyage, *Response* moved northward along the Eastern Shore, dodging crab pots in Hooper Strait and then finding an anchorage on Brooks Creek, in the Little Choptank River. After a visit to Cambridge, full of interesting sights and Chesapeake maritime history, the next stop was Oxford, an obligatory port of call for most yachtsmen because of its small-town charm and accessibility to boat people. From there the couple passed through Knapps Narrows, for a fueling stop and a shortcut to the bay. They did not anchor at Poplar Island, then much diminished by erosion since the earlier cruise. It was essential, however, for them to visit Annapolis to try to achieve what Dr. Rothrock had done in his time: visit the dome of the State House. The result, happily, was the same. After being told no, the public was no longer permitted to enter the dome, the officials relented and led them up the 413 steps to the dome and its view of the capital city and its maritime surroundings. From Annapolis, to Queenstown, and then back to St. Michaels in a few days completed the Rothrocks' challenging odyssey. These days, not many cruising sailors have the time or the endurance to spend one month, let alone three, circumnavigating the Chesapeake Bay, but to their credit the Rothrocks achieved their dream, as spoken in one of their final paragraphs:

> How it was is how it is for every Chesapeake sailor. It is a beautiful body of water to sail, at times looking like the painted flat of a stage set. Unhurried, there were no marching lines of houses, no tenements, no suburban stretches with gravel and smoke and

abandoned cars. We saw and experienced life on the water which is the side of life cared about and treasured by all boaters. Anyone who has ever cast off, even if only in a dinghy, knows something of how it was. Pleasure in the challenge, in the closeness that sailing brings, in the serenity of one's surroundings—all of those things we found.[23]

One of the most attractive stories of Chesapeake cruising is that of Robert de Gast, a Dutch-born photographer-essayist who sailed a small boat, single-handed, around the Eastern Shore peninsula, parts of Delaware, Maryland, and Virginia, shortened colloquially to *Delmarva.* He purchased a Sparkman and Stephens–designed Sailmaster 22 that had been built in Holland, so skipper and craft were well matched. His two basic requirements in the boat were a relatively short mast and shallow draft, with centerboard, and the capability of being driven by an outboard motor. He named the vessel *Slick Ca'm,* after the waterman's expression for a slick calm, when the water becomes mirrorlike for lack of wind. De Gast began at Annapolis and sailed around Delmarva clockwise, first northward along the Eastern Shore to the Chesapeake and Delaware Canal, eastward through the canal, and then down Delaware River and Bay until reaching the canals and marshes behind Delaware's Atlantic coast. He discovered the peaceful beauty of the Smyrna River when escaping the turbulent waters of Delaware Bay. In proceeding from there to Lewes, just inside Cape Henlopen, de Gast experienced a typical Delaware Bay choppy sea in a 25-knot breeze and was relieved to arrive finally at Roosevelt Inlet, the entrance to the inside passage, which would take him to the Lewes and Rehoboth Canal.

He had hoped to pass entirely south in the canal and bay system to Chincoteague Bay, but the bridges over the canal were too low for his mast, and if he took his mast down and waited for the lowest tide, he was in danger of running aground. Neither choice appealed to him so he took *Slick Ca'm* into the Atlantic through the Indian River Inlet for a seventeen-mile run in the ocean, passing by Fenwick Island and Ocean City's imposing hotels and high-rise condos. Fortunately, the wind had diminished and the sea swells were gentle. A friendly Coast Guardsman assured de Gast that the inlet was manageable, so he pushed out with his motor purring and sail hoisted, favored with a ten- to fifteen-knot breeze. Four hours later, he passed through the Ocean City Inlet and into Sinepuxent Bay, just west of Ocean City's barrier beach. On the following day, he was eager to get moving early to see Chincoteague Bay and its marshy islands, protected from the ocean by Assateague Island. He wrote later that he was struck by the vivid contrast between Ocean City, looking like Manhattan, with its tall buildings, and the deserted, barren vista of Assateague Island. Until 1965, a small population supported itself by fishing, hunting, and trapping there, but these people left and the entire area became part of the National Park Service's Assateague Island National Seashore. A northern portion of the island is also designated as Maryland's Assateague State Park.

De Gast motored south in *Slick Ca'm* until reaching Chincoteague Bay, whose width permitted him to sail, tacking as necessary to stay in navigable water. As he passed south, he observed a herd of the famous wild horses, which attract many tourists to the state park and to Virginia's Chincoteague Island. De Gast's destinations inside the bay included the Virginia village of Greenbackville, and then Chincoteague, as he threaded his way through the shallow channels separating Wallops, Assawoman, Metomkin, Parramore, Hog, and Cobb islands. All the while, he had to overcome the challenges of haze, fog, and the occasional squalls that suddenly sprang up. It is clear from his descriptions that he appreciated the quiet, serene beauty of the wetlands and the waterfowl that surrounded him. He met generally friendly receptions among local fishermen and Coast Guard personnel. De Gast and *Slick C'am* were several times objects of wonderment and comment, since sailboats rarely transited the area. He put in at Wachapreague for repairs to his centerboard by a scuba diver, as there were no boat lifts that could take *Slick Ca'm* on short notice. On reaching the tip of the Delmarva peninsula near Cape Charles, he motored through a cut and under the eastern span of the Chesapeake Bay Bridge. From there, de Gast cruised up the western side of the Eastern Shore, anchoring at Onancock, Tangier Island, on the Pocomoke River just short of Snow Hill, Somers Cove at Crisfield, Fishing Creek, La Trappe Creek off the Choptank, Dun Cove, and Wye River. He returned to Mill Creek off Whitehall Bay, near Annapolis.[24]

The entire cruise lasted twenty-four days. *Slick Ca'm* had covered nearly seven hundred miles, averaging twenty-eight miles per day. The actual circumference of the Delmarva peninsula is four hundred miles, but merely circumnavigating was not the object. De Gast was a dedicated "gunkholer"—he wanted to explore as many rivers and creeks as time permitted. Moreover, he made his cruise in May, a month known for near-freezing temperatures, lots of rain, and not much company in terms of other sailors. But de Gast enjoyed solitary moments and stated his desire to avoid the crowded anchorages that the Memorial Day holiday would inevitably bring. For those who like cruising and enjoy life on the water, uncomfortable though it may be at times, Robert de Gast set an example and wrote a beautifully illustrated book about his experience.

Recreational boating has been a partner in regional development and has stimulated establishment of boatyards, chandleries, yacht clubs, fuel docks, towboat services, marinas, and waterside restaurants. The 1996 edition of the *Guide to Cruising Chesapeake Bay* contains references to more than 430 marina services and facilities for the combined Maryland and Virginia portions of the bay, including 63 for the Potomac River. For Maryland alone, there are 266 marina facilities, including those on the Maryland side of the Potomac. The 2007 *Guide* updated the total number of Chesapeake Bay marinas to 440, with Maryland's share dropping to 260, and provided a guide to 220 waterfront restaurants.[25]

Rick Rhodes's *Discovering the Tidal Potomac: A Cruising and Boating Reference* (1998) covers 87 Maryland and Virginia marinas on or in the approaches to the Potomac. Statistics on the growth of recreational boating for previous decades are hard to obtain. During the 1980s, after several good seasons and the instituting of the Annapolis in-the-water boat shows, the Maryland marine trades industry experienced serious fluctuations. After peaking in 1988, U.S. retail expenditures for maritime recreation dropped suddenly because of a federal luxury tax that targeted new vessels costing over $100,000. In addition, there was a recession during 1990–91. The repeal of the luxury tax and the recovery of the U.S. economy in the middle

1990s produced a strong turnaround in the recreational boating industry. It is estimated that by 1993 there were 190,436 registered and documented boats in Maryland. The breakdown by type was as follows: trailered powerboats, 100,087; in-water powerboats, 60,021; and sailboats, 30,328. This water-oriented population provided a surprising amount of economic activity for the state. According to a recent study, the state benefited in 1985 from $400 million spent directly by boaters. The 1985 Annapolis-based sailboat and powerboat shows combined produced $14 million for the city of Annapolis alone and $1.8 million for the rest of Maryland.[26] The Sea Grant study on which this information is based estimated that boaters all together spent $1.01 billion in the state in 1993, and approximately one-third of that ended up as wages and compensation to Maryland employees. The study arrived at this figure by adding $428.5 million in boat-related expenditures, $438.5 million in boating-trip expenditures, and new and used boat sales expenditures of $144.5 million.[27] Some 18,000 full-time jobs in all sectors of the state's economy were attributed to spending by Maryland's registered recreational boaters. This does not include spending by transient boaters, that is, those from out of state who charter in the state or who transit the Chesapeake while following the intracoastal route, north or south.

A 1996 update of the 1993 study indicated that while there had been an increase in the number of boats registered, from 190,436 to 195,589, most of this growth had been in the smaller trailered boat and personal watercraft (PWC) categories. This represented a 2.5 percent increase and somewhat exceeds the rate of population growth in Maryland, which was 1.8 percent for the same period. Interestingly, this showed a 10.8 percent increase in trailered boats and PWCs and a 7.7 percent decrease in the number of in-water power and sailboats. There has been a dramatic increase in the number of registered personal watercraft since 1993, but the spending patterns of PWC owners are quite different and are lower than those of boat owners. Overall, maritime expenditures have increased since 1993. The six Maryland counties that enjoyed the greatest benefits from recreational boating expenditures were Anne Arundel, Baltimore, Cecil, Prince George's, Queen Anne's, and Calvert.[28]

The Marine Trades Association in Annapolis, assisted by the Maryland Sea Grants program, has provided the most recent information on the benefits accruing from boaters and the boating industries of Maryland.[29] The number of boat registrations in 2000 was 220,800, up 16 percent from 1993. The amount of spending generated by Maryland boaters in 2004 exceeded $2.2 billion, as compared with $1 billion in 1993. In addition, transient boaters generated approximately $154 million for Maryland, a figure that was not analyzed in the 1990s. Further analysis indicated that the boating industry was responsible for 27,000 jobs in Maryland. Each boat contributed an average of approximately $7,421 per year to the state's economy. Registration trends in the boating industry show that there has been an increase in the number of in-water powerboats as compared with trailered powerboats and sailboats. Further, there was a trend toward purchasing larger, costlier boats than in earlier years. Part of the increase in levels of boating money spent is accounted for by a 19.2 percent increase in overall price levels since 1993. Also, fuel prices went up by 40 percent between 1993 and 2000. Once again, Anne Arundel and Baltimore counties accounted for the bulk of the money spent on boats, boating equipment, and services in the state of Maryland.

In a 2004 update, Douglas Lipton noted that registrations decreased slightly—to 209,706—and that proportions by boat types had maintained their size, at 154,340 trailered powerboats, 40,726 in-water powerboats, and 14,640 sailboats. Thus, registered powerboats of all types outnumbered sailboats by 92 percent of the total.[30] By 2007, in the three years since Lipton's previous report, inflation had hit the marine industry. Costs of gasoline and marine diesel fuel had increased dramatically, as had prices at many marinas for boat slips, dry storage, materials, and labor. This may explain the overall decline in boat registrations, to 204,277. That is a loss of 5,429 registered boats, or 2 percent of the 2004 total. Within these parameters, the number of personal watercraft on the bay had increased to 15,015, which is 3,267 more than the reported numbers for 2002. As for auxiliary sailboats, there were 11,773, both inboard and outboard driven, as compared with 109,780 powerboats, including inboard, outboard, and stern-drive models. Thus, in 2007, the overall ratio of sailboats to powerboats on the bay was one sail to ten power. This indicates that there has been a small increase in sail as compared to power, perhaps due to increased fuel and associated costs.[31]

Little noticed in all the magazines, articles, and books about Chesapeake Bay is the sport of powerboat racing. With the application of gasoline engines to boats it was inevitable that numbers of people would, sooner or later, want to race them. In 1903, the American Power Boat Association (APBA) came into existence and began sponsoring races; the first Gold Challenge Cup was held at the Columbia Yacht Club, on the Hudson River, in 1904. The first races were intended for displacement boats only. As the years went by, the racing of outboard-driven boats increased, as did the numbers of hydroplane hulls and the speed at which they traveled. With a change in the rules in 1924, hydroplane hulls became eligible for the Gold Cup. There are many categories of powerboat in racing circuits, but the most popular in the Chesapeake is the stock outboard (hydroplane) racer.[32] The racing boats fell into various categories according to their engine displacement, as established by the APBA. The ranks, from small to large, run from the 1-liter hydroplane, which allows a maximum engine displacement of 1,200 cubic centimeters, to the 2.5-liter stock hydroplane (2300 cc.), 2.5-liter modified (155.5 cubic inches) hydroplane, 5-liter (305 ci.) stock hydroplane, 6-liter (368 ci.) hydroplane, and the 7-liter (454 ci.), or "Grand National," hydroplane.[33]

Although informal powerboat racing undoubtedly occurred in many areas around Chesapeake Bay, the Cambridge Yacht Club sponsored the first powerboat race under APBA rules. This set the standard for nearly a century of inboard powerboat racing on Chesapeake Bay.[34] As time went by the races became more popular, with more powerful engines and larger boats from around the nation entering the competition. Many other clubs sponsored powerboat racing on the Upper Chesapeake, including the Maryland Yacht Club, the Baltimore Yacht Club, the Stoney Creek Boat Club, and the Wilson Point Men's Club, which sponsored the

Middle River Regatta. The Havre de Grace Yacht Club ran these races, as did the Miles River Yacht Club, and a Chestertown Regatta ran races on the Chester River. The Kent Island Yacht Club sponsored races on Hog Bay until 1986, and the Kent Narrows Racing Association revived the race as the Kent Narrows Powerboat Challenge in 1990.

The Cambridge area was especially active, providing racers and boats that earned national titles and set world speed records. By the 1940s, the Chesapeake Bay Regattas, as they were called, had attracted the press, and the *Baltimore Sun* hired an airplane to take aerial photos of the action. The most famous powerboat races in the nation were the Gold Cup races, which were strictly for unlimited hydroplanes. Until 1948, these swift, powerful boats had not raced on the Chesapeake, so the Cambridge Yacht Club named its regatta of that year a Gold Cup Race. The famous orchestra leader Guy Lombardo was known to be a Gold Cup enthusiast, and he brought his boat *Tempo VI* to compete, but she came in second to a boat from St. Louis. Other "Gold Cup" races were held on the Choptank River in the early 1950s, but few of the racers were true unlimited hydroplanes.

Then things began to change for the traditional Cambridge powerboat regattas. By the 1960s, the APBA had published stricter rules, and insurance costs were rising. Larger crowds and more boats were attending the races, presenting logistical problems at the end of High Street, near the Cambridge Yacht Basin. In addition, recreational powerboat wakes from the Choptank River were rolling into the race course, creating a hazard for boats running at high speeds. This caused the organizers to move the race from the Choptank River into the more protected Hambrook Bay, adjacent to city-owned property. The Cambridge Yacht Club continued to sponsor the regatta until 1978 in this location. At that point, when the yacht club, for reasons not precisely revealed, decided to terminate its sponsorship, a group of powerboat enthusiasts formed the Cambridge Power Boat Regatta Association and worked hard to continue the tradition.[35]

Successful racing-boat skippers gained fame, if not fortune. The Gulf Oil Corporation, a major sponsor of powerboat racing in the 1940s and 1950s, offered to sponsor a Hall of Fame for the powerboat racers, and a number of Chesapeake men and a woman, in particular, were so honored. The corporation set up the Gulf Marine Racing Hall of Fame, in which some of the Chesapeake's fastest powerboaters were honored, including Polly Wright and W. Earle Orem, publisher of the *Cambridge Democrat and News.* Orem raced boats with the names *Seagull, Sea Flea,* and *Sea Turtle,* won nineteen of twenty races in 1940, set a world speed record of 50.183 miles per hour in a race on the Potomac in Washington, D.C., and was APBA Eastern Divisional Champion in 1941. Polly Wright was the first woman to be elected to the Gulf Marine Racing Hall of Fame. In 1940 she broke a record steering the 91-cubic-inch hydroplane *Scoundrel* going 56.04 miles per hour in a race at Havre de Grace. Originally from Philadelphia, she eventually moved to Cambridge. Another famous racer was Ed Nabb, who raced the boat *Black Magic,* a Pacific One Design, in which he frequently achieved 50 miles per hour. He won the APBA Eastern Divisional Championship in 1947 and, in recognition of his many wins, was elected to the Gulf Marine Racing Hall of Fame. Other local racers of note,

among many, were Lou Barrell, Elwood "Woody" Pliescott Sr., Calvert "Skeeter" Johnson, and George Cusick.

Hydroplane race on Hambrick Bay off the Choptank River, near Cambridge, ca. 1950s. Courtesy, Collection of the Historical Society of Talbot County.

These racers were bold and determined, and as racing speeds increased to well over 100 miles per hour, they risked injury or death—as many accidents have attested. Powerboat racers still recall with distaste the difficult President's Cup Regatta race held on the Potomac River, near Hains Point, Washington, D.C. On June 20, 1966, three race boat drivers died in crashes on the same day. From then on, race boat drivers have always referred to that day as "Black Sunday." As a writer reported on the day of that race:

> Death came to three hydroplane drivers in two stunning explosions Sunday at the President's Cup Regatta—a race "won" by one of the men who died. Ron Musson, 37, a three-time national driving champion from Seattle, was killed when his radically-designed new *Miss Bardahl* disintegrated at 160 mph. Later Rex Manchester of Seattle and Don Wilson of Palm Beach, Fla., died when Manchester's boat, *Notre Dame,* flew out of the water on the final beat, crashed back and exploded next to Wilson, driving *Miss Budweiser.* The race was ended after the Manchester-Wilson accident, which came during the first lap of the final heat.... Later, officials had no explanations for the accidents. "It's just what happens in racing," said regatta chairman Don Dunnington. "The water was calm. It was just one of those tragedies. It's a rather hazardous profession, and those kind of accidents are just the hazards of the game. These three drivers were the best in the business, but we don't really know what happened."[36]

Powerboat racing on Chesapeake Bay is apparently struggling for survival. It is an increasingly expensive and more complicated sport than it was in the 1950s or even in the 1970s. Safety regulations and insurance requirements have made the races harder for the spectators to see. Further, to take Cambridge as an example, the erosion of Rooster Island, which formerly sheltered Hambrook Bay, has created shallow areas near the course that may cost the regatta its APBA accreditation. Still, the sport has wide support among powerboat fans, although the general public has not been attracted, possibly because sports media generally do not cover the races. Every August the Kent Narrows Racing Association holds a series of races called Thunder in the Narrows, hosted by the Kent Island Yacht Club in Chester, Maryland, the site where powerboat racing is currently most active on Chesapeake Bay. These powerboat-racing events, still going on after a century, are now part of the bay's cultural heritage.

The latest trend in recreational bay boating, kayaks and canoes, reflects the public's interest in getting closer to nature in lightweight, inexpensive, self-propelled craft. This began in earnest at least thirty or forty years ago, when white-water rafting became a fascination for adventurous individuals. At first, this had nothing to do with Chesapeake Bay or its rivers and streams, but popular interest in getting on the water persuaded providers of canoes and kayaks that there was money to be made, and numerous providers of rentals and shuttling services established themselves near waterways on or near the Chesapeake's tributaries. In the last two decades, powerboat drivers and sailors became more aware of kayaks of many descriptions as they paddled along the edges of waterways and at times crossed channels crowded with faster and more substantial watercraft. Access to water has became a popular political issue, due to a shortage of launching ramps, combined with a general lack of waterfront property dedicated to public recreation on the bay. Kayaking enthusiasts can now find books, magazines, and Web sites that describe how and where kayaking can easily be done on the bay.[37] These publications describe in great detail where to find water access points on the Eastern and Western shores, where to launch, what to see, and what dangers to avoid—tugs and barges, summer afternoon thunderstorms, and Aberdeen Proving Grounds.

On the other hand, paddlers will delight in exploring the marshlands of Eastern Neck Island, Kent County, the Gunpowder Falls, on the Western Shore near Baltimore, areas as remote as the Transquaking River which empties into Fishing Bay at the head of Tangier Sound, and Nassawango Creek, on the Pocomoke River, all areas of rare beauty and tranquility. For the socially inclined, there are groups to join, for instance, the Chesapeake Paddlers Association, which advertises itself as offering "many diversified activities and benefits providing a way to safely enjoy sea kayaking within the Chesapeake Bay region." Furthermore, Maryland's Department of Natural Resources, in an effort to be of service to the boating public, created the Maryland Water Trails program in 2007. The goals of this program are to promote "the protection and creation of sites that provide public access to waterways and the development of water trails and other recreational boating opportunities throughout Maryland." This is in accordance with Chesapeake Bay Agreement goals for establishing new water trails, improving public access, and representing the DNR with the National Park Service's Gateways and Water Trails Workgroup.[38]

It will be interesting to watch the development of these new ways of enjoying the Chesapeake Bay region's waterways. Some may regret the presence of "more boats on the bay" and view paddlers as interlopers in what sailors and powerboaters have had to themselves for many decades. Others may see it as a way of finding more supporters for protection of the bay's environment, its natural beauty and resources. Either way, the increased access to the bay and popularity of light watercraft is a trend whose time has come—and not a moment too soon, as the bay's fragile ecology is something to be enjoyed before it is too late.

The Growth
of Recreational Boating

Chapter Ten

Naval Installations on Chesapeake Bay

$\approx\approx\approx\approx\approx\approx\approx\approx\approx\approx\approx\approx\approx\approx\approx\approx\approx$

Sixty miles northwest of the mouth of the Potomac River, near its confluence with the Anacostia River, the Washington Navy Yard stands as the oldest publicly established navy yard in the nation. In 1798, during the early days of his presidency, John Adams ordered the creation of the Navy Department, thereby separating the management of naval affairs from the War Department. The new nation was then on the verge of the Quasi-War with France, fought entirely with its infant navy and some ships donated by port cities and other vessels converted from use as merchant ships. Most of the first six frigates, *Constellation, United States, Constitution, Congress, President,* and *Chesapeake,* were either at sea or in the final stages of construction. Benjamin Stoddert, the first secretary of the navy, ordered a survey of sites likely to flourish as government-owned yards for the building and repair of future vessels, the accumulation of the essential shipbuilding timber, rope for ships' rigging and cables, and the manufacture of ordnance. The choice of Washington as the site of the first yard was logical and practical; at the very seat of government, it offered a ready means of access to the sea when the city of Washington itself was in its infancy and a means of defending the capital when crises arose. One of the more infamous events in the yard's early history occurred when the British Army invaded Washington briefly after the Battle of Bladensburg in 1814. Secretary of the Navy William Jones ordered the elderly commandant, Commodore Thomas Tingey, to burn the yard to prevent it falling into British hands. Tingey did as ordered, and the yard and the ships under construction went up in flames, but he made sure to spare his house from destruction. In later years, it was rumored that he claimed the house as his own and attempted to bequeath it to his heirs, even though it was government property.

Over its many years of service, the Washington Navy Yard became the focus of the navy's leadership. Many of the navy's more illustrious officers served as commandants of the yard, and they were in frequent contact with the bureaucrats and politicians who dominated the nation's policies and politics. President Lincoln, seeking relief from his onerous wartime duties, often visited the yard to converse with Capt. John Dahlgren when he was commandant. The Navy Yard was the official gateway to Washington for many foreign notables who arrived by sea during the nineteenth century. Until 1877, its workers primarily built and repaired ships, but thereafter, the yard's work concentrated on ordnance manufacture and testing, a function that had been Captain Dahlgren's principal interest. The yard's shops grew in number for varied industrial activities, including forges, machine shops featuring huge metal lathes for the boring of gun tubes, and optical shops for manufacturing the lenses for fire control equipment and submarine periscopes. The yard became so focused on the design and manufacture of weaponry during World Wars I and II that the navy renamed it the Naval Gun Factory.

In 1898, the naval constructor David Taylor built the Experimental Model Basin, housed in a long one-story building on the Navy Yard waterfront. There, in a long tank filled with water, equipped with current and wave-making apparatus, naval architects and marine engineers tested hull designs of future ships for stability and speed.[1] Forty years later, the navy built a larger and technically up-to-date Experimental Model Basin at the new Naval Ship Research and Design Center (named for Rear Admiral Taylor), located north of the Cabin John (American Legion) Bridge in Carderock, Maryland. The Navy Yard's four piers welcomed ships of all descriptions, subject to the decreasing depth of water over the years as upstream farms deposited silt along the Anacostia's banks. It was only after World War II demobilization that the navy gave up some of its buildings on the western end of the yard to the General Services Administration. During the 1960s and 1970s, the presence of other government agencies in these old buildings gave the yard a true polyglot character, along with its seemingly random numbering of the buildings, still in effect. After the end of the cold war, beginning in the 1990s, the Navy Department began to realign its activities and relocated some of its major commands, such as the Naval Sea Systems Command (formerly the Bureau of Ships) at the Washington Navy Yard.[2] During these same years, construction of new buildings brought to light deposits of hazardous materials on the sites of earlier intense industrial activity. The Environmental Protection Agency designated the Washington Navy Yard as a Superfund site to facilitate cleanup and remediation to protect the waters and sea life of the Potomac River.[3]

Meanwhile, with the onset of World War I, the navy's leadership had come to the conclusion that it needed to invest in research and development in technology if it were to challenge seriously the leading European nations for supremacy on the high seas. During World War I, Secretary of the Navy Josephus Daniels established the Naval Consulting Board to determine how to proceed in developing weapons for the future. With Thomas Edison as its head, this board recommended establishing the Naval Research Laboratory (NRL) on the Potomac near Washington, as well as the diesel-engineering program at the Engineering Experiment Station in Annapolis and the Naval Torpedo Factory in Newport, Rhode Island. Construction, postponed by the war, commenced in 1920, and four years later, the NRL opened its doors. Between the world wars, the NRL made its principal contribution in the fields of high frequency radio and underwater sound propagation. In the process it developed communications equipment, direction-finding devices, sonar sets, and the first practical radar built in the United States.[4]

The navy created other industrial research stations along the Potomac and on the Severn River, opposite the Naval Academy. The purpose of these establishments was to serve as naval research, development, test, and evaluation centers for naval vessels, vehicles, and logistics and also to provide support to the U.S. Maritime Administration. The first facility of this type had been built on the shores of the Anacostia River in the Washington Navy Yard, where, in 1898, the Experimental Model Basin was constructed for testing hull shapes under varying conditions. A few years later the navy's first wind tunnel was built in the same location, though in the 1940s both of these experiment stations were transferred to Carderock, Maryland. Near Annapolis, the navy built the Engineering Experiment Station (EES) for testing ship control, propulsion, habitability, marine corrosion, metal alloys, and silencing techniques. In 1963, it changed the name of the EES to the U.S. Navy Marine Engineering Laboratory and soon placed the David Taylor Model Basin, Carderock, and the facility on the Severn under the same command and added a mine warfare laboratory. In 1972, the entire complex became known as the David W. Taylor Naval Ship Research and Development Center, funded by the Naval Sea Systems Command.

The Naval Academy has unavoidably become a presence on Chesapeake Bay. The numerous on-water activities of the U.S. Naval Academy, whether in small-boat instruction, sail training in tall ships, summer cruises in battleships, training in yard patrol craft (YPs), or early naval aviation training on the river, justify its inclusion in a maritime history of Maryland. In its early years, the U.S. Navy notably lacked a professional, land-based training school for prospective officers. Secretary of the Navy George Bancroft established the Naval Academy in 1845 on the site of the Army's Fort Severn, near Annapolis.

The outbreak of the Civil War endangered the academy and its training ship, USS *Constitution*. Southern Maryland was a slave-oriented society, and the sympathies of many citizens surrounding the Naval Academy were favorable to the Confederacy, despite Annapolis's proximity to the federal capital. To assure the safety of the academy and "Old Ironsides," the secretary of the navy ordered the removal of both to the safer environment of Newport, Rhode Island. Once the Civil War had ended, the Naval Academy returned from Newport to its original seat on the banks of the Severn. The academy's discipline, faculty, and morale had suffered during the four-year sojourn in Rhode Island. To set things aright, Secretary of the Navy Gideon Welles appointed Radm. David Dixon Porter, one his most accomplished flag officers, as superintendent of the famous naval school. He soon recognized that larger facilities would be required to accommodate the 566 midshipmen authorized to attend the academy. More land was acquired, and new buildings soon adorned the campus.

Porter also modernized the school's curriculum, and giving it a practical direction, he acquired up-to-date ordnance and added double-turreted monitors to the frigates *Santee, Constitution,* and *Macedonian* and the sloops of war *Dale* and *Marion.* Midshipmen used the older ships for gunnery drill and as temporary barracks while the more maneuverable, shallow-draft vessels took the students on practice cruises on the bay. Porter's methods were occasionally criticized. Some ridiculed his institution with the name "dancing academy," but he succeeded in restoring the Naval

Academy's morale at a time when the navy had begun to suffer from a lack of national attention and its Civil War fleet had fallen into disuse and decay.[5]

Adm. John L. Worden, the first commanding officer of USS *Monitor,* succeeded Porter in 1869, and, though more conservative than Porter, he was determined to keep the Naval Academy on the same course. The academy grew little in size, but the faculty during the next years gained in distinction; Albert A. Michelson would win a Nobel Prize in Physics in 1907 for his experiments to determine the speed of light. Faculty members founded the U.S. Naval Institute on Naval Academy grounds in 1873; the institute became famous for its publication of the *Proceedings,* in which naval officers could express themselves on professional matters. The future historian and strategist Cdr. Alfred Thayer Mahan came to teach at the Naval Academy as head of the Ordnance Department during 1877–80.

A renaissance in American naval architecture began in the 1880s with the building of America's all steel navy, powered solely by coal and steam, equipped with heavier armor and more powerful ordnance. The beginning of America's age of imperialism also marked an age of affluence for the Naval Academy and other naval institutions on the shores of Chesapeake Bay. The most visible monument of the Naval Academy's good fortune in the late 1890s was Secretary of the Navy John D. Long's decision in 1898 to reconstruct everything on the grounds. In the process, this project would reshape the land on which the academy stood and change the environment of the town of Annapolis. The result was the completion, in 1906, of Bancroft Hall, in which the entire academy would be housed and fed, and of landfills to extend the academy grounds over the marshy shores of the Severn River.

The construction process included the demolition of quaint old Fort Severn in 1909. The new Naval Academy was completed at a cost of more than $8 million; the institution covered 111 acres, of which 45 were "reclaimed" land. Many of those buildings are still in use today and can be seen by mariners cruising on the bay. Another change took place when the familiar old training ship *Santee* sank at her moorings. She had been used as a gunnery and barracks ship for midshipmen under punishment since 1865. Her replacement was the captured Spanish cruiser USS *Reina Mercedes,* which arrived at Annapolis in 1912 and remained a station ship attached to the Naval Academy until 1957, when she was broken up.

Watermen who worked the Severn River and Chesapeake Bay for crabs and oysters in those days must have seen midshipmen receiving their practical training on summer cruises and experimenting in the early seaplanes as they got a taste of what active duty would bring. Between 1900 and 1909, midshipmen made their last training cruises under sail in square-rigged ships in USS *Monongahela,* USS *Severn* (formerly *Chesapeake*), and USS *Hartford,* Admiral Farragut's flagship during the Civil War. For the next few years, the cruises took place in battleships. In 1915, *Missouri, Wisconsin,* and *Ohio* took the midshipmen from Chesapeake Bay through the Panama Canal—the first time battleships had made such a transit. Likewise, the nation's first modern submarine, *Holland,* became a fixture at the academy for five years, from 1905 to 1910.

The nation's first naval air facility was established at Greenbury Point, on the

x

left bank of the Severn River, in 1911. The Wright brothers aircraft B-1 flew demonstrations at the academy that year, and in the next year, Lt. Theodore "Spuds" Ellyson made the first takeoff assisted by a compressed-air catapult from the *Santee*'s dock. In 1913, the Curtiss C-1 made its appearance on the Severn when Secretary Josephus Daniels and Assistant Secretary Franklin Roosevelt came to "take a spin" in the new aircraft.[6] Apparently convinced of the usefulness of this experimental aircraft, the navy transferred its aviators to the Glenn Curtiss Aviation Camp, San Diego. In 1912, the pilots returned to Greenbury Point, where they performed more flying experiments. Based on their experiences, the Navy Department created a Naval Aeronautical Service and ordered the establishment of a Naval Aeronautical Station at Pensacola, which opened in 1914.

Naval aviation continued at Annapolis as an offshoot of the academy's Department of Seamanship and Flight Tactics, which maintained a training squadron known as the Naval Air Detail. In 1937, the navy began construction of a ramp and a hanger for seaplanes next to the Naval Experiment Station. After World War II, the academy obtained the services of the escort carrier USS *Block Island* (CVE-106), moored in the Severn River. She provided instruction facilities in her combat information center and served as an Aviation Boatswains Mate School. Midshipmen needed training in other kinds of naval aircraft, and the academy made various attempts to acquire a land aviation facility, but all were deemed impractical. The Naval Air Facility at Annapolis was disestablished in 1961. Henceforth, all the midshipmen's aviation training took place at Pensacola.

≈≈≈

IN APRIL 1999, THE U.S. COAST GUARD celebrated the centennial of its establishment of the service's experimental shipyard at Curtis Bay, on the Patapsco River. This dates back to the Revenue Cutter Service lease of thirty-six acres of farmland embracing Arundel Cove for a Coast Guard Depot. Within a few years, Congress authorized the Coast Guard to purchase that parcel and, with the addition of more land, the depot became the Revenue Station at Curtis Bay. During its first decade, Coast Guardsmen repaired lifesaving boats, constructed other small craft needed by the service, and overhauled and painted its cutters.

As the years passed, the yard naturally grew, acquiring a boiler pump house, foundry, and shops for workers in sheet-metal, blacksmith, electrical, paint, and other trades, as well as buildings for mess halls, barracks, garages, storage, and recreation. When the United States entered World War I in 1917, the Coast Guard temporarily became part of the U.S. Navy. This meant that Coast Guard cutters and other vessels went under overall navy command, and some navy vessels were sent to the Curtis Bay Depot for repairs and conversion. During the postwar period, the depot gained personnel to keep up with the additional work that came with maintaining the cutters *Yamacraw, Seneca, Seminole,* and other smaller vessels. By 1930, this facility had grown to nearly five hundred service personnel and civilian employees. The Coast Guard modernized the depot in the following decade, constructing new machine shops, a gasoline-engine shop, boat shops and adding a 40-ton engine-driven marine railway. The Department of Commerce transferred its

Lighthouse Service to the Coast Guard in 1939, and with it came the responsibility to maintain the nation's aids-to-navigation system. The Curtis Bay Depot became a major buoy-construction facility.

When the United States entered World War II and the Coast Guard once again joined the Navy Department, the depot expanded its services and equipment, including a 3,000-ton floating dry dock, two shipways, and a 320-foot by 60-foot concrete pier with a tower crane. The Coast Guard Yard, as it was now called, facilitated the repairs of many large and small vessels, including submarines and buoy tenders, as well as the construction of cutters in the 225-foot range, the Coast Guard cutters *Mendota* and *Pontchartain.* To all this, the Coast Guard added one more responsibility to the yard: that of wartime training station ("boot camp"), which meant an increase of several hundred personnel and attention to their needs.

In the immediate post–World War II era, there was a necessary reduction of workforce to peacetime levels, but the yard continued its typical vessel overhaul and buoy construction. Yard personnel also participated in the building of 300 40-foot steel lifesaving patrol boats, the lightships *San Francisco* and *Ambrose,* and the lead vessel of a new class of 95-foot steel patrol boats. During the 1960s and 1970s, the yard produced 82-foot patrol boats for the Coast Guard's use in the Vietnam War, as well as the 210-foot cutters *Confidence, Resolute, Durable, Decisive,* and *Alert.* The 1980s saw the launching of nearly 300 rescue utility boats and renovation of the 95-foot patrol boats built some thirty years earlier. Periodically, too, the yard provided extensive repair and overhaul for the bark *Eagle,* the tall ship used for training Coast Guard Academy cadets. In 1997, the yard replaced its sixty-year-old dry dock with modern ship-lifting machinery. The Coast Guard's continuing missions involving the war on drug smuggling, rescues at sea, and the inspection of merchant ships involve hard use of its cutters and patrol boats. This burden has redoubled with the impact of the 9/11 attacks and the expanding global war on terrorism in the twenty-first century.[7]

The Coast Guard Yard at Curtis Bay has clearly accomplished much in its more than 110 years of service to the nation. With all this industrial activity, however, the Coast Guard created a harmful ecological legacy for the Patapsco River and Chesapeake Bay, one that it has struggled to mitigate. According to Environmental Protection Agency (EPA) reports, its preliminary assessment of the Curtis Bay Yard in 1993 identified thirteen potential sources of contamination. Investigators found earth samples with semivolatile organic compounds, metals, PCBs (polychlorinated biphenyls), pesticides, and dioxin. Samples taken from Curtis Creek contained elevated metals concentrations associated with dry-dock operations. As a result, after years of formal complaints and appeals, the EPA placed the Curtis Bay site on its National Priorities List in 2002.

The Coast Guard has taken steps to remedy the contamination, with the EPA's oversight. The Agency for Toxic Substances and Disease Registry's public health assessment as of 2007 found no harmful impact on workers or residents of the area. The experience of the Coast Guard Yard at Curtis Bay is similar to that of other naval industries in the Chesapeake Bay region and to the broader national experience. Nearly all naval industrial bases, such as the Washington Navy Yard and the

Naval Ordnance Station, Indian Head, whether involved in ship construction or the fabrication of combustible materials and propellants and the use of paints and solvents, have had to deal with the aftereffects of these toxic materials. While the cleanup is very expensive, the impact of not mitigating the damage would be equally if not more expensive for the bay's environment.[8]

One of the best-known naval enlisted training facilities in the United States was Bainbridge, formerly referred to as U.S. Naval Training Center, Bainbridge, Maryland. Located in Cecil Country in the northern Chesapeake, NTC Bainbridge made its home on the campus of the former Tome School for Boys, an expensive school built and endowed by millionaire Jacob Tome in 1894. For almost thirty years the school was a successful venture in American secondary education. It had a beautiful 100-acre campus designed by Frederick Law Olmsted, handsome granite buildings, spacious grounds, formal gardens, and ample athletic fields and tennis courts. Located on a bluff overlooking the Susquehanna River, it also had access to the river across Port Deposit's main street. During the Great Depression, however, it fell on hard times, and by the late 1930s, the Board of Trustees was ready to find a new use for the property. When Franklin D. Roosevelt was assistant secretary of the navy during the years 1912–20, he visited and delivered an address at the school. As President Roosevelt, he did not forget, and he was willing to acquire it for the federal government as a military base in 1941. In addition to the school's property, the government purchased another thousand-odd acres from nearby farmers to ensure adequate space to accommodate the thousands of servicemen who would pass through the training center. There was a brief competition between the army and the navy as to which service would receive the property, but the navy won out, and it named the new training center for Commodore William Bainbridge, commanding officer of USS *Constitution* in the War of 1812.[9]

Working at a forced-draft pace in 1942, fifteen thousand workmen built barracks, drill halls, and parade grounds at four separate camps on the property at a cost of $50 million over a six-month period. Bainbridge grew and grew until ultimately there were 506 buildings; built to last but ten years, they lasted over thirty years. The training center staff and their four thousand families lived on the base and enjoyed many amenities, such as a family service center, a hospital, libraries, chapels, swimming pools, a carpenter shop, an automobile hobby shop, riding stables, a pistol and rifle range, a boat dock, a movie theater, and a Navy Exchange with commissary. Naturally, the navy also provided an Officers Club, Chief Petty Officers Mess, Enlisted Club, as well as a nine-hole golf course and tennis courts. The facility served primarily as a boot camp, but there were also many different service specialty schools, such as the Naval Academy Preparatory School to prepare prospective midshipmen for the USNA, Enlisted Personnel Distribution Office, Radioman schools A (basic) and B (advanced), Yeoman's School, Fire Control Technician School, a Recruiter School, and in the 1960s, the Nuclear Power School, Naval Reserve Manpower Center, and the Wave Recruit Training Command (from the 1950s to 1972).

With the termination of the Vietnam War, the end of NTC Bainbridge was in sight as the navy downsized and closed many of its schools and training centers. The citizens of Port Deposit knew that the Navy Department was economizing when they could see less maintenance of the once-pristine buildings and grounds. Local residents who had worked at the NTC for years were furloughed, or they resigned to find other jobs. The Training Center closed officially in 1976 as the buildings deteriorated and the training grounds went back to nature. Nonetheless, NTC Bainbridge had a proud past and could boast of having trained half a million personnel during the thirty years of its existence.[10]

WORLD WAR II PROMPTED THE EXPANSION of naval aviation test facilities in southern Maryland, where the Patuxent River joins Chesapeake Bay. The facility was located at Cedar Point, where tobacco fields once flourished, approximately sixty-six miles from Washington, D.C. Fisherman and other mariners plying the bay and nearby rivers could not help but witness and be affected by the growth of the institution that became the Patuxent River Naval Air Station. Housing the Naval Air Test Center, built during 1942–43, it originally had a ten-thousand-foot runway, with access to fifty thousand square miles for air tests. Nearby were many tenant commands, including an aircraft intermediate-support facility, a naval aviation logistics center, a naval electronic systems engineering activity, and a naval oceanography command detachment. The NAS PAX River Air Traffic Control Center is an important feature and is responsible for the safety of its own aircraft and those of twenty-six other military and civilian airports within its area of control. One of the facility's best-known features is its Test Pilot School, where many of the navy's astronauts served in their earlier days.[11]

Navy aircraft from the Patuxent River Naval Air Station conducted live firing exercises over Chesapeake Bay in the area south of Smith and Tangier islands for the training of future carrier pilots. The targets for these exercises were three pre-dreadnought battleships, built before World War I, which had been sunk in the bay for that very purpose. The first of these was the first USS *Texas.* In February 1911, the navy decommissioned this ship and changed her name to *San Marcos* in order to make the name *Texas* available for the new battleship No. 35. Then, one month later, USS *New Hampshire* (BB-25) fired her 12-inch guns at *San Marcos,* sinking her southeast of Tangier Island.

These gunnery tests continued during the interwar era and into World War II. Gradually, gunfire and bombs shattered her superstucture, and *San Marcos* sank deeper into the mud—but not before the hulk had cost the federal government more than $100,000 in damages caused to private ships by this menace to navigation. *San Marcos*'s upper plating is reported to be sunk down to the mudline, twenty feet below the surface at low tide, and is marked as the "*San Marcos* wreck" on Chesapeake Bay navigational charts. Ordnance tests subjected two other pre-dreadnought battleships, USS *Indiana,* in 1920, and USS *Alabama,* in 1921, to a sinking near *San Marcos.* The planes that sank USS *Alabama* were those of the new U.S. Army Air Service. The navy sold the remains of these two target ships to salvage firms, which removed the hulks *Indiana* and *Alabama* before they, too, could become dangers to navigation.[12]

Some forty miles to the east of Washington, the navy in 1942 established the Solomons Island Amphibious Training Base near the mouth of the Patuxent River. This was intended for training the soldiers who would be embarking for operations in Africa and Europe. Solomons Island was chosen because it was the only area in the Chesapeake with beaches that could be used for amphibious landings. The Navy Department was hesitant to use the Atlantic beaches of North Carolina or Virginia because of the U-boat threat, which suddenly appeared in the spring of 1942. Solomons Island was safe from the U-boats, although realistic amphibious operations could not be conducted because of the lack of surf. There, on a narrow spit of land, located between Mill and Back creeks, the navy set up a primitive camp to serve as a base for more men and equipment than could be accommodated. It occupied approximately ninety-seven acres, taken by a petition of condemnation at a federal court in Baltimore on June 23, 1942, because of the landowners' reluctance to part with their property. The Navy Department had rented houses before the taking became official, and they began to bring amphibious ships and landing craft to Solomons Island even before constructing the camp facilities. The formal name of this installation was U.S. Naval Amphibious Training Base (ATB), Solomons, Maryland. The navy established a second ATB at Little Creek, Virginia, just east of Norfolk, a base that is still in operation almost sixty years later. The training began at Solomons in July 1942, with 3,300 enlisted men and officers arriving for eight weeks. Everything about the place was makeshift at first, and the navy conducted its training in a hasty, hurry-up mode because of President Roosevelt's commitment to launch an invasion of North Africa in October or November 1942. As the training got under way, the navy experienced severe administrative problems in setting up the living and working facilities for so many men in a remote rural setting. The actual landing exercises took place on the nearby beaches of Cove Point, with naval gunfire support exercises going into operation at Bloodsworth Island, directly across the bay from Solomons.

The inconveniences for those civilians who used to live and work at Solomons must have been many. To improve civil-military relations with the local landowners, the government set up the Solomons–Cove Point area as a Class B Restricted Area, effective on December 21, 1942. Eventually, facilities for 15,000 men were built, and landing craft, such as LCTs, LCIs, LSMs, and LCSs, were acquired so that men could be trained in their use for operations in the Mediterranean, on the Atlantic coast of Europe, and in the western Pacific. In the early days, morale suffered from lack of proper equipment, poor transportation, and overcrowding. Despite these obstacles, the Solomons Island facilities trained some 67,698 officers and men from 1942 to 1945. Seeing no need to retain this remote, poorly chosen site, the navy disestablished it before the end of the war.[13]

Although today there is no of evidence of the navy's activities at Solomons, its presence significantly disrupted the local population and its economy during the war. The town's small population of 300 expanded ninefold, to about 2,600, to say nothing of the thousands of sailors and soldiers who poured through each year. Local wells were taxed to the utmost and the digging of new ones caused collapse of the older, introducing saline contamination. Sanitation became a major issue, and a committee formed in the Solomons Island Yacht Club was about the only vestige of local government to be found in the small nonincorporated village of Solomons Island.

Naval ship traffic, almost constant from the Patuxent to Drum and Cove points and toward Norfolk in the lower bay, destroyed valuable oyster beds near the mouth of the Patuxent during those years. On the other hand, the wartime influx of personnel, the construction of administrative buildings and roads, and new contracts for local boat builders brought some prosperity. M. M. Davis and Son produced more than fifty 65-foot wooden personnel craft "T-boats" for the Army Transportation Corps, bringing new life for the boatyard, and "labor was no longer a problem. Men were eager to work in an industry so critical to the war effort because military deferments were almost automatic." The Davis company also benefited because, "for the first time, production lines were set up to build military craft. This change became permanent in the postwar era as the assembly line replaced the age-old craftsman approach of shifting skilled artisans from job to job as construction of a vessel advanced. M.M. Davis and Son, Inc. won several 'E' awards for its war work."[14]

On Cedar Point, across the river from Solomons Island, the Patuxent River Naval Air Station (commonly referred to as NAS Patuxent River) occupies an area of more than six thousand acres and is the site of intense naval aviation research, development, testing, and evaluation. As the headquarters of the Naval Air Systems Command, it is a growing complex whose requirements have totally changed the once-quiet landscape of the farmland on the bay that existed before World War II. At the beginning of the war, the navy's air-testing activities were scattered over the country, but with the need for improved aircraft, its leadership decided to consolidate these activities at this new and then-isolated location. At the end of the war, the navy formally established the Naval Air Test Center, including the Test Pilot Training Division. With the introduction of jet aircraft during the Korean War, the navy converted this facility to the Test Pilot School, adding the Weapons Systems Test Division in 1960. With continuing consolidation of naval aviation-related commands, NAS Patuxent River now has a population of approximately seventeen thousand service and civilian personnel working on the base.

The Naval Air Station is located near St. Mary's City, one of the earliest English settlements in America. Thus, when the U.S. Navy chose to build a base for its rapidly growing aviation branch in 1941 in this location, it knowingly acquired some very historic land, containing pre-contact Indian artifacts as well as those of colonial settlers. In 1981 the Maryland Historical Trust and the navy established a partnership that allows for the documentation of historic homes and archaeological excavations as long as they do not interfere with the navy's mission.

During the cold war, the navy became concerned about the potentially disabling effects of tactical and strategic nuclear weapons on its ships and aircraft. The primary methods used to determine vulnerability were simulations of base surge, air shock, underwater shock, and radiation. Test locations were far-flung in the continental United States and abroad. But testing for nuclear radiation effects on electronics took place at Solomons Island, Maryland. To calculate the impact of radiation on equipment based on solid-state electronics, the technicians at White Oak Laboratory near Silver Spring, Maryland, built an electro-magnetic pulse (EMP) radiation simulator for ships, code named EMPRESS, at Point Patience, in the Patuxent River. From there, the technicians could generate immense high-voltage pulses of electrical energy near anchored vessels, up to the size of a destroyer, located up to 1,200 feet away.

During the 1970s and 1980s, the navy conducted these tests against U.S. ships and those of NATO countries. The resulting data assisted in the "hardening" of ships at the platform level to produce virtual immunity to radiation. From the navy's viewpoint, "EMPRESS was a critical element in assuring survivability of the fleet's shipboard electronic systems against the 'cheap kill' from EMP generated by a high altitude nuclear burst."[15] Yet the navy had need of an even larger simulation system, one that could be used to generate a more powerful pulse against bigger ship targets. Over the period 1983 to 1988, the engineers decided to build EMPRESS II on a large barge that could be towed by an oceangoing tug to the open sea, where the new Arleigh Burke Class guided-missile destroyers, Aegis cruisers, and larger ships would be subjected to intensive pulses. The public at large became worried about the environmental impact of these high-energy pulses in the Solomons area, and there were public and political outcries against conducting these tests in populated areas. This undoubtedly had some influence on the navy's decision to move the tests to an ocean environment far from the Chesapeake Bay region.

Some forty miles upstream from the Potomac's mouth, the navy in 1890 established another base whose presence affected the maritime life on the bay. This site was originally known as the Naval Proving Ground at Indian Head, Maryland, where Ens. Robert Dashiell, a Marylander, served as first officer in charge. More precisely, where the Mattawoman Creek meets the Potomac, Dashiell's proving ground became the place where the navy tested the large gun barrels produced at the Washington Navy Yard. After 1898, Congress authorized the navy to set up a powder factory to produce smokeless powder. Many local residents became employees of the Proving Ground in seasons when farming and fishing failed to provide a livelihood.

Dashiell constructed a new 13,000-yard testing facility for gun ranging that soon outgrew its surroundings. For shorter-range weapons, the facility fired its shells down a small valley parallel to the Potomac River into butt emplacements holding 10- and 12-inch armor plates to test both shells and armor. But in long-distance down-range testing, guns had to be fired blindly over the south embankment and intervening land before reaching the open Potomac. The range set up a spotter downriver to report on river traffic and the shells' fall of shot. Officers in charge worried about stray shots, short rounds, flying pieces of armor, and rotating bands that spun off shells in flight. These posed a hazard for residents, farmers, fishermen, and vessels passing up and down the river. The navy in 1901 purchased 1,000 additional yards of land on Indian Head to allay the problem, but that did not last for long. Several incidents occurred, though no lives were lost, but the navy warned Congress in its annual reports that a more isolated location would be needed in the not-too-distant future. Yet no action was taken for another fourteen years. One of the close calls involved the presidential yacht *Mayflower.* President Woodrow Wilson was having a relaxing cruise in the summer of 1913, with Dr. Cary Grayson, his friend and personal physician. They were some distance below Indian Head when a 14-inch shell passed overhead and shed one of its components, probably a rotating band, which struck the water nearby. Again, no one was injured, but the president took note and the press publicized the bad news about the navy's carelessness.

Entry into World War I in 1917 increased the amount of testing done at Indian Head. By the end of the war they were testing the new 16-inch gun barrels and shells. In the process, the navy began testing naval railway guns to be dispatched to France for use in bombarding behind the German lines. These guns had to be tested at full elevation, and neither Indian Head's range nor the army's Aberdeen Proving Ground was adequate. Adm. Ralph Earle, the chief of the Bureau of Ordnance, ordered the officer in charge, Henry E. Lackey, to find a better location. He selected a piece of land on the Virginia side of the Potomac, lying along Machodoc Creek, twenty-two miles south of Indian Head, as nearly ideal. It boasted a 90,000-yard stretch of unimpeded river heading toward the bay. Thus was born the United States Naval Proving Ground, named for Adm. John Dahlgren, and as a result, the Indian Head facility changed its name to the Naval Powder Factory. But the transition was not an easy one, for the navy had to convince congressmen from Charles County, Maryland, that this change was absolutely necessary. Many months of wrangling followed during 1921 and 1922, and the navy was able to prevent closure of the new Dahlgren facility only with the help of southern Democrats, who faced down the Republicans who were trying to keep the facility at Indian Head from losing jobs in a declining postwar economy.[16]

Although the Powder Factory suffered during the lean years between the wars, World War II witnessed a period of expansion and increased complexity. Lower on the Potomac, at Piney Point, the navy established a Torpedo Testing Station and an Experimental Mine Development Unit, under the auspices of the Naval Powder Factory and the Naval Ordnance Laboratory (NOL) at White Oak, Maryland. The torpedoes that the navy used during the first two years of World War II were notoriously cranky and unreliable. When dropped from aircraft or fired from surface ships and submarines, either they did not explode or they exploded only when hitting their targets at an oblique angle. This was not only maddening to the firing crews but positively dangerous to the firing vessels, whose presence was instantly revealed to the enemy. When the navy finally determined that these failures were the fault, not of the men who fired them, but rather of poor manufacturing and faulty testing methods at the Newport Torpedo Station, several new testing ranges were established.

The Naval Ordnance Laboratory built one of these ranges in 1944 at Piney Point, Maryland, and others at Keyport and Port Orchard Inlet, Washington. The tracking range enabled NOL staff to measure torpedo speed and deflection angles at the launch point and then at distances set at 500, 1,000, 2,000, and so on, up to 6,000 yards. The 105-foot Navy tug *Sacagawea* (YT-241) was assigned to work with the ordnance personnel at Piney Point and at the Naval Torpedo Station, Alexandria, Virginia. During the 1930s, the navy established its Deep Sea Diving School at Piney Point. The department ordered the USS *R-10* (SS-87) and USS *S-22* (SS-127) in 1937 and 1938, respectively, to assist in training the divers and U.S. Naval Academy midshipmen. It was off Piney Point that the navy tested the captured German U-boat 1105 ("Black Panther") in the immediate postwar years and finally sank her in 1949. The State of Maryland's Maritime Archaeology Program converted this site to a Historic Shipwreck Preserve and Recreational Diving Site in 1995, with the approval and assistance of the navy's Historical Center in Washington, D.C.[17]

During the war, the navy added an Explosives Investigation Laboratory, where demolition experts dismantled and studied captured enemy ordnance. With the end of the war and the decline of the need for smokeless powder, the Indian Head facility sorely needed new projects. By 1947, enough political influence was brought to bear that the Powder Factory began to produce chemical propellants for rocket fuels. In 1958, the Naval Powder Factory changed its name to the Naval Propellant Plant and continued to house an Explosive Ordnance Disposal (EOD) School. With the creation of new and more elaborate explosive ordnance, as well as solid rocket fuels, the navy changed the name of the plant to Naval Ordnance Station in 1966. By the 1980s, NOS Indian Head's mission had come to include several modern technologies: production of guns, rockets, and missiles; energetic chemicals; ordnance devices; missile weapon simulators; explosive process development engineering; and explosive safety, occupational safety, and environmental protection.[18]

At the same time, the downside of this production of war materiel for local residents and workers at Indian Head was the contamination of the soil surrounding the area. The EPA reported that "manufacturing, testing, loading, and assembly operations have generated a variety of explosive, reactive, and hazardous wastes. In the past, some of these waste products were routinely dumped into pits and landfills on the facility or burned in open burning grounds. Industrial wastewaters were routinely discharged to septic systems and to open ditches and storm sewers that emptied directly into surrounding water bodies." These materials posed a potential danger to humans or wildlife ingesting groundwater or coming into contact with the soil in the Mattawoman Creek and Potomac River areas adjoining the Naval Surface Warfare Center (Indian Head). The EPA put the facility on its National Priorities List in 1995. As of 2007, NSWC had undertaken wellhead protection to assure that migration of groundwater from wells on the base will not pose a danger to the deeper aquifer. The EPA recommended testing soil in areas where lead has been found, voluntary screening of residents, and monitoring and sampling water from Mattawoman and Chicamuxen creeks to determine if heavy metals are entering the food chain through the fish in these waterways. The agency also recommended that NSWC develop an action plan in the event that contaminant levels exceed established public health standards.[19]

In the lower Chesapeake Bay, there is an elaborate complex of naval activities centered on the U.S. Naval Base at Norfolk. After the outbreak of World War I in Europe, the Dupont Corporation built a large powder and shell-loading plant on the York River, not far from Williamsburg. The navy undertook to assist the British by manufacturing and laying the mines for the North Sea Mine Barrage. The navy needed a plant on the Atlantic seaboard, where the mines could be stored, assembled, loaded, tested, and issued in quantities sufficient to meet the insistent demands of war. There, too, it could build up and train personnel in the adjustment and operation of mines. Thus, this tract of land, about eighteen square miles near Yorktown, Virginia, was selected as the best location on the East Coast to concentrate the navy's mine activities and was named the Navy Mine Depot.

During the interwar years, the plant closed and the land was either idle or used for farming, and the town faded away to a few hundred people. With the advent of World War II, the navy built a larger weapons-storage facility, along with warehouses for a wide variety of naval equipment. In 1942, federal officials condemned three thousand more acres (12 km^2) along the York River to establish the Naval Weapons Station. Part of the land that the Navy Department took at this time became the storage and shipping facility known as Cheatham Annex. This facility was commissioned in June 1943 as a satellite of the Naval Supply Depot in Norfolk to provide warehousing facilities in the Hampton Roads area. The supplies handled there included bulk storage of gasoline, diesel, and other fuels, and rural areas were used to dispose of toxic waste, such as medical materials from navy ships.

Cheatham Annex has continued as a navy supply depot right up to the present. The navy shifted oversight of the remaining Cheatham Annex facility to the adjacent Naval Weapons Station, Yorktown. In 2000, a portion of the Cheatham Annex complex was designated by the Environmental Protection Agency as a Superfund cleanup site. The Naval Weapons Station continues in operation. Its purpose is "to receive, store, and provide Naval and Marine Operating Forces with conventional ammunition, missiles, underwater weapons, and special weapons." It is equipped with extensive 1,200-foot-long deepwater piers to facilitate loading and unloading of sensitive, energetic materials.

The U.S. Naval Station, Norfolk, has grown from slender beginnings in 1917, following the Jamestown Exposition, to its current mammoth size. It is the world's largest naval base, covering 4,630 acres northwest of Norfolk, at the confluence of the James and Elizabeth rivers. Secretary of the Navy Josephus Daniels bought the original property, covering 474 acres, for $1.2 million, with an additional $1.6 million set aside for base development, including piers, aviation facilities, warehouses, fuel and oil storage, recruit training classrooms, submarine facilities, and recreation areas. Naval Aviation developed rapidly at NAS Norfolk during World War I and is now located at NAS Oceana, near Virginia Beach.

The magnificent natural harbor offered by the intersection of the James and Elizabeth rivers has deep roots as a naval depot. This reaches back to the establishment of Gosport (Portsmouth) on the east bank of the north-flowing Elizabeth River as a shipyard for the Royal Navy in 1767. Norfolk was already a thriving port at the time, virtually monopolizing the Chesapeake West India trade until overtaken by Baltimore in the late eighteenth century.[20] Shortly after the formation of the Navy Department in 1798, Secretary of the Navy Benjamin Stoddert identified Gosport as a preferred location for the building of a new navy yard. The federal government purchased the Gosport land from the Commonwealth of Virginia and began building a shipyard for the U.S. Navy in 1801. Secretary of the Navy Gideon Welles ordered the yard burned in 1861 to prevent Confederate use, though to little effect. It was from here that the CSS *Virginia* issued forth to give battle to the Atlantic Fleet in March 1862. Located in Portsmouth, on the Elizabeth River across from Norfolk, the Naval Shipyard grew to have eleven thousand employees in World War I and expanded again to forty-three thousand employees in World War II, when it built 6,850 vessels of all types. While no longer building ships, the shipyard provides repair and modernization services, primarily now for nuclear ships and nuclear support ships. The entire Naval Station area has severe ground-water contamination from its extensive industrial activities and since the 1990s has been the site of EPA Superfund investigations and remediation. The station is now the navy's primary operating base on the East Coast and the headquarters of the Commander, Fleet Forces Command (formerly CINCLANT-Commander in Chief, Atlantic Fleet).

The last Chesapeake naval installation considered here is the Naval Amphibious Base, Little Creek. It is a sprawling compound located on the southern shore of the bay, south of Thimble Shoal Channel, on the shores of Little Creek Inlet, on 2,120 acres within the city limits of Virginia Beach. Some of the beaches, named for the World War II invasion beaches Sicily, Anzio, Salerno, and Normandy, are still in use for amphibious landing exercises. In 1942, the Navy Department realized that the Solomons Island ATB was insufficient to train the large numbers of sailors and infantry who required amphibious training, so it acquired the farm acreage of the Whitehurst family, in Princess Anne County, east of Norfolk, and converted it into the Naval Amphibious Base, Little Creek. It had four components. The first, Camp Bradford, for the Construction Battalions (Seabees), soon changed into a training center for the crews of Landing Ships Tank (LSTs). Camp Shelton was an armed guard training center for bluejackets serving as gun crews on board merchant ships. The Frontier Base was the forwarding center for Amphibious Force personnel and equipment destined for the European Theater. The fourth was the Amphibious Training Center for crews of Landing Ship Medium (LSMs), Landing Craft Infantry (LCI), Landing Craft Utility (LCU), Landing Craft Mechanized (LCM), and Landing Craft Vehicle/Personnel (LCVP) boat crews. During World War II over 200,000 sailors and 160,000 army and Marine Corps infantrymen trained at Little Creek. In recent years, NAB, Little Creek, has continued its mission of training and support services to over 15,000 personnel of the twenty-seven home-ported ships and seventy-eight resident or supported activities. Its combination of operational, support, and training facilities, geared predominantly to amphibious operations, make the base unique among the United States Navy and the allied navies.[21]

The navy has had a presence on Chesapeake Bay for over two centuries. The many activities surveyed here provided an invaluable resource base, particularly in scientific and technical developments. But the navy's growth has also swelled the urban areas, helped expand the Washington and Baltimore suburbs toward the bay, and fed the real estate business's inevitable demand for "waterfront property." The navy's industrial activities in many locations have also had the deleterious effect of abusing the bay's tributaries as a means of flushing toxic waste products into the Patuxent, the Potomac, and the great Chesapeake estuary, which empties ultimately into the Atlantic Ocean. In the 1990s, the EPA made a major contribution by requiring federal facilities to investigate, identify, and mitigate the worst abuses of nature that were occurring at these locations. It is greatly to be hoped that these processes will continue, in tandem with the navy's progress in scientific research, technical development, and base operations.

Chapter Eleven

Maritime Archaeology and Cultural Resources

∾∾∾∾∾∾∾∾∾∾∾∾∾∾∾∾∾∾∾∾∾∾∾∾∾∾∾∾

THE MARITIME LORE OF CHESAPEAKE BAY abounds in stories about lost ships and sunken treasure. The avid student or enthusiast can glean these accounts by talking to watermen, reading old newspapers, or culling published articles and books on the history of Maryland. Yet there is a new source of information that can corroborate the oral and written history of the bay. This is the rapidly maturing field of underwater archaeology. In the 1980s, the underwater archaeologists increasingly raised concerns in Maryland and in other states about the need to protect shipwrecks that were being despoiled by treasure hunters and souvenir collectors.

Before the 1950s, underwater archaeology did not exist as a field of professional study. In the last half-century, however, many of the techniques of terrestrial archaeology have been modified to apply to artifacts embedded in the sediments of the numerous tributaries of the bay. A characteristic of underwater archaeology is that the material culture of the past has been preserved, to a certain extent, in the anaerobic (oxygen deprived) silt beneath the water's surface. Whether studied in situ or carefully recovered and conserved, these artifacts can add much to our existing core of historical knowledge about the maritime past. There is also a certain air of excitement and mystery surrounding the whole activity of underwater search and discovery. The public avidly watches television programs containing underwater video footage about shipwrecks and treasure hunters. Few shipwrecks contain the treasure they are reputed to hold within their crushed or battered hulls, but they often contain fascinating artifacts representing the maritime culture of their times. Plans are missing for ships constructed before the mid-nineteenth century and many small craft of more recent periods, but the discovery of their hulls preserved under water can help archaeologists reconstruct shipwrights' methods of bygone eras. It is normal procedure when archaeologists "document" a newly discovered shipwreck site to measure and sketch the remains before disturbing and recovering them. Thus, archaeologists can often recreate the "missing" plan or can better explain the circumstances under which a ship was storm-battered or otherwise destroyed.

Of the many wrecks that could be cited, the wreck of the steamboat *New Jersey* is evocative of what can happen to shipwrecks in a competitive human environment. By applying the methods of underwater archaeology and electronic technology, about thirty years ago underwater archaeologist Donald Shomette and his colleagues were able to revive a past era in maritime history; part of the story, however, is about the belated recognition that beneath Chesapeake waters many priceless time capsules are waiting to be discovered by the right people. Reading Shomette's account, one can sympathize with the keen disappointment felt by maritime historians and archaeologists because unauthorized divers took early advantage of the ship's discovery.[1] The state had no enforceable regulations to prevent wreck divers from absconding with artifacts from the sunken ship and its cargo.

The *New Jersey* was a propeller-driven, steam-propelled freight hauler, 166 feet in length, 23 feet in the beam, and 8 feet in the hold. She also had three schooner-rigged masts, which could be utilized in case the engine malfunctioned. This ship was built during the Civil War and was intended for use in canals and inland waters. Surveyed in December 1862, she entered into government service for the army in 1863 and continued until the end of the war, in 1865. In 1867, she entered commercial service for the Baltimore Steam Packet Company, more popularly known as the Old Bay Line. Her final voyage took place on February 25, 1870. She was scheduled to make the run from Baltimore to Norfolk with a cargo of grain, guano, meat, bacon, and pork. In mid-afternoon, the *New Jersey* departed, and by 12:30 a.m. was between Poplar Island and Sharps Island. Suddenly the crew smelled smoke, and all hands were called to fight the fire. With the fire soon out of control, the captain and crew abandoned ship but stood by in hope of rescue. The ship drifted close to Sharps Island, but the captains of other vessels passing in the night failed to render assistance, perhaps in fear of grounding. A pungy schooner came in close and rescued the crew, but nothing could be done for the *New Jersey*.

During the next 105 years, *New Jersey* was lost from memory. Capt. Varice Henry, of the fishing vessel *Bammy II*, rediscovered her by fathometer in 1973. When Donald Shomette heard the news of Captain Henry's discovery, he was initially skeptical, but the size of the wreck and its height above the surface of the bay bottom provoked his curiosity. On October 4, 1975, Shomette and Jay Cooke, of the National Institutes of Health, dived on the wreck from Henry's boat. They found that the wreck Henry had discovered was a mid-nineteenth century steamboat, filled with commercial goods and not yet despoiled by pothunters, or wreck strippers. Shomette identified her as *New Jersey* because of her location, on the slope of the main channel near the Sharps Island lighthouse, and a date on an artifact that placed the wreck not earlier than May 11, 1869. The significance of this wreck, it later turned out, was its undisturbed nature and relatively intact structure. *New Jersey* was, as Shomette stated, "a gigantic cultural and technological warehouse" reflecting mid-nineteenth-century seafaring on Chesapeake Bay. Unfortunately, before adequate safeguards could be put in place, clusters of divers began to visit and strip *New Jersey* of her cargo and nautical artifacts. What was desperately needed was a state regulatory program to evaluate and protect Maryland's submerged cultural resources. Interestingly enough, the *New Jersey* came to be one of the causes célèbres that would precipitate the need for federal legislation as well as an organized state program in underwater archaeology. Gov. William Donald Schaefer visited Shomette's research vessel on February 27, 1987, and was so impressed by what he saw that he immediately adopted the cause of underwater archaeology as his own and accepted a proposal that the Maryland Historical Trust create a state maritime archaeology program. In addition, he pushed the construction of a state conservation and curation laboratory suitable for the acceptance of large-scale artifacts from underwater sites.[2]

This eventually occurred, as the acquisition and construction of Jefferson Patterson Archeological Park and Museum became a reality. The Maryland Archeological Conservation Laboratory, or MACLAB, as it is called, opened its doors in 1995–97. In the meantime, however, the struggle to enact the Abandoned Shipwreck Act of 1987 in the U.S. Congress proceeded; it became law in 1988, partially in response to Governor Schaefer's earnest advocacy of such a move. At about the same time, the governor established the Maryland Maritime Archeology Program and an oversight body, the governor's Advisory Committee on Maritime Archeology, which comprises underwater archaeologists, conservators, and representatives of commercial and recreational diving interests. This committee provided recommendations that resulted in the Maryland Submerged Archeological Historic Property Act, which became law in 1988, soon after passage of the federal Abandoned Shipwreck Act. In retrospect, it is clear that the state was able to adopt these measures because an archaeological crisis had occurred in the discovery and subsequent looting of the *New Jersey* site during the late 1970s. Maryland officials, lacking enforcement authority, were unable to intervene, and in the debates that preceded passage of the Abandoned Shipwreck Act, this case was cited as an example of bad things that can happen when private interests obtain access to historic sites and can use the latest in SCUBA and site-excavation equipment.

As of the year 2000, more than a dozen years later, the state's officials in the Maritime Archeological Program had much better control over potential archaeological sites. They now have the authority to issue and review diving, dredging, and construction permits, to monitor, and to intervene in unauthorized site plundering in the underwater environment. In 1988, the Office of Archeology found a new home in the Maryland Historical Trust. This agency is endowed with powers to enforce implementing regulations directly or through the Department of Natural Resources (DNR)'s Marine Police. The program officials are empowered to identify, document, and nominate properties eligible for the Maryland Register of Historic Properties and the National Register of Historic Places. They must also do fundamental research, synthesize existing data, and encourage research by representatives of other state historical and scientific institutions. The program is mandated to do educational outreach, participate in conferences, and cooperate with regional and national organizations.[3] These include the Maryland State Highway Administration, the state's Department of the Environment, the U.S. Army Corps of Engineers, the National Park Service, the U.S. Fish and Wildlife Service, the U.S. Department of Defense Cultural Legacy Management Program, and the Department of the Navy's Naval Historical Center.

The Maryland Maritime Archeology Program (MMAP) has many significant achievements to its credit since its establishment in 1989. Considering the vast area of the state covered by water—12,327 square miles, or nearly a quarter of its total—

and the 8,000-mile shoreline of the bay and its tributaries, MMAP officials face a continuing challenge of implementing a submerged cultural resource program. The dynamic river flow and tidal action of the bay's waterways have caused a tremendous amount of erosion over time, cutting away riverbanks and consuming whole islands over the space of two or three lifetimes. One has only to refer to the disappearance of Sharp's Island off the mouth of the Choptank River, the Three Sisters off the West River, the shrinkage of James Island near the Little Choptank River, and the erosion that has cut away the coastline of Kent Island to show how dramatically the bay's landscape has changed.[4] The natural alteration of the margins of the bay accelerates with the development of waterfront residential property, the building of access roads, the construction of marinas, and the dredging of channels, to say nothing of the clearing of forested acreage and of damage done to wetlands. In effect, the bay is getting wider and shallower as the effects of natural and manmade erosion take place, and significant amounts of cultural material are being displaced and swallowed up in the process.[5]

The Maritime Archeology Program's small staff, which has reviewed an average of 250 applications per year for the past twelve years, gives a high priority to survey work in areas prone to high-development activity. As of 1997, the program had surveyed seventeen of the twenty-four major rivers that empty into the bay and discovered 237 prehistoric sites, 209 historic sites, and 217 remote-sensing targets. Four major sites are in the process of being added to the National Park Service's National Register of Historic Places.[6] Another major task of the Maritime Archeology Program is to review National Historical Preservation Act Section 106 permit applications, which pertain to waterway disturbance. Section 106 requires a permit application if a project would intrude into or disturb federally owned submerged historic properties or waterways. The criteria for determining whether a property is historic or not is contained in the National Park Service's guidelines for placing a property on the National Register. If a property has been placed on the National Register or if it is not on the register but can be considered eligible for being put on the register, then it is considered "historic." Involvement in this process does take a fair amount of staff time, but that is considered acceptable because of the potential danger to historic resources if the process were not undertaken. This would also put the program into noncompliance with a federal requirement that makes the state vulnerable to costly lawsuits.

In order to protect historic underwater sites, the state has to demonstrate its possession of submerged historic resources by locating, documenting, and identifying them by remote sensing equipment and by photography, if possible. To accomplish this, it is also beneficial if the MMAP officials and staff maintain cordial relations with businesses, agencies, and individuals who work on or about the bay. MMAP itself has too small a staff to do compliance-mandated research, surveys, or investigations. For these projects, the state contracts with private firms, develops scopes of work, monitors the process, and evaluates the results. The MMAP staff did take on the management of several sites during the 1990s, among them the Stephen Steward Shipyard, which played a role in the Revolutionary War; the state maritime police vessel *Governor Robert M. McLane;* the SS *Columbus,* a nineteenth-century steamboat; the *U-1105* recreational diving site; the USS *Tulip*, a Civil War Union gunboat that sank in the Potomac River in 1864 after a boiler explosion (see Chap. 5); and the Chesapeake Flotilla, a squadron of War of 1812 gunboats scuttled in the Patuxent River in 1814 under the command of Commodore Joshua Barney.[7]

The stories of the *U-1105,* SS *Columbus,* and Barney's Chesapeake Flotilla exemplify what underwater archaeologists have accomplished in Maryland during the last thirty years. The *U-1105* was one of the late-model submarines developed by the German navy in its continuing struggle against the Allies in the Battle of the Atlantic. The war against the U-boats was in part one of scientific ingenuity and engineering in developing counter-weapons against the ever-inventive German submarine service. The Allies had developed sonar and radar to the extent that, by mid-1943, they had reached the turning point in the Battle of the Atlantic. Unable to use their U-boats in surfaced condition because of the possibility of airborne detection, the Germans had developed the snorkel, a breathing device that allowed the boats to cruise at shallow depth with just a large air-intake tube piercing the surface of the sea; further, they developed an artificial rubber coating for the exterior of the submarine to deaden the sonar reflections aimed at locating the U-boats. The snorkel was not a final answer to the Allies' radar devices, which were continually being refined and could pick up echoes from the snorkel tube. The Germans used the labor-intensive Alberich process of rubber-coating their Type VII U-boats. The *U-1105* was a Type VII-C/41, of which only ten were modified with this process. She was ordered in 1941, laid down in 1943, launched in 1944, and was in her second war patrol in April 1945, when she sank a destroyer in the Irish Sea. Immediately, two British destroyers counterattacked as *U-1105* dove deep and avoided detection, perhaps due to her stealth technology. When the war ended for Germany only three weeks later, the commander of *U-1105* surfaced his boat and surrendered to the British in Loch Eribol, Scotland. After study, the British transferred *U-1105* to the U.S. Navy for further study and testing in the Patuxent and Potomac rivers.

The sailors at the Naval Mine Warfare Station at Solomons Island subjected the U-boat to explosive tests, sinking her in 1946 off Point No Point, in Chesapeake Bay, not far from Patuxent Naval Air Station. They recovered the submarine and sank her again in the Potomac River off Piney Point, with a two-stage depth charge that broke her keel. She would not surface again, but remained undetected at a depth of about sixty feet in the dark and swift currents of the lower Potomac for thirty-six years. In the records of where she was located, the navy listed the coordinates of her position with two digits exchanged so that anyone looking for the derelict would be going out to sea, but photographs of her last explosion showed shoreline in the distance. Anyone who saw that would understand that the U-boat was not really so far away or inaccessible. In 1986, sport diver Uwe Lovas and two friends found *U-1105* as the navy's divers had left her, with her hatches sealed. Prying their way in, they found the interior in good condition. For several years, they kept her location secret, but ultimately and perhaps inevitably, the news spread. When this was brought to the attention of the Naval Historical Center and the Maryland

Underwater Archaeologist in 1991, these two agencies took steps to assert control. If no steps were taken, the submarine site would undoubtedly soon be swarming with curiosity seekers and wreck strippers. Donald Shomette, a freelance historian and underwater archaeologist, studied the site under contract to the navy and made recommendations for actions that would provide a path to management of this newly found cultural resource. In a paper delivered to the Society for Historic Archaeology in 1997, Shomette stated:

> The State and the Navy entered into a Memorandum of Agreement governing the stewardship and management of the site on 18 November 1993. With financial support provided by a Navy Legacy grant, the site was sealed from entry, hazardous features recorded and removed, significant artifacts recovered for preservation by the Trust's conservator, and a marker buoy for divers affixed to the wreck. Brochures featuring the ship's history, diving information, and emergency numbers were published, and a permanent exhibit on the ship was erected in the museum's Piney Point Lighthouse Museum Annex. Diving safety and emergency management guidelines, for dissemination throughout the sport diving community, were commissioned by the Trust. On 8 May 1995 the *U-1105* Shipwreck Preserve was officially opened to the public. To date, the site has been visited by an estimated 3,000 divers. Monthly inspections of the wreck are now being carried out by the Maritime Archaeological and Historical Society [MAHS], a not-for-profit organization, under the supervision of the State Underwater Archaeologist's Office.[8]

Under federal law, the navy had ownership of the submarine as a prize of war and as former German and British property, deserving of preservation and protection as a historic artifact. In 1995, the navy granted a permit to the State of Maryland to establish state custody, and in conjunction with the MMAP, declared *U-1105* a historic site and recreational diving preserve under the control of the Maryland MMAP. This required the underwater archaeologist to mark the location of the sub with a buoy, to establish rules for the safety of the diving public, and to protect the submarine from pilfering and damage. Today, anyone wishing to dive on *U-1105* must first sign in at the Piney Point Lighthouse.

A second shipwreck of archaeological importance to Maryland was the steamboat *Columbus,* whose remains were discovered in 1991 as the result of an Army Corps of Engineers survey, "The Baltimore Harbor and Channels Fifty-foot Project in the Chesapeake Bay." The Maryland and Virginia Steamboat Company contracted with James Beacham and George Gardner to build the vessel in 1828. They subcontracted with George Reeder's firm to build a crosshead engine for her, rated at 100 horsepower. Completed within a year, *Columbus* made a fine impression as she ended her sea trial from Baltimore to Poole's Island and back, registering an average speed of 12 knots. She measured 137 feet long, with a copper-sheathed hull, a 30-foot beam, and nearly 11 feet in the hold. Soon this handsome vessel began her runs between Baltimore and Norfolk, carrying primarily tobacco hogsheads, cotton bales, and cattle, although she had some premier passenger accommodations as well. In making her Norfolk run, she also put in at City Point and Richmond on the James River, and she carried excursion parties within a day's run of Richmond or

Norfolk. To take the Norfolk to Baltimore passage, people would pay seven dollars; to go from Norfolk to Richmond cost three dollars. *Columbus* had her share of close calls on the bay. In March 1831, the steamer *Rappahannock* rammed her off Smith Point at the mouth of the Potomac, but she survived. Later that year, she got caught in a December snowstorm and just managed to escape being trapped in an ice floe. The passengers later awarded their captain a silver urn for his "skill and intrepidity" in successfully negotiating the ice in a violent storm.

The ship was also host to important celebrations, such as the anniversaries of the Battle of North Point, and on another occasion she carried a band of Sauk Indians and their chief, Black Hawk, after their release from imprisonment at Fort Monroe (a result of the Black Hawk War of 1832 in Illinois) to a tour of the Norfolk Navy Yard to see the ship of the line USS *Delaware,* with her Indian figurehead. Gooding and Company of Baltimore made repairs and enlarged the *Columbus* in 1836 by almost 40 feet, to 174 feet overall, enabling her to undertake coastal navigation between Norfolk and Charleston. But the Maryland and Virginia line fell on evil days in 1839 because of intense competition and soon went into receivership. The Baltimore Steam Packet Company took over the M&V Line's assets and put the *Columbus* in the Powhatan Line, one of their subsidiaries. Soon she was back on her old route and faithfully steamed the miles between Baltimore and Norfolk until her last voyage, on November 25, 1850.

Departing Baltimore on a cold and blustery Wednesday afternoon, she began her passage to Norfolk carrying only a few passengers and some horses and light cargo. Nearing Smith Point, on the Virginia side of the mouth of the Potomac River, there was an explosion in the engine room. The engineer immediately notified the captain that the ship was on fire. The captain notified his crew and the passengers. The helmsman turned the ship downwind to minimize the rush of the flames. The crew could launch only one of the ship's boats, owing to the intensity of the fire. Only seven persons survived the fire; nine others, including the captain and first mate, were lost, either in the fire or in the frigid waters. The engineer, Lloyd Lecompte, survived with a few of the hands in the lifeboat. Days later the *Baltimore Sun* published his graphic account of the ship's demise:

> We rowed in the wake of the burning steamer, hoping that we could rescue anyone trying to save themselves. When the upper works collapsed, we turned toward the Smith Point Lightship and reached it after much effort. There we stayed because of the rough weather until the next day, when the *Georgia* coming up from Norfolk took us off for Baltimore. In the meantime, the wreck, a mass of flames, drifted so close to the lightship that we could feel the intense heat. At 8 o'clock in the morning the wreck was still puffing steam or smoke and drifting about, and we watched her with binoculars, but around 11 a.m. she disappeared.[9]

Engineer Lecompte provided an answer as to the cause of the fire. A spark arrestor in the stack had malfunctioned, blocking the draft on the furnace and forcing a blowback in the engine room, where the wood fuel caught fire. The *Columbus,* sinking at mid-century, disappeared from public notice and memory until the Corps of Engineers project discovered her remains in 1990. By this time, federal and state laws were in place requiring an archaeological survey before removal or destruction of the wreck. The corps called on the firm of Christopher Goodwin and Associates to carry out an archaeological survey, documenting the wreck. R. Christopher Goodwin Jr. was the principal investigator, and archaeological field operations were under the control of Stephen R. James Jr., of Pan-American Consultants. The army provided reservists to man equipment, and army divers came from Fort Eustis to assist archaeologists Jack Irion and David Beard. Goodwin also contracted diver-photographer Mike Pohuskie to assist with the documentation work.

For three months during the summer and fall of 1992 they worked in the open bay, nine miles from Point Lookout, an area notorious for contrary wind and current. The wreck was at a depth of sixty feet and in total darkness. Much of the wooden ship had burned and disintegrated, creating a wide debris field, and the metal remains were encrusted with sea life, making them difficult to identify. Gradually, inspection of some pieces of the wreck allowed the team to eliminate the possibilities of her being some other ship. Measurements of what was left of the hull, the copper plating, the crosshead steam engine's piston cylinder diameter and her stroke, and the starboard paddle wheel enabled the archaeological team to firmly identify the ship as *Columbus*.[10]

Consultations among experts from the Maryland Historical Trust and the MMAP determined that the most valuable elements of the historic crosshead engine of 1828 should be recovered and conserved with a view to eventual display for the benefit of the public. The storms of late fall 1992 postponed completion of the job until 1993. The corps then moved the engine artifacts by barge to Curtis Bay, off the Patapsco River. From there the artifacts would be transported to the International Artifact Conservation and Research Laboratory in New Orleans for the lengthy and costly conservation process. The long-range plan provided that these artifacts be put on display in the Columbus Center for Marine Research and Exploration in the Baltimore Inner Harbor. Events were to conspire against this grand scheme, however. The magnitude and costs of the conservation and display effort created political opposition and essentially cut off further funding at the state level. The remains of the *Columbus's* engine may now be seen at the Maryland Archaeological Conservation Laboratory at Jefferson Patterson Park, in Calvert County, Maryland.

A third major effort to use underwater archaeology to reveal Maryland's hidden past took place on the Patuxent River in the late 1970s. As related in Chapter 3, the Royal Navy invaded the Chesapeake Bay as part of their strategy to humiliate and defeat the United States during the War of 1812. Most of the U.S. troops were fighting the British on the Canadian border during the months of August and September 1814. To create a diversion, a British squadron with troop transports under the overall command of Vadm. Alexander Cochrane entered the bay in August 1814. His immediate second in command was Radm. Sir George Cockburn, whose ships and marines had been raiding and terrorizing the inhabitants of the bay region since the spring of 1813. Lt. Gen. Robert Ross commanded the British Army troops in the transports. To face these redoubtable elements, the Americans in the Chesapeake had very few federal troops and almost no U.S. Navy ships. Instead, Joshua

Barney, a veteran sailor of the American Revolutionary War, had suggested to Secretary of the Navy William Jones in July 1813 that a flotilla of gunboats and barges armed with cannon and small arms be created to take advantage of the shallow waters of the bay during the light winds of summer. Jones approved the idea and appointed Barney to command, with the rank of master commandant (later promoted to captain, dating from April 25), and to supervise the building of the flotilla's barges, commencing at Baltimore during 1813.

Barney's flotilla was nearing completion as the summer of 1814 approached, and his main task was recruitment of sailors and marines to man his barges. Secretary Jones ordered the sloop *Scorpion* from Norfolk to serve as Barney's flagship. *Scorpion* reported for duty in February 1814. She was of modest size: 48 feet in length, 18 feet of beam, and drawing 4 feet 6 inches. Although sloop rigged, she came equipped with oars and could be rowed in calms by her complement of twenty-five sailors. For ordnance, she carried one long 24-pounder, one 18-pounder, and two 12-pounder carronades. Barney chartered at least one schooner to serve as a supply vessel, carrying provisions and munitions. The flotilla, as of the end of April, comprised *Scorpion,* two navy gunboats (*No. 137* and *No. 138*), an unnamed "lookout boat," the schooner *Asp* (used as a supply vessel), and twelve barges. Barney carried on board a navy surgeon borrowed from the frigate *Ontario,* then under construction in Baltimore; naturally, the surgeon carried with him his kit of surgical instruments. This is mentioned here because the instruments will miraculously "surface" at a later date. The *Scorpion* and the flotilla, after several confrontations in St. Leonard's Creek during June, retreated up to the head of navigation near St. Anne's Bridge, between Anne Arundel and Prince George's counties. There they remained until the British advance by water and by land from Benedict, toward Bladensburg, where they would clash with the Maryland militia and Commodore Barney's sailors and marines on August 24. Barney's burning of the Chesapeake Flotilla in the shallow waters of the upper Patuxent eventually led to its rediscovery.

Some 165 years later, Barney's flotilla became famous in a different way, in the annals of nautical archaeology. In 1977, Donald Shomette, Ralph Eshelman, Fred Hopkins, and others in the firm Nautical Archaeology Associates decided to explore the Patuxent River and its tributaries for evidences of the historic past. At about the same time, the State of Maryland was developing an archaeological master plan for the state. Part of this plan would be a submerged cultural resources database, which would require the establishment of an inventory and a mapping of representative portions of Maryland's underwater territory. It was essential, if this plan were to be fulfilled, that some undiscovered sites be discovered and surveyed as a baseline. Shomette and his colleagues selected four sections of the Patuxent River for further survey and analysis.[11] These were St. Leonard's Creek, Nottingham, Lyons Creek, and the upper Patuxent between Selby's Landing and the northern end of Spyglass Island (just north of the current Route 4 bridge, formerly Hill's Bridge, near Wayson's Corner). The Maryland Historical Trust awarded Nautical Archaeology Associates a matching grant to carry out the survey in 1979.[12]

After a careful survey, working upriver with a magnetometer to locate anomalies, Shomette noticed the magnetometer's needle vibrating, indicating the presence of metal submerged below. The team set up a cofferdam around the site, located about a mile south of Spyglass Island, where during a previous visit they had located the remains of a vessel that came to be known as the "Turtle Shell" wreck.[13] Now they had to probe the site with pipe and hose, moving sediments out of the way. The cofferdam was intended to keep water currents and debris from further contaminating the site while the divers worked down through the sediment within the cofferdam, layer by layer, until they reached the solid framework of the vessel lying beneath them. Naturally, when a wooden boat has been underwater for 170 years, the structure collapses; the upper levels drop down and the bulkheads lose their vertical orientation. The entire vessel loses its integrity and splays outward, looking very little like an upright boat. Another event that damaged these vessels was the sudden shock of explosions from the charges placed by Barney's crews in 1814. The archaeologists had to take these factors into account as they probed deeper into the Turtle Shell wreck.

The most exciting result of the search was the discovery of a trove of well-preserved artifacts that clearly proved the vessel belonged to Barney's Chesapeake Flotilla. These included a munitions box labeled to indicate it had come from the arms contractor Christopher Deshon, of Baltimore, and a group of surgical instruments, including a dental tooth key, dental forceps, a bullet probe, surgical scissors, a scalpel, surgical knives, and cauterizers. Some of these surgeon's tools carried the maker's mark, showing they had been manufactured by Hague and Nowill, a leading surgical manufacturer in England; others had been produced by John Evans and Company, a supplier of surgical instruments for the Royal Navy. Barney may have taken the surgeon's kit when he captured HM packet *Princess Amelia* during his cruise in the privateer *Rossie* in 1812. It is also possible that the kit may have come from the surgeon of the U.S. Navy sloop of war *Ontario,* then fitting out in Baltimore.

Other finds included an apothecary's jar and wooden stopper, a mixing spatula, an apothecary plate, a swivel-gun grip, a gunner's pick, a swivel-gun shot partially surrounded by wood, indicating that the British had fired and hit the vessel during the Battle for St. Leonard's Creek, and a musket ball flattened on one side, indicating that it had hit and perhaps been kept as a souvenir. The archaeologists found tools in the forward section of the boat that may have been part of a carpenter's kit. These included a drawknife, a punch, and a clump of white clayish substance that may have once, in liquid form, been white lead paint. The Turtle Shell wreck also yielded up domestic items like those probably carried by sailors, including a Liberty-head penny, a leather shoe fragment, buttons, ceramic bowls, eating utensils, cups, a pair of padlocks, and a small sandstone portable galley stove. They found a few maritime artifacts, such as a sounding lead; a wooden block, which would have served as part of a pulley system to haul spars or lift cargo or guns; a conical covered "Paul Revere" lantern; a companion way ladder; and an oarsman's bench, of which there might have been as many as ten. From the profusion, condition, and nature of these artifacts it was evident that Shomette's group had found an important vessel belonging to Barney's flotilla. Still not satisfied that they had discovered Barney's flagship, they did further research in naval records, considered the measurements taken on site, and found corroboration in the work of naval architect-historian Howard Chapelle.[14] Shomette's conclusion: they had found US block sloop *Scorpion,* the flagship of the Chesapeake Flotilla. Following the excavation and recovery of artifacts from *Scorpion* it was only natural that Shomette's discovery became an object of public and media curiosity. Barney's flotilla had become famous once again, and several popular and scholarly publications spread the word.[15]

Yet for the Nautical Archaeological Associates there was still urgent work to do. Having removed a number of artifacts from the wreck site, the team hastened to backfill and close the excavation to prevent further degradation of the site and to protect it against curiosity seekers and wreck strippers. Next, they were concerned to conserve the artifacts, which had spent 170 years in the protective sediments of the Patuxent River, in their new environment. They had previously approached the Calvert Marine Museum on Solomons Island for permission to use a portion of the J. C. Lore Oyster House Museum as an improvised conservation laboratory. They then transferred all the artifacts and began the varied treatments that objects of differing elements demanded. Artifacts of wood, leather, ceramic, and metal all require specific chemical treatments to arrest deterioration and to bring them to a point of stabilization before they can be exhibited to the public. Finally, as with all important archaeological excavations, once completed, there was a major report to write to fulfill the conditions of the Maryland Historical Trust grant and to provide a research resource for those who wished to pursue the subject further. Selected conserved artifacts from the Chesapeake Flotilla collection are on display at the Calvert Marine Museum and the National Museum of the U.S. Navy at the Washington Navy Yard, Washington, D.C. The artifacts found on board the US block sloop *Scorpion* are navy property, on loan to the Calvert Marine Museum.

One further example of Maryland's Maritime Archeology Program is demonstrated in the discovery of CSS *Favorite,* a Confederate schooner carrying a cargo of coal that was found on the bottom of Swan Cove, on the north bank of the Potomac River in May 1994. The team that made this discovery was led by Maryland's assistant underwater archaeologist, Bruce Thompson, with the help of volunteers from the Maritime Archaeological and Historical Society (MAHS). The team's archival research revealed that the U.S. Navy steam tug *Yankee,* under the command of Capt. Tunis Craven, had captured the *Favorite* in the Yeocomico River while patrolling the south shores of the Potomac on July 14, 1861. *Yankee* at that time had been assigned to the Potomac Flotilla, whose job it was to clear the Potomac of enemy vessels and destroy the Confederate defenses along the indented Virginia shoreline. Having towed the *Favorite* into Swan Cove, Captain Craven made the mistake of anchoring the schooner without leaving any sailors on board to protect her. She sank on the night of July 18. Perhaps she was involved in a collision, or more likely, she was sabotaged by some of the many Confederate sympathizers in southern Maryland.

For the next 133 years, *Favorite* lay apparently undisturbed. Having located the shipwreck by side-scan sonar, the team did further research and tentatively identified the vessel as a Confederate schooner. Since she had been taken as a prize by the USS *Yankee,* the *Favorite* was considered to be federal property. As such she fell under the custody of the Naval Historical Center (now the Naval History and Heritage Command), which acts on behalf of the General Services Administration when government-owned shipwrecks are discovered. Five years later, Thompson and the MAHS volunteers took a closer look. By this time, they had in place an ad hoc agreement among the Maryland Historical Trust, the Naval Historical Center, and the MAHS to visit, document, and recover a few items from the remains of *Favorite.* During three days in August 1999, the team measured the dimensions of the vessel, identified and recorded two anchors, and found a cache of ceramic artifacts: a pitcher, a jug, and three saucers. Returning to the site in 2001, the team conducted an underwater video survey from stem to stern on the port side, including the centerboard. A year later, they returned to conduct a remote sensing, full side-scan coverage, and testing of the schooner's remains. At this time, they removed the ceramic artifacts, made a drawing of the site, and collected some hull fasteners. With these products and the documentary research previously performed, they concluded that the wreck was indeed the schooner *Favorite,* very similar in her lines to the George Steers–designed schooner *Sunny South,* built in New York in 1855.[16]

In the long run, MMAP has plans to develop research into prehistoric sites on the Eastern Shore, gold-mining remains in the Potomac River in Montgomery County, and sites drowned by reservoir construction. In partnership with the National Park Service, the MMAP staff will do further surveying on the Atlantic Coast of Assateague National Seashore to assess and document cultural remains from shipwrecks along the barrier beaches.[17] Other likely targets for further underwater archaeological research are Commodore Barney's War of 1812 flotilla in the Patuxent River and the earlier Revolutionary War schooner wrecks of *Cato* and *Hawke,* which belonged to the Maryland State Navy of that era. Of more recent vintage are the World War II–era aircraft wrecks in the bay and its tributaries, which often attract individuals interested in salvaging them for possible restoration and display. These, however, are likely to belong to the government, which, in the case of the U.S. Navy, cannot be intruded upon without an archaeological permit obtained from the navy. There are many willing volunteers among the SCUBA-diving population of Maryland. One of the most active groups is the Maritime Archaeological and Historical Society, whose members include experienced divers and amateur archaeologists. MAHS produced a twelve-week underwater archaeology course that meets undergraduate standards and is recognized by national SCUBA-certification agencies. Such groups can be very helpful to the MMAP because they are sensitive to the need to protect underwater sites and in many cases have adopted stewardship and site monitoring as one of their missions.[18]

Among the cultural resources that Maryland offers the public for the interpretation of its marine environment are the maritime museums on the bay's eastern and western shores. Students of the maritime past can visit these sites for an appreciation of the local watercraft, fishing traditions, boatbuilding styles, and regional history. The leading museum in terms of its wealth of maritime artifacts is the Radcliffe Collection of the Maryland Historical Society. For many years, this collection was available for study in the basement of the society's headquarters at 201 West Monument Street, in Baltimore. Mary Ellen Hayward, the society's former maritime curator, wrote an illustrated guide to the collection that also serves as a short history of the state's maritime heritage. Published in 1984, this guide contains photographs of early ship paintings, models of the various local watercraft common to Maryland waters, and artifacts such as scrimshaw, carved from whalebone and seal tusks by sailors in their few idle hours. There are photographs recording the work of oyster tongers, shipwrights, ship carvers, and decoy carvers, as well as of nautical tools and instruments normally found in ship chandleries. In addition, the Radcliffe Collection includes paintings and photos of the steamboats that plied the waters of the Chesapeake from about 1813 to 1962, taking goods to market and bringing manufactured wares to isolated villages along the many creeks and rivers of the bay. The collection's images and models also record the dramatic enlargement of the port of Baltimore to accommodate the huge containerships and loading facilities that now serve the city on a daily basis.[19]

In the 1990s, the Maryland Historical Society undertook a redesign and reorganization of its exhibits, attempting to integrate the separate collections to describe Maryland's history in new ways. One of these acts dismantled the Radcliffe Collection, removing it from the basement display area and integrating some of the objects in other collections. The rest were either put in storage or installed in a newly acquired building on the Fells Point waterfront. In collaboration with the Society for the Preservation of Fells Point, the Maryland Historical Society established the Fells Point Maritime Museum in a former trolley barn and ship chandlery at 1724 Thames Street, not far from the old Recreation Pier. This new museum opened its doors in 2002 with considerable fanfare, featuring exhibits of the early history of Fells Point and the shipbuilding industry that flourished there for many years, from the late eighteenth to the mid-nineteenth century. The privateering business, in which merchants collaborated with the builders of pilot schooners and aggressive sea captains looking to turn a dollar with patriotic pride, flourished in Fells Point during the War of 1812. It was this Fells Point "nest of pirates" that the British wanted to burn when they attacked Baltimore in 1814. Thus, the museum was a perfect fit for the waterfront history of Fells Point and a welcome cultural upgrade for a somewhat raffish area. Unfortunately, this brief flourish ended in 2007, when the Maryland Historical Society's overall finances fell into difficulties and the Fells Point Maritime Museum was not attracting a sufficient number of visitors year-round to justify its continued operation. The historical society decided to regroup and focus its attention on the main buildings at West Monument Street. Thus, having retrieved the artifacts and art from Fells Point, the society reopened its maritime exhibits on the main floor of its headquarters in an exhibit called "Work and Play on the Bay" in November 2008. This will be a changing exhibit, which will continue to show the different phases of maritime activity throughout Maryland's waters.

For the benefit of tourists and maritime history buffs, Baltimore has several museum ships and one historic lighthouse on display, known collectively as the Baltimore Maritime Museum. These are the former U.S. Coast Guard Cutter *Taney,* a veteran of the Pearl Harbor attack; the World War II–era submarine USS *Torsk;* the Lightship *Chesapeake,* which served off the Fenwick Island Shoal and the Virginia Capes until World War II; and the Seven Foot Knoll Lighthouse, a screwpile light that marked shoals at the mouth of the Patapsco River from 1855 until 1988, when it was moved to the Inner Harbor. This museum is part of the National Historic Seaport of Baltimore, a partner of the Living Classrooms Foundation, which manages four vessels that are of particular relevance to an interpretation of Chesapeake maritime culture: the pungy schooner *Lady Maryland,* the buyboat *Mildred Belle,* and the skipjacks *Sigsbee* and *Minnie V.* These vessels make up the Living Classrooms' educational fleet, which serves to educate people of all ages about Chesapeake Bay.[20]

Standing proudly in Baltimore's Inner Harbor, the sloop of war USS *Constellation* is a virtual icon of the city. Although built in Gosport, Virginia, in 1854, she has long been associated with the history of Baltimore, as was her namesake, the US frigate *Constellation.* The sloop of war was the last U.S. Navy sailing warship; all the later vessels operated under a combination of sails and steam or steam only. She served successively in the Mediterranean during the Civil War, as a training ship at the U.S. Naval Academy, and as the reserve flagship of the Atlantic Fleet in Newport, Rhode Island, during World War II. Since the 1950s, she has had a place of honor in Baltimore harbor. Forty years later, an inspection found her to be severely hogged and her rigging in bad shape. This was not a peaceful time for the old veteran. There had been a prolonged and heated debate about whether she was a rebuilt version of the original frigate or a purpose-built sloop of war, circa 1854. In the minds of many, the sloop-of-war argument won out.[21] An energetic funding campaign in the 1990s enabled a $9 million renovation and brought her back to visiting condition. She now serves the public well as an educational ambassador for the Historic Naval Ships Association and the Historic Seaport of Baltimore.[22]

Quite a different example of ship restoration is on display at the Baltimore Museum of Industry, where the steam tug *Baltimore* is moored. The Skinner Shipbuilding Company launched the tug in 1906, and for many years she did the harbor work typical of tugs: assisting larger vessels to their piers, getting others under way, moving barges and lighters, breaking ice, and providing tours around the harbor. The constructors built her hull of wrought-iron plate, the pilothouse of Georgia pine, and the wheelhouse and saloon of finished oak. She has two coal-fired Morrison furnaces and a Scotch boiler, with a compound, surface-condensing engine that generated 330 horsepower. Her dimensions: length 88 feet, beam 18 feet 6 inches, and depth 9 feet, with gross tonnage of 81, net tonnage of 55, and a top speed of 11 knots. The owners converted the tug to burn oil in 1957, and in 1963 they sold her to S. F. Dupont. He sold her in 1972, but through mishap she sank in the Sassafras River, where she lay for two years until the McClearn Contracting Company recovered her and brought her to the Baltimore Museum of Industry. There the tug gradually came back to life, thanks to the generosity of the museum's patrons and the hard work of many volunteers. Restoration work continues on the vessel. The National Park Service designated the tug *Baltimore* a National Historic Landmark in 1993, and in January 2009, the Save America's Treasures program awarded the Museum of Industry a matching grant of $250,000 to continue the tug's renovation.

In 1976, the City of Baltimore contracted for the construction of *Pride of Baltimore,* a re-creation of the War of 1812 pilot-schooner *Chasseur,* based on a draft by naval architect Thomas Gillmer. *Pride*'s dimensions indicated that she was built with a higher center of gravity and less depth of hold than her early-nineteenth-century predecessors. She served well on her goodwill missions but fell victim to a "white squall," capsized, and sank in 1986, with the loss of her captain and three of the crew. In 1988, Gillmer redesigned *Pride* to conform to Coast Guard regulations, with watertight bulkheads and heavier ballast to make her safer and stiffer. *Pride of Baltimore II,* now affiliated with the Living Classrooms Foundation and the National Historic Seaport of Baltimore, has successfully sailed the world's oceans as a seafaring representative of Baltimore ever since.

Farther down the bay, on the Miles River, stands one of the best-known maritime museums of the region, the Chesapeake Bay Maritime Museum. This relatively young institution aspires to interpret the entire bay and does an excellent job in demonstrating what such museums do best. Concerned citizens of St. Michaels, Easton, and the surrounding area gathered in 1963 to discuss what might be done to preserve the ancient ways of life, which had begun to disappear. It was only some ten years since the Chesapeake Bay Bridge had been built, bringing thousands of new visitors across the bay on their way to Ocean City. Others came looking for places to build homes in an idyllic environment near quiet creeks and scenic wetlands. They looked at places like Kent Island, Queen Anne's County, and Talbot County as suitable for development. Those concerned citizens decided to invest their resources in the creation of the Chesapeake Bay Maritime Museum, and in 1965, the museum opened to visitors. Beginning with only two acres and centered in the Dodson House of St. Michaels, the museum soon became popular, hosting ten thousand visitors in its first six months and enlisting nearly six hundred members by the end of its first year.

Under the inspired leadership of executive director R. J. "Jim" Holt, the museum grew to acquire more land and buildings at the water's edge, on the west side of St. Michaels harbor, including Navy Point and Fogg's Landing. In a dramatic move, the museum obtained the transfer of the Hooper Strait Lighthouse to Navy Point in 1966. The light had been manned and maintained by the U.S. Coast Guard for years, but it had outgrown its usefulness. Far better for the old screwpile lighthouse to find a new home than be destroyed or left to disintegrate. The Hooper Strait Lighthouse stands as an icon of the museum as well as a demonstration of an aid to navigation from a bygone era. In the 1970s, the museum built a new marine railway, a boat-repair shop, and a boat shed, where a visitor can examine original types of bay craft in a protected setting. Those interested in studying how wooden boats are built and repaired can visit the boat shop, whose staff restores commercial skipjacks and preserves the museum's own fleet of bay craft. To encourage the

preservation of wooden-boatbuilding skills, the museum has a Shipwright Apprentice Program, in which bona fide graduates of boatbuilding courses can get on-the-job training and experience under the eyes of master shipwrights.

The museum maintains a large collection of in-the-water historic vessels that can be visited and studied. As with all old wooden vessels, the effort to preserve and maintain is a continuing process and fits in well with the museum's apprentice shipwright program. These vessels include the *Old Point,* a 1909 crab dredger formerly owned by the Old Dominion Crab Company. She worked the lower bay from 1909 to 1956, dredging crabs in the winter, hauling fish in the summer, and dredging oysters in the fall. Anther is the skipjack *Rosie Parks,* constructed by Bronza Parks, widely known on the Eastern Shore for his boatbuilding skills. The *Rosie Parks* worked for many years dredging oysters and also gained fame as a racing skipjack. The collection also has the *Delaware,* a rare example of an early-twentieth-century river tug built in 1912; the *Edna Lockwood,* a John B. Harrison–built bugeye that worked out of Tilghman Island from 1889 to 1967; the *Isabel,* a 38-foot Matthews-built recreational powerboat that is now part of the "At Play on the Bay" exhibit; the *Martha,* a Bronza Parks–built Hooper Island workboat known as a "draketail" because of its aft-sloping stern; and *Mister Jim,* a replica buyboat similar to the vessels that served the watermen on oystering dredges and tonging skiffs by collecting and buying their catches and taking them to resell at market prices.

The museum's library and archives are open to visitors at the Breene M. Kerr Center for Chesapeake Studies. This is an appropriately quiet building that houses valuable collections where the serious student can do research in books, documents, and images under professional supervision. The Eastern Shore region, rich in rivers, creeks, and wetlands, has long been a place where thousands of geese and ducks have

Steam tug *Baltimore.* Built and launched in 1906, this vessel is the oldest hand-fired, steam-operated tugboat in the United States. She is listed on the National Register of Historic Places. Courtesy, Maryland Historical Society Z24–625.

wintered over. Wildfowl hunters have enjoyed their pastime during the permitted seasons, and the museum has recognized this hobby by establishing a large collection of wildfowl hunting decoys, weapons, and gunning boats in a dedicated gallery that houses nearly three hundred decoys carved by regional artists. In recent years, Chesapeake Bay has become a "playground" for recreational boating, whether by sail or power, and the museum has recognized this in "At Play on the Bay," an exhibit that includes images and accounts of steamboat excursions, sailboat racing, fishing, and tours of the Eastern Shore. The Chesapeake Bay Maritime Museum celebrates the past but at the same time is concerned about the present and the future. This theme is carried forward in exhibits on the natural environment that speak about shrinking wetlands, overdevelopment, the presence of toxic wastes in regional waters, and the ever-diminishing stocks of oysters, crabs, fish, and wildlife—resources that once made the Eastern Shore seem like a paradise.

The Calvert Marine Museum, located at Solomons Island, is another example of a Chesapeake maritime museum that has served the public, interpreting the watermen, watercraft, and natural environment of its region, the mid-bay Western Shore. As in the case of St. Michaels, citizens of Solomons Island looked at the changes taking place around them and decided in 1970 that their locality needed a maritime museum to preserve artifacts, watercraft, and watermen's memories and to interpret the unique natural environment of the Calvert Cliffs. Solomons Island, located in Calvert County near the mouth of the Patuxent River, was once a thriving shipbuilding and commercial fishing port, but as these activities diminished in the second half of the twentieth century, the town developed into a location that features a number of marinas servicing both sailboats and powerboats, as well as recreational fishing.

The Patuxent River is one of nineteen major tributaries to Chesapeake Bay. A total of 110 miles in length, it runs from Parrs Ridge, in Carroll County, to Drum Point, where the river enters the bay. For some three hundred years before Europeans arrived, the Patuxents, an Algonquin-speaking tribe, settled and traded along the river. They farmed and fished, much as did the Englishmen who supplanted them.[23] From the early seventeenth century, settlers on both sides of the Patuxent developed their lands as a rich agricultural area with ample access to the river and Chesapeake Bay for ease of transport and communication. As in most other tidewater locations, tobacco was the crop of choice, and the Patuxent River provided excellent access for ships bound to or coming from England. Just as often, farmers resorted to fishing, not only to vary their family's fare but also to hedge against the evil days when farm prices dropped. Near the mouth of the Patuxent River lies Solomons Island, a smoking pipe–shaped spit of sand that shelters the mouths of several small creeks. In the early days of settlement, it was known as Bourne's Island; it was Somervell's Island in the eighteenth and early nineteenth centuries, and Sandy Island from 1827 to 1865.

From 1654 to 1657, during the period of Cromwell's rule in England, Maryland's colonial government moved from St. Mary's City to the home of a Protestant member of the colony's governing commission, Richard Preston, who lived on a neck of land on the Patuxent River between St. Leonard's and Hellen creeks. The

Maryland Assembly and Provincial Court met at Preston's house during that turbulent time. The American Revolutionary War wrought few changes to the area, which was largely bypassed. However, during the War of 1812, British warships were much in evidence as they pursued Joshua Barney's Chesapeake Flotilla into the Patuxent. After the battles of St. Leonard's Creek, Barney sailed his gunboats and barges as far north as he could and then burned them, to keep them out of enemy hands. As the British pursued, in late August 1814, they landed some four thousand troops at Benedict and marched toward Bladensburg, ultimately winning that battle and burning government buildings in the City of Washington before returning to Benedict to board their ships and continue their Chesapeake rampage as far as Baltimore, where they were repulsed. The British beat a hasty retreat in late September 1814, never to return to the Chesapeake in battle array.

The Civil War did not touch the Patuxent militarily, but since most of the tobacco farmers were slave owners, their sentiments largely favored the Confederacy. Just before the Civil War, there were 4,600 slaves in Calvert County, and if you add the county's 1,800 freedmen, African Americans made up 61 percent of the total population of approximately 10,500 souls. With the war over, economic depression came to agriculture in southern Maryland. Many of the people, black as well as white, turned to the water to make a living. It was fortunate that during the years 1872–92 the oyster fishery enjoyed good times. The oystermen rarely produced fewer than 10 million bushels annually during that twenty-year period, and the Patuxent River was reputed to have some of the best oyster beds in the state. In Calvert County, the number of tonging licenses issued rose from 145 in 1870 to 521 in 1890. In St. Mary's County, the same thing happened: tonging licenses rose from 267 to 757 for the period. The increased demand for oysters went hand in hand with the development of the canning industry in Baltimore, where New Englanders went to set up plants after their own region's oyster production declined.[24]

Isaac Solomon was one Baltimore's successful canners at this time, and his enterprising spirit led him to purchase Sandy Island, where he opened the Patuxent's first oyster-packing house. He anticipated that a railroad would be built connecting Solomons Island to Baltimore and its oyster distribution system, which was spreading nationwide. But the railroad never came, so Solomon sold his property and left for Philadelphia. His name, however, lived on, as the name of the island and the town, and others came to take his place. From New Jersey came J. C. Lore, who in 1888 developed a business of shipping fresh oysters to his uncle, a seafood packer in Philadelphia. Lore's successful business lasted until 1978, and the building he erected in 1934 now stands offsite as part of the Calvert Marine Museum.[25]

The Calvert Marine Museum possesses nine acres of land located just north of Solomons Island Road. With seven buildings on the campus and two offsite facilities, the visitor is welcomed into the 29,000-square-foot exhibition hall, where one quickly catches sight of the mission statement plaque: "Our mission is to collect, preserve, research, and interpret the cultural and natural history of Southern Maryland. We are dedicated to the presentation of our three themes: regional paleontology, estuarine life of the tidal Patuxent River and adjacent Chesapeake Bay, and maritime history of these waters." This is a challenging and worthwhile task, entirely appropriate to a local and regional nonprofit museum. Through the presence of the looming Calvert Cliffs, which anyone who has passed up or down the bay will recognize, the long duration of geological time makes itself felt.

Inside the museum, the exhibit "Treasure from the Cliffs" interprets these impressive natural wonders. Using fossils from the cliffs, wall panels explain the passage of immense periods of geological time and the tumultuous movements of earth and oceans that shaped the Chesapeake land- and waterscape. Scientists have identified over six hundred species of sea creature that must have inhabited this area, judging from the fossils that survive, and among them over four hundred types of mollusk shell (including clams, oysters, scallops, snails, and mussels). The cliffs have yielded up some complete vertebrate fossils of marine mammals, making this area one of the most diverse groupings of extinct whales and dolphins in the world. Among the most spectacular fossils are the sharks' teeth, from a wide variety, including angel, basking, cow, mako, giant white (larger than today's great white), sand, tiger, and whale sharks.

Turning its attention to the Patuxent River as an estuary, another exhibit examines "A River and Its Life." Defining an estuary as an inlet of the sea reaching into a river valley to the limit of tidal rise, the Patuxent estuary exhibit panels discuss the range of creatures that exist along the various ranges of salinity as the estuary reaches the upper stages of the river, where the water changes from saline to brackish to fresh. In each of these areas different species of sea life breed, reproduce, and grow. As the creature grows, depending on its nature, it may migrate from saline to fresh water or from fresh to saline. These include species such as rockfish (striped bass), perch, and bluefish. The exhibit panels define the marine food chain, in which plankton is the basic food for many of the bay's sea creatures. One variety of plankton is a microscopic plant alga that provides food for zooplankton or microscopic animals, fish, and invertebrates, such as clams and oysters. The up-to-now-plentiful menhaden, the main food for rockfish, feeds exclusively on plankton. Sea life in the bay is divided into the free-swimming nekton community and the benthic community of bottom-dwelling invertebrates. Some of these, like oysters, clams, and mussels, have played an important role in filtering bay water. In the distant past, such filtering organisms were numerous enough to keep the bay water clear, but now that these are fewer, the bay's water is murky, dense, and dark. Communities of bay grasses are also important to the estuary, providing submerged hiding places where young species can escape predators, feed, and grow. These communities are in a delicate balance, contending with both man and nature. Human, industrial, and agricultural effluvia can make the waters inhospitable for these communities, and hurricanes, nature's most violent storms, can also upset the balance, burying wetlands and oyster beds with sediment brought by surges of fresh water and making the marine environment unhealthy for saline-dependent sea life.

Other exhibits cover the steamboats that frequented the Patuxent River, boatbuilding in the yards of M. M. Davis, James T. Marsh, and Thomas R. Moore, the changes wrought by the navy's three bases—Patuxent Naval Air Station, the Mine Warfare Test Station, and the Amphibious Training Base—as well as the development of Solomons Island into a maritime recreation area after World War II. The museum has energetically collected examples of small craft typical of the region, such as log canoes, a five-log brogan, a bugeye hull, an oyster skiff, a clam dredger workboat, a draketail workboat, and a Potomac River dory boat. The Drum Point Lighthouse has been a popular attraction since its construction in 1883, as one of forty-two screwpile lighthouses built on the bay. The lantern room contains a fourth-order Fresnel lens, which was installed in the lighthouse in 1899. The lighthouse was listed on the National Register of Historic Places in 1973, and the museum acquired the decommissioned lighthouse and moved it to the museum's waterfront in 1975. Another museum property, acquired in 2000, is the Cove Point Lighthouse, complete with keeper's house, light tower, and fog-signal building. At first manned by civilian keepers and later by the U.S. Coast Guard, this lighthouse served bay navigators from 1828 until 1986.

Museum visitors can enjoy a visit to the *Wm. B. Tennison,* a 60-foot converted nine-log bugeye built in Somerset County in 1899. Her owners used it first as an oyster dredge boat, and later they took out one of its masts and added an engine and pilothouse. In this new life *Tennison* became an oyster buyboat and carried freight when oysters were not in season. In 1945, J. C. Lore & Sons bought the boat for their own use as a buyboat and oyster dredge in private Patuxent oyster beds. She now occasionally takes passengers from the museum on short cruises, weather permitting. The Calvert Marine Museum is a fine example of how a community that cares about its past can harness and interpret maritime cultural resources for the benefit of current and future generations.

ONE OF THE NOW ALMOST FORGOTTEN but once famous cultural offerings on the Chesapeake Bay was the James Adams Floating Theater, later known as "The Original Showboat." James Adams was a showman who had made a fortune in vaudeville and carnivals. He created the first showboat on saltwater in 1914. Showboats had been running on the western rivers for years, but Adams's was the first and only one to appear on the North Carolina sounds and Chesapeake Bay. He hired Bill Chauncey of Washington, North Carolina, to build a barge to accommodate both a theater and lodgings for the theater company. She measured 128 feet long by 34 feet wide and held an auditorium that could seat 850. In those segregated days, the auditorium was for whites, and blacks sat in the balcony. The barge lacked propulsion; she was towed from port to port by a tugboat, usually the *Elk* or the *Trouper.* Normally, the barge would spend the winters at Elizabeth City, North Carolina, hold the show's premiere in that location, start her seasonal tour of ports in the sounds, and then move north through the Intracoastal Waterway to Norfolk. For most of the summer she would work her way visiting Chesapeake ports, up one side of the bay and down the other.[26]

The troupe that lived on board also had an orchestra, which would board the tug when they arrived at a town. The tug would then run gaily along the shore and up and down the neighboring creeks, playing all the while, to announce the arrival of the *Playhouse,* for that was her official name, and the register of American merchant vessels listed her as such. As time passed, ads placed in local papers would announce the scheduled arrival time and the theatrical offerings, usually melodramas or light comedies. Normally, the *Playhouse* would spend a week at each port and perform every night at 8:15, except Sundays, when they would hold a matinee. Admission fees were set at thirty-five or forty cents to attract all sorts of people for whom plays were the major attraction, but the *Playhouse* also featured concerts or vaudeville acts after the plays. The performers participated in repertory style. The director and leading man for many years was Charles Hunter, whose wife, Beulah, James Adams's daughter, played the leading lady in many plays. She was called the "Mary Pickford of the Chesapeake." In 1925, novelist Edna Ferber visited the *Playhouse* in North Carolina and stayed for four days to gather material for her book *Showboat.*[27] Ferber had been researching stories of floating playhouses for many months before she arrived at Bath, a small port on the Pamlico River, for her visit, but this was the first time she had actually been invited to come aboard and live among the actors, musicians, and tugboat hands. She was enthralled. "On her third morning in Bath, North Carolina, where the *Playhouse* was expected, Edna finally beheld the arrival of the massive show boat. The 'James Adams Floating Palace Theatre came floating majestically down the Pamlico and tied up alongside the rickety dock.' The long rectangular barge—a full two stories high—kindled in Edna Ferber all of the romance and river lore that her studies had yielded thus far: 'There began, for me, four of the most enchanting days I've ever known.'"[28]

The success of the novel caused Adams to paint a huge announcement—"James Adams Showboat"—on the side of the barge, but public tastes in entertainment soon featured movies, especially as talking films began to circulate. Automobiles changed audience habits, too, making day trips and other attractions more available. In 1933, as the Depression hit and times got harder, Adams sold the barge to Nina Howard, of St. Michaels. She and her son, Milford Seymoure, the new director, continued the *Playhouse*'s circuits around the bay and changed her name to *The Original Showboat.* Howard's most spectacular run occurred over twelve weeks in Baltimore during 1939, when the troupe produced eight different plays, but still its days were numbered. The gradual decline of steamboat commerce also affected the *Playhouse* in the 1930s. Steamboat landings, where the barge moored during visits, fell into disrepair.

By 1941, the *Playhouse* virtually ceased productions, and an announcement in *Billboard* (magazine) mentioned that she would be turned into a floating movie house in the Chesapeake, but this did not come to pass. A new owner ordered the vessel towed to Savannah, Georgia, where her days ended when she caught fire on November 14, 1941. Nonetheless, for some thirty years she had been a remarkable success and a unique moment in the history of American theater in the Chesapeake region.[29]

Thus, it is one of the complexities of history that the material and cultural threads of human events intertwine. The continuing search for material artifacts in the underwater world of the Chesapeake yields up evidence of human activity both known and unknown and adds explanations for the disappearance of vessels and cargoes of long ago. So, too, historians and educators seek to describe and explain to a curious public why the beloved and cherished traditions of Chesapeake lives and livelihoods on the water are disappearing. Here the bay's greater and smaller maritime museums play a role that other public and private educational institutions lack the time, funds, and trained staff to carry out. Likewise, the James Adams showboat brought literature and drama to remote hamlets, villages, and towns up and down the bay and its tributaries; furthermore, its existence formed a link between the maritime cultures of the North Carolina, Virginia, and Maryland tidewater regions.

Epilogue

Our Diminishing Maritime Environment

〜〜〜〜〜〜〜〜〜〜〜〜〜〜〜〜〜〜〜〜〜〜〜〜〜

A N ENVIRONMENTAL HISTORIAN RECENTLY WROTE of the "tragedy of the commons," comparing the Great Plains and the Chesapeake Bay region of the years before the Civil War with what they became later. "Until the economic boom of the post Civil War era," he wrote, the areas "functioned reasonably well as a commons because ecological stresses were manageable. But later as Americans locked themselves in a system by which each man sought to gather as much wealth as was humanly possible, whether by shooting buffalo or gathering oysters, there came the inevitable tragedy."[1] Men believed that both resources were there for all to exploit and that they were inexhaustible. Events in our era demonstrate the folly of this view. Today we bear witness to the diminution of almost all species of finfish, shellfish, and wildfowl in the Chesapeake Bay estuary.

This statement does not imply that the root of the problem rests solely with the commercial watermen, the harvesters of the bay, and the amateur and professional hunters who view the bay's wildfowl as their personal preserve. But those who have enjoyed and exploited this area for hundreds of years have spread a belief that an apparently unending abundance of natural wealth is man's birthright. There has also been, until recently, a publicly embraced attitude that no matter what environmental harm people, governments, and industries do in this technologically advanced world, there is a fix to be found. Americans are a pragmatic people who have come to believe that science, engineering, and technology will always be here to heal and improve what nature is unable to do. The Industrial Revolution brought steam engines, canning, mechanized dredging, industrial waste, the gasoline-combustion engine, and use of the rivers as sewers for burgeoning cities and suburban areas. Technology advanced the way commercial fishermen harvested fish, brought concrete roads and highways to the water's edge, improved agricultural techniques and developed fertilizers to improve vegetable and animal produce, developed new technologies in home building, and indeed, built whole communities in but a few months time in places where before there had been family farms or wooded areas in which regional flora and fauna thrived. Many of these developments are seen as beneficial to society as a whole. Unfortunately, there is a dark side to these outwardly positive developments.

The great question about Chesapeake Bay now is not whether it can replenish itself, but whether we humans can alter our own behavior as a society to assist the natural processes. The environmental condition of the bay has not materially improved in recent years, and there is still much to be concerned about as population pressure and residential development builds up on the margin of the sensitive Chesapeake tidelands. In recent years, the Chesapeake Bay Foundation and concerned citizens have made public statements about the persistence in the bay of dead zones, where the lack of oxygen has killed and driven away a wide variety of fish species. In July 2007, former Maryland state senator Gerald W. Winegrad drew attention to the need for greater efforts on the part of the state to control pollution and farm runoff. He stated that the bay cleanup that has been envisioned for so long has proven much harder than anyone anticipated, with rapid population growth in the Chesapeake region yielding an 8 percent increase in the 1990s, and with increasing housing development has come the addition of more impervious surfaces, such as roads and parking lots, which sluice unfiltered runoff into the bay. He argues that the state must improve the way it manages growth and place more effective controls on the protection and enhancement of forests. Maryland's progress in controlling nutrient pollution falls far short of the goals set for achievement in 2010. The state's legislature has funded subsidies to assist farmers but has been lax in enforcing controls. The weakness in the state's program for bay cleanup resides in the lack of penalties for noncompliance by developers, industries, and agribusinesses.[2] In a prescient essay written for the Abell Foundation, journalist Tom Horton points out that the one big issue policy makers have avoided is the impact of population growth around the bay. Without some limits to population growth, the bay will continue to be subject to pressures brought by development. He places the blame on popular attitudes involved in the phrase "grow or die"; in other words, it is the attitude that communities that are merely stable are failing. Developers, Realtors, and vendors of all types have an unreasoning faith in growth as an economic panacea to society's problems. The unseen or unrealized aspect of this is that the push for ever more waterfront and waterview properties is driving down the environmental health of the bay, and a healthy bay is, paradoxically, what nearly everyone says they want. This reflects a conflict of values whose resolution requires self-imposed limits.[3]

Chesapeake Bay and its many tributaries have brought to Maryland great opportunities in their natural abundance of shellfish and finfish, as highways to the hinterlands and to markets when roads were lacking, and as a means of waging war and of self-defense in times of national crises—the American Revolution, the War of 1812, and the Civil War. The early maritime traditions of Maryland include the voyages of John Smith, the ships and captains of the tobacco trade, the slave trade, the influx of indentured servants and propertied families. Britain's Royal Navy supported the colonies in combating piracy and controlling smuggling on the bay, but it also tried to thwart Maryland's patriots during the Revolutionary War. Maryland's navy of schooners, sloops, row galleys, and armed barges defended the bay, opposing Tory barges and raiding parties. The state's trading vessels supported not only the state's revolutionary government but that of the fledgling United States as well, importing war materiel and providing transportation for the Continental and

French armies during their march toward Yorktown. Maryland's letter of marque traders and privateers raided British merchant ships on the high seas.

During the War of 1812, Maryland's Fells Point seafarers once more gained fame as privateers bedeviling Britain's commerce, and Commodore Joshua Barney's flotilla men fought well in battles on the Patuxent, at Bladensburg, and at the battle for Baltimore. As the Industrial Revolution of the eighteenth and nineteenth centuries progressed, bringing steamboats, railroads, and lighthouses, transportation improved. Advances in food processing, preservation, and refrigeration created the demand that sent Maryland's seafood across the nation.

The Civil War virtually cleaved this border state in twain, with terrible consequences. The bay and rivers again became a naval highway, and although Union gunboats predominated, pro-slavery and secessionist mariners found ways to interrupt commerce, smuggle goods, and transport spies between Maryland and Virginia, along the Potomac River and on the Eastern Shore. Rebel sailors destroyed aids to navigation, seized steamboats, and staged small-boat raids on Virginia's Northern Neck. The steamboat traffic that had prospered for forty years became subject to the demands and ravages of war. Both Generals McClellan and Grant and their naval counterparts made good use of the Potomac, York, and James rivers to transport troops, artillery, and gunboats. In the end, the Union's use of sea power on Chesapeake Bay ensured defeat of the Confederacy in the Eastern Theater of the war.

The nation and Maryland recovered slowly from the disruptions of the Civil War. Trade and industrial activity regained momentum. Baltimore's trade with southern states and South American ports blossomed, with imports of coffee and nitrates leading the way. Shipbuilding and exports of seafood, vegetables, and manufactured goods were key money makers. Prosperity followed, enabling leisure-time activities, bay resorts, and vacation homes on the waterfront. But, even as the seafood industry flourished, stocks of oysters began to decline noticeably, producing competition for scarcer resources, as witnessed in the "oyster wars." Centuries of wooden boat building and sailing-rig technology gradually gave way to the diesel and gasoline engines still used in maritime labor and industry. There was a time, perhaps up to the 1970s, when watermen could make a living wage working the bay in all seasons. As the fisheries declined, the scarcity of species of nearly all types made bay-harvesting on an individual basis a difficult-to-impossible way of making a living. Thus, many watermen are now reconciled to working ashore while waiting for conditions to improve. The ubiquitous Chesapeake steamboats disappeared, unable to compete with trucks, automobiles, and railroads. Construction of the bay bridge from Sandy Point to Kent Island in the 1950s and 1960s sped transportation across the bay while changing vacation lifestyles and bringing sudden population growth to the Atlantic beaches and the Eastern Shore.

At the same time, there was a steady increase in recreational sailing, powerboating, and kayaking. These revived old industries with new materials—fiberglass-boat manufacturing, synthetic sail–making for local and international customers, computerized yacht design, yacht brokers, modern mechanized boatyards, and overcrowded marinas. These have been so successful, in fact, that at peak usage times, the bay can be a dangerous place because of the numbers of reckless, negligent, and speeding boaters. Baltimore is still a great shipping port, as can be seen in the large number of containerships usually waiting at anchorages off Annapolis. While some of this lag in ship loading and unloading operations is due to the slow economic climate, another reason is the continuing need for dredging in the Port of Baltimore and the northern bay channels, as the siltation process is ever present and hulls of ships grow longer and deeper.

Popular nostalgia toward aspects of the Chesapeake as it was "in the old days," as seen in maritime museum exhibits and regional publications, has never been greater. The times of the Baltimore clippers, locally built wooden sloops, pungy schooners, bugeyes, and skipjacks that swarmed in great numbers across the bay are long past. Even so, and despite all the alarming news about the bay's health, the bay and its rivers and creeks still provide beautiful places to go for a day of fishing, racing, cruising, or merely to view from a buyboat while sightseeing on the rivers of the Eastern Shore. And there is still much history to be written and many stories to be told. A compendium could be written about Chesapeake Bay–based literature, which is centuries old and continues to evolve. The bay gives up her treasures reluctantly and then only to those who do the research and make the effort to travel its remote byways or dive into its depths to search for early shipwrecks and primitive or obsolete bay craft.

In these early years of the twenty-first century, new concerns will demand the attention of historians as well as ecologists and politicians. The impacts of industrial development and urbanization on the maritime activities of the bay are of utmost importance. As chemical pollution of the bay weakens the state's fishing industries and as silt runoff from community development and highway construction clogs the bay's streams, creeks, and rivers, navigation will be adversely affected. Restrictions on dredging operations, whether from lack of public funds or from fears that dredging spoil will damage fragile environments, contribute to this problem. As these trends will eventually become part of the maritime traditions of Maryland, so will the methods Marylanders use to confront them. In this context, history is a continuum of human and ecological problems, solutions, disasters, and successes. A consciousness of our dependence on the maritime past may help us realize how much future generations will depend on how we deal with our contemporary maritime culture.

NOTES

Chapter 1. Colonial Maritime Heritage

1. John Capper, Garrett Power, and Frank R. Shivers Jr., in *Chesapeake Waters: Pollution, Public Health, and Public Opinion, 1607–1972* (Centreville, MD: Tidewater Press, 1983), claim the "currently prevalent" figure of eight thousand miles of shoreline.

2. Arthur P. Middleton, *Tobacco Coast: A Maritime History of Chesapeake Bay in the Colonial Era* (Baltimore: Johns Hopkins Univ. Press, 1989), 382.

3. Robert J. Brugger, *Maryland: A Middle Temperament, 1634–1980* (Baltimore: Johns Hopkins Univ. Press, 1988), 348.

4. Middleton, *Tobacco Coast,* 387.

5. Helen Rountree, Wayne Clark, and Kent Mountford, *John Smith's Chesapeake Voyages, 1607–1609* (Charlottesville: Univ. of Virginia Press, 2007), 75–135.

6. Timothy B. Riordan, *The Plundering Time: Maryland and the English Civil War, 1645–1646* (Baltimore: Maryland Historical Society, 2004), 258–75.

7. Ibid., 323.

8. Ibid., 328–29.

9. Al Luckenback, *Providence: The History and Archaeology of Anne Arundel County, Maryland's First European Settlement* (Crownsville, MD: Maryland State Archives and Maryland Historical Trust Press, 1995), 4–5; David Gadsby and Jane Cox, eds., "Providence: Maryland's Seventeenth Century Maritime Community" (unpublished Lost Towns Project Research Report, 2005), 26–27.

10. Luckenback, *Providence,* 8–23.

11. Clayton Colman Hall, ed., *Narratives of Early Maryland, 1633–1684* (1910; repr., New York: Barnes & Noble, 1967), 233–308.

12. John F. Wing, *Bound by God . . . for Merryland: The Voyage of the Constant Friendship, 1671–1672* (Annapolis: Maryland State Archives and the Maryland Historical Trust, 1995), 1–8.

13. Nancy T. Baker, "Annapolis, Maryland 1695–1730," *Maryland Historical Magazine* 81, no. 3 (1986): 191.

14. Anthony D. Lindauer, *From Paths to Plats: The Development of Annapolis, 1651 to 1718* (Crownsville, MD: Maryland State Archives and Maryland Historical Trust, 1997), 1–14.

15. John F. Wing, "The Colonial Tobacco Fleet," *Nautical Research Journal* 48, no. 1 (2003): 3–14.

16. Ibid., 7–8.

17. Middleton, *Tobacco Coast,* 336–79.

18. Ibid., 161–65.

19. Ibid., 150–51, 483.

20. Wing, "Colonial Tobacco Fleet," 8–11.

21. V. J. Wyckoff, "Ships and Shipping of Seventeenth-Century Maryland," *Maryland Historical Magazine* 34, no. 3 (1939): 272–75.

22. William J. Kelley, "Shipbuilding at Federal Hill" (unpublished typescript, Maryland Historical Society, Baltimore), 21–31.

23. Arthur P. Middleton, "Ships and Shipbuilding in the Chesapeake Bay and Tributaries," in *Chesapeake Bay in the American Revolution,* edited by Ernest MacNeill Eller, 98–132 (Centreville, MD: Tidewater Press, 1981).

24. Edward C. Papenfuse, *In Pursuit of Profit: The Annapolis Merchants in the Era of the American Revolution, 1763–1805* (Baltimore: Johns Hopkins Univ. Press, 1975), 77–131.

25. Baker, "Annapolis, Maryland," 199–200.

26. Vaughan W. Brown, *Shipping in the Port of Annapolis, 1748–1775* (Annapolis: U.S. Naval Institute Press, 1965), 11–13.

27. Ibid., 13. See also the remarkably complete list of every ship that cleared Annapolis from June 1748 to July 1775 contained in Brown's appendix, 37–71.

28. Ibid., 17, 29–30; Middleton, *Tobacco Coast,* 199–200.

29. Nancy T. Baker, "The Manufacture of Ship Chandlery in Annapolis, Maryland, 1735–1770" (research paper prepared under a grant for the Early American Industries Association in the William Paca House files, Historic Annapolis, 1981), 8–10. Published (abbreviated format) in the *Chronicle of the Early American Industries Association* 35, no. 4 (1982): 61–71.

30. Baker, "Manufacture of Ship Chandlery," 13–19.

31. Ibid., 43. The difference between imported English cordage and colonial cordage is found in the greater diameter and length of the English variety, said to be available from 800 to 1,000 and more feet long and thus more useful for running rigging where splicing is undesirable.

32. Ibid., 28–43.

33. Ibid., 44–45.

34. Ibid., 46.

35. Mechelle L. Kerns Nocerito, "Trade in Colonial Anne Arundel County: The Tobacco Port of London Town," *Maryland Historical Magazine* 98, no. 3 (2003): 325–44.

36. Andrew Burnaby, *Travels through the Middle Settlements in North America* (London, 1775), 67.

37. Baker, "Manufacture of Ship Chandlery," 53–54.

38. Bruce Thompson and Brian Prince, Video: *Where Ships Were Borne: The Stephen Steward Shipyard* (Crownsville, MD: Maryland Historical Trust, 1997).

39. Jason Moser and Jane Cox, eds., "Colonial Trades and Shipbuilding in Anne Arundel County, Maryland" (unpublished research paper produced under the auspices of Anne Arundel Country's Lost Towns Archaeology Project), 33–51. Cited with the permission of the Annapolis Maritime Museum. See also Bruce Thompson, "Preliminary Report of Archaeological Investigations at the Stephen Steward Shipyard Site (1993)." File 18AN817, Maryland Historical Trust, Crownsville, MD.

40. Moser and Cox, "Colonial Trades and Shipbuilding," 52–56.

41. Middleton, *Tobacco Coast,* 241–43.

42. Brugger, *Maryland,* 125–26.

43. Adam Goodheart, "Tea and Fantasy: Fact, Fiction, and Revolution in a Historic American Town," *American Scholar* 74, no. 4 (2005): 21–34.

44. Papenfuse, *In Pursuit of Profit,* 46–50; Jane McWilliams and Morris L. Radoff, "Annapolis Meets the Crisis," in Eller, *Chesapeake Bay in the American Revolution,* 407–8.

1. Norman K. Risjord, *Builders of Annapolis: Enterprise and Politics in a Colonial Capital* (Baltimore: Maryland Historical Society, 1997), 92.

2. Myron J. Smith Jr. and John G. Earle, "The Maryland State Navy," in *Chesapeake Bay in the American Revolution,* edited by Ernest MacNeill Eller, 204–16 (Centreville, MD: Tidewater Press, 1981).

3. William S. Dudley, "Maryland at War on the Chesapeake, 1775–1783," in *New Aspects of Naval History: Selected Papers Presented at the Fourth Naval History Symposium, 25–26 October 1979,* edited by Craig Symonds, 102–21 (Annapolis, MD: Naval Institute Press, 1981). For general accounts of the state navies, see Charles Oscar Paullin, *The Navy of the American Revolution* (1906; repr., New York: Haskell House, 1971), and Gardner Weld Allen, *A Naval History of the American Revolution,* 2 vols. (Boston, 1913). Probably the best treatment of a single state navy is John W. Jackson's *The Pennsylvania Navy, 1775–1781: The Defense of the Delaware* (New Brunswick, NJ: Rutgers Univ. Press, 1974).

4. Smith and Earle, "The Maryland State Navy," in Eller, *Chesapeake Bay in the American Revolution,* 211–15. The types of war material imported included gunpowder, flints, saltpeter, brimstone, guns with bayonets, salt, medical supplies, blankets, and canvas.

5. Capt. Andrew Snape Hamond, RN, to Capt. Matthew Squire, RN, Feb. 26, 1776, in *Naval Documents of the American Revolution* (hereafter cited as *NDAR),* Vol. 4, edited by William Bell Clark (Washington, DC: GPO, 1969), 92–93.

6. Journal of HM sloop *Otter,* Mar. 4–9, 1776, Capt. Matthew Squire, in ibid., 270–72.

7. Proceedings of the Maryland Convention, 24 May 1776, in *NDAR,* Vol. 5, edited by William Bell Clark and William James Morgan (Washington, DC: GPO, 1970), 235–36.

8. Journal and Correspondence of the Maryland Council of Safety, vols. 21 and 73, Maryland State Archives, Annapolis.

9. Edwin M. Jameson, "Tory Operations on the Bay from Lord Dunmore's Departure to the End of the War," in Eller, *Chesapeake Bay in the American Revolution,* 378–402; Richard Arthur Overfield, "A Patriot Dilemma: The Treatment of Passive Loyalists and Neutrals in Revolutionary Maryland," *Maryland Historical Magazine* 68, no. 3 (1973): 140–59; and idem, "The Loyalists of Maryland during the American Revolution" (PhD diss., University of Maryland, 1968).

10. Joseph Dashiell to Gov. Thomas Johnson, June 10, 1777, in *NDAR,* Vol. 9, edited by William James Morgan (1986), 84; Worcester County Committee to Gov. Thomas Johnson, June 28, 1777, in ibid., 185; Henry Stevenson to Gen. Sir William Howe, Jan. 12, 1778, in *NDAR,* Vol. 11, edited by Michael J. Crawford (2005), 102–3.

11. Roger Novak, "The Mermaid of Assateague," *Maryland Historical Magazine* 102, no. 3 (2007): 194–203; Donald G. Shomette, *Shipwrecks, Sea Raiders, and Maritime Disasters along the Delmarva Coast, 1632–2004* (Baltimore: Johns Hopkins Univ. Press, 2007), 68–70.

12. Arthur Pierce Middleton, "Ships and Shipbuilding in the Chesapeake," in Eller, *Chesapeake Bay in the American Revolution,* 128–29.

13. "Action between American and British Barges in the Chesapeake Bay, November, 1782," *Maryland Historical Magazine* 4, no. 2 (1909): 115–33.

14. Jerome R. Garitee, *The Republic's Private Navy: The American Privateering Business as Practiced by Baltimore during the War of 1812* (Middletown, CT: Wesleyan Univ. Press, 1977), 11–21.

15. Richard K. Hart, "Maryland's Maritime Enterprises During the Revolution" (M.A. thesis, University of Maryland, 1947); Bernard C. Steiner, "Maryland Privateers in the American Revolution," *Maryland Historical Magazine* 3, no. 2 (1908): 99–103. See also Radm. Elliot Snow, "Lists of Public and Private Armed Vessels of the North American Colonies Fitted Out in the United States during the Revolutionary War, 1776–1783" (vertical file, Maryland Historical Society, Baltimore).

16. Edward C. Papenfuse, *In Pursuit of Profit: The Annapolis Merchants in the Era of the American Revolution, 1763–1805* (Baltimore: Johns Hopkins Univ. Press, 1975), 156–68.

17. Ibid., 172–73.

18. Benjamin Stoddert (1751–1813), who was born in Charles County, Maryland, became a wealthy Georgetown merchant after the Revolution and was the first secretary of the navy (1798–1801).

19. Hulbert Footner, *Sailor of Fortune: The Life and Adventures of Commodore Joshua Barney, U.S.N.* (New York, 1940). This event was replicated in 1987–88, during the bicentennial of the ratification, with the building of a full-size replica of the *Maryland Federalist*. Naval architect Melbourne Smith designed the miniature vessel, Allan Rawl built her, and Fred Hecklinger sailed her from Baltimore to Mount Vernon, with many stops for rest and refreshment along the way.

20. Donald M. Dozer, *Portrait of the Free State* (Chestertown, MD: Tidewater Publishers, 1976), 296.

21. Fred Leiner, *The End of Barbary Terror: America's 1815 War against the Pirates of North Africa* (New York: Oxford Univ. Press, 2006), 1–4.

22. *Maryland Gazette,* no. 2626, Thursday, May 11, 1797.

23. In the *Essex* case, the British High Court of Admiralty decided that the Royal Navy had the right to stop, search, and seize ships that were evading the "continuous voyage" doctrine so as to trade with French and Spanish colonies in the Caribbean. For a discussion, see William S. Dudley, ed., *The Naval War of 1812: A Documentary History,* Vol. 1 (Washington, DC: GPO, 1985), 16–23.

24. Spencer C. Tucker and Frank T. Reuther, *Injured Honor: The Chesapeake Leopard Affair, June 22, 1807* (Annapolis: Naval Institute Press, 1996), 67–68.

25. Ibid., 185–88.

26. Gary Lawson Browne, *Baltimore in the Nation, 1789–1861* (Chapel Hill: Univ. of North Carolina Press, 1980), 26–29.

27. James S. Van Ness, "Economic Development, Social and Cultural Changes: 1800–1850," in *Maryland: A History, 1632–1974,* edited by Richard Walsh and William Fox, 175–77 (Baltimore: Maryland Historical Society, 1974).

28. John Schroeder, *Commodore John Rodgers: Paragon of the Early American Navy* (Gainesville: Univ. Press of Florida, 2006), 2–8.

29. Ibid., 68.

30. Secretary Hamilton to Commodore Rodgers, June 9, 1810, in Dudley, *Naval War of 1812,* 1:39–40.

Chapter 3. The War of 1812 in Chesapeake Bay

1. Cdr. Arthur Bingham, RN, to Vadm. Herbert Sawyer, RN, May 21, 1811; Commo. John Rodgers to Secretary of the Navy, May 23, 1811; Secretary of the Navy Hamilton to Commo. Rodgers, May 28, 1811, in *The Naval War of 1812: A Documentary History,* Vol. 1, edited by William S. Dudley (Washington, DC: GPO, 1985), 41–49.

2. James F. Zimmerman, *Impressment of American Seamen* (New York: Columbia Univ. Press, 1925), 246–75.

3. Lawrence S. Kaplan, *Entangling Alliances with None: American Foreign Policy in the Age of Jefferson* (Kent, OH: Kent State Univ. Press, 1987), 111–28.

4. Ibid., 129–30.

5. For the best single volume treatment of the war, see Reginald Horsman, *The War of 1812* (New York, 1969).

6. Hamilton to Hull, 18 June 1812, in Dudley, *The Naval War of 1812,* 1:135–36; Linda M. Maloney, *The Captain from Connecticut: The Life and Naval Times of Isaac Hull* (Boston: Northeastern Univ. Press, 1986), 170.

7. Hamilton to Charles Stewart, June 22, 1812, NA, RG45, Letters from the Secretary of the Navy to Captains, Ships of War. National Archives, Record Group 45, Washington, DC.

8. Geoffrey M. Footner, *USS* Constellation: *From Frigate to Sloop of War* (Annapolis, MD: Naval Institute Press, 2003), 75; Charles Stewart to Paul Hamilton, Nov. 12, 1812, in *American State Papers,* 6, *Naval Affairs* 1:278–79 (1789–1825). Stewart sent this letter to Hamilton in response to his request in answering House of Representatives Naval Committee Chairman Burwell Bassett's queries concerning future naval construction. Capts. Isaac Hull and Charles Morris concurred in Stewart's statement.

9. Lords Commissioners of the Admiralty to Adm. Sir John B. Warren, Dec. 25, 1812, Adm. 2/1375 (Secret Orders and Letters), UkLondon National Archives, 337–38; see also Dudley, *Naval War of 1812,* 1:633–34.

10. Capt. John Cassin to Sec. William Jones, June 23, 1813, in William S. Dudley and Michael J. Crawford, eds., *Naval War of 1812,* Vol. 2 (Washington, DC: GPO, 1992), 359–60; Footner, *Constellation,* 93–98.

11. John P. Cranwell and William B. Crane, *Men of Marque: A History of Private Armed Vessels out of Baltimore during the War of 1812* (New York, 1940).

12. William M. Marine, *The British Invasion of Maryland, 1812–1815* (Baltimore, 1913). See also Michael J. Crawford, *The Naval War of 1812,* Vol. 3 (Washington, DC: GPO, 2002), 1–367.

13. Jerome R. Garitee, *The Republic's Private Navy: The American Privateering Business as Practiced by Baltimore during the War of 1812* (Middletown, CT: Mystic Seaport and Wesleyan Univ. Press, 1977), 103–26, 238–44. This is probably the best book ever written about American privateering in any war. The appendixes are particularly valuable for lists of commissions, investors, proceeds, and vessels.

14. Ibid., 149–52.

15. Radm. Sir George Cockburn to Vice Admiral Warren, Apr. 19, 1813, in Dudley and Crawford, *Naval War of 1812,* 2:340–41.

16. Cockburn to Warren, May 3, 1813, in ibid., 341–44.

17. Midn. Frederick Chamier of HMS *Menelaus,* as quoted in Christopher George, *Terror on the Chesapeake: The War of 1812 on the Bay* (Shippensburg, PA: White Mane Books, 2000), 29.

18. Cockburn to Warren, May 3, 1813, in Dudley and Crawford, *Naval War of 1812,* 2:343.

19. Earl Arnett, Robert J. Brugger, and Edward C. Papenfuse, *Maryland: A New Guide to the Old Line State,* 2nd ed. (Baltimore: Johns Hopkins Univ. Press), 164.

20. Vice Admiral Warren to First Secretary of the Admiralty John W. Croker, July 29, 1813, in Dudley and Crawford, *Naval War of 1812,* 2:368–69.

21. William Calderhead, "Naval Innovation in Crisis: War in the Chesapeake, 1813," *American Neptune* 36, no. 3 (1976): 206–21.

22. Commo. Joshua Barney to William Jones, July 4, 1813, in Dudley and Crawford, *Naval War of 1812,* 2:373–76.

23. Jones to Barney, Aug. 20 and 27, 1813, in ibid., 376–78.

24. Scott S. Sheads, *The Rockets' Red Glare: The Maritime Defense of Baltimore in 1814* (Centreville, MD: Tidewater Publishers, 1986), 13–17.

25. Lt. James Polkinghorne to Cdr. Henry Baker, Aug. 10, 1813, in Dudley and Crawford, *Naval War of 1812,* 2:381.

26. George, *Terror on the Chesapeake,* 62–64, 183–84 n. 54; Norman Plummer, "Another Look at the Battle of St. Michaels, *Weather Gauge* 31, no. 1 (Spring 1995): 10–17.

27. Warren to Croker, Aug. 23, 1813, in Dudley and Crawford, *Naval War of 1812,* 2:382–83.

28. Jones to Morris, Aug. 12 and 20, 1813, in ibid., 383–84.

29. Barney to Jones, Dec. 15, 1813, and Jones to Barney, Dec. 17, 1813, in ibid., 398–400.

30. Roger Morris, *Cockburn and the British Navy in Transition: Admiral Sir George Cockburn, 1772–1853* (Columbia: Univ. of South Carolina Press, 1997), 84–97.

31. Ibid., 100.

32. Barney to Jones, Apr. 15, 18, 22, and 29 and May 1 and 11, 1814, in Dudley and Crawford, *Naval War of 1812,* 2:55–59.

33. Cockburn to Barrie, June 3, 1814, in Crawford, *Naval War of 1812,* 3:82–83.

34. Donald G. Shomette, *Flotilla: The Patuxent Naval Campaign in the War of 1812* (repr., Baltimore: Johns Hopkins Univ. Press, 2009).

35. Sheads, *Rockets' Red Glare,* 47–48.

36. Anthony S. Pitch, *The Burning of Washington: The British Invasion of 1814* (Annapolis: Naval Institute Press, 1998), 39–40.

37. Barney to Jones, Aug. 29, 1814, in Crawford, *Naval War of 1812,* 3:207–8.

38. The leading recent study is Pitch's *Burning of Washington,* but see also Walter Lord, *The Dawn's Early Light* (New York: Norton, 1972), James Pack, *The Man Who Burned the White House: Admiral Sir George Cockburn, 1772–1853* (Annapolis: Naval Institute Press, 1987), and William Marine, *British Invasion of Maryland, 1812–15* (Baltimore, 1913).

39. Pitch, *Burning of Washington,* 54, 146–47.

40. Donald Hickey, *Don't Give Up the Ship: Myths of the War of 1812* (Champaign: Univ. of Illinois Press, 2006), 84, 88. See also Ralph J. Robinson, "New Facts in the National Anthem Story," *Baltimore* 49, no. 3 (1956): 33, 35, 37, 58. Hickey clears up many mistaken ideas about the War of 1812. The author verifies that it was the packet sloop *President,* rather than the *Minden,* that delivered Key and Skinner to the flagship.

41. Muller, *The Darkest Day: The Washington-Baltimore Campaign* (Philadelphia, 1963), 197–205.

42. Parker to Cochrane, Aug. 29 and 30, 1814, and Lt. Henry Crease to Cochrane, Sept. 1, 1814, in Crawford, *Naval War of 1812,* 3:232–35.

43. Capt. Alfred Grayson to Col. Franklin Wharton, Aug. 28, 1814, as quoted in Sheads, *Rockets' Red Glare,* 65.

44. General Smith to Secretary Monroe, Sept. 1, 1814, as quoted in ibid., 69.

45. Smith to Rodgers, Sept. 2, 1814, in Crawford, *Naval War of 1812,* 3:262.

46. Jones to Rodgers, Sept. 4, 1814, in ibid., 250.

47. Capt. David Porter to Jones, Sept. 7, 1814, in ibid., 251–55.

48. Capt. James Alexander to Vadm. Alexander Gordon to Cochrane, Sept. 9, 1814, in ibid., 238–42.

49. George, *Terror on the Chesapeake,* 146.

50. Cochrane to Cockburn, Sept. 13, 1814, and Lt. Col. Arthur Brooke, British Army, to Cochrane, Sept. 14, 1814, in Crawford, *Naval War of 1812,* 3:277–79.

51. For coverage of Baltimore's successful defense, see William D. Hoyt Jr., "Civilian Defense in Baltimore, 1814–1815," *Maryland Historical Magazine* 39, no. 3 (1944): 199–224, and 40, no. 1 (1945): 293–309; Muller, *The Darkest Day;* and Lord, *Dawn's Early Light.* See also George, *Terror on the Chesapeake,* and Sheads, *Rockets' Red Glare.*

52. Robert G. Stewart, "The Battle of the Ice Mound, February 7, 1815," *Maryland Historical Magazine* 70, no. 4 (1975): 372–78.

Chapter 4. The Surge of Maritime Baltimore under Sail and Steam

1. Jerome B. Garitee, *The Republic's Private Navy: The American Privateering Business as Practiced by Baltimore during the War of 1812* (Middletown, CT: Mystic Seaport and Wesleyan University Press, 1977), 224–29; Charles Carroll Griffin, *The United States and the Disruption of the Spanish Empire, 1810–1822: A Study of the Relations of the United States with Spain and the Rebel Spanish Colonies* (New York, 1937), 104–26; Arthur P. Whitaker, *The United States and the Independence of Latin America, 1800–1830* (New York, 1964), 139, 219. See also David Head, "Baltimore Seafarers, Privateering, and the South American Revolutions, 1816–1820, *Maryland Historical Magazine* 103, no. 3 (2008): 269–94, and Fred Hopkins, "For Freedom and Profit: Baltimore Privateers in the Wars of South American Independence, 1815–1824," in William S. Dudley and Roger Sarty, eds. *Troubled Waters: New Aspects of Maritime and Naval History. The Proceedings of the North American Society for Oceanic History, 1999–2005,* published as a double edition of *Northern Mariner* 18, nos. 3 and 4 (2008): 93–104.

2. See correspondence of James H. McCulloch, Collector of Customs, Baltimore, contained in National Archives Record Group 56, General Records of the Treasury Department, and RG 60, Attorney General Papers, Maryland Correspondence, 1812–62.

3. Howard I. Chapelle, *The Baltimore Clipper: Its Origin and Design* (1930; repr., Hatboro, PA: Tradition Press, 1965), 144–45.

4. Marion Brewington, *A Pictorial History of Chesapeake Bay* (New York: Bonanza Press, 1953), 10.

5. Thomas Gilmer, *Chesapeake Bay Sloops* (St. Michaels, MD: Chesapeake Bay Maritime Museum, 1982), 38–55.

6. Ibid., 18–36.

7. The use of the term *clipper* is rife with controversy, thanks in part to Howard Chapelle, who used the term indiscriminately to describe all types of Chesapeake schooners. *Clipper* or *Baltimore clipper* should apply only to Chesapeake schooners of the largest size constructed after 1830. Likewise, the common use of the term *clipper ship* has little relation to the sharp-built Chesapeake pilot schooner. The classic clipper ship is a bulk cargo-carrying square-rigged ship typically constructed at New York, Boston, or in Maine in the mid-nineteenth century, the prototype of which is probably Gordon McKay's New York–built *Flying Cloud.* The first use of the word *clipper* as applied to Chesapeake schooners was found in the language of British naval officers in describing the speed over the water attained by Baltimore privateer schooners during the War of 1812. See Geoffrey M. Footner, *Tidewater Triumph: The Development and Worldwide Success of the Chesapeake Bay Pilot Schooner* (Centreville, MD: Tidewater Publishers, 1998), 167.

8. Footner, *Tidewater Triumph,* 10. Footner revises Howard I. Chapelle's theories on the development of schooner design, as found in the latter's essays in *The National Watercraft Collection* (Washington, DC: Smithsonian Institution Press, 1976).

9. Footner, *Tidewater Triumph,* 72–73.

10. The Venice draft of *Enterprize* was located in 1994 during the research project of CDR Michael L. Bosworth, USN, who had written to the Venice Arsenal with the knowledge that *Enterprize,* when commanded by Thomas Robinson Jr., in 1805, put in for extensive repairs. His letter reached Dr. Mario Marzini, the biographer of Andrea Salvini, who happened to have made two drafts, one of which Marzini believes to be that of *Enterprize.* See Footner, *Tidewater Triumph,* 87–90. Annapolis ship surveyor Fred Hecklinger takes issue with this and believes it highly unlikely that this drawing was of the *Enterprize.*

11. Footner, *Tidewater Triumph,* 121.

12. Frederick C. Leiner, *The End of Barbary Terror: America's 1815 War against the Pirates of North Africa* (New York: Oxford Univ. Press, 2006).

13. Footner, *Tidewater Triumph,* 135.

14. Geoffrey M. Footner, "John Robb: Shipbuilder of Fells Point: His Work as a Study of Nineteenth-Century Naval Architecture," *Nautical Research Journal* 50, no. 3 (2005): 131–32.

15. Footner, *Tidewater Triumph,* 141.

16. Ibid., 146.

17. Josephine Pacheco, *The Pearl Failed Slave Escape* (Chapel Hill: Univ. of North Carolina Press, 2005).

18. Daniel Drayton, *The Personal Memoir of Daniel Drayton: For Four Years and Four Months a Prisoner (for Charity's Sake) in a Washington Jail* (N.p., 1854). Project Gutenberg online books, 2008, 8.

19. For detailed information on schooner *Pearl's* origin and dimensions, see Master Abstracts of Enrollments, Maine to Ohio, Ship Enrollments, 1844–87, entry 7 for 1846, Record Group 41, National Archives and Records Administration.

20. Mary Kay Ricks, *Escape on the Pearl: The Heroic Bid for Freedom on the Underground Railroad* (New York: HarperCollins, 2007).

21. Footner, *Tidewater Triumph,* 174–76.

22. Ibid., 128–32, 182–88. See Jean Baptise Marestier, *Mémoire sur Bateaux à Vapeur des Etats Unis d'Amérique,* 2 vols. (Paris: Le Ministre de la Marine et des Colonies, 1824).

23. Footner, *Tidewater Triumph,* 196–202.

24. Frederick Fitzgerald de Roos, *Personal Narrative of Travels in the United States, with Remarks on the Present State of the American Navy* (London, 1827).

25. K. Jack Bauer, *A Maritime History of the United States: The Role of America's Seas and Waterways* (Columbia: Univ. of South Carolina Press, 1987), 50–103.

26. William Armstrong Fairburn, *Merchant Sail,* 6 vols. (Carter Lovell, ME, 1945–55), 5:2747–48.

27. Donald M. Dozer, *Portrait of the Free State* (Cambridge, MD: Tidewater Publishers, 1976), 399–400.

28. Pete Lesher, "A Load of Guano: Baltimore and the Growth of the Fertilizer Trade," *Maryland Historical Magazine* 99, no. 4 (2004): 480–90.

29. John Fitch, operating on the Delaware River, deserves credit for inaugurating the first regular steamboat passenger service in the United States. His stern-paddle steamboats operated between Philadelphia and Trenton, New Jersey, in the summer of 1790. The company failed for lack of passengers. His competitor, Robert Fulton, who became more famous

and more successful, is more often referred to as the "father" of steamboat transportation in the United States.

30. Brewington, *A Pictorial History of Chesapeake Bay,* 43–44.

31. Alexander Crosby Brown, *Steam Packets on the Chesapeake: A History of the Old Bay Line since 1840* (Cambridge, MD: Cornell Maritime Press, 1961), 14.

32. David C. Holly, *Tidewater by Steamboat: A Saga of the Chesapeake: The Weems Line on the Patuxent, Potomac, and Rappahannock* (1991; repr., Baltimore: Johns Hopkins Univ. Press, 2000), 1–25.

33. David C. Holly, *Chesapeake Steamboats: Vanished Fleet* (Centreville, MD: Tidewater Publishers, 1994), 42–51.

34. Ibid., 243–56.

35. William J. Kelley, "Shipbuilding at Federal Hill, Baltimore" (unpublished typescript, 1956, on file at the Maryland Historical Society).

36. Ibid., 79–81.

37. Irving H. King, *The Coast Guard Expands, 1865–1915: New Roles and New Frontiers* (Annapolis: Naval Institute Press, 1996), 226–27.

38. Robert H. Burgess, *This Was Chesapeake Bay,* as excerpted in "Nautical Monster of an Age," *Waterways* 5, no.1 (2007): 14–15.

39. Alexander Crosby Brown, *The Old Bay Line* (Richmond, VA, 1940).

40. The utility of such a canal during the two wars of American independence, 1775–83 and 1812–15, became clear when the British navy blockaded the entrances to Chesapeake and Delaware bays. Needed at the time, it was too late for action when the wars arrived. Several years were required to engineer, dig, and arrange financing for the canal. It is of passing interest to note that Canada's Rideau Canal, linking the Ottawa River and the St. Lawrence River, was constructed after the War of 1812 for similar reasons. Communications between Quebec, Montreal, and Upper Canada could continue uninterrupted no matter who controlled Lake Ontario.

41. Frederick Erving Dayton, *Steamboat Days* (New York, 1925), 310.

42. Burgess, *This Was Chesapeake Bay,* 78.

43. James Dugan, *The Great Iron Ship* (New York: Harper & Bros., 1953), 5.

44. Ibid., 72.

45. Burgess, *This Was Chesapeake Bay,* 18–21.

46. Kelley, "Shipbuilding at Federal Hill," 150–51.

47. Ibid., 153–54.

48. Robert de Gast, *The Lighthouses of Chesapeake Bay* (Baltimore: Johns Hopkins Univ. Press, 1973), 3.

49. Ibid., 4–5.

50. Mary Bellis, "A History of Buoys and Tenders," *About.com* Web site: http://inventors.about.com/library/inventorsblbuoys1.htm=1 (accessed Sept. 21, 2008).

51. See "Inventory of Historic Light Stations, Maryland Lighthouses," National Park Service Web site: www.nps.gov/history/maritime/light/md.htm (accessed Sept. 16, 2008).

52. Irving H. King, *The Coast Guard Expands, 1865–1915: New Roles, New Frontiers* (Annapolis: Naval Institute Press, 1996), 196–203; Bob Stevens, *A History of the U.S. Life Saving Service,* www.ocmuseum.org/uslss/history1.asp (accessed Aug. 30, 2008).

53. Nan DeVincent-Hayes and John E. Jacob, *Ocean City,* Vol. 1, Images of America Series (Charleston, SC: Arcadia Books, 1999), 9–11; see also John R. Wennersten, *Maryland's Eastern Shore: A Journey in Time and Place* (Centreville, MD: Tidewater Publishers, 1992), 254–63.

54. George M. and Suzanne Hurley, *Shipwrecks and Rescues: Along the Barrier Islands of Delaware, Maryland, and Virginia* (Norfolk, VA: Donning Co., 1984).

55. King, *The Coast Guard Expands,* 192–244.

56. Jane W. McWilliams, *Bay Ridge on the Chesapeake: An Illustrated History* (Annapolis, MD: Brighton Editions, 1986), 39–106.

57. David C. Holly, *Steamboat on the Chesapeake: Emma Giles and the Tolchester Line* (Chestertown, MD: Tidewater Publishers, 1987), 17–18.

58. Burgess, *Chesapeake Circle,* 51–53.

59. Robert Burgess and H. Graham Wood, *Steamboats Out of Baltimore* (Centreville, MD: Tidewater Press, 1968), 63.

60. Michael Buckley, ed., *Voices of the Chesapeake Bay* (Annapolis: Geared Up, 2008), 178–79; Holly, *Steamboat on the Chesapeake,* 197–98; Burgess and Wood, *Steamboats Out of Baltimore,* xiii–xv; Holly, *Chesapeake Steamboats,* 220–26.

61. Burgess and Wood, *Steamboats Out of Baltimore,* 127.

62. The *President Warfield* was the most notable of these. She was under the control of the U.S. Navy and was used as a transport to Omaha Beach a month after D-Day and later on the Seine River. After the war, individuals sympathetic to the Zionist cause purchased her, renamed her *Exodus 1947,* and sent her to Europe to carry Jewish refugees illicitly from France to Haifa. There she confronted British destroyers, which sent boarding crews to take over the vessel. The British removed the passengers and sent them back to Europe. The ship caught fire and burned at Haifa, where she was scrapped, thus ending a highly eccentric career for a Chesapeake Bay steamboat.

63. David C. Holly, *Exodus 1947* (Annapolis: Naval Institute Press, 1998).

64. Scott M. Kozel, "Chesapeake Bay Bridge History," *Roads to the Future.com,* 1–5 (accessed June 9, 2007).

65. Maryland Department of Transportation, Transportation Authority, *Task Force Report, Task Force on Traffic Capacity across the Chesapeake Bay* (Annapolis, July 2006), 2–61.

Chapter 5. Civil War on Chesapeake Bay

1. David C. Holly, *Chesapeake Steamboats: Vanished Fleet* (Centreville, MD: Tidewater Publishers, 1994), 103–4.

2. Naval History Division, *Civil War Naval Chronology, 1861–1865,* 5 vols. (Washington, DC: GPO, 1965), 1:7.

3. Jack Sweetman, *The U.S. Naval Academy: An Illustrated History* (Annapolis: Naval Institute Press, 1979), 61–63.

4. Naval History Division, *Civil War Naval Chronology, 1861–1865,* 1:22.

5. Eric Mills, *Chesapeake Bay in the Civil War* (Centreville, MD: Tidewater Publishers, 1996), 57–62. At the outbreak of the Civil War, Hollins was one of the few remaining U.S. Navy veterans of the War of 1812 and was in command of USS *Susquehanna* in the Mediterranean. He returned to the United States, resigned his commission, and accepted the rank of captain in the Confederate States Navy as of June 20, 1861. He later served as commander of that navy's New Orleans Station and on the Upper Mississippi and participated in the defense of New Orleans during Admiral Farragut's invasion of April 1862.

6. Ibid., 78–79.

7. Ibid., 95–97.

8. Allan Nevins, *The War for the Union: The Improvised War, 1861–1862* (New York: Charles Scribner's Sons, 1959), 404–5.

9. Allan Nevins, *The War for the Union: War Becomes Revolution, 1862–1863* (New York: Charles Scribner's Sons, 1960), 34–49.

10. Charles Dana Gibson and Kay Gibson, *Assault and Logistics: Union Army Coastal and River Operations.* The Army's Navy Series. Vol. 2, *Union Army Coastal and River Operations, 1861–1866* (Camden, ME: Ensign Press, 1995), 191–207, app. P, 618–19.

11. Nevins, *War Becomes Revolution,* 130.

12. Naval History Division, *Civil War Naval Chronology,* 2:93.

13. Mills, *Chesapeake Bay in the Civil War,* 183–87.

14. Nevins, *War Becomes Revolution, 1862–1863,* 184–88.

15. Mills, *Chesapeake Bay in the Civil War,* 187–89.

16. Naval History Division, *Civil War Naval Chronology,* 3:16.

17. Jeffrey D. Wert, *General James Longstreet, The Confederacy's Most Controversial Soldier: A Biography* (New York, 1993), 229–38; *Civil War Naval Chronology,* 3:63, 66.

18. Mills, *Chesapeake Bay in the Civil War,* 202–4.

19. Naval History Division, *Civil War Naval Chronology,* 3:140–41.

20. U.S. Office of Naval Records and Library, *Official Records of the Union and Confederate Navies in the War of the Rebellion,* 1st ser., 27 vols.; 2nd ser., 3 vols. (Washington, DC: GPO, 1894–1922), 1st ser., 9:206, 222–23. Hereafter cited as ORN.

21. Robert de Gast, *The Lighthouses of Chesapeake Bay* (Baltimore: John Hopkins Univ. Press, 1973).

22. Frank E. Vandiver, *Jubal's Raid: General Early's Famous Attack on Washington in 1864* (Westport, CT, 1960), 25–58.

23. Mills, *Chesapeake Bay in the Civil War,* 244–45.

24. Daniel Carroll Toomey, *The Johnson-Gilmor Raid, July 9–13* (Baltimore: Toomey Press, 2005), 14–30.

25. Raimundo Luraghi, *A History of the Confederate Navy,* trans. Paolo Coletta (Annapolis: Naval Institute Press, 1996), 309–19.

26. Gen. U. S. Grant to Gen. H. T. Halleck, July 7, 1864, *ORA.* U.S. War Department, *The War of the Rebellions: A Compilation of the Official Records of the Union and Confederate Armies,* 1st ser., 53 vols.; 2nd ser., 8 vols., 3rd ser., 5 vols.; 4th ser., 4 vols. (Washington, DC: GPO, 1880–1902), 1st ser., 37:98; Ulysses S. Grant, *Memoirs and Selected Letters, 1839–1865,* edited by Mary D. and William S. McFeely (New York: Library Classics of America, 1990), 605–6, 801–2.

27. Naval History Division, *Civil War Chronology,* 4:86–87; *ORA,* 1st ser., 37:98.

28. Bruce F. Thompson, Principal Investigator, "The Terrible Calamity on the Lower Potomac: An Historical and Archaeological Assessment of the Shipwreck U.S.S. *Tulip,* Potomac River, St. Mary's County, Maryland," prepared for the U.S. Naval Historical Center, 1996, rev. 1998. 212 pages. See also Bruce Thompson, "Legacy of a Fourth Rate Steam Screw," *Naval History* 10, no. 3 (1996): 36–39.

29. Naval History Division, *Civil War Naval Chronology,* 5:87–91.

30. ORN, 1st ser., 5:578.

Chapter 6. Oysters, Crabs, Fish, and Watermen

1. Edmund A. Nelson, "The Chesapeake Bay Oyster Industry, 1800–1900" (unpublished paper, Maryland Historical Society Library, Baltimore, 1994).

2. Ibid.

3. John R. Wennersten, *The Oyster Wars of Chesapeake Bay* (Chestertown, MD: Tidewater Publishers, 1981), 13–14.

4. Ibid., 16–17.

5. Victor S. Kennedy and Linda L. Breisch, "Sixteen Decades of Political Management of the Oyster Fishery in Maryland's Chesapeake Bay," *Journal of Environmental Management* 16 (1983): 153–71.

6. Ibid., 163.

7. Ibid., 166.

8. Maryland Oyster Advisory Commission 2007 Interim Report Concerning Maryland's Chesapeake Bay Oyster Management Program, www.md.dnr.state.md.us/fisheries/oysters/oac.

9. U.S. Army Corps of Engineers, Notice of Intent to Prepare an Environmental Impact Statement for the Proposed Introduction of the Oyster Species *Crassostrea ariakensis, Federal Register* 6, no. 2 (2004). See also Maryland DNR Web site: www.dnr.state.md.us/dnrnews/infocus/notice_of_intent2.asp.

10. Erica Goldman, "A Model Scientist: Following Oysters from Spawning to Settlement," *Chesapeake Quarterly* 4, no. 3 (2005): 4–10.

11. Mark Luckenbach, "*Crassostrea ariakensis:* Panacea or Pandora?" Virginia Institute of Marine Science, www.ian.umces.edu/pdfs/iannewsletter (accessed Oct. 14, 2008).

12. The Maryland Department of Natural Resources sponsored a series of public meetings to provide comment on the draft EIS report in November 2008. The final report was published in spring 2009. See www.dnr.state.md.us/dnrnews/infocus/oysters.asp (accessed Oct. 16, 2008). Gov. Martin O'Malley announced on April 7, 2009, that Maryland, Virginia, and the U.S. Army Corps of Engineers had agreed on a preferred oyster restoration program. Web site accessed Dec. 13, 2009.

13. "Maryland Hatchery Rears Record Number of Oysters," *Bay Journal* 18, no. 7 (2008): 16.

14. Cynthia Barry, "A Homecoming for Oysters: Nurturing Millions of Spat, Experts Learn What Works," *Save the Bay* 34, no. 3 (2008): 10–12.

15. William W. Warner, *Beautiful Swimmers: Watermen, Crabs, and the Chesapeake Bay* (Boston: Little, Brown, 1976, 1994), 77.

16. Ibid., 78.

17. Paula J. Johnson, ed., *Working the Water: The Commercial Fisheries of Maryland's Patuxent River* (Charlottesville: Univ. Press of Virginia and Calvert Marine Museum, 1988), 14–16.

18. Mick Blackistone, *Dancing with the Tide: Watermen of the Chesapeake* (Centreville, MD: Tidewater Publishers, 2000), 181–88.

19. Katie Arcieri, "Watermen Blues: Higher Gas, Bait Costs Take Toll on Crabbers," *Sunday Capital* (Annapolis), July 29, 2007, B1–B2.

20. Blackistone, *Dancing with the Tide,* 185.

21. Johnson, *Working the Water,* 56–64.

22. Mark E. Jacoby, *Working the Chesapeake Bay: Watermen on the Bay,* 2nd ed. (College Park, MD: Maryland Sea Grant College, 1993), 2–5.

23. Johnson, *Working the Water,* 60.

24. Ibid., 64.

25. Jacoby, *Working the Chesapeake Bay,* 51–59.

26. Karl Blankenship, "America's Shad Decline a Mystery," *Bay Journal* 18, no. 6 (2008): 1, 8–9.

27. "Atlantic Sturgeon," Chesapeake Bay Field Office, U.S. Fish and Wildlife Service, www.fws.gov/chesapeakebay/sturgeon.html (accessed Sept. 26, 2008).

28. "Striped Bass," Chesapeake Field Office, U.S. Fish and Wildlife Service, www .fwsgov/chesapeakebay.striper.html (accessed Sept. 24, 2008).

29. "Bacterial Disease Fatal to Rockfish," *Washington Post,* Dec. 28, 2008; "Striped Bass Health: All About Mycobacteria"; www.dnr/state.md.us/dnrnews/infocus/striped_ bass_health.asp (accessed Nov. 30, 2008).

30. "Alewife and Blueback Herring," Chesapeake Bay Field Office, U.S. Fish and Wildlife Service, www.fws.gov/chesapeakebay/herring.html (accessed Sept. 24, 2008).

31. William H. Wroten Jr., *Assateague* (Centreville, MD: Tidewater Publishers, 1972), 22–25.

32. Daybreak, "Ocean City Maryland Scallop Boats," www.commercial-fishing.org/ business/ocean-city-maryland-scallop-boats (accessed Sept. 24, 2008).

33. U.S. Department of Commerce, NOAA, National Marine Fisheries Services, Statistics and Economics Division, *Fisheries of the United States, 1998* (July 1999).

34. Blackistone, *Dancing with the Tide,* 206–7. For harvests in Maryland's commercial fisheries, see www.dnr.state.md.us/fisheries/commerical/chbayharvest.html; and for harvests in Maryland's recreational fisheries: www.st.nmfs.noaa/st1/recreational/queries/catch/ time_series.html. Online commercial catch data is not up to date; tabular data reflect totals only to 2004. One must contact DNR directly for more current data.

35. Jacoby, *Working the Chesapeake Bay,* ix.

36. Marion E. Warren, with Mame Warren, *Bringing Back the Bay: The Chesapeake in the Photographs of Marion E. Warren and the Voices of Its People* (1983; repr., Annapolis: Time Exposures Limited, 2002), 1.

37. Ibid., 8.

38. Ibid., 221.

39. Harold Anderson, "Slavery, Freedom and the Chesapeake," *Maryland Marine Notes Online* 16, no. 2 (1998), www.mdsg.umd.edu/MarineNotes/MarApr98/side1 (accessed Mar. 10, 2009).

40. Anderson, "Black Men, Blue Waters: African Americans on the Chesapeake," *Maryland Marine Notes Online,* www.mdsg.umd.edu/MarineNotes/Mar-Apr98/.

41. Ibid.

42. Ibid.

43. Vincent O. Leggett, "Sixty Years on the Bay with Earl White," *Blacks of the Chesapeake,* www.dnr.state.md.us/irc/boc.html (accessed Dec. 13, 2009).

44. Philip L. Brown, *The Other Annapolis, 1900–1950* (Annapolis: Annapolis Publishing, 1994), 40.

45. Jefferson Holland, "McNasby Oyster Company," *What's Up Magazine,* August 2007.

46. Annapolis Maritime Museum, Eastpoint Walking Tour, Site 10, "The McNasby Oyster Company," www.annapolismaritimemuseum.org/EWT/ewt10.htm (accessed Mar. 15, 2008, 4 pages).

47. Phyllis Leffler, "Maritime Museums and National Identity," in *Public Historian* 6, no. 4 (2004).

Chapter 7. Maritime Commerce after the Civil War

1. Eleanor Bruchey, "Industrialization of Maryland," in *Maryland, A History: 1632– 1974,* edited by Richard Walsh and William Lloyd Fox (Baltimore: Maryland Historical Society, 1974), 462.

2. Ibid., 463–64.

3. Ibid., 469–76.

4. Harold Kanarek, *The Mid-Atlantic Engineers: A History of the Baltimore District U.S. Army Corps of Engineers, 1774–1974* (Washington, DC: GPO, 1976); Joseph L. Arnold, *The Baltimore Engineers and the Chesapeake Bay, 1961–1987* (Baltimore: U.S. Army Corps of Engineers, 1988).

5. For a detailed history of the canal, see Ralph D. Gray, *The National Waterway: A History of the Chesapeake and Delaware Canal, 1769–1965* (Urbana: Univ. of Illinois Press, 1967).

6. Ibid., 257–58.

7. Donald M. Dozer, *Portrait of the Free State* (Centreville, MD: Tidewater Publishers, 1976), 503.

8. Mark Reutter, *Sparrows Point: Making Steel—The Rise and Ruin of American Industrial Might* (New York: Summit Books, 1988), 107.

9. Elmer J. Hall, *Shipbuilding at the Sparrows Point Yard: A Century of Pride and Transition* (Indiana, PA: Gazette Printers, 2007), 139–50.

10. Robert H. Burgess, *Sea, Sails, and Shipwreck: Career of the Four-Masted Schooner Purnell T. White* (Centreville, MD: Tidewater Publishers, 1970).

11. Robert H. Burgess, *This Was Chesapeake Bay* (Centreville, MD: Tidewater Publishers, 1963), 43–46.

12. Quentin Snediker and Ann Jensen, *Chesapeake Bay Schooners* (Centreville, MD: Tidewater Publishers, 1992), 136–37, 197–98.

13. Dozer, *Portrait of the Free State,* 511.

14. Hall, *Shipbuilding at the Sparrows Point Yard,* 139–50.

15. See foreign trade figures as listed in the *Foreign Commerce Statistical Reports,* various years, Maryland Port Administration, World Trade Center, Baltimore.

16. Ibid., 1989, 13–14.

17. Maryland Port Authority Web sites: www.marylandports.com/welcome/govindex.htm; www.marylandports.com/CIC/Seagirt.htm; and Maryland State Archives Web site: www.msa.md.gov.manual/01glance/html/port.html.

18. Mary Butler Davies, *Time and Tide: A Centennial History of the Vane Brothers Company* (Baltimore: Vane Brothers Publishers, 1998), 1–5.

19. Robert J. Brugger, *Maryland: A Middle Temperament, 1634–1980* (Baltimore: Johns Hopkins Univ. Press, 1988), 438.

20. Kelley, "Shipbuilding at Federal Hill," 261–64.

21. Davies, *Time and the Tide,* 9.

22. Ibid., 21–25. For a select sample of Robert Burgess's publications, see *This Was Chesapeake Bay* and *Chesapeake Circle* (Cambridge, MD, 1965). For Aubrey Bodine's photographic work, see *Chesapeake Bay and Tidewater* (New York: Hastings House, 1954).

23. Kelley, "Shipbuilding at Federal Hill," 262.

24. Davies, *Time and the Tide,* 51–69; see also the Vane Brothers Web site: www.vanebrothers.com/assets (accessed Mar. 20, 2008).

Chapter 8. The Decline of Working Sail

1. Pete Lesher, "Apprenticeships and the Shipbuilding Trade: Robert Lambdin of St. Michaels," *Weather Gauge* 36, no. 2 (2000): 19–26.

2. Robert Dawson Lambdin, "Early Shipbuilding in Maryland: A Special Reference for the Chesapeake Bay Log Canoe: Autobiography of Robert Dawson Lambdin," 1935

(unpublished manuscript, vertical file, Chesapeake Bay Maritime Museum Library, St. Michaels, MD).

3. Pete Lesher, "Thomas Kirby and the Decline of Shipbuilding in Talbot County," *Maryland Historical Magazine* 97, no. 3 (2002): 359–68.

4. Pete Lesher, "The Industrious Shipbuilder: Joseph W. Brooks," *Weather Gauge* 36, no. (2000): 3–4.

5. Ibid., 10–11.

6. Marion V. Brewington, *Chesapeake Bay Log Canoes and Bugeyes* (Centreville, MD: Tidewater Publishers, 1963), 39.

7. Pete Lesher, "From Bugeyes to Skipjacks: John Branford Master Carpenter," *Weather Gauge* 34, no. 2 (1998): 18–24.

8. Brewington, *Log Canoes and Bugeyes,* 100–110 (app. 5).

9. Geoffrey M. Footner, *The Last Generation: A History of a Chesapeake Shipbuilding Family* (Solomons, MD: Calvert Marine Museum Press, 1991), 178–81.

10. Quentin Snediker and Ann Jensen, *Chesapeake Bay Schooners* (Centreville, MD: Tidewater Publishers, 1992), 138–45.

11. Ibid., 145–46.

12. Burgess, *This Was Chesapeake Bay* (Centreville, MD: Tidewater Publishers, 1963), 130–31. A reprint of Robert Burgess's article from *This Was Chesapeake Bay* gives his version of the visit in "Nautical Monster of an Age," *Waterways* 5, no. 1 (2007): 18–21.

13. Ibid., 144–47.

14. Robert H. Burgess, *Chesapeake Circle* (Centreville, MD: Tidewater Press, 1965), and idem, *Chesapeake Circle* (Cambridge, MD: Cornell Maritime Press, 1965), 185–94.

15. Burgess, *This Was Chesapeake Bay,* 110–11.

16. Ibid., 145–47.

17. Mark E. Jacoby, *Working the Chesapeake Bay: Watermen on the Bay,* 2nd ed. (College Park: Maryland Sea Grant College, 1993), 119–31.

18. Doug Stephens, *Workin' with the Wind: Portrait of a Chesapeake Bay Skipjack* (Salisbury, MD: Factor Press, 2004). This is an account of the *Caleb W. Jones,* one of the few surviving skipjacks from the lower Eastern Shore of Maryland.

19. Pat Vojtech, *Chesapeake Bay Skipjacks* (Centreville, MD: Tidewater Publishers, 1993), 127–40.

20. Ralph Eshelman, "Chesapeake Skipjack *Hilda M. Willing,* National Landmark Study," National Park Service Web site, 1–7: www.nps.gov/history/maritime/nhl/Willing .html (accessed Aug. 14, 2007).

21. Pete Lesher, "Maryland Oyster Dredging Fleet Surviving Today" (handout distributed at the annual meeting of the National Maritime Historical Society, St. Michaels, MD, May 30, 2008).

22. Robert Barrie and George Barrie Jr., *Cruises, Mainly on the Bay of the Chesapeake,* 3rd ed. (Bryn Mawr, PA: Franklin Press, 1909), 209–13. For an appreciation of the Barries' book, see Burgess, *This Was Chesapeake Bay,* 178–79.

23. Michael F. Miron, "Historic Boat Yards of Eastport, Spa Creek," *Publick Enterprise,* 1996. Miron, the director of economic development for the City of Annapolis, devoted much time and effort to gathering the personal stories of men who had owned the boatyards of Annapolis during the first half of the twentieth century. In spring 1996, he published these stories in a series of articles in the *Publick Enterprise,* a freely distributed local newspaper no longer in circulation.

24. This statement is unconfirmed. Although Bill Mason may have competed, there is no mention of the boat or the driver in the official President's Cup results for 1946.

25. For a complete listing of both the Chance and Annapolis Yacht Yard boats, see "Chance Marine Construction, Annapolis MS," http://shipbuildinghistory.com/history/shipyards/6yachts/inactive/trumpymd.html.

26. Michael Miron, "History: John Trumpy and Sons," *Boater's Life,* www.boaterslife .com (accessed Jan. 2008); Lisa Larsen, "The Trumpy Story: Relaunching an Icon," http://trumpyyachts.net/RelaunchingAnIcon.html.

Chapter 9. The Growth of Recreational Boating

1. Kenneth Grahame, *The Wind in the Willows* (1908), chap. 1.

2. Robert Barrie and George Barrie Jr., *Cruises, Mainly in the Bay of the Chesapeake* (Bryn Mawr, PA: Franklin Press, 1909), 1–42.

3. Richard Henderson, *Chesapeake Sails: A History of Yachting on the Bay* (Centreville, MD: Tidewater Publishers, 1999), 24.

4. Geoffrey M. Footner, *The Last Generation: A History of a Chesapeake Shipbuilding Family* (Solomons, MD: Calvert Marine Museum Press, 1991), 39–40.

5. Ibid., 40–41.

6. Henderson, *Chesapeake Sails,* 15.

7. Footner, *The Last Generation,* 53.

8. Ibid., 88.

9. John Rousmaniere, *The Low Black Schooner: Yacht America, 1851–1945* (Mystic, CT: Mystic Seaport Museum Stores, 1986), 49–50.

10. Robert W. McNitt, *Sailing at the U.S. Naval Academy: An Illustrated History* (Annapolis: Naval Institute Press, 1996), 40–42.

11. Ibid., 47–48.

12. Ibid., 68–69.

13. Henderson, *Chesapeake Sails,* 58.

14. Marion V. Brewington, *Chesapeake Bay Log Canoes and Bugeyes* (Centreville, MD: Tidewater Publishers, 1963), 22–24.

15. Robert H. Burgess, *This Was Chesapeake Bay* (Centreville, MD: Tidewater Publishers, 1963), 119–20.

16. Robert H. Burgess, *Chesapeake Sailing Craft: Recollections of Robert H. Burgess,* ed. William A. Fox, rev. ed. (1957; Centreville, MD: Tidewater Publishers, 2005), 1–12. See also the Web site of the Chesapeake Bay Log Sailing Canoe Association: www.logcanoes .com/canoes.html.

17. George J. Collins and Kathy Alexander, *Chessie Racing: The Story of Maryland's Entry in the 1997–1998 Whitbread Round the World Race* (Baltimore: Johns Hopkins Univ. Press, 2001).

18. Laurence Hartge, *A History of the Hartge Yacht Yard,* 3rd ed. (Galesville, MD, 2000), 21–30.

19. Henderson, *Chesapeake Sails,* 264–65.

20. Barrie and Barrie, *Cruises, Mainly in the Bay of the Chesapeake,* 249–50.

21. Ibid., 229–30.

22. Joseph T. Rothrock, *Vacation Cruising in Chesapeake and Delaware Bays* (Philadelphia, 1884). There is a new edition of this book available (as of 2008) in paperback, published by BiblioBazaar.

23. Joseph T. Rothrock and Jane C. Rothrock, *Chesapeake Odysseys: An 1883 Cruise Revisited* (Centreville, MD: Tidewater Publishers, 1984), 135.

24. Robert de Gast, *Western Wind, Eastern Shore: A Sailing Cruise around the Eastern Shore of Maryland, Delaware, and Virginia* (Baltimore: Johns Hopkins Univ. Press, 1975).

25. Chesapeake Bay Magazine's *Guide to Cruising Chesapeake Bay* (Annapolis: Chesapeake Bay Magazine, 2007), 361–81.

26. Douglas W. Lipton and Scott Miller, *Recreational Boating in Maryland: An Economic Impact Study, 1993–94,* A Maryland Sea Grant Extension Program Publication (College Park: University of Maryland, 1995), 36 pages.

27. Lipton and Miller, *Recreational Boating,* 15.

28. Douglas W. Lipton, *Economic Impact of Maryland Boating, 1993–1995,* A Maryland Sea Grant Extension Program Publication (College Park: University of Maryland, Oct. 1996).

29. Douglas W. Lipton, *Boating 2000: A Survey of Boater Spending in Maryland,* A Maryland Sea Grant Extension Program Publication (College Park: University of Maryland, 2003), 1–7.

30. Lipton, *Economic Impact of Maryland Boating in 2004* (Maryland Sea Grant Extension Web site): www.mdsg.umd.edu/programs/extension/communities/boating/index.php (accessed July 2006), 1–2.

31. "Report of Certificates of Number Issued to Boats, Recreational Boats Only," Jurisdiction of Maryland, U.S. Coast Guard, Department of Homeland Security, 2002–7.

32. William W. Mowbray, *Power Boat Racing on the Chesapeake* (Centreville, MD: Tidewater Publishers, 1995), 20.

33. Ibid.

34. Ibid., 27–28.

35. Ibid., 36–37.

36. Web site: www.hydroplanes in history (accessed July 24, 2007).

37. John Page Williams Jr., *Exploring the Chesapeake in Small Boats* (Centreville, MD: Tidewater Publishers, 1992); Michael Savario and Andrea Nolan, *Sea Kayaking Maryland's Chesapeake Bay: Day Trips on the Tidal Tributaries and Coastlines of the Western and Eastern Shore* (Woodstock, VT: Backcountry Guides, 2003); *Seakayaker* magazine; and www.kayak academy.com.

38. For text of the Chesapeake Bay Agreement, see the Web site of the Chesapeake Bay Program: www.chesapeakebay/net/publications/net/publiations/83agree.htm; "Water Trails," *Maryland's Statewide Water Trails Program* (Maryland Department of Natural Resources; updated Aug. 13, 2008), Web site: www.dnr.state.md.us/greenways/watertrails .html (accessed Sept. 30, 2008).

Chapter 10. Naval Installations on Chesapeake Bay

1. David Watson Taylor began his naval career after graduating from Randolph-Macon College in 1881. He graduated from the U.S. Naval Academy in 1885 and then studied advanced naval construction and marine engineering at the Royal Naval College, Greenwich, England, earning the highest grades achieved until then at both institutions. Instrumental in convincing Congress of the value of towing tanks and model tests in support of our nation's defense mission, naval constructor Taylor designed and supervised construction of the Washington Navy Yard's Experimental Model Basin (EMB). Taking charge of the Experimental Model Basin in 1899, Taylor undertook experiments to discover what char-

acteristics of a ship's hull govern its water resistance. By a method internationally known since 1910 as the Taylor Standard Series Method, he determined the actual effect of changing those characteristics, making it possible to estimate in advance the resistance of a ship of given proportions. His *Speed and Power of Ships* (1910), setting forth this knowledge, is still informative. For fifteen years he remained in charge of the EMB, during which time more than a thousand ship designs for all navy and for many civilian vessels were tested. Taylor was promoted to rear admiral in 1914 and served as chief constructor and chief of the Bureau of Construction and Repair from 1914 to 1922. During this time he held responsibility for the design and construction of naval aircraft as well as ships. He also designed and supervised construction of the navy's first wind tunnel at EMB, contributing greatly to the advance of aeronautic research and development in the United States.

2. Edward J. Marolda, *The Washington Navy Yard: An Illustrated History* (Washington, DC: Naval Historical Center, 1999).

3. Mid-Atlantic Superfund, "Anacostia River Initiative," Current Site Information on Web site: www.epa.gov.reg3hwmd/superDC/Anacostia-river/pad.htm, updated June 2008.

4. Rodney P. Carlisle, *Navy RDT&E Planning in an Age of Transition: A Survey Guide to Contemporary Literature* (Washington, DC: Naval laboratory/Center Coordinating Group and the Naval Historical Center, 1997), 1–7. See also the NRL's Web site: www.nrl.navy.mil.

5. Jack Sweetman, *The U.S. Naval Academy: An Illustrated History* (Annapolis: Naval Institute Press, 1979), 83–111.

6. Ibid., 165–66.

7. "The United States Coast Guard Yard," U.S. Coast Guard Web site: www.uscg.mil/hq/cg4/yard/history.asp.

8. "Curtis Bay Coast Guard Yard," Environmental Protection Agency Web site: www.govreg3hwmd/npl/MD4690307844.htm.

9. Erika L. Quesenbery, *United States Naval Training Center, Bainbridge* (Charleston, SC: Arcadia Press, 2007), 11–26.

10. Ibid., 49–86.

11. Paolo E. Coletta and K. Jack Bauer, eds., *United States Navy and Marine Corps Bases, Domestic* (Westport, CT: Greenwood Press, 1985), 625.

12. John C. Reilly and Robert L. Scheina, *American Battleships, 1886–1913* (Annapolis: Naval Institute Press, 1980), 45–48, 62, 108.

13. Merle T. Cole, *Cradle of Invasion: A History of the U.S. Naval Amphibious Training Base, Solomons, Island, Maryland, 1942–1945* (Solomons, MD: Calvert Marine Museum, 1984), 20–21.

14. Geoffrey M. Footner, *The Last Generation: A History of a Chesapeake Shipbuilding Family* (Solomons, MD: Calvert Marine Museum Press, 1991), 163.

15. William B. Anspacher et al., *The Legacy of the White Oak Laboratory* (Dahlgren, VA: Naval Surface Warfare Center, 2000), 104–7.

16. Rodney P. Carlisle and James P. Rife, *The Sound of Freedom: Naval Weapons Technology at Dahlgren, Virginia, 1918–2006* (Washington, DC: GPO, 2007).

17. For additional information, see the Web sites for the Maryland Historical Trust: www.marylandhistorical trust.net/u1105.html; and the Naval Historical Center: www.history.navy.mil/branches/org12-5.htm.

18. Rodney Carlisle, *Powder and Propellants: Energetic Materials at Indian Head, MD, 1890–1990* (Indian Head, MD: Naval Ordnance Station, 1990).

19. "Indian Head Naval Surface Warfare Center," Current Site Information, Environmental Protection Agency Web site: www.epa.gov/reg3hwmd/npl/MD7170024684.htm, updated June 2007.

20. Arthur P. Middleton, *Tobacco Coast: A Maritime History of Chesapeake Bay in the Colonial Era* (Baltimore: Johns Hopkins Univ. Press, 1989), 49–50.

21. William L. Tazewell and Guy Friddell, *Norfolk's Waters: An Illustrated History of Hampton Roads* (Sun Valley, CA: American Historical Press, 2000), 116–40. See also the Web site of the Naval Amphibious Base Little Creek: www.cnic.navy.mil/littlecreek/AboutCNIC/GeneralInformation/index.htm.

Chapter 11. Maritime Archaeology and Cultural Resources

1. Donald G. Shomette, *The Ghost Fleet of Mallows Bay and Other Tales of the Lost Chesapeake* (Centreville, MD: Tidewater Publishers, 1996).

2. Ibid., 100.

3. Susan B. M. Langley, "Maryland/Chesapeake Region," in *Handbook of International Underwater Archaeology,* edited by Carol V. Ruppe and Janet F. Barstad (Portsmouth, UK: Nautical Archaeology Society, 2002); "Maryland Supports Unique Maritime Archaeology Program," *Public History News* 15, no. 2 (1995): 6; see also Donald G. Shomette, *Tidewater Time Capsule: History Beneath the Patuxent* (Centreville, MD: Tidewater Publishers, 1995), ix–xii. Susan B. M. Langley, PhD, is the Maryland State underwater archaeologist.

4. Shomette, *Ghost Fleet of Mallows Bay,* 189–200.

5. William B. Cronin, *The Disappearing Islands of the Chesapeake* (Baltimore: Johns Hopkins Univ. Press, 2005).

6. Bruce F. Thompson, "Maryland's Maritime Archaeology Program: The Formative Years," *INA* [Institute of Nautical Archaeology] *Newsletter* 19, no. 1 (1992): 4–9; *Maryland Maritime Archeology Program: Statistics and Data Sheets, 1988–1997* (Crownsville, MD: Maryland Historical Trust, 1997), 1–3.

7. Bruce F. Thompson, Maryland State assistant underwater archaeologist, principal investigator, is author of the following reports, which can be consulted at the Maryland Historical Trust, Crownsville, MD: "The Terrible Calamity on the Lower Potomac: An Historical and Archaeological Assessment of the Shipwreck U.S.S. *Tulip,* Potomac River, St. Mary's County, 1996, rev. 1998"; "Phase I Survey for Submerged Archaeological Resources within Maryland's Susquehanna Drainage Basin and Easter Shore Coastal Plain Province," Dec. 2000, 315 pages, and "Phase I Survey for submerged Archaeological Resources within Maryland's Northwestern Shore, Patuxent, and Potomac Drainage Areas," July 2001, 146 pages; "The Bungay Creek Wreck, Kent County, Maryland," Apr. 2002, 19 pages; "The Martinak Boat, Caroline County, Maryland," 22 pages, Nov. 2005. In "Pig Iron," *Maryland Archaeology* 40, no.2 (2004): 31–34, Thompson analyzes a bar of pig iron used for ballast found at Stephen Seward's shipyard. It probably originated at the Legh Masters iron furnace northwest of Baltimore during the years 1765–67.

8. Donald G. Shomette, "The U.S. Navy Shipwreck Inventory Project in the State of Maryland" (paper read at the Society for Historical Archaeology Conference on Historic and Underwater Archaeology at Corpus Christi, Texas, Jan. 10, 1997). See the Naval Historical Center Web site: www.history.navy.mil/branches/org12-7a.htm.

9. David C. Holly, *Chesapeake Steamboats: Vanished Fleet* (Centreville, MD: Tidewater Publishers, 1994), 89–102

10. R. Christopher Goodwin & Associates, "Data Recovery on the Wreck of the Steamship *Columbus,* 18ST625, of St. Mary's County, Maryland." Final Report, May 1995, U.S.

Army Corps of Engineers, Baltimore District. Filed in Maryland Historical Trust Library, Crownsville, MD.

11. Ralph E. Eshelman and Donald G. Shomette, "A Proposal for the Survey of the Submerged Archaeological Resource Base of the Patuxent River, Maryland, Phase I, 1 June 1979–30 September 1979" (Crownsville, MD: Maryland Historical Trust, 1979).

12. Donald G. Shomette, *Tidewater Time Capsule: History beneath the Patuxent* (Centreville, MD: Tidewater Publishers, 1995), 187–91.

13. Ibid., 201–4.

14. Howard. I. Chapelle, *The History of the American Sailing Navy: The Ships and Their Development* (New York: Bonanza Books, 1949), 226–27.

15. For further information on continuing investigations of the Turtle Shell Wreck and related sites in the Patuxent River, see the Web site of the Maryland Historical Trust: www.marylandhistoricaltrust.net/flotilla.html.

16. See Thompson's report on CSS *Favorite,* held at the Maryland Historical Trust Library: Swan Cove Wreck (18ST643) Project, St. Mary's County, Maryland; published in the journal of the Archaeological Society of Maryland, *Maryland Archaeology* 38, no. 1 (2002). For a recent article based on an interview with Bruce Thompson, read Ann E. Dorbin, "Underwater Rescue: Marine Archeologist Bruce Thompson Sinks to New Depths to Recover Lost History," *Chesapeake Life,* Oct. 2005, 64–65.

17. Susan B. M. Langley, PhD, Principal Investigator, "Archaeological Remote Sensing Survey for Maritime Resources off Assateague Island National Seashore, Worcester County, Maryland." This survey occurred during 2002–3 and was undertaken by the Maryland Historical Trust for the U.S. Department of the Interior, National Park Service, and State of Maryland, and the Commonwealth of Virginia Department of Historic Resources. The study area encompassed the length of Assateague Island, approximately thirty-seven miles, and a breadth of one-half mile from the land base seaward.

18. Ibid., 30.

19. The Radcliffe Collection has its origins in the Radcliffe boatbuilding family of Dorchester County, on the Eastern Shore, where three brothers, John, William, and Nehemiah Radcliffe, began in 1847 to build schooners that were used in the bay coasting trade. The original tools and shed in the collection belonged to John Anthony LeCompte Radcliffe, the father of the late senator George L. Radcliffe (1877–1974), for whom the society's maritime collection and museum were named. See Mary Ellen Hayward, *Maryland's Maritime Heritage* (Baltimore: Maryland Historical Society, 1984), 23.

20. See www.livingclassrooms.org.

21. Dana M. Wegner, *Fouled Anchors: The Constellation Question Answered* (Carderock, MD: Naval Ship Research and Development Center, 1991).

22. See www.baltimoremaritimemuseum.org/museums. See also Historic Naval Ships Association Web site: www.hnsa.org/ships/constellation.htm.

23. G. Terry Sharrer, "The Patuxent Fisheries: Transformations of a Rural Economy, 1880–1985," in *Working the Water: The Commercial Fisheries of Maryland's Patuxent River,* edited by Paula J. Johnson (Charlottesville, VA: Calvert Marine Museum and the Univ. Press of Virginia, 1988), 1–4.

24. Ibid., 4–5.

25. C. Douglas Alves et al., eds., *Calvert Marine Museum* (Lawrenceburg, IN: Creative Company, 2002), 20.

26. Robert H. Burgess, *This Was Chesapeake Bay* (Centreville, MD: Tidewater Publishers, 1963), 188–89.

27. C. Richard Gillespie, *The James Adams Floating Theatre* (Centreville, MD: Tidewater Publishers, 1991), 103–18.

28. Mark A. Moore, "Edna Ferber and the Showboat," North Carolina Web site: http://nchistories.org/bath/edna-ferber.htm; Michelle F. Lawing, "Edna Ferber's Visit to Bath, N.C." (unpublished research report, North Carolina Historic Sites, Office of Archives and History Raleigh, NC, 1979).

29. Robyn Quick, "James Adams Floating Theatre," *Maryland Online Encyclopedia:* www.mdoe/adams_theatre.html (accessed Apr. 18, 2008).

Epilogue. Our Diminishing Maritime Environment

1. John R. Wennersten, *The Chesapeake: An Environmental Biography* (Baltimore: Maryland Historical Society, 2001), 109–10.

2. Gerald W. Winegrad, "What Will It Take to Restore the Bay?" *Baltimore Sun,* Sunday, July 15, 2007.

3. Tom Horton, "Growing, Growing, Gone: The Chesapeake Bay and the Myth of Endless Growth," *Abell Report* 21, no. 2 (2008): 1–7. In the same vein, see also the photo essay by David W. Harp and Tom Horton entitled *The Nanticoke: Portrait of a Chesapeake River* (Baltimore: Johns Hopkins Univ. Press, 2008).

GLOSSARY OF NAUTICAL TERMS

bald-headed: Said of a schooner having no topmasts.

barge: A sloop or schooner-rigged or unrigged craft of full body and heavy construction used for transporting bulky freight; in the naval sense, it would be armed with a long gun or carronade, would be rowed by seamen, and would carry infantry.

bateau: A planked hard-chine boat with a shallow V-bottom; a two-sail vessel known as a skipjack.

beat to windward: To sail, "work," or make progress by alternating tacks in the direction from which the wind is blowing.

block: A mechanical device made up of one or more grooved pulleys mounted in casings, fitted with a hook or some other means of attaching, and used to transmit power or change the direction of motion of rope or chain run through it.

boom: A spar or pole that anchors the foot of a fore-and-aft sail.

bowsprit: A large spar projecting from the bow of a sailing vessel. It supports headsails and the foremast by means of headstays.

brig: A two-masted, square-rigged vessel.

bugeye: A three-sail, round-bilge workboat, with raking masts and a foremast taller than the main. It usually carried sharp-headed triangular sails and was called *square-rigged* when carrying gaff-headed sails.

bulwarks: The extension of a vessel's side above the weather deck to prevent persons or objects from going overboard.

buyboat: A vessel engaged in buying and carrying oysters from dredgers to packinghouses.

capstan: A vertical shaft or drum used as a spindle for winding rope or anchor cable.

carronade: A short powerful cannon used in fighting at close range.

cathead: A timber or piece of iron projecting from either side of the bow, used in hoisting the anchor from the water and supporting it when stowed.

centerboard: A movable board of wood or metal, enclosed in a watertight casing or trunk, that can be raised or lowered through a slot in the bottom of a vessel. It provides lateral stability and enables a vessel to work in either deep or shallow water.

chandler: A harbor merchant, so-called originally because he supplied ships with candles, although he later supplied nearly everything needed at sea, including clothing, equipment, and food staples.

chine: Where the bottom and sides of the hull meet; called *hard chine* when they meet in a sharp angle and *soft chine* when the meeting point is curved or rounded.

clipper: A sharp-built, fast-sailing schooner or brig, with especially fine lines and high rig, that evolved from the Virginia pilotboat of colonial times.

close-hauled: When sails are trimmed for heading as close as possible into the direction from which the wind is coming; also called *on the wind.*

cutwater: A timber bolted to the foreside of the stem for added strength, especially in the ornamental curve of a clipper bow.

deadrise: The relative angle of a vessel's hull between the keel and the water line.

displacement: The volume or weight of water displaced by the hull of a vessel, which is equal to the weight of that hull.

draft: Depth of the hull measured from the water line to the bottom of the keel; also, the depth of water needed to keep a vessel afloat.

fathom: The nautical measure for cordage, anchor chains, lead lines; also, the depth of water at sea, equivalent to six feet.

fore-and-aft: Running from stem to stern, or lengthwise, parallel to a vessel's keel.

forecastle, fo'c'sle: Forward living compartment for crew, usually below; in larger schooners, sometimes in the forward deckhouse.

foremast: The mast closest to the stem.

forestay: The heaviest of standing rigging. It supports the foremast and runs from the masthead to the stem, or knighthead.

freeboard: The height of a vessels's sides from the deck to the water's surface.

gaff: The spar to which the upper edge of the four-sided sail on a schooner is attached. The outer end is the peak; the forward end, at the mast, the throat.

gross tonnage: Measure of the internal volume of a vessel for registry.

gunwale: The top planking on a vessel's side, capped by a rail, usually on small craft.

halyard: A rope or tackle used to hoist or set sails.

hatch: An opening in the deck of vessel, usually covered.

headsails: The sails forward of the foremast, such as jibs and staysails.

heeling: When the force of the wind against sails causes a vessel to lean to one side.

hogging: The tendency of a vessel's hull to droop in both bow and stern, caused by insufficient longitudinal strength in the keel and hull supports, as well as lack of buoyancy in the stem and stern to support their weight.

hold: Cargo space below deck.

inside ram: A type of ram (schooner) with a beam less than the 24-foot width of the Chesapeake & Delaware Canal. Sailed primarily in the Chesapeake Bay and inland waterways from the Carolinas to Philadelphia.

jib: A triangular-shaped sail set forward of the forestay.

jibboom: A spar secured to and extending forward from the bowsprit.

jib-headed: A general term for all sails of triangular shape. The term *sharp-headed* is also used on Chesapeake Bay.

keel: The backbone of a vessel, forming the bottom centerline.

keelson: The internal reinforcing structure running parallel and bolted to the keel, usually on top of floors.

ketch: A two-masted vessel of colonial origin with a square sail on one mast and a gaff sail on the other; also, a modern two-masted vessel with foresail larger than main and with the helm located aft of the mainmast.

lateen sail: Shaped like a 45-degree right-angled triangle. Used in the Mediterranean as early as the twelfth century. The rig is exceptionally good for sailing close-hauled or on a beam reach with wind blowing at a right angle to a vessel's course.

lee, leeward: The side away from the direction of the wind. The opposite of *weather.*

letter of marque (and reprisal): A document issued by state or national governments authorizing owners of privately armed vessels to seize vessels and properties of other countries; also, the private armed vessel itself, primarily a vessel engaged in trade and authorized to seize only those enemy ships encountered on a voyage.

lighter: A scow, barge, or other boat used to carry cargo or other materials between a vessel and shore.

loft: The open upper floor of a shipyard building, clear for preparing rigging and laying out molds or sails. Also, the process of drawing a vessel's lines full size to establish molds or patterns used in making parts for construction.

log canoe: A small bay-sailing vessel, usually sharp on both ends, constructed from shaped logs. Style varies regionally, but it usually carries two sails, leg-of-mutton cut, although more sails and springboards are added for racing.

mainmast: The principal mast in a sloop; the second and taller mast in a two-masted schooner, the second mast on a multimasted schooner, and the aftermast on a bugeye.

mast: A vertical wood or metal pole that supports booms, gaffs, yards, and gear for carrying sails.

mizzenmast: The third mast from forward, or aftermost on a three-masted vessel; *mizzen* can also refer to the sail on the third mast.

oakum: A tarred hemp fiber used for caulking a ship's seams.

outside ram: A larger type of schooner (see *inside ram*), with beam of up to 34.5 feet, used coastwise and occasionally for oceangoing trade.

packet: A fast-sailing or steam vessel running on a regular schedule to carry passengers, mail, and cargo.

peak: The topmost end of the gaff or the sail on the gaff; the upper corner of a triangular sail, usually called *head* on a jib.

pilot: A person possessing knowledge of local navigational conditions, qualified or licensed to guide vessels through unfamiliar waters.

pilotboat: A sharp-built, fast-sailing sloops or schooner used to transport pilots to inbound vessels.

privateer: A privately owned armed vessel commissioned by federal and state governments to seize or destroy an enemy's merchantman or warship.

prize: A vessel or property seized by a navy warship, a privateer, or letter of marque trader under wartme conditions.

pungy: A shoal-draft-keel schooner with a long, low hull and raking masts, the final variant of the clipper schooner. Used for freight-carrying and oyster-dredging on Chesapake Bay.

ram: A narrow, shoal-draft, wall-sided schooner developed by J. M. C. Moore for traversing the Chesapeake & Delaware Canal.

reach: The point of sailing when neither beating to windward nor running before the wind. A *close reach* occurs when wind is forward of the beam; *broad reach* is when wind is abaft the beam, but not running.

reef: To take in part of the sail in order to reduce the area of canvas exposed to the wind; also, that part of the sail that has been taken in.

reef point: A short piece of line sewn into a sail for securing the section to be reefed.

rig: A particular arrangement of masts and sails that distinguishes a vessel type.

rigging: The collective term for mast, spars, sails, stays, shrouds, and other equipment.

rise: The angle at which the floor rises from keel to chine.

run: The underwater shape of the after part of a hull from its widest point to the stern. A "fine" run tapers aft.

schooner: A fore-and-aft-rigged vessel with two or more masts, headsails, and a jib.

schooner barge: A type of seagoing barge usually towed but fitted with masts and fore-and-aft sails to assist with steering.

scow: A wide, flat-bottomed vessel with a square bow and stern, used for freight, like a lighter, or a ferry. A scow schooner carries a schooner rig.

scuppers: Waterways along the side of the deck with openings through which water can flow off the deck.

shallop: A small colonial vessel carrying a fore-and-aft rig on one or two masts.

sharp-built: A vessel designed for speed and built with fine lines, a narrow bow, and a long run aft.

sheer: Line of the deck from stem to stern; it can be curved or flat.

sheet: A rope or line, leading from a sail's clew—the outboard end of sail on a spar— or from the boom near the clew, used to take in or ease off sail as needed.

ship: A large seagoing square-rigged sailing vessel with three or more masts.

shoal: A shallow.

shroud: A rope or wire that is part of standing rigging to support the mast in an athwartships position, as opposed to a *stay,* which is a fore-and-aft rig support.

skeg: Deadwood next to the stern post.

skipjack: A single-masted, hard-chine, usually sloop-rigged workboat used for dredging oysters; it carries leg-of-mutton sail and jib.

sloop: A single-masted fore-and-aft-rigged vessel.

snow: A type of brig with a jack mast aft of the main.

spanker: A fore-and-aft sail set below a square-rigged topsail on the mizzen of a three-masted ship, or the fourth mast on a four-masted schooner.

spar: A boom, mast, gaff, yard, or other round pole used in conjunction with sailing rig.

spritsail: Similar to gaff-rigged sail, except that the spar reaches diagonally from tack to peak.

square rig: Having square (or rectangular) sails set at right or oblique angles to a vessel's centerline. *Square-rigged* can also refer to Chesapeake Bay boats, if gaff-rigged.

standing rigging: The collection of shrouds and stays used to support masts, the bowsprit, and the jibboom.

stay: A rope or wire that is part of standing rigging to support the mast in a fore-and-aft position, as opposed to a *shroud,* which is a lateral support.

staysail: A fore-and-aft triangular sail, not a jib, which is spread from a stay.

stem: A structural upright timber at the bow of a vessel; to make progress against a headwind, tide, or current.

step: The block, socket, or platform on which a mast or stanchion rests; also, to place the mast in its position.

sweep: A long oar with a broad blade, used to row or steer a vessel.

tack: The direction of a vessel's head relative to the trim of its sails. *Starboard tack* is with the wind coming over the starboard side; *port tack* is with the wind coming over the port side. To change course when sailing by heading into the wind; to "go about"; the lower forward corner of a fore-and-aft sail.

throat halyard: A line or rope for hoisting the throat, or upper forward end, of the gaff; the upper corner next to the mast.

tiller: The helm; an arm as opposed to a wheel; for shifting rudder position to adjust a vessel's course.

top hamper: The upper rigging of a vessel.

topmast: The second mast, extending from and above the lower mast.

topsail schooner: A fore-and-aft-rigged schooner with square sails set on the fore-topmast; sometimes found with square sails also set on the main topmast.

trailboard: An ornamental plank on either side of the cutwater.

trunk: A between-decks enclosure for a hatchway; part of a cabin extending above deck; the walls of a watertight box enclosing the centerboard.

tuck: Where planking meets the overhang of the stern.

tumblehome: Where the hull turns inward above the water line.

waist: Midship, or widest part of deck.

waterway: Two or more wide strakes of deck planking along the edge of the deck at the side of a vessel to carry water off through scuppers or freeing ports.

weatherly: Capable of sailing close to the wind.

weather side: The side toward the direction of the wind (see *lee, leeward*).

winch head: The top of the capstan, used for hoisting anchors, yawl boats, and other heavy objects on board a vessel.

windlass: A horizontal winch for hauling in the anchor.

windward: Direction from which the wind is blowing.

wing-and-wing: Set of the sails when a vessel is running before the wind with one sail set to starboard and the other to port.

yard: A horizontal spar for carrying the head of a square sail.

yawl boat: A small auxiliary-powered boat carried on stern davits and lowered to push or pull a sailing vessel when there is not enough wind to move her or in close quarters.

ESSAY ON SOURCES

This book is a synthesis of selected published works and unpublished materials that will be of interest to the general reader and students concerned with Maryland's maritime history and heritage. The following titles reflect those most useful to the author and include many specialized works: monographs, journal articles, newspaper articles, and transcriptions of oral histories. Readers will notice that references to Internet Web sites are becoming increasingly pervasive as sources. While rapidity and ease of access is a benefit, this Web site material at times presents research problems associated with rapid technical changes in electronic communications, which can result in the disappearance of a Web site or in the unexplained deletion of data or information formerly contained on that Web site. Obsolescence in the forms of software utilized or lack of interface between commercially developed hardware systems can also interfere with this form of research.

As this work focuses primarily on the early national and contemporary eras in Maryland's maritime history, the colonial period is presented most concisely. Foremost is Arthur P. Middleton's classic, *Tobacco Coast: A Maritime History of Chesapeake Bay in the Colonial Era* (Baltimore: Johns Hopkins Univ. Press, 1989). As a comprehensive general work covering Maryland's history, Robert J. Brugger's *Maryland: A Middle Temperament, 1634–1980* (Baltimore: Johns Hopkins Univ. Press, 1988) is without peer in providing the political, social, and economic context for the state's maritime history. The early days of Maryland's exploration and settlement can be studied through the documents in Clayton Colman Hall's *Narratives of Early Maryland, 1633–1684* (1910; repr., New York: Barnes & Noble, 1967). Helen Rountree, Wayne Clark, and Kent Mountford's *John Smith's Chesapeake Voyages, 1607–1609* (Charlottesville: Univ. of Virginia Press, 2007) provides a modern interpretation of the explorer's observations of the terrain and Native American peoples of colonial Maryland. Timothy B. Riordan's *The Plundering Time: Maryland and the English Civil War, 1645–46* (Baltimore: Maryland Historical Society, 2004) explains the disruptions in Lord Baltimore's colony introduced by partisans of Oliver Cromwell. See also archaeologist Al Luckenback, *Providence: The History and Archaeology of Anne Arundel County: Maryland's First European Settlement* (Crownsville, MD: Maryland Historical Trust, 1995), and Anthony D. Lindauer, *From Paths to Plats: The Development of Annapolis, 1651–1718* (Crownsville, MD: Maryland State Archives and Maryland Historical Trust, 1997). John F. Wing presented a study of the colonial tobacco trade in *Bound by God . . . for Merryland: The Voyage of the Constant Friendship, 1671–1672* (Annapolis, MD: Maryland State Archives and Maryland Historical Trust, 1995) and idem, "The Colonial Tobacco Fleet," *Nautical Research Journal* 48, no. 1 (2003): 3–14, based on research in British and

Maryland's Archives. Likewise, for a broader view, see V. J. Wyckoff, "Ships and Shipping of Seventeenth-Century Maryland," *Maryland Historical Magazine* 34, no. 3 (1939): 270–83.

Vaughan W. Brown, *Shipping in the Port of Annapolis, 1748–1775* (Annapolis, MD: Naval Institute Press, 1965), and Nancy T. Baker, "The Manufacture of Ship Chandlery in Annapolis, Maryland, 1735–1770," in the *Chronicle of the Early American Industries Association* 35, no. 4 (1982): 61–71, treats the development of shipping and the maritime trades in the Anne Arundel County and Annapolis areas. In the article "Trade in Colonial Anne Arundel County: The Tobacco Port of London Town," *Maryland Historical Magazine* 98, no. 3 (2003): 325–44, Mechelle L. Kerns Nocerito presents an important statement concerning the flourishing trade on the South River during the early eighteenth century. William J. Kelly presented considerable data on early shipbuilding in the Baltimore and Patapsco River region in "Shipbuilding at Federal Hill" (unpublished MS, Maryland Historical Society Library, Baltimore), 21–31. Resistance to colonial status came gradually to Maryland. For pertinent studies, see Edward C. Papenfuse, *In Pursuit of Profit: The Annapolis Merchants in the Era of the American Revolution, 1763–1775* (Baltimore: Johns Hopkins Univ. Press, 1975); Norman K. Risjord, *Builders of Annapolis: Enterprise and Politics in a Colonial Capital* (Baltimore: Maryland Historical Society, 1997); Arthur Meier Schlesinger, *The Colonial Merchants and the American Revolution, 1763–1776* (New York: Columbia Univ. Press, 1918); Adam J. Goodheart, "Tea and Fantasy: Fact, Fiction, and Revolution in a Historic American Town [Chestertown, MD]," *American Scholar* 74, no. 4 (2005): 21–34; and Jane McWilliams and Morris L. Radoff, "Annapolis Meets the Crisis," in *Chesapeake Bay in the American Revolution,* edited by Ernest MacNeill Eller (Centreville, MD: Tidewater Publishers, 1981), 403–31.

With the advent of the American Revolution, Maryland supported the Continental Army, and its militias contributed to the national defense. Maryland seafarers played an important role as importers of munitions, transporters of troops, and warriors on the high seas in privateers and in the ships of the Continental Navy. A valuable resource is *Naval Documents of the American Revolution,* a multivolume series edited by William Bell Clark and William J. Morgan, which includes documents drawn from the Archives of Maryland, the Proceedings of the Maryland Convention, and the Journal and Correspondence of the Maryland Council of Safety. These topics are studied by William S. Dudley, "Maryland at War on the Chesapeake, 1775–1783," in *New Aspects of Naval History: Selected Papers Presented at the Fourth Naval History Symposium, October 25–26, 1979,* edited by Craig Symonds (Annapolis, MD: Naval Institute Press, 1981), 102–21, and Myron G. Smith and John G. Earle, "The Maryland State Navy," in *Chesapeake Bay in the American Revolution,* edited by Ernest MacNeill Eller (Centreville, MD: Tidewater Publishers, 1981), 211–15. E. Gordon Bowen-Hassell, in "Lambert Wickes," focuses scholarly attention on this Kent County native of Eastern Neck Island in *Sea Raiders of the American Revolution: The Continental Navy in European Waters* (Washington, DC: Naval Historical Center, 2003), 1–15; and see Arthur P. Middleton, "Ships and Shipbuilding in the Chesapeake," in Eller, *Chesapeake Bay in the American Revolu-*

tion, 98–132. Edwin M. Jameson analyzed Maryland's seagoing Loyalists in "Tory Operations on the Bay from Lord Dunmore's Departure to the End of the War," also in Eller, *Chesapeake Bay in the American Revolution,* 378–402. See also Richard Arthur Overfield, "A Patriot Dilemma: The Treatment of Passive Loyalist and Neutrals in Revolutionary Maryland," *Maryland Historical Magazine* 68, and idem, "The Loyalists of Maryland during the American Revolution" (PhD diss., University of Maryland, 1968). A study of events at Sinepuxent Bay on Maryland's Atlantic shore can be found in Robert Novak's "The Maid of Assateague," *Maryland Historical Magazine* 102, no. 3 (2007): 194–203, and in Donald Shomette's broader work, *Shipwrecks, Sea Raiders, and Maritime Disasters along the Delmarva Coast, 1632–2004* (Baltimore: Johns Hopkins Univ. Press, 2007). The last Revolutionary War battle on the bay is covered in Bernard C. Steiner's article "Action between American and British Barges in the Chesapeake Bay, November 1782," *Maryland Historical Magazine* 4, no. 2 (1909): 115–33.

The postwar recovery of maritime commerce and the rapid growth of Baltimore dominated the nearly three decades between the American Revolution and the War of 1812. Gary Lawson Browne's *Baltimore in the Nation, 1789–1861* (Chapel Hill: Univ. of North Carolina Press, 1980) provides a context for the transition to the early national period, as does James S. Van Ness, in "Economic Development, Social and Cultural Changes, 1800–1850," in *Maryland a History, 1632–1974,* edited by Richard Walsh and William Lloyd Fox (Baltimore: Maryland Historical Society, 1974). The role of Maryland's Benjamin Stoddert as the first secretary of the navy is examined in Michael A. Palmer, *Stoddert's War: Naval Operations during the Quasi-War with France, 1798–1801* (Columbia: Univ. of South Carolina Press, 1987). Official documentation concerning the growth of the U.S. Navy in the early years of the nineteenth century is contained in *American State Papers,* 6, *Naval Affairs,* Vol. 1 (Washington, DC: Gales and Seaton, 1834). For political, diplomatic, and naval developments as tensions grew between the new American nation and Great Britain, see Dumas Malone's *Jefferson the President; Second Term, 1805–1809* (Boston: Little, Brown, 1974); Lawrence S. Kaplan, *Entangling Alliances with None: American Foreign Policy in the Age of Jefferson* (Kent, OH: Kent State Univ. Press, 1987); James F. Zimmerman, *Impressment of American Seamen* (New York: Columbia Univ. Press, 1925), and Spencer C. Tucker and Frank T. Reuther, *Injured Honor: The Chesapeake Leopard Affair, June 22, 1807* (Annapolis, MD: Naval Institute Press, 1996).

As the War of 1812 bicentennial approaches, a new generation of studies is making its appearance. Those seeking an overview of the entire war could do no better than to read Reginald Horsman, *The War of 1812* (New York, 1969), and Donald R. Hickey, *The War of 1812: A Forgotten Conflict* (Urbana: Univ. of Illinois Press, 1989). For a maritime perspective, readers can avail themselves of the multivolume series published under the auspices of the Naval Historical Center: William S. Dudley and Michael J. Crawford, eds., *The Naval War of 1812: A Documentary History,* 3 vols. (Washington, DC: GPO, 1985–). Volume 3 is especially valuable for the documents pertaining to the War of 1812 on Chesapeake Bay. William M. Marine's classic *The British Invasion of Maryland, 1812–1815* (Baltimore, 1913) is still useful. Of similar quality is John P. Cranwell and William B. Crane's *Men of Marque: A History of Private Armed Vessels out of Baltimore during the War of 1812* (New York, 1940). Jerome B. Garitee's *The Republic's Private Navy: The American Privateering Business as Practiced by Baltimore during the War of 1812* (Middletown, CT: Mystic Seaport and Wesleyan Univ. Press, 1977) is irreplaceable for its thorough research and comprehensive treatment of the subject. The history of Baltimore's favorite frigate is revealed in Geoffrey M. Footner's *USS Constellation: From Frigate to Sloop of War* (Annapolis, MD: Naval Institute Press, 2003). Although his study ranges well beyond the War of 1812, Footner recounts the story of the ship's construction and the difficulties that resulted in her spending the war blockaded at Norfolk in the Elizabeth River, where her guns and crew played a salutary role in defeating the British at the Battle of Craney Island.

Joshua Barney, one of Maryland's most famous seafarers, is the subject of two good biographies, Hulbert Footner's *Sailor of Fortune: The Life and Adventures of Commodore Joshua Barney, U.S.N.* (New York, 1940) and Louis Arthur Norton's *Joshua Barney: Hero of the Revolution and 1812* (Annapolis, MD: Naval Institute Press, 2000). The historian John Schroeder has provided a modern interpretation of the life of John Rodgers, another Maryland sea warrior who dominated the U.S. Navy after the War of 1812, in *Commodore John Rodgers: Paragon of the Early American Navy* (Gainesville: Univ. Press of Florida, 2006). For biographies of the most prominent British naval leader in the War of 1812, see James Pack, *The Man Who Burned the White House, Admiral Sir George Cockburn, 1772–1853* (Annapolis, MD: Naval Institute Press, 1987), and Roger Morriss, *Cockburn and the British Navy in Transition: Admiral Sir George Cockburn, 1772–1853* (Columbia: Univ. of South Carolina Press, 1997).

To view British operations during the Chesapeake campaign from a Maryland perspective, see Christopher T. George, *Terror on the Chesapeake: The War of 1812 on the Bay* (Shippensburg, PA: White Mane Books, 2000). Two other useful studies of the campaign are Walter Lord, *The Dawn's Early Light* (New York: W. W. Norton, 1972), and Anthony S. Pitch, *The Burning of Washington: The British Invasion of 1812* (Annapolis, MD: Naval Institute Press, 1998). Two works focusing on specific battles of the Chesapeake campaign in Maryland are Donald G. Shomette's revised and enlarged *Flotilla: The Patuxent Naval Campaign in the War of 1812* (1986; Baltimore: Johns Hopkins Univ. Press, 2009), and Scott S. Sheads's *The Rocket's Red Glare: The Maritime Defense of Baltimore in 1814* (Centreville, MD: Tidewater Publishers, 1986). Donald Hickey's recent *Don't Give Up the Ship: Myths of the War of 1812* (Champaign: Univ. of Illinois Press, 2006) is cast broadly in both Canada and the United States, but it does skewer a few Maryland myths about the war. An account of the last battle of the war on Chesapeake Bay is found in Robert G. Stewart's "The Battle of the Ice Mound, February 7, 1815," *Maryland Historical Magazine* 70, no. 4 (1970): 372–78.

Newspapers announced the end of the War of 1812 to a grateful public in February 1815 with the exchange of ratifications of the Treaty of Ghent. Many Baltimore merchants hastened to return to transoceanic and coastal trade, but a few shipowners and commanders sought to continue the search for privateering profits by enlisting their vessels in the Latin American struggle for independence. Accounts of American privateers in the service of the newly independent Latin American republics are contained in Charles Carroll Griffin, *The United States and the Disruption of the Spanish Empire, 1810–1822: A Study of the Relations of the United States with Spain and the Rebel Spanish Colonies* (New York, 1937); Arthur P. Whitaker, *The United States and the Independence of Latin America, 1800–1830* (New York, 1964); David Head, "Baltimore Seafarers, Privateering, and the South American Revolutions, 1816–1820," *Maryland Historical Magazine* 103, no. 3 (2008); Fred Hopkins, "For Freedom and Profit: Baltimore Privateers in the Wars of South American Independence, 1815–1824," in *Troubled Waters: New Aspects of Maritime and Naval History. The Proceedings of the North American Society for Oceanic History, 1999–2005,* edited by William S. Dudley and Roger Sarty, published as double edition of the *Northern Mariner* 18, nos. 3 and 4 (2008): 93–104.

During the antebellum period, from 1815 to 1860, America spread her sails. No longer restricted by Barbary corsairs and European wars, the U.S. merchants sent their schooners and ships coastwise and around the globe. Maryland's shipowners and sea captains, who had made their profits and reputations during the War of 1812, sought to increase their share of the nation's commerce. Howard Chapelle chronicled the evolution of the schooner from pilotboat to trading vessel in *The Baltimore Clipper: Its Origin and Design* (1930; repr., Hatboro, PA: Tradition Press, 1965). To consult more recent interpretations, read Quentin Snediker and Ann Jensen's *Chesapeake Bay Schooners* (Centreville, MD: Tidewater Publishers, 1992) and Geoffrey M. Footner's *Tidewater Triumph: The Development and Worldwide Success of the Chesapeake Bay Pilot Schooner* (Centreville, MD: Tidewater Publishers, 1998). Footner followed this major study with an interesting article, "John Robb: Shipbuilder of Fells Point: His Work as a Study of Nineteenth-Century Naval Architecture," *Nautical Research Journal* 50, no. 3 (2005): 131–32. Marion V. Brewington, former maritime curator at the Maryland Historical Society and the Chesapeake Bay Maritime Museum, authored a valuable illustrated survey of Chesapeake maritime history entitled *Chesapeake Bay: A Pictorial Maritime History* (New York: Bonanza Books, 1953). Robert H. Burgess's *Chesapeake Bay Watercraft* (Centreville, MD: Tidewater Publishers, 1975), and the expanded version, edited by William A. Fox (Centreville, MD: Tidewater Publishers, 2005) is a beautifully illustrated survey of a wide variety of the bay's sailing vessels. A useful short study of an important bay vessel is Thomas Gilmer's *Chesapeake Bay Sloops* (St. Michaels, MD: Chesapeake Bay Maritime Museum, 1982).

Maryland's schooners had many and varied missions on the high seas during this period. Some merchants and sea captains participated in the African slave trade despite its having been declared illegal in 1807. In 1820 the U.S. Congress made transporting slaves by sea an act of piracy punishable by death, but the law was difficult to enforce. The schooner *Amistad* incident is a case in point. Snediker and Jenson, *Chesapeake Bay Schooners,* assert that *Amistad* was built in Baltimore in the 1830s. The bay schooner *Pearl* was put to an unusual use in the attempt to facilitate an escape of slaves from Washington, D.C., in 1848. Josephine E. Pacheco has documented this in her account *The Pearl: A Failed Slave Escape on the Potomac* (Chapel

Hill: Univ. of North Carolina Press, 2005). Another version is that of Mary Kay Ricks, *Escape on the Pearl: The Heroic Bid for Freedom on the Underground Railroad* (New York: Harper Collins, 2007). The account of a key participant in the escape is Daniel Drayton's *The Personal Memoir of Daniel Drayton: For Four Years and Four Months a Prisoner (for Charity's Sake) in a Washington Jail* (Np., 1854, Project Gutenberg on-line books, 2008).

Full-rigged ships gradually supplanted schooners as ocean-voyaging, cargo-carrying vessels, as documented in William Armstrong Fairburn, *Merchant Sail, 6* vols. (Center Lovell, ME, 1945–55), and K. Jack Bauer, *A Maritime History of the United States: The Role of America's Seas and Waterways* (Columbia: Univ. of South Carolina Press, 1987). Donald M. Dozer, *Portrait of the Free State* (Centreville, MD: Tidewater Publishers, 1976), describes Baltimore's mid-nineteenth-century business expansion and trade patterns. The growth of steamboat operations on the Chesapeake Bay and rivers is recorded in Alexander Crosby Brown, *Steam Packets on the Chesapeake: A History of the Old Bay Line* (Cambridge, MD: Cornell Maritime Press, 1961); Robert H. Burgess, *Chesapeake Circle* (Centreville, MD: Tidewater Publishers, 1965); Robert H. Burgess and H. Graham Wood, *Steamboats Out of Baltimore* (Centerville, MD: Tidewater Publishers, 1968); David C. Holly, *Chesapeake Steamboats: Vanished Fleet* (Centreville, MD: Tidewater Publishers, 1994); idem, *Tidewater by Steamboat: A Saga of the Weems Line on the Patuxent, Potomac, and Rappahannock* (1991; repr., Baltimore: Johns Hopkins Univ. Press, 2000); and idem, *Steamboat on the Chesapeake: Emma Giles and the Tolchester Line* (Centreville, MD: Tidewater Publishers, 1987). Michael Buckley's useful *Voices of the Chesapeake Bay* (Edgewater, MD: Geared Up, 2008) provides transcriptions of oral histories told by specialists from many fields.

The building and repair of steamboats on the Patapsco at Federal Hill is covered well in William J. Kelley's unpublished typescript held in the Maryland Historical Society Library. James Dugan's The *Great Iron Ship* tells the story of the British-built *Great Eastern,* an enormous steamship that visited Chesapeake Bay in 1860.

Robert de Gast's illustrated *Lighthouses of Chesapeake Bay* (Baltimore: Johns Hopkins Univ. Press, 1973) discusses the establishment of a national system of lighthouses and aids to navigation material. The National Park Service provides a helpful inventory of Maryland Light Stations and on its maritime heritage Web site: www/nps.gov/history/maritime/light/md.htm. Mary Bellis's useful article "A History of Buoys and Tenders" can be found at www.about.com/library/inventors/blbuoys. Readers may consult the history of the Steamship Inspection Service at the U.S Coast Guard Web site, www.uscg.mil/history/articles/Steamboat_Inspection_Service.asp.

The work of Sumner Kimball in establishing the Life Saving Service under the Revenue Marine is described in Irving H. King's *The Coast Guard Expands, 1865–1915: New Roles, New Frontiers* (Annapolis, MD: Naval Institute Press, 1996). See also Bob Stevens's *A History of the U.S. Life Saving Service* at the Ocean City Life-Saving Station Museum Web site: www.ocmuseum.org/uslss/history.

The maritime activities of Marylanders who lived on the Eastern Shore's Atlantic coast are an important part of the state's history. John R. Wennersten's *Maryland's Eastern Shore: A Journey in Time and Place* (Centreville, MD: Tidewater Publishers, 1992) provides a brief overview of the settlement and ways of life of this once-isolated location on southern Fenwick and Assateague islands. Nan DeVincent-Hayes and John Jacob present an illustrated history in the first volume of *Ocean City,* Images of America Series, 2 vols. (Charleston, SC: Arcadia Books, 1999). See also Nan DeVincent-Hayes and Bo Bennett's *Chincoteague and Assateague Islands* (Charleston, SC: Arcadia Books, 2000). George M. and Suzanne Hurley tell of the dangerous work of the Revenue Marine's lifesaving teams stationed along these beachy strands in *Shipwrecks and Rescues: Along the Barrier Islands of Delaware, Maryland, and Virginia* (1984; Norfolk, VA: Donning Co., 1995).

As the steamboat era entered the twentieth century, the owners of a number of these vessels, such as *Emma Giles* and *Westmoreland,* put them into the excursion trade, carrying work-weary city dwellers to recreation destinations on the bay. Jane McWilliams, *Bay Ridge on the Chesapeake: An Illustrated History* (Annapolis, MD: Brighton Editions, 1986), provides an excellent example of a Western Shore resort. Janet Freedman's *Kent Island: The Land That Once Was Eden* (Baltimore: Maryland Historical Society, 2002) describes the Love Point Hotel and Resort, which flourished from about 1900 to the 1930s but went into decline and closed in 1947. As the steamboat lines diminished, ferries brought clients to the hotel, but railway connections extending to the Atlantic beaches and the completion of the Chesapeake Bay Bridge spans ended the days of most bay resorts. A description of the impact of the bridges on steamboat and ferry traffic is to be found in Scott M. Kozel, "Chesapeake Bay Bridge History," on the Web site: www.roads to the future.com.

The service of ferries on Chesapeake Bay and its tributaries has been essential to settlers and travelers in the region from the earliest years of the colony, when bridges were nonexistent, but only a few such services remain. With now overcrowded bridges and frequent accidents, there is occasional talk of using high capacity–high speed ferries, as in the Maryland Department of Transportation, Transportation Authority Task Force Report, *Task Force on Traffic Capacity across the Chesapeake Bay* (Annapolis, MD, 2006). For a concise but thorough view of these valuable linkages, see the forthcoming work of Clara Ann Simmons, *Chesapeake Ferries: A Waterborne Tradition, 1636–2000* (Baltimore: Maryland Historical Society, 2009). A final word on the most famous of Chesapeake steamboats is contained in David Holly's *Exodus, 1947* (Annapolis, MD: Naval Institute Press, 1998), in which he recounts the tragic tale of the *President Warfield,* in which this large bay steamer, which carried troops to Europe in World War II, ends her days in a heroic attempt to bring Holocaust survivors to settle in Israel.

The number of works on the Civil War in the Chesapeake Bay region is vast, so one must be selective in choosing those most helpful to following its course. The core documentation was published in United States, Naval War Records Office, *Official Records of the Union and Confederate Navies in the War of the Rebellion* (Washington, DC: GPO, 1894–1922). An edited selection of these documents is contained in the Naval History Division's *Civil War Naval Chronology, 1861–1865* (Washington, DC: GPO, 1971). Allan Nevins's multivolume *The War for the Union*

is a useful, detailed analysis of political, military, and naval events of the war. Eric Mills's *Chesapeake Bay in the Civil War* provides a readable account both U.S. Navy operations and Confederate maritime guerrilla activity, as well as war-stimulated smuggling activity on the bay.

Charles Dana Gibson and Kay Gibson's *Assault and Logistics: Union Army Coastal and River Operations,* the Army's Navy Series, vol. 2, *Union Army Coastal and River Operations, 1861–1866* (Camden, ME: Ensign Press, 1995), gives an impressive picture of the extent to which U.S. military operations depended on control of the rivers. Frank E. Vandiver, *Jubal's Raid: General Early's Famous Attack on Washington in 1864* (Westport, CT, 1960) portrays the fright given Washington, D.C., in July 1864 and the associated Confederate plan to attack the U.S. prisoner of war camp at Point Lookout. Daniel Carroll Toomey provides an even more detailed focus in *The Johnson-Gilmor Raid, July 9–13, 1864* (Baltimore: Toomey Press, 2005). Mary D. and William S. McFeely, eds., *Ulysses S. Grant, Memoirs and Selected Letters, 1839–1865* (New York: Library Classics of America, 1990), gives us General Grant's own account of his thoughts and actions during Early's raid. Royce G. Shingleton's portrait, *John Taylor Wood: Sea Ghost of the Confederacy* (Athens: Univ. of Georgia Press), details the life of the man who bedeviled the Union Navy's Potomac Flotilla with overland boat raids and cutting-out expeditions along Virginia's indented Chesapeake coast.

Among a wealth of sources on oysters and oystering in Chesapeake Bay, the following selected works have been useful: John R. Wennersten, *The Oyster Wars of Chesapeake Bay* (Centreville, MD: Tidewater Publishers, 1981); Victor S. Kennedy and Linda L. Breisch, "Sixteen Decades of Political Management of the Oyster Fishery in Maryland's Chesapeake Bay," *Journal of Environmental Management* 16 (1983): 153–71; Edmund A. Nelson, "The Chesapeake Bay Oyster Industry, 1800–1900" (unpublished paper, Maryland Historical Society Library, Baltimore, 1994). In *Chesapeake Bay Buyboats* (Centreville, MD: Tidewater Publishers, 2003), Larry S. Chowning has written on a distinctive class of freight vessels that hauled oysters, crabs, fish, and other commodities to market. Their captains played an important role as middlemen in the bay's economy.

The drastic decline in native oyster harvests over the past forty years has led to a debate among scientists, politicians, and watermen as to the wisdom of introducing an Asian oyster variety into the bay. The debate can be followed in these reports: Department of Defense, Department of the Army; Corps of Engineers, "Notice of Intent to Prepare an Environmental Impact Statement for the Proposed Introduction of the Oyster Species *Crassostrea ariakensis*"; *Federal Register* 6, no. 2 (2004). See the Maryland Oyster Advisory Commission, 2007 Interim Report Concerning Maryland's Chesapeake Bay Oyster Management Program Web site: www.md.dnr .us/fisheries/oysters/oac. See also the Maryland Department of Natural Resources Web site: www.dnr.me.us/dnrnews/infocus/notice_of_intent2.asp; Erica Goldman, "A Model Scientist: Following the Oysters from Spawning to Settlement," *Chesapeake Quarterly* 4, no.3 (2005), 4–10; Mark Luckenbach, "*Crassostrea ariakensis*: Panacea or Pandora?" Virginia Institute of Marine Science Web site: www .ian.umces.edu/pdfs/iannewsletter. For a more up-to-date report, see "Maryland

Hatchery Rears Record Number of Oysters," *Bay Journal* 18, no. 7 (2008), and Cynthia Barry's article "A Homecoming for Oysters: Nurturing Millions of Spat: Experts Learn What Works," in *Save the Bay* 34, no. 3 (2008), 10–12, which shows scientists and watermen working together in efforts supported by the nonprofit Chesapeake Bay Foundation.

The place to start in understanding the blue crab industry is William W. Warner's *Beautiful Swimmers: Watermen, Crabs, and the Chesapeake Bay* (1977; repr. Boston: Little, Brown, 1994). Paula J. Johnson, ed., *Working the Water: The Commercial Fisheries of Maryland's Patuxent River* (Charlottesville: Univ. Press of Virginia and the Calvert Marine Museum, 1988), provides other perspectives. Also informative on harvesting crabs as well as several other types of sealife is Mark E. Jacoby's *Working the Chesapeake Bay: Watermen on the Bay,* 2nd ed. (College Park, MD: Maryland Sea Grant College, 1993). Mick Blackistone's *Dancing with the Tide: Watermen of the Chesapeake* (Centreville, MD: Tidewater Publishers, 2000) presents the viewpoint of those who work the water and have traditionally opposed the governmental approach to regulating the state's crabbing industry. Terry Noble's *Starting at Sea Level* (Mcleod, MT: Foggy River Books, 2007) provides valuable insight from the viewpoint of a native of the Eastern Shore who grew up in the Tangier Sound area of Deal Island, the Manokin River, and Smith Island. His father was a supervisor of inspectors of the Maryland Tidewater Fisheries Commission; in other words, he was a marine policeman charged with enforcing the state's seafood-harvesting laws. Journalist Tom Horton's memoir *An Island Out of Time: A Memoir of Smith Island in the Chesapeake* (New York: Vintage Books, 1996) records his three years on Smith Island as an employee of the Chesapeake Bay Foundation. He details the plight of watermen and their families who live on Smith Island, near Crisfield, but still isolated from the mainstream, as they cope with the pressures of modern times. Paula J. Johnson has written about Smith Island's watermen and their livelihoods in *The Workboats of Smith Island* (Baltimore: Johns Hopkins Univ. Press, 1997), in which she documents the variety of wooden deadrise workboats, crab scrapes, and skiffs still in use during the 1990s.

Finfisheries in the Chesapeake have to cope with the same pressures of overharvesting, water pollution, algae growth, and oxygen starvation as do shellfisheries. Fewer books have been published on the finfisheries, but considerable information is available on-line. Both Paula Johnson's *Working the Water* and Mark Jacoby's *Working the Chesapeake Bay* have useful chapters on harvesting finfish. Karl Blankenship's interesting article "American Shad Decline a Mystery," *Bay Journal* 18, no. 6 (2008) records the virtual disappearance of a once-prolific and much sought-after species. The famed but rarely landed Atlantic sturgeon is discussed on-line at "Atlantic Sturgeon," on the Chesapeake Bay Field Office, U.S. Fish and Wildlife Service Web site: www.fws.gov/chesapeakebay/sturgeon.htm. The popular Maryland rockfish (otherwise known as striped bass) has had considerable attention from anglers and lawmakers during the past thirty years, since its fortunes declined in the 1980s, before imposition of a statewide moratorium. Its recovery a few years later was hailed as a success for those who see regulation as a panacea. See "Striped Bass," on the same Web site: www.fws.gov/chesapeakebay.striper.htm. But the health of this species is still a matter for concern, as reported in "Bacterial Disease Fatal to Rockfish," *Washington Post,* Dec. 28, 2008, and on the Maryland Department of Natural Resources Web site: "Striped Bass Health: All about Mycobacteria," www.dnr.state.us/dnrnews/infocus/striped_bass_health.asp. The U.S. Fish and Wildlife Service tracks commercially landed alewife and herring species, which are also listed as matters of concern on the Web site: www.fws/chesapeakebay/her ring.htm. Maryland's Atlantic shore fisheries have historical importance as well. William H. Wroten's *Assateague* (Centreville, MD: Tidewater Publishers, 1972) describes the work of pound fishing off the beach and the nearby processing plants in the early twentieth century. The sea scallop industry is still vibrant, though under strict regulations, according to the article by "Daybreak," "Ocean City Maryland Scallop Boats," *Commercial Fishing,* Jan. 27, 2009, on the Web site: www .commercial-fishing.org/business/ocean-city-maryland-scallop-boats.

On the lives and work of Chesapeake Bay watermen, there is a wealth of material in Marion E. Warren, with Mame Warren, *Bringing Back the Bay: The Chesapeake in the Photographs of Marion E. Warren and the Voices of Its People* (1994; repr., Annapolis, MD: Time Exposures Limited, 2002). Anthropologist Harold Anderson offers information on African American watermen in "Slavery, Freedom, and the Chesapeake" and "Black Men, Blue Waters: African-Americans on the Chesapeake," *Maryland Marine Notes Online* 16, no. 2 (1998) at: www.mdsg.umd/ MarineNotes/Mar-Apr98. Another source is Vincent Leggett, "Sixty Years on the Bay with Earl White," *Blacks of the Chesapeake* Web site: www.dnr.state.md.us/ programs/nr/nrboc.html. On black watermen working at Annapolis, see Philip L. Brown, *The Other Annapolis, 1900–1950* (Annapolis, MD: Annapolis Publishing, 1994), Jefferson Holland, "The McNasby Oyster Company," *What's Up Magazine,* Aug. 2007, and the Annapolis Maritime Museum's Web site: www.amuseum.org. For an interesting comment on museums and the reflection on their role interpreting maritime history, read Phyllis Leffler, "Maritime Museums and National Identity," in *Public Historian* 6, no. 4 (2004).

Industrialization brought Maryland's society into the modern era, and it had a major impact on trade, the fisheries, and the bay's watercraft. Eleanor Bruchey's essay "The Industrialization of Maryland, 1860–1914," in *Maryland: A History, 1632–1974,* edited by Richard Walsh and William L. Fox (Baltimore: Maryland Historical Society, 1975), 396–498, gives a useful overview of the period. The important work of the U.S. Army Corps of Engineers in Chesapeake Bay channel dredging is the subject of Harold Kanarek's *The Mid-Atlantic Engineers: A History of the Baltimore District, U.S. Army Corps of Engineers, 1774–1974* (Washington, DC, 1978). Ralph D. Gray's *The National Waterway: A History of the Chesapeake and Delaware Canal, 1769–1965* (Urbana: Univ. of Illinois Press, 1967) is essential reading for those interested in the origins, gradual expansion, and use of the canal linking Chesapeake and Delaware bays. A key corporate history for the steel shipbuilding industry is Mark Reutter's *Sparrows Point: Making Steel—The Rise and Ruin of American Industrial Might* (New York: Summit Books, 1988). But Elmer J. Hall's profusely illustrated *Shipbuilding at the Sparrows Point Yard: A Century of Pride and Transition* (Indiana, PA: Gazette Printers, 2007) is essential for tracing

274

Essay on Sources

the enormous production of ships constructed at Sparrows Point. Mercantile shipping from Baltimore abroad has varied over the years, according to national and international trends, competition with other U.S. ports, and the capacity of Baltimore's terminals to handle new methods of bulk shipping in extremely large vessels. For export and import data for the port of Baltimore, see *Foreign Oceanborne Commerce, Foreign Commerce Statistical Report,* various years, Maryland Port Administration, World Trade Center, Baltimore. Visiting ships need prompt services of all types. In former times, ship chandleries provided such needs. The Vane Brothers Company of Fairfield, once located in Fells Point, is a contemporary version that offers a variety of marine fuels and other services and now has operations in Philadelphia, Norfolk, and other East Coast ports. Mary Butler Davies, *Time and the Tide: A Centennial History of the Vane Brothers Company* (Baltimore: Vane Brothers Publishers, 1998) provides a portrait of this family-owned company that has endured since 1898.

During the late nineteenth and twentieth centuries, the technologies associated with the era of working sail went into decline as wood and coal-fired steam, diesel, and internal combustion engines replaced sails. Then, auxiliary steam engines and electrical machinery replaced some of the human power required for deck operations. But before the end of the sailing era, Chesapeake shipwrights constructed remarkably effective sailing vessels, which earned fame for their beauty and the work they did. The evolution of the bugeye from its log canoe and brogan origins is lovingly covered in Marion V. Brewington, *Chesapeake Bay Log Canoes and Bugeyes* (Centreville, MD: Tidewater Publishers, 1963). Pete Lesher's articles on Eastern Shore shipbuilding cover the more renowned shipbuilders: "From Bugeyes to Skipjacks: John Branford Master Carpenter," *Weather Gauge* 34, no. 2 (1998): 18–24; "Apprenticeships and the Shipbuilding Trade: Robert Lambdin of St. Michaels," *Weather Gauge* 36, no. 2 (2000): 19–26; "The Industrious Shipbuilder: Joseph W. Brooks," *Weather Gauge* 26 (Spring 2000), 3–4; "Thomas Kirby and the Decline of Shipbuilding in Talbot County," *Maryland Historical Magazine* 97, no. 3 (2002): 359–68; and "Shipbuilding Powerhouse on the Banks of the Pocomoke," *Waterways* 5, no. 2 (2007): 6–9 (about the work of E. James Tull, 1850–1924).

Geoffrey M. Footner's *The Last Generation: A History of a Chesapeake Shipbuilding Family* (Solomons, MD: Calvert Marine Museum Press, 1991) chronicles the remarkable boat- and shipbuilding work of the Davis family yard at Solomons Island over two generations. On the building and career of the oyster-dredging skipjack (bateau), consult Howard I. Chapelle's booklet, *Notes on Chesapeake Bay Skipjacks* (St. Michaels, MD: Chesapeake Bay Maritime Museum, a reprint of an article published originally in the *American Neptune* in 1944); Pat Vojtech's *Chesapeake Bay Skipjacks* (Centreville, MD: Tidewater Publishers, 1993); and Doug Stephens's *Workin' with the Wind: Portrait of a Chesapeake Bay Skipjack* (Salisbury, MD: Factor Press, 2004).

In the Annapolis region, other boatbuilders were at work during the late nineteenth and early twentieth centuries, all of them located along placid Spa Creek (Carroll's Creek in colonial days). These included Heller's, James Chance, Benjamin Sarles's, Mason and Sons, Owens Yacht Company, John Trumpy and Company, and the Annapolis Yacht Yard. Michael Miron researched the subject, interviewing local boatyard workers and descendents of former owners. He published these sketches in the *Publick Enterprise,* a freely distributed local newspaper, in the spring of 1996. These articles are no longer in print, but on-line versions are available through the Annapolis Maritime Museum. Robert Tolf's *Trumpy* (St. Michaels, MD: Tiller Publishing, 1996) provides a more complete narrative of the Trumpy family boatbuilding story, from Bergen, Norway, to Annapolis, Maryland. See also Lisa Larsen, "The Trumpy Story: Relaunching an Icon": http://trumpy yachts.net/RelaunchingAnIcon.html.

By the late nineteenth century, the continuing Industrial Revolution, the rise of affluence and leisure time, and the expansion of yachting as a popular activity brought recreational boating to Chesapeake Bay. Geoffrey M. Footner's *The Last Generation* provides a sketch of what recreational yachting consisted of in those early days, as do Robert Barrie and George Barrie Jr. in their celebrated *Cruises, Mainly in the Bay of the Chesapeake* (Bryn Mawr, PA: Franklin Press, 1909). Richard "Jud" Henderson's *Chesapeake Sails: A History of Yachting on the Bay* (Centreville, MD: Tidewater Publishers, 1999) gives readers a sweeping chronicle of a sailor's view of cruising and racing on the bay, including the yacht races from Gibson Island to New London and back, the Newport-Annapolis and Annapolis-Newport races, and many intrabay races. An early view of cruising on the bay can be found in Joseph T. Rothrock and Jane C. Rothrock, *Chesapeake Odysseys: An 1883 Cruise Revisited* (Centreville, MD: Tidewater Publishers, 1984), wherein a couple in the 1980s, having read a great-grandfather's cruise journal, re-create that gentleman's circuit of the bay a century later, visiting many of the same rivers and ports. Great-grandfather Joseph T. Rothrock's original cruise journal was published as *Vacation Cruising in Chesapeake and Delaware Bays* (Philadelphia: J. B. Lippincott, 1884); a reprint can be obtained in a BiblioBazaar paperback. Robert de Gast's record of a single-handed cruise around the Delmarva peninsula can be read in his *Western Wind, Eastern Shore: Sailing Cruise around the Eastern Shore of Maryland, Delaware, and Virginia* (Baltimore: Johns Hopkins Univ. Press, 1975). The schooner *America,* of America's Cup fame, arrived in Chesapeake Bay during the 1920s as a donation to the U.S. Naval Academy. Sailor-historian John Rousmaniere details her career and demise in *The Low Black Schooner: Yacht America, 1851–1945* (Mystic, CT: Mystic Seaport Museum Stores, 1986).

In recent years, the Naval Academy sailing teams have done well in intercollegiate competition, but it has not always been that way. Radm. Robert McNitt's *Sailing at the U.S. Naval Academy: An Illustrated History* (Annapolis, MD: Naval Institute Press, 1996) recounts the navy's variable attitude toward competitive sailing on Chesapeake Bay and other venues. The racing of sailing log canoes is a highly specialized sport, popular mainly on the Eastern Shore on the Chester, Miles, and Choptank rivers. An excellent source for a brief history of this subject is *Chesapeake Sailing Craft: Recollections of Robert H. Burgess,* ed. William S. Fox, rev. ed. (1975; Centreville, MD: Tidewater Publishers, 2005). The Web site of the Chesapeake Bay Log Sailing Canoe Association is also a good source of current and historical information: www.logcanoes.com/history.htm.

For recreational powerboaters, William W. Mowbray's *Power Boat Racing on the Chesapeake* (Centreville, MD: Tidewater Publishers, 1995) is a good resource. There is also the Web site of the Hydroplane and Race Boat Museum: www.thun derboats.org/history/history0225.html. Hydroplane racing on the Kent Narrows at Kent Island is featured on the Web site of the Kent Narrows Racing Association Web site: http://kentnarrowsracing.com/index.php. Those interested in the current boating opportunities on Chesapeake Bay should consult the monthly issues of *Chesapeake Bay* magazine, which often have historical notes and articles, as well as the annual *Chesapeake Bay Magazine's Guide to Cruising Chesapeake Bay* (Annapolis, MD: Chesapeake Bay Communications, 2007). This useful guide contains advice on entering ports, the locations of marinas, fuel docks, and pump-out facilities, and water's-edge restaurants for the entire bay and its rivers. It also contains tide charts and cruise-planning information, depending on what locations and how many days' cruising range are within a boater's reach. Since the early 1990s, Douglas Lipton has compiled statistics on the economic impact of recreational boating in the state, as seen, for example, in Lipton's *Economic Impact of Maryland Boating in 2007,* published on the Maryland Sea Grant Extension Program Web site: www .mdsg.umd.edu/programs/extension/communities/boating. Another informative Web site is the U.S. Coast Guard, Department of Homeland Security's "Report of Certificates of Number of Boats, Recreational Boats Only."

Traditional boaters may have been surprised in recent years to see the number of small self-propelled watercraft that have appeared along the margins of the Chesapeake Bay, its rivers and creeks. The outdoors movement is characterized by the use of canoes and the increasingly popular kayaks, as reflected in John Page Williams Jr.'s *Exploring the Chesapeake in Small Boats* (Centreville, MD: Tidewater Publishers, 1992), as well as in Michael Savario and Andrea B. Nolan's *Sea Kayaking Maryland's Chesapeake Bay: Day Trips on the Tribal Tributaries and Coastlines of the Western and Eastern Shore* (Woodstock, VT: Backcountry Guides, 2003), *Seakayaker Magazine,* and the Web site: www.kayakacademy.com. See also "Water Trails," *Maryland's Statewide Water Trails Program* (Maryland Department of Natural Resources), published on the Web site: www.dnr.state.md.us/greenways/ watertrails.html.

The U.S. Navy's historic presence on Chesapeake Bay can be detected in facilities located principally on its Western Shore rivers and concentrated in the southern, Norfolk region. Starting on the Potomac River at Washington, D.C., the Naval Surface Warfare Center, Carderock Division (NSWC, CD), established in 1940 and located north of the American Legion (Cabin John) Bridge, has had several names, the best known of which was the David Taylor Naval Ship Research and Development Center (DTNSRDC). Rodney Carlisle's *Where the Fleet Begins: A History of the David Taylor Research Center* (Washington, DC: Naval Historical Center, 1998) is the main source for the background of this important institution. Farther down the Potomac is the oldest government Navy Yard, founded in 1799. The history of this multifaceted activity is well told by Edward J. Marolda, *The Washington Navy Yard: An Illustrated History* (Washington, DC: Naval Historical Center, 1999). Rodney Carlisle describes the navy's scientific and engineering research activities in *Navy RDT&E [Research, Development, Testing, and Evaluation] Planning in an Age of Transition: A Survey Guide to Contemporary Literature* (Washington, DC: Naval Laboratory/Center Coordinating Group and the Naval Historical Center, 1997). See also the Naval Research Laboratory Web site: www .nrl.navy.mil (re: About NRL History); William B. Anspacher et al., *The Legacy of the White Oak Laboratory* (Dahlgren, VA: Naval Surface Warfare Center, 2000); Rodney Carlisle and James P. Rife, *The Sound of Freedom: Naval Weapons Technology at Dahlgren, Virginia, 1918–2006* (Washington, DC: GPO, 2007); and Rodney Carlisle, *Powder and Propellants: Energetic Materials at Indian Head, MD, 1890–1990* (Indian Head, MD: Naval Ordnance Station, 1990).

For a history of naval institutions on the Severn River, see Jack Sweetman, *The U.S. Naval Academy: An Illustrated History* (Annapolis, MD: Naval Institute Press, 1979), which describes research activities at the U.S. Naval Station, including the U.S. Naval Engineering Experiment Station and Testing Laboratory (EES) near Greenbury Point. This activity, now a detachment of the NSWC, CD, was originally set up to do experiments with steam engineering and ships' machinery. When World War II erupted and the navy had an immediate need for additional training facilities, President Franklin D. Roosevelt suggested a location near the head of the bay. Erika L. Quesenbury has written a study of one of these: *United States Naval Training Center, Bainbridge* (Charleston, SC: Arcadia Press, 2007). *Bainbridge,* as it was casually called, was located adjacent to Port Deposit, near the mouth of the Susquehanna River. It became far more than a mere training center and did not close its doors until 1976.

As a necessity to train sailors and soldiers for amphibious warfare on the coasts of Africa, Europe, and Asia, the navy selected a remote site on the Patuxent River to begin the process. Merle T. Cole tells this story in *Cradle of Invasion: A History of the U.S. Naval Amphibious Training Base, Solomons Island, Maryland, 1942–1945* (Solomons, MD: Calvert Museum, 1984). The context of this site can be found in Richard J. Dodds, *Solomons Island and Vicinity: An Illustrated History and Walking Tour* (Solomons, MD: Calvert Marine Museum, 1995). In 1941, the navy decided to establish the Patuxent River Naval Air Station as a consolidated aircraft test and evaluation center on Cedar Point, across the river from Cove Point. Naval gunfire training and bombing practice targeted early navy pre-dreadnought battleships sunk in the lower bay for precisely that purpose. For further information, consult John C. Reilly and Robert L. Scheina, *American Battleships, 1886–1913* (Annapolis, MD: Naval Institute Press, 1980), 45–48, 62, and 108. Background on this now huge facility is only sparsely published, but some historical information can be gleaned from its Web site: www.globalsecurity.org/military/facility/Patuxent-river.htm.

Although not part of the history of the Maryland Chesapeake, other Chesapeake Bay naval installations that should be mentioned are located on the York and James rivers and in the Norfolk–Hampton Roads region. The histories of the Norfolk Naval Base, Norfolk Naval Shipyard at Portsmouth (Gosport), Naval Weapons Station, Yorktown, and Amphibious Training Base, Little Creek, Virginia, can be consulted in Paolo E. Coletta and K. Jack Bauer, eds. *United States Navy and Marine Corps Bases, Domestic* (Westport, CT: Greenwood Press, 1985).

William L. Tazewell and Guy Friddell, *Norfolk's Waters: An Illustrated History of Hampton Roads* (Sun Valley, CA: American Historical Press, 2000), provides an excellent overview of the navy's impact on this important region.

Sources for underwater archaeology research and interpretation in Chesapeake Bay can be found in Donald G. Shomette's works, *Tidewater Time Capsule: History beneath the Patuxent* (Centreville, MD: Tidewater Publishers, 1995); *The Ghost Fleet of Mallows Bay and Other Tales of the Lost Chesapeake* (Centreville, MD: Tidewater Publishers, 1996); and "The U.S. Navy Shipwreck Inventory Project in the State of Maryland," a paper read at the Society for Historical Archaeology Conference on Historical and Underwater Archaeology at Corpus Christi, Texas, Jan. 10, 1997; see also Shomette's *Flotilla: The Patuxent River Naval Campaign in the War of 1812* (Baltimore: Johns Hopkins Univ. Press, 2009). In addition, see the Naval Historical Center Web site: www.history.navy.mil/branches/org12-7a.htm; Maryland state underwater archaeologist Susan B. M. Langley, "Maryland/Chesapeake Region," in *Handbook of International Underwater Archaeology,* edited by Carol V. Ruppe and Janet F. Barstad (Portsmouth, UK: Nautical Archaeology Society, 2002); Langley's "Maryland Supports Unique Maritime Archaeology Program," *Public History News* 15, no. 2 (1995); Maryland assistant state underwater archaeologist Bruce F. Thompson, "Maryland's Maritime Archaeology Program: The Formative Years," *INA Newsletter* [Institute of Nautical Archaeology–Texas A&M University] 19, no. 1 (1992): 4–9; *Maryland Maritime Archeological Program: Statistics and Data Sheets* (Crownsville, MD: Maryland Historical Trust, 1997); Report, "The Terrible Calamity on the Lower Potomac: An Historic and Archaeological Assessment of the Shipwreck USS *Tulip,* Potomac River, St. Mary's County, Maryland," prepared for the U.S. Naval Historical Center, 1996, rev. 1998; and "Legacy of a Fourth Rate Steam Screw," *Naval History* 10, no. 3 (1996): 36–39.

David C. Holly tells the story of the disastrous fire and sinking of the Baltimore-based steamboat *Columbus* in *Chesapeake Steamboats, Vanished Fleet* (Centreville, MD: Tidewater Publishers, 1994). R. Christopher Goodman and Associates provided a report following the recovery of artifacts from the steamboat entitled "Data Recovery on the Wreck of the Steamship *Columbus,* 18S625, off St. Mary's County, Maryland." Final Report, May 1995, U.S. Army Corps of Engineers, Baltimore District, filed in the library of the Maryland Historical Trust, Crownsville, MD. The most exciting Chesapeake underwater discovery to date was finding Commodore Joshua Barney's flagship of his War of 1812 flotilla in the upper Patuxent River. Donald Shomette and Ralph Eshelman's plan to survey that location was contained in "A Proposal for the Survey of the Submerged Archaeological Resource Base of the Patuxent River, Maryland, Phase I, 1 June 1979–30 September 1979" (Crownsville, MD: Maryland Historical Trust, 1979). Shomette first described the history of Barney's flotilla and the excavation of the wreck of the vessel he identified as probably USS *Scorpion* in *Flotilla: The Battle for the Patuxent* (Solomons, MD: Calvert Marine Museum Press, 1981). This shipwreck, also known as the "Turtle Shell Wreck," and continuing investigations on the Patuxent are the subject of a Maryland Historical Trust Web site: www.marylandhistoricaltrust.net/flotilla.html (last updated Sept. 15, 2005).

The major museum maritime collections of the Maryland mid-bay area are located at the Maryland Historical Society, the Chesapeake Bay Maritime Museum, and the Calvert Marine Museum. These collections are described in Mary Ellen Hayward's *Maryland's Maritime Heritage* (Baltimore: Maryland Historical Society, 1984) and on the Maryland Historical Society Web site: www.mdhs.org; the Chesapeake Bay Maritime Museum's Web site: www.cbmm.org/index.html; and C. Douglas Alves et al., eds., *Calvert Marine Museum* (Lawrenceburg, IN: Creative Company, 2002) and the museum's Web site: www.calvertmarinemuseum.com/cmm-history.htm. For further information on the maritime museum attractions in Baltimore harbor, readers should visit the Web sites of the Baltimore Maritime Museum, the National Historic Seaport of Baltimore, and the Living Classrooms Foundation. To delve more deeply into the *Constellation* debate, consult Dana M. Wegner, *Fouled Anchors: The* Constellation *Question Answered* (Carderock, MD: Naval Ship Research and Development Center, 1991); for other dissenting views, see William M. P. Dunne, "The Frigate *Constellation* Clearly Was No More, or Was She?" *American Neptune* 53, no. 2 (1993): 77–97; and Geoffrey M. Footner, "The Impact of Redesigning and Rebuilding the U.S. Frigate *Constellation* in 1812, 1829, and 1839 on Currently Held Theories Concerning Her Age," *American Neptune* 61, no. 4 (2001): 453–63.

The floating theater phenomenon, already present on the rivers of the Midwest, made its appearance on the East Coast in the North Carolina sounds and on the Chesapeake Bay during the early twentieth century. C. Richard Gillespie provides an authoritative history in *The James Adams Floating Theater* (Centreville, MD: Tidewater Publishers, 1991); see also Mark A. Moore, "Edna Ferber and the Showboat," and Michelle F. Lawing, "Edna Ferber's Visit to Bath, N.C." (unpublished research report, North Carolina Historic Sites, Office of Archives and History, Raleigh, NC, 1979). See the Web site: http://nchistoricsites.org/bath/ednaferber.htm; and Robyn Quick, "James Adams Floating Theater," Maryland Online Encyclopedia Web site: www.mdoe.adams_theater.html.

There are many sources on the ecological decline of Chesapeake Bay. A good place to begin is with John R. Wennersten, *The Chesapeake: An Environmental Biography* (Baltimore: Maryland Historical Society, 2001), and Steven Davison et al., *Chesapeake Waters: Four Centuries of Controversy, Concern, and Legislation,* 2nd ed. (Centreville, MD: Tidewater Publishers, 1997). The Maryland Department of Natural Resources Web site, www.dnr.state.md.us/nrp/history.html, provides good background on the role of the Natural Resources Police. See also, Report of the Conservation Department, Maryland Manual, 1922. See Archives of Maryland online, vols. 0453 and 0454. On the importance of the work of Reginald V. Truitt, see Remarks by Dr. Kevin Tenore, former director of the Chesapeake Biological Laboratory (CBL), which was quoted on the University of Maryland Center for Environmental Studies Web site: www.cbl.cmes.edu/About-CBL/Facilities/R.V.Truitt-Controlled-Environment-Laboratory.html (accessed Aug. 15, 2006). Robert C. Keith, *Baltimore Harbor: A Picture History,* rev. ed. (Baltimore: Johns Hopkins Univ. Press, 1991), illustrates and discusses the industries, industrial waste, and shipwrecks along the shores of the Patapsco River. Tom Horton's *Bay*

Country (Baltimore: Johns Hopkins Univ. Press, 1987, 1994) gives a vivid account of the environmental and social costs of pollution in the regions' waters and wetlands. Susan Q. Stranahan, *Susquehanna: River of Dreams* (Baltimore: Johns Hopkins Univ. Press, 1993), provides a stunning account of how misuse of the Susquehanna River has fouled the waters and damaged the fisheries of Chesapeake Bay. Linda Lear's biography *Rachel Carson, Witness for Nature* (New York: Henry Holt, 1997) highlights how much we owe to this brave scientific writer for revealing the chemical industry's negligence in marketing products harmful to the environment. A still-timely article by Victoria Churchville, "The Poisoning of Chesapeake Bay: Pollution Permit System Abused by Industry, Sewage Plants," *Washington Post,* Sunday, June 1, 1986, sec. A, 1, 14–15 represented two years of research in environmental records. Accompanying the article was a graphic entitled "The Slow Death of Chesapeake Bay."

For a much more recent account, see reporters Rona Kobell and Timothy B. Wheeler, "Bay Protection Eroded, Bit by Bit," *Baltimore Sun,* Jan. 21, 2008, 1A and 8A. Michael W. Fincham, Erica Goldman, and Jack Greer, "Whatever Happened to Pfiesteria?" *Chesapeake Quarterly* (Maryland Sea Grant College) 6, no. 1 (2007) analyze the aftermath of the outbreak of this alarming algae-related disease in 1997. Maryland legislator Gerald W. Winegrad's "What Will It Take to Restore the Bay," *Baltimore Sun,* Sunday, July 15, 1997, set out an agenda to reverse current trends in the bay's decline. Finally, Tom Horton, in "Growing, Growing, Gone: The Chesapeake Bay and the Myth of Endless Growth," *Abell Report* 21, no. 2 (2008): 1–7, points out that a major factor in the deterioration of the bay's ecology is population growth, a subject policy makers have failed to address. To read a superb example of this thesis as applied to a beautiful river on the Eastern Shore, see David W. Harp and Tom Horton's photo essay entitled *The Nanticoke: Portrait of a Chesapeake River* (Baltimore: Johns Hopkins Univ. Press, 2008).

Essay on Sources

INDEX